The Cost of Racial Equality

The Cost of Racial Equality

MAJOR G. COLEMAN

CASCADE *Books* · Eugene, Oregon

THE COST OF RACIAL EQUALITY

Copyright © 2025 Major G. Coleman. All rights reserved. Except for brief quotations in critical publications or reviews, no part of this book may be reproduced in any manner without prior written permission from the publisher. Write: Permissions, Wipf and Stock Publishers, 199 W. 8th Ave., Suite 3, Eugene, OR 97401.

Cascade Books
An Imprint of Wipf and Stock Publishers
199 W. 8th Ave., Suite 3
Eugene, OR 97401

www.wipfandstock.com

PAPERBACK ISBN: 979-8-3852-2032-8
HARDCOVER ISBN: 979-8-3852-2033-5
EBOOK ISBN: 979-8-3852-2034-2

Cataloguing-in-Publication data:

Names: Coleman, Major G., author.

Title: The cost of racial equality / Major G. Coleman.

Description: Eugene, OR : Cascade Books, 2025 | Includes bibliographical references and index.

Identifiers: ISBN 979-8-3852-2032-8 (paperback) | ISBN 979-8-3852-2033-5 (hardcover) | ISBN 979-8-3852-2034-2 (ebook)

Subjects: LCSH: Race discrimination—United States. | Racism—Philosophy. | Racism—United States—History. | United States—Race relations.

Classification: LC213.2 .C645 2025 (paperback) | LC213.2 .C645 (ebook)

VERSION NUMBER 10/08/25

Para Sandra Regina
Por nossa vida juntos

The real cost lies ahead. The stiffening of white resistance is a recognition of that fact. The discount education given Negroes will in the future have to be purchased at full price if quality education is to be realized. Jobs are harder and costlier to create than voting rolls. The eradication of slums housing millions is complex far beyond integrating buses and lunch counters.

MARTIN LUTHER KING JR., *WHERE DO WE GO FROM HERE: CHAOS OR COMMUNITY?* (1968)

Contents

List of Illustrations | viii

Preface and Acknowledgments | xiii

List of Abbreviations | xv

Chapter One	You Get What You Pay For	1
Chapter Two	Black Deficiency Theory and Cost	31
Chapter Three	White Cultural Belief Systems: A Glass Half Empty	71
Chapter Four	The Costs of the Law	103
Chapter Five	How Much Affirmative Action Costs America	146
Chapter Six	The Price of Wage Discrimination, Poverty, and Wealth Inequality	177
Chapter Seven	Trouble Ahead: The Danger of Political Power on the Cheap	199
Chapter Eight	The Fierce Urgency of Now: K–12 Education	248
Chapter Nine	High-Cost Equality: Welfare, Social Security, and Reparations	283
Chapter Ten	Penny Wise and Pound Foolish	319

Bibliography | 351

Index | 383

Illustrations

FIGURES

1	Strategic Equality Model, Black to White Family Income Ratio and Non-Hispanic White Population Percentage, 1947–2060	5
2.1	Black/White Median Family Income, 1880–2022	38
2.2	Life Expectancy at Birth for Males	51
2.3	Race and Receipt of AFDC/TANF Payments	63
2.4	Ratio of Blacks to Whites Receiving AFDC/TANF	64
2.5	Female-Headed Families That Are Poor	65
2.6	Ratio of Black to White Female Heads Who Are Poor	67
3.1	Persons Aged 25 and Over with Bachelor's Degree or Higher	74
3.2	Ratio of Persons Aged 25 and Over with Bachelor's Degree or Higher	75
3.3	Safest Equality Route and Strategic Equality Gap for Baccalaureate or More Completion Rate	77
3.4	Diversity in Neighborhoods by Race	80
3.5	Income Ratios for Non-White Male Workers as a Percentage of White Male Workers	92
3.6	Income Ratios for Non-White Female Workers as a Percentage of White Female Workers	92
3.7	Black and White Male Unemployment Rate and Ratio, 1972–2022	97

ILLUSTRATIONS

4.1 White Men in Philadelphia Construction Craft and Labor Occupations as a Percentage of All White Men in Construction in Philadelphia | 141
4.2 Blacks in Construction Craft and Construction Labor Occupations as a Percentage of All Blacks in Construction in the US | 142
4.3 Black Men in Philadelphia Construction Craft and Labor Occupations as a Percentage of All Black Men in Construction in Philadelphia | 143
5.1 Worst-Case Gain or Loss from Return on Capital for Black Employment, 1990–2002 | 172
5.2 Worst-Case Market to Book Ratio for Black Employment, 1990–2002 | 173
5.3 Worst-Case Sales per Employee for Black Employment, 1990–2002 | 174
6.1 Poverty and Race in the US, 1959–2022 | 178
6.2 Ratio of Black to White Poverty in the US, 1959–2022 | 179
6.3 Black Male Wages as a Percentage of White Male Wages by Years of Education, 1966–2006 | 186
7.1 EEOC Budget in Current and Constant Dollars, 1966–2023 | 207
7.2 EEOC Budget as Percentage of GDP, 1966–2023 | 208
7.3 White (Non-Hispanic) Votes as a Percentage of Major Party Coalitions, 1948–2024 | 229
8   Funding per Pupil by Source, 1919–2021, in Constant 1982–84 Dollars | 253
9.1 Weekly Wages for Manufacturing and Private-Sector Production Non-Supervisory Workers, and All Industries, All Occupations, in Constant 1982–84 Dollars | 300
9.2 Black Poverty, 1959–2021 | 301
9.3 Black Male Log Wage Coefficient, 1963–2014 | 302
9.4 Black Female Log Wage Coefficient, 1963–2014 | 303
9.5 Social Welfare Spending as a Percent of GDP, 1933–2020 | 308

ILLUSTRATIONS

TABLES

1 The Cost of Racial Equality | 14
2.1 Female Headedness on Race, Human Capital, Marital Status, Labor Market, and Geography, 2013, Logit Odds Ratios | 48
2.2 AFDC Status Regressed on Race and Other Factors, Logit Odds Ratios | 59–62
2.3 Poverty and AFDC/TANF Status Regressed on Race, Human Capital, Marital Status, Labor Market, and Geography, Logit Odds Ratios | 66
3.1 Residential Segregation for Blacks or African Americans in Large Metropolitan Areas: 1980, 1990, and 2000, Dissimilarity Index | 78–79
3.2 Affirmative Action (AA) and Non–Affirmative Action (N–AA) Firms by Race, Gender, and Occupation of Workers | 87–88
3.3 Male Employment on Government Contractor Status | 89
3.4 Female Employment on Government Contractor Status | 90
4.1 Race and Immigration into the US, 1820–2000 | 122–23
4.2 US Immigration by Area, 2017 | 124
5.1 Summary of Major Studies of Affirmative Action Costs | 156–59
5.2 Financial, Market, and Productivity Performance on Black Labor, 1990–2002 | 161–62
5.3 The Cost of Black Employment, 1990–2002 | 163–64
5.4 Government Contractor Financial, Market, and Productivity Performance on Black Labor, 1990–2002 | 165–66
5.5 The Cost of Black Employment for Government Contractors, 1990–2002 | 166–67
5.6 Non-Contractor Financial, Market, and Productivity Performance on Black Labor, 1990–2002 | 168
5.7 The Cost of Black Employment for Non-Contractors, 1990–2002 | 169–70
6 Wages on Race, Human Capital, Demographics, Labor Market, and Poverty, 2006 | 182–85
7.1 Presidential Vote by Party and Race, 1948–2024 | 210–11

ILLUSTRATIONS

7.2   Voters and Non-Voters by Race and Year in the South: Percentages | 216
7.3   Presidential Vote by Race and Gender, 1948–2024 | 227–28
7.4   Democratic Party Voting on Race | 239–41
7.5   Democratic Party Voting on Latino Nationality | 244–46
9.1   Social Welfare Spending in the US | 288
9.2   Race and TANF Receipt | 290–92
9.3   Historical Trends in AFDC/TANF Enrollments | 297–98
9.4   Social Welfare Spending as a Percent of GDP, 2019 | 308–9
9.5   Index of Income Inequality, 2019–22 | 310–11

Preface and Acknowledgments

I ORIGINALLY HAD NO intention of writing a book of such scope and breadth. My original plan was just to deal with the problems surrounding affirmative action and merit. Working with the late Jeannette Hopkins changed all of that. I gave her all of my scribbling to see what she could make of it. Jeannette's skill and passion for writing are what changed this book into a project that addresses more than just one area of social concern into a general study of cost. Jeannette's toughness and demands that a book be approached correctly are what allowed me to tackle a job that I never believed possible. I will always be in her debt for believing in my work when I had so many doubts. Jeannette sent me looking for my voice. Had I not started looking for it, I could never have found it. Jeannette passed away on August 4, 2011, and I miss her greatly.

I will probably never be able to name all the people who helped me along the way but I must take that risk and name those for whom, without their support, I would never have started or completed this book. Paula McClain was the first to recognize that this idea was book material and her support and encouragement often cheered me along. Ronald Edwards, formerly with the EEOC, was an early supporter. Deborah Freund and Howard Johnson saved my life when I was without a friend. Johnny Yinger and Dave Richardson spent many hours working with me as I developed into a political economist who could stand the rigor of their examination. They never coddled or patronized but always demanded that the numbers be as good as the ideas and theories from which they sprang. Johnny and Dave didn't always know the answers but they never failed to get me on the path to finding the answer. William A. Darity Jr. gave me a physical place to work and provided an intellectual home for me when it was hard to find anyone with anything more than idle curiosity and a scathing rebuke for the political scientist who would stoop to do something as "disgusting" as labor economics. Frank Baumgartner, Errol Henderson, and James B.

Stewart never failed to read and comment when I needed their help the most. I also thank the ARC for support. Stephen Halpern spent so much effort preparing for my entry into academia. I will always be grateful for his stern words of guidance; I have never forgotten them. Christian Winting's careful reading made the book much stronger. Richard Holway always believed this was possible. I cannot forget those mentors who set me on my path with so many good wishes, great ideas, and a desire that I never stop moving forward—Gary Orfield, Stephen Holmes, Edgar Epps, Charles Lipson, and Lucius Barker. John Witte Jr. and the Center for the Study of Law and Religion (CSLR) at Emory University School of Law provided very generous funding to support this project. Thanks to Sally Wolff King and Mary Beth Hinton for editorial consulting.

Abbreviations

AAA	Agricultural Adjustment Act
ADC	Aid to Dependent Children was changed to AFDC in the mid-1960s amid fears of encouraging out-of-wedlock births.
AFDC	Aid to Families with Dependent Children
AFQT	Armed Forces Qualification Test
AIDS	Acquired immunodeficiency syndrome
AIG	American International Group
AYP	Adequate yearly progress
BAMN	By any means necessary
CARES	Coronavirus Aid, Relief, and Economic Security Act
CCC	Civilian Conservation Corps
CDC	Centers for Disease Control and Prevention is part of the Department of Health and Human Services and is the leading public health organization in the US and the world.
CES	Committee on Economic Security
COPOC	Fictional civil rights group: Coalition of Oppressed Peoples of Color (in ch. 9)
CORE	Congress of Racial Equality
COVID-19	Coronavirus disease, 2019, is an infectious disease that began in Wuhan, China, in December 2019. The World Health Organization declared COVID-19 a pandemic. Millions of people have been infected and tens of thousands have died from the pandemic as of 2020.

ABBREVIATIONS

CPS	Current population survey
CRA	Civil Rights Act
CSLR	Center for the Study of Law and Religion, Emory University Law School
CWA	Civil Works Administration
DEA	Drug Enforcement Administration
DEI	Diversity, equity, and inclusion
DI	Disability insurance
DNA	Deoxyribonucleic acid
DoD	Department of Defense
DOJ	Department of Justice
EEOC	Equal Employment Opportunity Commission
EITC	Earned income tax credit
ESEA	Elementary and Secondary Schools Act
FCC	Federal Communications Commission
FDR	Franklin Delano Roosevelt, 32nd president of the US
FEPC	Fair Employment Practice Committee
FERA	Federal Emergency Relief Administration
FHA	Federal Housing Administration
GATBY	General Aptitude and Test Battery
GDP	Gross domestic product
GI	Government Issue, used to refer to people in the military or veterans
GOP	Grand Old Party, the traditional name of the Republican Party
GSS	General Social Survey, compiled by the National Opinion Research Center at the University of Chicago
Hamas	Acronym for Harakat al-Muqawama al-Islamiya, Palestinian political group
IOM	Institute of Medicine
JFK	John Fitzgerald "Jack" Kennedy, 35th president of the US
LBJ	Lyndon Baines Johnson, 36th president of the US
LEAA	Law Enforcement Assistance Administration
LFPR	Labor force participation rate

ABBREVIATIONS

MCSUI	Multi-City Study of Urban Inequality
MLK Jr.	Martin Luther King Jr.
N95	An N95 face mask is a piece of personal protective equipment that covers the nose, mouth, and chin and is not (N) resistant to oil but which blocks at least 95 percent of very small (0.3 micron) test particles.
NAACP	National Association for the Advancement of Colored People
NCES	National Center for Education Statistics
NCLB	No Child Left Behind
NES	National Election Study
NFA	Net financial assets
NIRA	National Industrial Recovery Act
NLRB	National Labor Relations Board
NRA	National Recovery Administration
NWRO	National Welfare Rights Organization
NYA	National Youth Administration
OASI	Old-Age and Survivors' Insurance
OECD	Organisation for Economic Co-Operation and Development; mostly European, North and South American nations
OEO	Office of Economic Opportunity
OFCC	Office of Federal Contract Compliance
OFCCP	Office of Federal Contract Compliance Programs
OIC	Opportunities Industrial Corporation
OOP	Out-of-precinct voting
POEs	Points of entry
POVs	Personally owned vehicles
PPE	Personal protective equipment, such as masks, gowns, and gloves for hospital workers
PRWORA	Personal Responsibility and Work Opportunity Reconciliation Act
PWA	Public Works Administration
SCLC	Southern Christian Leadership Conference

ABBREVIATIONS

SCOTUS	Supreme Court of the United States, report drafted in 2021 to study court expansion
SDA	Seventh-day Adventist
SES	Socioeconomic status
SFFA	Students for Fair Admissions
SIPP	Survey of Income and Program Participation
SNAP	Supplemental Nutrition Assistance Program, formerly known as Food Stamps
SNCC	Student Nonviolent Coordinating Committee
SSA	Social Security Act
SSI	Supplemental security income
SURR	Schools under registration review
TANF	Temporary assistance to needy families
UI	Unemployment insurance
VRA	Voting Rights Act
VSL	Value of a statistical life
WIC	Women, Infants, and Children; a federal food nutrition program
WPA	Works Progress Administration

Chapter One
You Get What You Pay For

AMERICA MAY CHOOSE TO pay a price to achieve the goal of racial equality, and that price may be high, medium, low, or anything in between. The fundamental problem for America is not that the nation is choosing a certain level of cost for racial equality. The problem is that America is choosing to pay no costs at all. America has three options when it comes to racial equality: 1) do nothing; 2) continue with non-substantive but symbolic overtures (like high-level political appointments) to peoples of color, while the dangers of political instability and racial polarization continue; or 3) choose a certain level of racial equality (low, medium, or high) to pursue and stay the course of that policy until certain goals are met.

The thesis of *The Cost of Racial Equality* is that America is choosing a combination of the first two options above. America spends little on the problem of racial inequality, in comparison to the size of the problem, and refuses to pursue racial equality, while at the same time the white population dwindles and the ratios of peoples of color increases. This combination of demographic changes with concentrations of economic and political power in a soon-to-be racial minority (whites) portends difficult times ahead. Not only is America ignoring costs, but also most of America does not know what those costs and dangers are. Examining the different types and levels of costs and fixes necessary to achieve racial equality is the focus of this book.

The no-cost option is an illusion when applied to racial equality because a no-cost option assumes that some level of stasis, stability, balance, or equilibrium is present in America with most of the nation comprised of Blacks, Latinos, Asians, and American Indians, but with most of the money, political power, and wealth in the hands of whites. Below in this chapter, table 1 will list racial programs with low economic cost, which have outsized benefits for low levels of racial equality: 1) political equality, 2) school bussing for integration, 3) affirmative action in education and employment, and 4) EEOC funding for strong antidiscrimination enforcement. These four programs are low-to-no economic cost but have a proven record of assisting marginalized populations. Most of white America has soundly rejected all of them, however. To make matters worse, in 2024, whites were the only identifiable racial group to vote for a president who openly opposes DEI and identifies unearned historic and contemporary white privileges as merit (table 7.3).

First, political equality in terms of voting and elections is already the law and therefore carries low intrinsic political costs and also low economic costs. Table 7.2 shows that in some years in the South, when controlled for income and education, Blacks vote at higher rates than do whites. Because of this record, the US Supreme Court found cause to rule in *Shelby County v. Holder* that section 4(b) of the 1965 VRA was unconstitutional because the VRA singled out the Southern states for federal monitoring.

Voting is not controlled by income and education, however, and most of the violations of the VRA still come from the South. Justice Kagan's dissent in *Brnovich v. Democratic National Committee* showed that race remains a powerful variable in voting, and any laws that negatively impact peoples of color and the franchise are highly suspect. The unsubstantiated challenges to the 2020 presidential election of President Biden in Wisconsin and Pennsylvania attacked mostly Black votes in Milwaukee and Philadelphia. Nearly two-thirds of whites in 2024 in table 7.3 voted for a political party that does not mention a single racial group or address racial inequality in its 2016, 2020, and 2024 party platforms. Peoples-of-color groups are represented in low single digits in the Republican Party coalition. The 2020 and 2024 Democratic Party platforms were the first major party platforms to put the issue of reparations for slavery on the agenda. Generally, however, Black equality issues are rarely on any political agenda. Racial political polarization, attacks on the Black franchise, and refusals to even acknowledge racial inequality are dangerous no-cost choices for political equality as America approaches becoming a majority minority.

Second, the leading social indicators are those institutions we look to when we want to know what the future holds for America. Unfortunately, the leading social indicators, K–12 education and the church, are the most racially segregated major institutions in the nation. The economic cost of integrating all of America's K–12 schools is only the price of gasoline. Matthew F. Delmont has made it clear that America has never opposed bussing. Before *Brown v. Board of Education*, white kids rode the bus, while Black kids walked.[1] What white America opposes is bussing to integrate schools, and once bussing was linked to racial integration, that practice was doomed. Most studies show that K–12 school integration, even with its problems of tracking, continues to pay big benefits for Black and Latino children, with no harm to white children. "Republican administrations [have been] hostile to desegregation efforts, and neither the Clinton nor the Obama Administrations had substantial initiatives for desegregation, except for a small effort at the very end of the Obama period."[2] When the Department of Education under President Biden asked for comments on "Proposed Priorities—American History and Civics Education," to "Incorporate Racially, Ethnically, Culturally, and Linguistically Diverse Perspectives into Teaching and Learning,"[3] and teach in the K–12 curriculum that racism is a systematic and structural problem in America, twenty-eight states passed laws, proposed resolutions, or issued rules restricting such teaching.[4] By rejecting bussing for integration, or even the concept of structural bias, white America is choosing to pay not low cost, but no cost for racial equality.

Third, 75 percent of white America opposes affirmative action in employment, when using GSS results as a guide. Of the most serious cost studies undertaken for affirmative action, in table 5.1, only one found significant costs associated with the program, and that lone study was flawed in many ways. The overwhelming evidence from the affirmative action cost studies is that on average, affirmative action is costless. In a worst-case scenario, affirmative action has very low cost, and in the most likely scenarios, affirmative action pays big dividends for American business because of the superior productivity of Black workers. With all of these free benefits from affirmative action, America nonetheless looks this gift horse in the mouth and says no.

In 2014, the US Supreme Court held that the courts could not set aside the amendment to the Michigan Constitution that prohibited race-based affirmative action in public education, employment, and contracting, thus allowing white majorities in states to block routes toward correcting historic and contemporary racial disparities.[5] Again in the 2020 elections, the California Proposition 16 to repeal the 1996 Proposition 209, which banned the use of race-based and sex-based affirmative action in state college admissions and California state government contracts, failed to pass

1. Delmont, *Why Busing Failed*.
2. Orfield and Jarvie, "Black Segregation Matters," 15.
3. Ryder, "Proposed Priorities," 20349.
4. Stout and LeMee, "Efforts to Restrict Teaching."
5. *Schuette v. Coalition*.

with 57 percent voting no and only 42.8 percent voting yes.[6] The rejection of affirmative action by white America is another example of an approach that is penny wise and pound foolish.

Fourth, antidiscrimination in many areas, such as employment, is the law, so antidiscrimination enforcement carries low intrinsic political cost. A nationwide comprehensive testing program that would essentially eliminate racial discrimination in employment is only $500 million. Law notwithstanding, antidiscrimination enforcement via testing by the top enforcement agency in the nation, the EEOC, has essentially been banned for decades. Antidiscrimination enforcement carries high-perceived political costs because strict enforcement from the federal government would expose the breadth and depth of racial discrimination in the United States. The breadth and depth of racial discrimination in the United States desperately need to be exposed. With the population of peoples of color exploding upward, figure 7.2 shows that as a percentage of GDP, the budget for antidiscrimination enforcement is dropping like a rock. The more antidiscrimination enforcement America needs, the less antidiscrimination enforcement America wants.

A QUESTION OF COST

Failure to know how much a computer, couch, or car costs is itself problematic. Failure to know how much racial equality costs can be catastrophic for democracy and could threaten the future of America. Armed militias are just one example of the developing crisis—a warning given a quarter of a century ago.[7] The Black Lives Matter movement is also evidence that Black groups are no longer led by respected religious leaders who hold the moral high ground and are philosophically committed to nonviolent change. Failure to recognize that a Black, Latino, and Asian majority is the future of America, and ignoring racial inequality under the mistaken assumption that no costs will arise for inaction, will be a costly error.

Sometime around 2045, a little over twenty years from now or maybe less, America officially will become mostly non-white for the first time in its history. On that date, the United States will enter what figure 1 calls "supercritical conditions." Figure 1 shows the rapid decline of the non-Hispanic white population since the 1940s.

Figure 1 also shows the Black to white family income ratio since the 1940s projected out to mid-century at current rates of change. The Black

6. M. Powell, "Liberals Envisioned a Multiracial Coalition."
7. Rowan, *Coming Race War in America*.

to white family income ratio is stagnant and generally hovers between 50 and 65 percent. Prior to the passage of the Civil Rights Act of 1964 and the Voting Rights Act of 1965, America was in what figure 1 calls "historic conditions," little changed since the end of the Civil War, with large percentages of Blacks trapped in poverty and oppressed by Jim Crow in the South and nearly universal de facto segregation in the North. These were the historic conditions from which contemporary white privileges emerged.

Figure 1 Strategic Equality Model, Black to White Family Income Ratio and Non-Hispanic White Population Percentage, 1947–2060

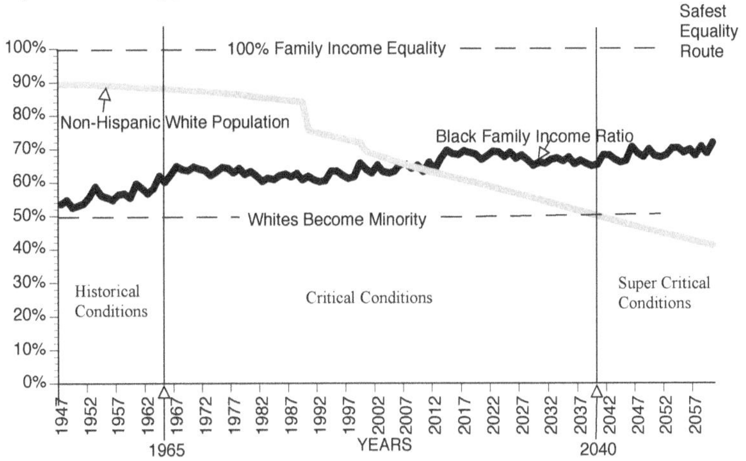

Source: Coleman, "At a Loss."

The passage of the major civil rights legislation moved the nation from historic conditions to "critical conditions" and created the immediate economic changes in figure 1, but those changes did not last long. The shortest and safest route to equality would have been to stay on the route begun in the 1960s toward 100 percent substantive racial equality with whites, not just improvements in Black conditions. The safest equality route was not taken, and the gap between Black family income and the safest equality route continues to widen.

THE DANGER AHEAD AND BEHIND

Failure to pursue racial equality and fix the problem of racial inequality may lead to destabilization of the state. Few American statesmen saw the American Civil War coming, and few people envisioned the January

6, 2021, deadly attack on the Capitol of the United States involving white supremacist protestors. Most leaders and common people in the antebellum period took a no-cost-option approach to race relations, similar to today. No real race relations existed before the Civil War. For the most part, Blacks were slaves, American Indians were savages, and the brutal murder of millions was thought to continue forever. For anyone who was observing closely, however, storm clouds clearly were gathering. The slave revolt near the Stono River, southwest of Charleston, South Carolina, on September 9, 1739, came to be known as the Stono Rebellion and cost the lives of twenty whites and at least sixty Blacks. The incident illustrated that enslaved Blacks could organize and conduct warfare. Whites should have been alarmed at the growing power of enslaved Blacks in Charleston but, says Peter Wood, "even after the systematic enumeration of slaves had begun, it was hard for Europeans to come to terms directly with the demographic situation which was so thoroughly apparent around them."[8] As Hoffer points out about Stono—

> In all, then, most likely it was contingency that marked every step of the Stono Rebellion. Contingency is a synonym for chance.... Many revolts began as more or less spontaneous acts of desperation. But ... desperation [is] common, whereas revolts are not. Contingency requires a trigger. Many little things coming together may tip the scales ... change so often happens ... quickly and ... unexpectedly ... things can happen all at once, and little changes can make a huge difference. The tipping point—the big change—comes when enough little changes have occurred to tip the balance, and trigger a big change. It's the boiling point. It's the moment on the graph when the line starts to shoot straight upwards. No one at the time knows when or how many of these little changes are necessary for the big change. But put them together and the unexpected at the time becomes the inevitable in hindsight.[9]

Gabriel's Richmond, Virginia, insurgency in 1800, Denmark Vesey's 1822 revolt, again in Charleston, South Carolina, were warnings. Nat Turner's 1831 uprising in Southampton, Virginia, cost sixty whites their lives and some two hundred Blacks, although only about seventy-five slaves joined Turner. These were the most well-known examples of Blacks' ability to liberate themselves. Hundreds more insurrections of enslaved Blacks

---

8. Wood, *Black Majority*, 218.
9. Hoffer, *Cry Liberty*, 76–77.

are recorded.[10] Few wrote of them as passionately as David Walker did in 1830: "You will scarcely ever find a paragraph respecting slavery, which is ten thousand times more injurious to this country than all the other evils put together. . . . I tell you Americans! that unless you speedily alter your course, you and your Country are gone!!!!! For God Almighty will tear up the very face of the earth!!!!"[11] In hindsight, all these events were prophetic warnings, but at the time, these warnings were taken as mere editorializing, sermonizing, and pontificating.

Nevertheless, the voices during the Jim Crow era were just as mighty, prophetic, and strong as those that came before. Henry McNeal Turner cried: "We are bitten, we are poisoned, we are sick and we are dying. We need a remedy. Oh for some Moses to lift a brazen serpent, some goal for our ambition, some object to induce us to look up. Have we that object here [in America]? Is there any possibility of getting it here [in the US]? I do not see it."[12] W. E. B. Du Bois counseled, "The problem of the Twentieth Century is the problem of the color line."[13] Reverdy Ransom pleaded, "In dealing with this question, the history of our past is well known. The Race problem in this country is not only still with us as an unsolved problem, but it constitutes perhaps the most serious problem in our country today. . . . American Christianity will un-Christ itself if it refuses to strive on, until this Race Problem is not only settled, but settled right; and until this is done, however much men may temporize and seek to compromise, and cry 'peace! peace!' there will be no peace until this is done."[14]

All of these men were ignored until the prophet-pastor of America, Martin Luther King Jr., on August 28, 1963, in his "I Have a Dream" speech, demanded that "justice roll down like waters and righteousness like a mighty stream," and that the "whirlwinds of revolt will continue to shake the foundations of our nation until the bright day of justice emerges."[15] The urban unrest that followed two years after King's prediction left nearly a hundred dead in Los Angeles, Newark, Detroit, and Chicago, and forced America to hear King's voice. Nonetheless, America refused to pay his bill. Chapter 9 shows that King asked for only $500 billion in the late 1960s, spread out over ten years, as the cost of racial equality. King never received

---

10. Carroll, *Slave Insurrections*.
11. Walker, "Our Wretchedness," 197.
12. H. Turner, "Emigration to Africa," 291.
13. Du Bois, *Souls of Black Folk*, 5.
14. Ransom, "Race Problem in a Christian State," 339.
15. King, "I Have a Dream," 218–19.

even a pittance of his request. The entire cost for the Great Society was only around $50 billion, less than a tenth of what King requested.

Blacks were not the only ones upset by Jim Crow oppression. Whites were equally upset by Black progress and their rise from slavery. White race riots, which left hundreds dead in Wilmington, North Carolina, in 1898; Atlanta, Georgia, in 1906; and Tulsa, Oklahoma, in 1921, showed the tenacity of white supremacy in American culture. In 1996, two books, both containing the title *The Coming Race War*, seemed again to prophesy the future of America.[16] Now we have Black Lives Matter, the Department of Homeland Security warning about the rise of white terrorist groups, and a nation polarized by racial and political division. The March 4, 2015, DOJ *Investigation of the Ferguson Police Department* revealed a Black community terrorized by the Ferguson police, the courts, and the municipal government. The DOJ report found "Ferguson's police and municipal court practices both reflect and exacerbate existing racial bias, including racial stereotypes. Ferguson's own data establish clear racial disparities that adversely impact African Americans. The evidence shows that discriminatory intent is part of the reason for these disparities. Over time, Ferguson's police and municipal court practices have sown deep mistrust between parts of the community and the police department, undermining law enforcement legitimacy among African Americans in particular."[17]

Black anger and rage over white oppression has been a frequent focus of writers.[18] But now white rage has come into focus and just as with white race riots early in the twentieth century, "the trigger for White rage, inevitably, is Black advancement. . . . White rage is not about visible violence, but rather it works its way through the courts, the legislatures, and a range of government bureaucracies. It wreaks havoc subtly, almost imperceptibly," says Anderson.[19] Anderson's description of white rage is appropriate, but not only is white rage very violent, white rage is far more violent than Black rage. And it is mostly white rage, and the impact of white rage, that threatens American democracy. A month before the events in Ferguson, Missouri, Eric Garner, a forty-three-year-old unarmed Black man, essentially died of strangulation by New York City police officers on Staten Island. A Staten Island grand jury did not indict the officer involved, and that conclusion set off protests and rallies around the country with people chanting, "I

---

16. Delgado, *Coming Race War*; Rowan, *Coming Race War in America*.

17. United States Department of Justice, *Investigation of Ferguson*, 2.

18. Cose, *Rage of a Privileged Class*; P. Harris, *Black Rage Confronts the Law*; Grier and Cobbs, *Black Rage*.

19. Anderson, *White Rage*, 3.

can't breathe," Eric Garner's last words as he died. On December 20, 2014, less than six months after Eric Garner's death, Ismaaiyl Brinsley assassinated two NYPD officers by shooting them in the head and upper bodies as they sat peacefully in their car. Brinsley had made statements on social media that he intended to kill police officers in revenge for the death of Eric Garner and the shooting in Ferguson. Some readers may not understand the connection between the enslavement of Black Americans, slave revolts, Jim Crow, white race riots, Black Lives Matter, and the failure to pay or to know the cost to repair this damage to racial equality. Perhaps Martin Luther King Jr. said it best when he said "the all too prevalent method of physical violence and corroding hatred['s] chief legacy will be an endless reign of chaos."[20] Violent oppression begets violent resistance, hatred begets hatred, and rage begets rage.

Few have forgotten Dylann Roof, the twenty-three-year-old white supremacist who killed nine Black churchgoers in Charleston, South Carolina, on June 17, 2015. Roof claimed that he wanted to start a race war. Many people also recall the five white police officers killed in Dallas on July 7, 2016, at a protest rally against police shootings of Black people. A Black suspect, who allegedly killed the five white officers, claimed he was acting in revenge for the shootings of Black people by police officers.

No doubt still fresh in recent memory also is the shooting of fifty-year-old Walter Scott, another unarmed Black man, shot in the back as he ran away from a white police officer in North Charleston, South Carolina, on April 4, 2015. Michael Slager was sentenced to twenty years in federal prison for the shooting of Walter Scott, and this instance was a rare one in which a police officer received a conviction for a shooting death that occurred while he was on duty.

Also memorable is the white supremacist rally in Charlottesville, Virginia, on August 12, 2017, in which one person died. So great was the fear of Florida Governor Rick Scott, that on October 16, 2017, two months after the Charlottesville white supremacist rallies, Scott declared a state of emergency in anticipation of a rally by white nationalist Richard Spencer at the University of Florida, Gainesville.

Many of the other recent racial incidents in the national news have likely been forgotten, however, such as: Colin Ferguson, a Black West Indian immigrant who in 1993 committed a racially motivated murder of six white passengers, wounding nineteen others, on a Long Island Rail Road train; the thirty-three-year-old former Los Angeles police officer, Christopher Dorner, who systematically attacked other LAPD officers in February

---

20. King, "Nonviolence and Racial Justice," 59.

of 2013 and allegedly was fired in retaliation for reporting racial incidents by other officers; the three white and one Asian officers from Oakland, California, killed by Lovelle Mixon, a Black man, in March 2009; Maurice Clemmons, a Black man, who killed four white police officers in Lakewood, Washington, in November 2009. News reports in both the Mixon and Clemmons cases stated that community and family members, apparently because of antagonism toward the police, assisted the perpetrators in their escapes. If any of these reports are even half true, they are not good signs for the future of America.

No one can count all of the incidents of unarmed Black men killed by the police, for example: the death of Freddie Gray at the hands of the Baltimore police in April 2015; the shooting of Akai Gurley on November 20, 2014, by an NYPD officer in a dark stairwell; Sean Bell on November 25, 2006; and Amadou Diallo on February 4, 1999. Some cases are too fresh to know fully their long-term implications: the murder of Botham Shem Jean on September 6, 2018, in his own apartment, while he was eating ice cream, shot by Amber Guyger, a white female officer who entered his apartment claiming she thought it was hers. Guyger was convicted of murder and sentenced to ten years in prison. Atatiana Jefferson was also killed in her home, on October 12, 2019, by a white Fort Worth, Texas, police officer, Aaron Dean, who was eventually convicted of manslaughter and sentenced to nearly twelve years in prison. Ahmaud Arbery, unarmed, was shot and killed while jogging by two white men, one a former police officer, in Glynn County, Georgia. No arrests were made in the Arbery case for months until the state attorney general and the Georgia Bureau of Investigations entered the case. In late May 2020, forty-six-year-old George Floyd, a Black man, who was handcuffed with his hands behind his back, was suffocated to death after a white police office pinned him to the ground with the full weight of the officer's body on Mr. Floyd's neck. Mr. Floyd reportedly cried out numerous times that he could not breathe, all to no avail. Mr. Floyd died from his injuries. The police officer was sentenced to twenty-two and a half years in prison for the Floyd killing. In August 2020, white seventeen-year-old Kyle Rittenhouse was arrested for killing two people protesting the shooting multiple times in the back of a Black man, Jacob Blake, in Kenosha, Wisconsin. On March 13, 2020, Breonna Taylor, a Black twenty-six-year-old emergency room technician, was shot to death in a botched police raid on her apartment.

Ferguson, Missouri; Trayvon Martin; Christopher Dorner; Eric Garner; Walter Scott; the shootings of police officers in Washington, Dallas, New York; the white supremacist rallies in Charlottesville and Gainesville; the unarmed, law-abiding Black people shot in their own homes—perhaps all these incidents may be isolated and unrelated. However, the racial events in Ferguson and the rest of the nation spurred protests on some of the most elite colleges and university campuses in the nation, which seemed to explode with racial tension. Between September and November 2015, a series of incidents at the Columbia campus of the University of Missouri resulted in the resignation of the president of the main campus and the University of Missouri system chancellor. Black students at Harvard, Yale, Duke, and Claremont McKenna College protested for various reasons. Jack Dickey, writing for *Time* magazine on May 31, 2016, said, "At more than 50 schools in all, student protesters made demands to right what they see as historic wrongs. . . . It's been a half century since we've seen US colleges so roiled."[21]

Eight years later, elite colleges and universities across the nation have been again rocked by protests not seen since the 1960s. The terrible attacks by Hamas against those perceived to be their enemies and the horrifying violence against Palestinians by the Israeli military have led to marches, tent encampments, protests, and arrests. The racial implications are hard to ignore. Perhaps, however, these incidents are not isolated but instead are symptomatic of larger problems of both inequality and the increasing power of out-groups and the voices of peoples of color to impact the social and political system in ways unimagined prior to the twenty-first century. Government officials, journalists, community leaders, and organizers are all wondering aloud about a race war and whether Dylann Roof might succeed after all.

The December 26, 2015, *Washington Post* article "A Year of Reckoning: Police Fatally Shoot Nearly 1,000" found that while "the kind of incidents that have ignited protests in many U.S. communities—most often, white police officers killing unarmed black men—represent less than 4 percent of fatal police shootings. . . . Race remains the most volatile flash point in any accounting of police shootings. Although black men make up only 6 percent of the U.S. population, they account for 40 percent of the unarmed men shot to death by police this year."[22]

Rather than newspaper reports, however, scholars should cite Department of Justice reports on the incidence of white on Black police shootings, but no such comprehensive Department of Justice report exists. On October 13, 2016, Barack Obama's former attorney general, Loretta E. Lynch, outlined a plan to start collecting nationwide data on the use of force. That is, until recently, no one has been counting the cost of all this violence, as difficult as that may be to believe.

21. Dickey, "Revolution on America's Campuses," para. 2.
22. Kindy et al., "Year of Reckoning," paras. 3, 5.

Former president Joe Biden has named his top three priorities as: 1) COVID-19, 2) racial inequality, and 3) climate. Biden's recognition that racial equality is one of the most important goals is also a recognition that the nation has not solved the fundamental racial equality issues of the 1960s, when race relations was the top concern of most Americans and provided the impetus for the major civil rights legislation.

THE SOLUTION

At the very least, Americans should know the costs for varying levels of racial inequality in America. Beyond that, America should quickly be buying up low-cost equality programs like there is no tomorrow, because tomorrow may not arrive. The assumption here is that America does not want to pay high costs for racial equality because, heretofore, America has avoided or disdained even the lowest-cost programs. If this assumption is correct, the best solution to avoiding high-cost fixes is not only to pay the low-cost fixes, but to pay them early. If people do not want the expense of a new automobile, certainly they should be religious about regular oil changes and maintenance on the old clunker. This low-cost solution metaphorically does not suggest eradicating racial equality any more than regular maintenance of an old clunker will give the look and feel of a brand new automobile. The purpose of the low-cost solution is to avoid a major life-threatening catastrophe.

Many books and newspaper articles have been written about the two radically different worldviews of Blacks and whites in America. The works of Richard Morin, Andrew Hacker, Donald Kinder and Lynn Sanders, Joe Feagin and Melvin Sikes, William Darity and Samuel Myers, the National Advisory Commission on Civil Disorders, and others come readily to mind.[23] These differing worldviews of Blacks and whites stem from the racial inequality between them. Black and white worldviews are so at odds with each other that only one can be correct. Further, these Black and white perspectives are on a collision course that threatens not only our civic culture and discourse but democracy itself and the physical survival of the nation. Chapter 5 shows why only Black worldviews are supported by the best social science.

Nevertheless, this book does not specifically focus on the differing views of Blacks and whites, the abuses Blacks normally suffer at the hands

23. Atkinson, *Inequality*; Darity and Myers, *Persistent Disparity*; Feagin and Sikes, *Living with Racism*; Hacker, *Two Nations*; Hajnal, *Dangerously Divided*; Kerner, *Kerner Report*; Kinder and Sanders, *Divided by Color*; Morin, "Distorted Image of Minorities"; Piketty, *Economics of Inequality*; Shapiro, *Toxic Inequality*; Stiglitz, *Price of Inequality*.

of whites, the incidents of Black retaliation, or racial disparities in the COVID-19 crisis. Neither is this book about President Donald Trump's felony convictions, legal woes, a level of racial animosity not seen perhaps since Andrew Johnson, or the riot by Trump supporters at the Capitol and the battle to reconstruct the nation. President Trump's 2024 presidential election win is not a main focus here. The lack of a strong connection between racial equality and which party controls the White House may be difficult for readers to understand. Figures 7.1 and 7.2 help to make this clear. In figure 7.1 the annual inflation-adjusted budget for the EEOC, the nation's premier antidiscrimination enforcement agency, has not increased since the Great Society years or the end of the 1970s. Neither Presidents Obama, Trump, nor Biden changed this fact. In figure 7.2, compared to the nation's GDP, the EEOC budget has decreased markedly since the 1970s, regardless of who occupies the White House.

Table 1 The Cost of Racial Equality (M=Million, B=Billion, T=Trillion)						
	Economic Cost	Impact on Racial Equality	Other Costs			
	Column 1	Column 2	Column 3	Column 4	Column 5	Column 6
			Intrinsic Political Cost (IPC)	Perceived Political Cost (PPC)	Social (Group) Cost (SGC)	Cultural (Individual) Cost (CIC)
Low Economic Cost Equality	Low economic cost—under $100B Equality under the law=$0 Political equality=$0 School bussing=$500M Affirmative action=$0–52B EEOC funding=$500M	Low. Current affirmative action programs are merit based and do not work to equalize the lower human capital of Blacks or impact persons outside the labor market.	Low IPC. Voting rights and affirmative action have been supported by both major political parties.	High PPC. The Black franchise and affirmative action are used to create racial block voting and to rally voters by race.	Low SGC. Voting rights, diversity and antidiscrimination are widely accepted and actually improve social conditions.	High CIC. Large changes in white attitudes, thinking, and behavior are required to end racial voting polarization, support school integration and affirmative action.

THE COST OF RACIAL EQUALITY

Table 1
The Cost of Racial Equality
(M=Million, B=Billion, T=Trillion)

	Economic Cost	Impact on Racial Equality	Other Costs			
	Column 1	Column 2	Column 3	Column 4	Column 5	Column 6
Medium Economic Cost Equality	Medium economic cost—$100B–$800B Wage discrimination=$180B Poverty equalization=$134B Poverty elimination=$791B K–12 equality=$650B Racial wealth equality=$123B–$232B Opioid crisis=$100B–$504B	Medium. Ending wage discrimination, equalizing or eliminating poverty and providing high-quality K–12 education will remake the American racial landscape much as it began to do in the Great Society.	Low to medium IPC. Antidiscrimination in wages, poverty elimination, K–12 equality, and wealth redistribution have had some political support at one time or another. Overcoming white voter resistance requires bold leadership.	High PPC. Strong antidiscrimination enforcement, school bussing, and income transfer programs are opposed by most whites.	Low SGC. Poverty elimination, K–12 equality, and other redistribution programs have high social value and few costs.	High CIC. White responses about the relationship between poverty and race, Black stereotypes, rejection of government integration programs, and blaming the victims of discrimination require much reeducation and training.
High Economic Cost Equality	High economic cost—$1.5T–$12T Social welfare=$2T Reparations, low estimate=$3.5T Reparations, high estimate=$12T Contemporary wage reparations=$11.7T	High. Social welfare is already a great racial equalizer. Black reparations start at the level of social welfare and go up.	Low IPC. All major political parties support social security and the welfare state. Black reparations are an exception.	Low PPC. All major political parties support social security and the welfare state. Black reparations are an exception.	Low SGC. Almost all countries with socialized medicine and high welfare costs have high life quality.	High CIC. Americans have become acculturated to a hierarchy of inequality with Blacks and Latinos on the bottom. These lifestyles will not change easily.

This book concerns instead what the cost will be to fix the economic, political, social, and cultural problems of historic and contemporary racial inequality that lay at the root of Black and white differing worldviews and hostility. This is a book about the long-term costs of ignoring racial inequality under the mistaken assumptions that no one has costs to pay, or that costs may be avoided indefinitely. Many of the most recent racial incidents are evidence that much of America, including white, Black, Latino, Asian, and American Indian, are mistaken about the real costs ahead.

This book argues that racial equality has differing levels of cost: high, medium, and low. America should be purchasing low-cost programs not only to avoid the possibility of high-cost programs, but also to avoid the social, political, and economic disruption that results from large-scale racial inequality.

The most conservative Americans should be the grandest supporters of low-cost equality programs, such as affirmative action, school integration, and voting rights, not only because these programs are relatively inexpensive, but also because racial inequality breeds social, economic, and political disruption. Costs may be avoided in the short run, but to ignore them, as chapter 10 makes clear, is penny wise and pound foolish. Paying the low costs early rather than the high costs later is a better option for those who are risk and cost averse.

Waiting to pay high costs later not only involves all the natural cost expenses of the programs, but also the clean-up, if possible, of the social, economic, and political damage. The evidence for the costs of racial equality lie in an analysis of Black and white culture, the law, affirmative action, wealth and poverty, political polarization, K–12 education, and the welfare state.

HOW COST IS MEASURED

This book divides racial equality programs into low, medium, and high cost, based primarily on their dollar costs, which relate to their ability to eliminate racial inequality. Table 1 shows the three levels of economic cost (low, medium, and high) in columns 1 and 2 and the four other types of cost (intrinsic political costs, perceived political costs, and social and cultural costs) in columns 3–6. Theoretically, each type of cost could be applied to every equality program and then analyzed, but this task quickly becomes awkward. Rather, targeted examples in each category are revelatory.

ECONOMIC COST

Economic costs are simply the dollar costs of the programs. Economic costs are the financial, market, or productivity outlays for the relevant programs. As a rule of thumb, in column 1 of table 1, low-cost equality is any racial equality program under $100 billion. Medium-cost equality is any program over $100 billion but under $1 trillion. High-cost equality is any program over $1 trillion. While these dollar amounts are convenient estimates, the amount of money spent on a program does matter.

THE COST OF RACIAL EQUALITY

Affirmative action programs, to the surprise of many, are low-dollar-cost programs, and they make money for the United States, which is probably why they are still here in spite of all the complaining and objections. Even a worst-case cost for affirmative action is only $52 billion per year, about as much as Wall Street bonuses before the Great Recession, which began in December 2007.

Affirmative action economic costs are low because they are merit-based labor and education market programs. The GOP should be the greatest supporter of low-cost racial equality programs, such as affirmative action, because of the programs' natural alignment with their constituency—whites who do not want to pay large sums for social programs for the poor non-white, Black, or Latino. Because so much of racial inequality takes place outside the labor and postsecondary education markets, the ability of most low-cost programs to affect racial equality is somewhat limited.

Table 1, column 1, also illustrates examples of medium-cost economic programs: racial equalization of wages ($180 billion), equalizing poverty across races ($134 billion), poverty elimination ($791 billion), K–12 racial equality ($650 billion), and racial wealth equality ($123–$232 billion). Social welfare ($2 trillion) and reparations for slavery and contemporary discrimination ($1.5–$12 trillion and up) top the list for high economic cost equality in column 1 of table 1.

Column 2 of table 1 shows that economically, racial equality is much the same as any product—usually you get what you pay for. In column 2, low-cost programs generally have a low impact on racial equality. Affirmative action is low cost because it is merit based and assists only the skilled who just happen to be Black. Affirmative action thus has a limited ability to impact racial inequality. This limitation is not a fault of affirmative action programs, but rather a reality of their nature.

Exceptions always exist to this broad general rule of the market that you get what you pay for. School bussing for integration is a bargain and costs only $500 million per year for the whole country and by most measures pays large benefits on the educational outcomes for Black and Latino children, without harming white children.

In column 2 of table 1, ending racial inequality in the labor market has a medium impact on racial inequality only because most racial inequality takes place outside the labor market. Examples of racial inequality outside the labor market are poverty, K–12 education, and wealth inequality.

OASI, at a cost of nearly three-quarters of a trillion dollars per year, is only one part of the much larger $2-trillion social welfare system that is progressive and returns more to poorer workers than those who are better off. Racial equality may not be exactly like a product a person can buy from the shelf in the market, but the point is that market costs can be calculated.

Besides economic costs, however, political, social, and cultural costs also arise. Columns 3–6 of table 1 go along with buying racial equality because racial equality in the United States is a sociopolitical problem. All social programs involve political, social, and cultural as well as economic costs.

POLITICAL COSTS

In table 1, political costs may be intrinsic (column 3) or perceived (column 4). Intrinsic political cost is how much a political party would have to change in fundamental ideology or ideas to support an equality program. Intrinsic political cost measures how different the racial equality program is from the beliefs of the party's most loyal constituents. If all major parties support or have supported such a program at one time or another, little essential or intrinsic political cost accrues, since the program is not naturally partisan.

Perceived political costs are those costs that a political party would have to pay in votes, public education, or influence should they decide to support such a program. Once an issue becomes a political football and the parties take sides to attract a voter base, the perceived cost can be very high.

This distinction between intrinsic and perceived political costs is apparent in affirmative action and social welfare programs. Both programs were supported by both major parties over the last forty years, but the enfranchisement of Black voters after 1965 changed the political landscape. The parties became racially polarized and the perceived political cost went up substantially. Thus, the GOP does not support affirmative action, even though Richard Nixon, a Republican, supported it to such a degree that he is often mistakenly believed to be its inventor.

In column 3 of table 1, antidiscrimination enforcement in the labor market also has low to moderate intrinsic political costs, since the FEPCs set up by the federal government and the states during and after WWII crossed party lines. However, labor market antidiscrimination enforcement has high perceived political costs in table 1, column 4. Social welfare, particularly for the middle class, is broadly supported across party lines and has low intrinsic and perceived political costs in columns 3 and 4 of table 1, even though these programs carry some of the highest economic costs.

SOCIAL COSTS

The terms "social" and "cultural deficiency" usually apply to theories of racial inequality. In this context the term "social" may imply the behaviors of racial groups of people. Social costs are the behavioral changes racial groups and societal structures must navigate to create a level of racial equality. For example, employment discrimination against Blacks in firms of fifteen or more people is already a violation of the law. Social security, a program with high economic costs, is already a legal entitlement. Because of the high level of support for social welfare, particularly for the middle class, these programs have low social group costs in column 5 of table 1.

A few small groups want to end antidiscrimination laws and social security, but these programs are widely accepted and approved. Thus, the group behavior (social) costs of implementing antidiscrimination in employment or social security are low to nonexistent in column 5 of table 1.

Column 5 of table 1 also shows that medium economic cost programs, such as poverty elimination and K–12 racial equality, have low social costs since they involve few changes in group behaviors; most peoples, regardless of race or party, want high-quality education for their children and oppose racial discrimination. Group ideas, however, are not tantamount to individual behaviors.

Sometimes common terms have specific meanings in certain fields. The terms "speech," "privacy," or "liberty" have specific meanings in the law and refer to freedoms in the Bill of Rights (the first ten amendments) of the Constitution of the United States. Whenever a term of art is used for a specific field, this will be noted in the text. "Affirmative action" is one such term and was coined in the Wagner Labor Relations Act of 1935, officially the National Labor Relations Act of 1935. The term "social costs" has a very specific meaning in the field of economics. In economics, social costs refer to "the total cost of any activity. This includes private costs which fall directly on the person or firm conducting the activity, as well as external costs outside the price system which fall on other people or firms."[24] Social cost may also be defined as "the sum of money which is just adequate when paid as compensation to restore to their original utility levels all who lose as a result of the production of the output. The social cost is the opportunity cost to society (i.e., to all individuals in society) rather than just to one firm or individual. One of the major reasons why social costs differ from the

---

24. Hashimzade et al., "Social Cost," para. 1.

observed private costs is due to the existence of externalities or external costs."[25]

Social costs, and cultural costs discussed below, refer to the effort required to eradicate the social and cultural deficiencies used in the field of sociology and made popular by Mario Barrera.[26] Social cost is the amount of social or group deficiency and how much effort is involved in changing the deficits or defects of a racial group. Classic Black social deficiencies were thought to be female-headed families, male role confusion, poor socialization, weak family structure, sexual promiscuity, or crime. How much effort (cost) is involved in changing these deficiencies, if they exist at all, is what is meant by social cost. The sociological and economic terms are not totally unrelated in that they both refer to a type of aggregate costs for changes in society. The economic concept of social costs tends to be monetary. The sociological concept of social deficiency costs may ultimately be synthesized into monetary costs but here should be thought of in terms of low, medium, or high societal effort to conform a group's behavior or ideas to fit some social science reality. Social and cultural deficiency is usually thought to apply only to people of color. Here, the concepts are applied with equal force to whites.

CULTURAL COSTS

Cultural costs refer to individual behaviors in which people must engage. Antidiscrimination in employment may be the law, but discrimination in employment is still widely practiced and rarely enforced. Because of this, a white person automatically is part of the system of white privilege, even unwittingly. By contrast, a Black person cannot help but be a part of the system of racial oppression, no matter from which class. Also a substantial number of whites are active participants in the racist system. In column 6 of table 1, changes to the cultural belief systems and individual behaviors of whites, even for a low-cost program like affirmative action, are high. Likewise, individual white ideas about Black stereotypes, Blacks as the cause of higher rates of Black poverty, and white rejection of large-scale government intervention to alleviate racial inequality mean that changes to white ideas in these areas involve high cultural costs in table 1. Cultural costs here refer to the effort involved (high, medium, or low) in changing individual behaviors to match some standard of acceptable behavior that matches some type of politico-economic reality.

25. Pearce, *MIT Dictionary*, 398.
26. Barrera, *Race and Class*, 176.

EQUALITY AND INEQUALITY

Absolute equality means that no statistically significant economic, political, social, or cultural differences exist among racial groups, and if statistically significant differences do occur among racial groups, these differences are practically insignificant. If race were not a factor in any decision made at any personal, corporate, or governmental level, no statistically significant differences would exist between racial groups. Absolute equality is a society at its best. While other measures of equality exist, few have been as profound as MLK Jr. when he said, "Most whites in America . . . including many persons of good will, proceed from a premise that equality is a loose expression for improvement."[27] Fixing inequality is very different from creating equality. Inequality implies social systems that are operating with bias, discrimination, prejudice, racism, and maybe even bigotry. Attacking inequality involves removing these system imbalances.

Creating a type of procedural equality involves removing inequality or barriers to achieving equality. The focus of this book is not on procedural equality or simply removing barriers that create inequality. Equality assumes a type of make-whole relief that corrects and compensates for the past wrongs and enforces the present to assure compliance. This book discusses levels of equality but always in the sense of compensatory relief, which operates to force the oppressor to disgorge some or all of the ill-gotten gains of oppression and not to reward but to reimburse the oppressed.

Some of the greatest legal philosophers of the twentieth century, from many different perspectives, have recognized the concept of recompense. H. L. A. Hart explained, "The distinctive features of justice and their special connection with law begin to emerge if it is observed that most of the criticisms made in terms of just and unjust could almost equally well be conveyed by the words 'fair' and 'unfair.' . . . Hence what is typically fair or unfair is a 'share' . . . when some injury has been done and compensation or redress is claimed."[28] John Rawls's "difference principle" recognized that even if everyone entered this world not knowing what their station in life would be (the "veil of ignorance"), differences and inequalities would be present, such as race and gender. Thus, according to John Rawls:

> The difference principle gives some weight to the considerations singled out by the principle of redress. This is the principle that undeserved inequalities call for redress; and since inequalities of birth and natural endowment are undeserved, these inequalities

---

27. King, *Where Do We Go from Here*, 8.
28. Hart, *Concept of Law*, 158.

are to be somehow compensated for. Thus, the principle holds that to treat all persons equally and provide genuine equality of opportunity, society must give more attention to those with fewer native assets and those born into the less favorable social positions. The idea is to redress the bias of contingencies in the direction of equality.[29]

Although Robert Nozick admits he is uncertain how far back the concept of compensation should go, nevertheless "the principle of rectification presumably will make use of its best estimate of subjunctive information about what would have occurred . . . if the injustice had not taken place."[30]

In MLK Jr.'s last book, *Where Do We Go from Here*, written in 1968, King identified "the problems of inequality [as] meaningless unless a time dimension is given to programs for their solution."[31] King used the word "inequality" only twice in his last book, choosing instead to focus on the solution of "equality" and using the term some forty-one times in connection with the programs that would bring equality. King was clear. Equality meant integration, economic parity, prioritizing Black problems, justice, immediacy, cultural equivalency, the complete elimination of poverty and war in the US and the world, educational expenditures, Black preferences in hiring before credentials, rights for welfare recipients—and the list went on and on. Absolute parity in every economic, social, political, and cultural area is beyond the level of reparations. Anything less than parity is a type of compensation. Chapter 10 closes with the concept of atonement, which may be the only real way to achieve absolute parity.

CHAPTERS

Chapter 2, "Black Deficiency Theory and Cost," explains why Black cultural change carries very little if any cost in achieving racial equality. Most Black cultural pathology is a response to white oppression, that is, little evidence supports any inherent Black social, cultural, or biological deficiency. In addition, because of oppression, Blacks have been forced to outperform whites in many areas, including voting, savings, education, and skill.

Further, concentrating on Black social and cultural deficiency as a solution to inequality is counterproductive. As Blacks and other out-groups achieve white educational credentials, training, and skill, they face the structural and systemic barriers that always were present and find they are

29. Rawls, *Theory of Justice*, 86.
30. Nozick, *Anarchy, State, and Utopia*, 152–53.
31. King, *Where Do We Go from Here*, 87.

further behind their white peers than before. This creates justifiable frustration and anger, which may hamper racial reconciliation.

Social, cultural, and biological deficiency theories posit that Blacks have bad social structures (female-headed families), bad culture (present-time orientation, lazy), or bad genes (less inherent intelligence), which cause bad behavior and low performance, and result in racial inequality. Cultural and social deficiency theories are inherently weak explanations, however, for the racial inequality in American society.

Rather, structural and bias theories are the strongest explanations for Black inequality. Slavery and the aftermath of slavery—poverty, violence, and massive discrimination—created the conditions present today. All contemporary racial inequality involving Blacks is directly traceable to the slave past. The best theory illustrates that racial inequality is caused by white racism and practice. Racial inequality is not caused by welfare, Black deficiency, or Black family life, as some whites have argued.

The Black and white public disagree as much as the experts do about what causes racial inequality and how to implement equality. Simple majority rule usually settles this difference of opinion. Unfortunately, white public opinion has little to contribute when it comes to ideas about racial equality. White opinion is both a cause of the problem and an impediment to the solution. This white ignorance is what increases cultural costs for racial equality in table 1.

Many whites even have difficulty believing that racial inequality exists. Chapter 2 demonstrates how important good theory is in social science and why all information must be interpreted through good theory. Rules exist for good theory, and timing, process, parsimony, and prediction all support structural and bias theories as the best for explaining contemporary and historic Black inequality.

Chapter 3, "White Cultural Belief Systems: A Glass Half Empty," challenges many ideas about race held by whites and explains why eliminating white privileges carries high cultural costs. Changing cultural beliefs and ideas involves little economic cost, which is one reason why chapter 3 is located in the low-cost part of the book.

Another reason chapter 3 is in the low-cost section of the book is that these belief systems must be demystified early, before other issues can be addressed. Low economic cost, however, in no way means that a racial equality program is costless. Belief systems, particularly in the white community, have been resistant to change precisely because the major social institutions (media, schools, churches, government) lend support to these ideas.

Cultural belief systems about race and racial equality that lack empirical support are inherently dangerous when combined with the penchant in America for anti-Black thought. First, erroneous belief systems block knowledge of the truth. Second, belief systems based more on prejudice and bias than on real evidence eliminate the ability to correct the initial error.

Beliefs about the inherent rightness of American democracy, that equal opportunity exists for all, that color blindness is possible in a society built on white racial superiority, and the ability of any president, Obama, Trump, Biden, or whoever, to institute substantive racial equality without major system changes, all must be corrected to enhance understanding regarding the economic, cultural, political, and social cost for equality. The white majority firmly holds most of these cultural beliefs, and that situation increases the cultural costs of change.

Scholars also hold some of these cultural beliefs, accept that Blacks are culturally or socially deficient, and take issue with the concept of large-scale government economic support for Black equality because it is presumed that these deficiencies are not easily remedied. Many of the ideas held about the Black poor lack empirical support. Most of the poor are not Black. No objectifiable evidence is apparent that Blacks prefer welfare to work, and most of the poor either have jobs or are looking for work.

Many have argued that welfare causes nonwork. While not much empirical data supports this contention, chapter 3 argues that welfare should cause nonwork. Many people should be protected from predatory employers: children, the sick, mothers with young children, the elderly, and caregivers, most of whom are women. Little empirical evidence supports the centuries-old idea that welfare for the poor, provided at subsistence levels, is sufficient to keep large numbers of people out of the labor market. Neither is there solid information that welfare destroys Black families.

Rather, the refusal of non-Black men to marry Black women and the lack of suitable Black partners seems to be the biggest reason for the declining marriage rate among Black women, on welfare or not. The ready acceptance of these erroneous ideas, mainly by the white public, is a central reason why the glass of racial equality appears half empty and not half full.

Chapter 4, "The Costs of the Law," explains why the law carries high perceived political and cultural costs. Martin Luther King Jr. explained that it costs no money to integrate lunch counters. Convincing whites, however, that their economic and political advantages are not based on merit, but on the oppression of others, will challenge the foundations of American government and law.

Most white affirmative action is not defined as such. White affirmative action and privilege is defined as merit because it passes from generation to generation. White affirmative action is difficult for most whites to see. The difficulty many have in seeing white privilege makes the political cost of eliminating white affirmative action high, even though the overall economic costs to the society at large are low. Society as a whole would benefit from a leveling of the playing field, so that more groups could participate.

The US Constitution is an excellent example of the interaction of social and political costs. The Constitution wrote into the supreme law of the land the subjugation of Blacks and the superior position of whites. Even today the difficulty of changing the Constitution works against institutional change. If we define generic affirmative action as the operation of governments, institutions, and business to advance the interests of racial groups, in most of American history, institutions are accustomed to assuring that the interests of whites advance above those of other groups. Historic white privileges from the wealth cotton provided to the nation and the one-drop rule, which defined any individual with Black ancestry as Black, regardless of their skin color, assured that Blacks would enter society severely hampered and trapped by how society and law defined them.

Black affirmative action programs began with free Blacks in the North and South before the Civil War and continued during the period of Reconstruction. Overall, however, Black affirmative action programs have been limited in comparison to programs favoring whites. The high tide of Black affirmative action is thought to have been Richard Nixon's Philadelphia quota plans. The Philadelphia Plan never approached representative numbers of Blacks in the skilled construction trades. Nevertheless, the data shows that the Philadelphia Plan was meritorious, broke down the racial caste system in the construction industry, and was one of the most successful examples of low-cost, substantive equality programs.

Chapter 5, "How Much Affirmative Action Costs America," illustrates that despite wild claims to the contrary, affirmative action carries surprisingly low, if any, financial cost and returns large productivity gains. The economic cost for affirmative action can be measured three ways: worst case, average case, and best case. The average case should be what people focus on, since the average cost is the most likely cost. On average, affirmative action makes money for America because Blacks often are the most productive workers firms have. Blacks are relatively more productive and tend to be better trained than equivalent whites for the jobs they hold because Blacks are discriminated against and not promoted as quickly as whites and thus have more experience and skill relative to their jobs. Plus, administrative costs for affirmative action compliance are statistically zero.

Research studies show that few people are interested in the average costs for affirmative action. They want the worst-case costs. Even the worst-case costs are low. America should be more than happy to pay these expenses. The most conservative political parties should embrace these costs because low-cost equality is a cheap way of avoiding the potentially high-cost programs. The only reason low-cost equality programs are opposed is that most Americans believe they will never have to pay for the high-cost programs. Most of the historical evidence shows the possibility of avoiding all costs are highly unlikely.

Chapter 6, "The Price of Wage Discrimination, Poverty, and Wealth Inequality," begins the medium-cost section of the book. Chapter 6 shows why eliminating poverty, equalizing wealth, and ending wage discrimination would remake the racial landscape, even though most racial discrimination takes place outside the labor market.

Poverty is a type of inequality that takes place outside the labor market. Since poverty is measured at a subsistence level, official poverty levels lead to erroneous ideas about who the poor are. A more realistic poverty level, those within 150 percent of the official poverty line, would contain about 25 percent of the US population. Most people are only a job loss away from poverty, as the Great Recession and COVID-19 pandemic have shown. For Blacks and whites to have the same level of poverty would mean the Black poor need to receive an additional $134 billion. To eliminate poverty for everyone would cost $791 billion in transfers from those who have to those who do not have.

Americans seem to be fascinated with wealth. Most wealth is not earned, but inherited. Wealth is the best measure of the historic racial injustices in the US. Wealth is the difference between what an individual owns and what that person owes.

Wealth is difficult to measure because most of it is hidden. Table 1 shows that wealth inequality between Blacks and whites costs Blacks up to $232 billion. Even the Black middle class have less wealth than the white poor because the wealth of most people is in home equity.

Discrimination against Blacks in the labor market costs them $180 billion in wages and salaries, more than what Blacks receive in welfare payments from the government. If anyone ever thought that affirmative action and welfare were sufficient reparations for the discrimination Blacks receive, they are sadly mistaken.

Chapter 7, "Trouble Ahead: The Danger of Political Power on the Cheap," measures the intrinsic and perceived political cost of racial equality. Chapter 7 is in the medium-cost section of the book and based primarily on the intrinsic and perceived political costs. American racial political polarization costs little economically, but perceived political costs for ending the nightmare of racial block voting are very high. The most recent evidence of this phenomenon is the Trump 2016 election and Supreme Court rulings on voting rights and affirmative action from a court recently packed by political skullduggery.

Nonetheless, the election of Barack Obama shocked nearly everyone. The most farsighted never expected to see a Black US president in their lifetimes. Barack Obama the man is even more fascinating than his election. In fundraising, Obama seemed to have few peers. He energized a class of voters, the young, even more than the star power of Bobby Kennedy could manage. His Nobel Prize signified that around the world he represented hope for the future.

After Obama came Trump. Unlike for Obama, most voters did not vote for President Trump in 2016 or 2020. Whites have been the only racial group who voted mostly for Trump. In many respects, however, Donald Trump must be as fascinating as Obama. Trump defied his own party's elected leaders. Trump won the presidency even though Hillary Clinton spent twice as much money as Donald Trump in nearly every category, including money from super PACs in 2016. And not even claimed meddling by Vladimir Putin explains why Hillary Clinton's pull among Black voters ranked among the lowest percentages for the Democratic Party in over half a century. Trump pressed on and won in spite of the polls that predicted his failure in 2016.

Trump's loss in the 2020 election and his 2024 felony convictions in New York as he sought a second term change none of the foregoing. For the second time in 2020, Trump stunned the polls, which had predicted a nearly catastrophic loss. Instead, Trump garnered the second highest number of votes in election history, losing by only 2.7 percent of the popular vote to Joe Biden. And Trump would have won a second time in 2020 had it not been for the loss of five states (Arizona, Georgia, Michigan, Pennsylvania, and Wisconsin) that voted for him in 2016. Even more impressive is that Trump put together what must be considered in some sense a multiracial coalition in 2020, which was 81.6 percent white, 3.3 percent Black, 8.8 percent Latino, 2.6 percent Asian, and 3.4 percent others (table 7.1).

Whatever losses Trump suffered in 2020, he reversed most of them in 2024. Arizona, Georgia, Michigan, Pennsylvania, and Wisconsin all went for Trump in 2024. And Trump's 2024 multiracial coalition must be considered impressive for a GOP candidate with 80 percent white, 3 percent Black, 10 percent Latino, 2 percent Asian, and 3 percent others (table 7.1). Blacks voting for Trump were sufficient to provide the margin of victory, supplying 3 percent of the 1.8 percent needed for Trump to win. This is amazing for a GOP candidate.

Trump's March 2024 felony convictions were predicted to inhibit his goals to regain the White House in November of that same year. It was said that no president or former president has ever been a convicted criminal, not even Richard Nixon. Yet Trump strengthened his support among his strongest supporters. Trump's support among white, Black, and Latino males increased from 2020. Trump even increased his support among Latinas (table 7.3). Political scientists are as of yet grappling to fully understand the phenomena known as Trumpism.

Chapter 7 explains that for all of Obama's star power, Trump's tenacity, Biden's physical and political stumbles, and Harris's adaptability and courage in switching quickly from vice presidential to presidential candidate, the US buys political power on the cheap. While certainly the racial and political differences between Obama and Trump are profound, nevertheless, when it comes to support for antidiscrimination enforcement funding for the EEOC, the very essence of DEI, and the antithesis of Trump politics and policy, there is little practicable difference between Trump and Obama in policy outcomes for EEOC funding (figs. 7.1 and 7.2). This is political power on the cheap. This chapter concerns the racial polarization that threatens to destroy the nation if not remedied. This polarization is apparent in the party platforms and racial makeups of the party coalitions. The political polarization that occurred after the Black vote was enfranchised has raised the stakes for the perceived political costs to the highest level. To support political issues perceived to favor Blacks is to lose white votes. Failure to mention specific programs favorable to Blacks is to ensure that few Blacks or other minorities will rally to a specific cause. Such choices encourage the GOP to pander to white voters simply because they are white.

The Democratic Party fares little better than the GOP with the perceived cost of specific programs favorable to Blacks. The Democratic Party's deal with the coalition of Black voters seems to center upon verbal support for programs of low or no economic cost (affirmative action, ghetto enrichment for K–12 schools, and voting rights). Support by Democratic candidates at the national level for any program seriously addressing Black economic and political inequality and white advantages is perceived as high cost because it would seriously jeopardize the possibility of whites remaining in the coalition.

For this reason, real Black political interests are almost never on the ballot; nationally elected Black officials are only a small fraction of their population percentage. Blacks are no longer the margin of victory in close elections because of racial polarization, and Blacks are taken for granted in a political party that is not viable without their votes. For all of President Obama's brilliance, Obama won the lowest percentage of white votes for any president in Democratic Party history of the last sixty years, and President Joe Biden received the second lowest (fig. 7.3).

THE COST OF RACIAL EQUALITY

America is teetering on the precipice of a political crisis as the minority population nears a majority in less than thirty years. The shrinking economic pie, white racial bigotry, racially polarized voting, and the failure of presidential leadership to teach the white electorate that substantive equality is in their interest have created a volatile mixture of racial antagonism that is never good for political stability. The handwriting is already on the wall. While the 2024 presidential election seems to have left Blacks and their allies in disarray, the wins of the GOP cannot be sustained if America is to remain a democracy. The shrinking white voter base in both major parties means that the United States must find a way around racially polarized politics or fail as a democratic nation state (fig. 7.3). Figure 7.2 (low support of the EEOC) and the 2024 election of Trump with a strong anti-DEI agenda portend a direction toward failure rather than success.

Chapter 8, "The Fierce Urgency of Now: K–12 Education," argues that racial equality is a low-cost fix that every American should jump at if they want a bright future for America. Chapter 8 calculates mainly the economic cost of K–12 educational equality and places K–12 education as medium-high cost.

High-quality K–12 education should be a right that every American child receives at birth regardless of their gender, language, race, or region. Unfortunately, we stack the odds against poor Latino and Black children by keeping most of them in dilapidated schools with little chance for escape. Wyandanch, New York, the poorest and Blackest school district in the state, is a perfect example of the type of education America gives to its Black children. Because so many Black children are poor, they need not just equal education, but a better education than their white, middle-class peers. These poor Black children have so much to overcome, equal is simply not good enough.

America spends about $500 billion per year to educate children. That is a lot of money. Ten times the cost of worst-case affirmative action. But chapter 8 shows that we spend it grudgingly. Full equality for Black school children in table 1 would cost another $145 billion so that each Black child would be at the 99th percentile of school spending, and a mere $500 million to transport each and every Black child to a high-quality white school.

School integration is not a popular topic because ghetto enrichment (trying to create high-quality racially segregated schools in poor Black and Latino neighborhoods) is the order of the day. However, for the large masses of Black and Latino children there is no evidence that money spent on segregated schools produces the equivalent of a white education. Separate still seems to be inherently unequal.

Chapter 9, "High-Cost Equality: Welfare, Social Security, and Reparations," charges that by balking at low-cost programs, America unwittingly accepts high-cost programs as the only available option. Social security costs a lot of money, but is one of the most equal economic programs in the US. The cost only goes up from here if you want real racial equality.

Social welfare programs are almost always high cost and dwarf other types of equality programs in dollars spent. Social welfare in the US cost about 10 percent of GDP or $2 trillion in table 1. The US is near the bottom of the list in much of the industrialized West in terms of percent of GDP spent for social welfare and equality achieved in society. Infant mortality, a basic measure of social well-being, is surprisingly high in the US compared to nations with far fewer resources.

You might think that social welfare, with its high economic price tag, would also come with a high political and social price tag, but you would be wrong. Only social welfare for the poor is controversial and has high political cost. Poor peoples' welfare is only a minor part of what we spend. Welfare for the middle class and the rich are where more than two-thirds of the dollars go and there is little complaining. Social security and other programs not based on having low income are so ingrained into the American psyche that the spending is written into law and is not even voted on from year to year.

Chapter 9 closes with the issue of reparations for slavery, labor market discrimination, and state-sponsored apartheid. This apartheid was officially endorsed by culture and by law until the 1960s. Black reparations are not considered a serious issue by most white or Black voters. However, the same could be said of voting rights, equal employment, and affirmative action for Blacks in the South in 1906.

Chapter 10, "Penny Wise and Pound Foolish," argues that the nation needs to think about the costs for racial equality not in bits and pieces, but holistically. Seeing the trees, differing levels and types of cost, is important, but understanding the entire forest, the ability to compare, contrast, and weigh one cost and its impact against another cost or multiple costs and their impact, is what allows us to take action. The price of failing to institute substantive racial equality is higher than any of the costs estimated here. The price is the destruction of the nation. Politics can and will change, this is all that is certain. The political coalition in 2045 will be very different than it is today, and as 30 percent of the minority coalition, Blacks will be a force to contend with. In table 1, the price tag for reparations starts at about $1.5 trillion and goes up to more than one year GDP, combined with a strong antidiscrimination enforcement apparatus. This price sounds high, but it is not as high as the rending of the nation that might take place with most of the political power, media control, and money in the hands of a future racial minority, whites. The willingness of the leaders of today's racial majority to pack courts and ignore the law can just as well be exercised by the leaders of tomorrow's racial majority.

Americans should not operate on the assumption that they will always dodge the bullets of political chaos, civil war, ethnic conflict, social crises, and worst of all, natural disasters and pandemics that infect so much of the world. In the long run, reparations and high social welfare payments may be the most economical solution.

Chapter Two

Black Deficiency Theory and Cost

BLACK KNUCKLEHEADS

For many, the solution to Black inequality, self-help, and pulling yourself up follows logically from the cause, individual Black deficiency. Many prominent political commentators and most of the public think that social and economic inequality between groups has its cause in the defective and deficient behaviors of individual group members of particular racial groups rather than outside forces such as oppression and racism.[1] In 2004, Bill Cosby stated:

> These people are not parenting. They are buying things for kids—$500 sneakers for what? And won't spend $200 for "Hooked on Phonics." They're standing on the corner, and they can't speak English, I can't even talk the way these people talk: "why you ain't," "where you is." And I blamed the kid until I heard the mother talk. And then I heard the father talk. . . . Everybody knows it's important to speak English except these knuckleheads. You can't be a doctor with that kind of crap coming out of your mouth.[2]

Most people do not believe that white racial discrimination causes racial inequality. The 1977 General Social Survey (GSS) asked people whether a lack of "motivation and will power to pull themselves up out of poverty" caused the worst jobs, income, and housing of Blacks.[3] Sixty-five percent of

---

1. Carson, *One Nation*, 31; McWhorter, *Losing the Race*; Mead, *Beyond Entitlement*; Riley, *Please Stop Helping Us*, ch. 2.
2. Badie, "Cosby's Rant Got People Talking."
3. T. Smith et al., "General Social Surveys, 1972–2018," mnemonics race, racdif4.

respondents in 1977 responded that yes, the cause for racial inequality in jobs, income, and housing between Blacks and whites was a lack of motivation and willpower on the part of Blacks. Fifty percent of people surveyed in 2012 said the cause for racial inequality is deficient Black motivation and willpower. By 2018, 37.91 percent of people surveyed said lack of motivation and willpower was the reason for racial inequality.[4] However when asked in 2018 if racial inequality is caused by discrimination, 52.37 percent said no.[5]

Since most people dismiss bias and discrimination as the cause of racial inequality and a significant percentage accept cultural deficiency as the reason, no wonder their solution is that Blacks simply should pull themselves up by their bootstraps. In his now famous October 8, 1995, *Washington Post* newspaper article titled "Distorted Image of Minorities," Richard Morin found that 82 percent of the least-informed whites believed that minorities can overcome prejudice and work their way up without special help from the government.

Two-thirds of whites in Morin's *Washington Post* survey said the federal government had no responsibility to ensure racial equality. Writes Morin, "Many Whites in the survey minimized the importance of any past discrimination and traced the source of Black problems to Blacks themselves, with 58 percent of Whites citing the breakup of the Black family as a major cause of problems in the Black community."[6]

The GSS supports Morin's findings about white attitudes about the solutions to racial inequality. The GSS asked respondents if they agreed with the statement that "Irish, Italian, Jewish and many other minorities overcame prejudice and worked their way up. Blacks should do the same without special favors." In 2018, 59 percent of people surveyed agreed Blacks should pull themselves up.[7]

These ideas about self-help versus welfare are strong, particularly when race is involved. For whites, over 73 percent think whites prefer self-help over welfare, but only 13 percent of whites think Blacks prefer self-help over welfare. For Blacks, 64 percent think whites prefer self-help over welfare, but only 22 percent of Blacks think Blacks prefer self-help over welfare.[8]

4. T. Smith et al., "General Social Surveys, 1972–2018," mnemonics racecensus, racdif1.

5. T. Smith et al., "General Social Surveys, 1972–2018," mnemonics racecensus, workwayup.

6. Morin, "Distorted Image of Minorities," para. 27.

7. T. Smith et al., "General Social Surveys, 1972–2018," variables farewhts and fareblks.

8. T. Smith et al., "General Social Surveys, 1972–2018," variables farewhts and fareblks.

White and Black people are incorrect on all counts: first, nearly all the research confirms that the cause of racial inequality between Blacks and whites is white racial discrimination, rather than Black deficiency. Second, given the first point, the logical solution to racial inequality is to stop white bias from actualizing into racialization. Third, few people, .2 percent of whites and 1 percent of Blacks in 2013, receive what is commonly thought of as welfare for the poor—AFDC or TANF (fig. 2.3). Whites rather than Blacks benefit most from welfare. Most people are incorrect about the cause for racial inequality because they do not have good theoretical concepts or understand social science.

The solution to racial inequality follows logically from the cause assuming that the cause is correctly interpreted. The logical solution to white racial discrimination is antidiscrimination enforcement rather than the attempt to fix supposed Black deficiencies. If the government designs social programs based on common understandings of the problem of racial inequality, we will not only waste money but also create what we seek to avoid: racial animosity, division, and alienation, which in turn negatively impact individual behavior. We also fail to rectify the problem of increasing racial inequality as the minority population ratio rapidly increases.

Fixing Black deficiencies carries low cultural costs because little credible evidence exists that racial inequality has its cause in the independent and deficient behaviors of individual Black persons. Because racial differences between Blacks and whites do not stem from Black deficiency, but rather white racial bias, less needs to be changed in Black culture other than the removal of white racial bias. For the most part, Blacks have responded to racial oppression with a diligence, skill, and fortitude that surpasses that of whites in similar circumstances. Blacks vote, save, and achieve educations at higher levels than whites, once starting conditions are controlled. Blacks even outperform whites in job performance.[9]

THE GOOD, THE BAD, THE UGLY: STUDYING RACE IN AMERICA

Erroneous and misguided methods have affected few areas of research as much as racial equality studies. Most people writing about racial inequality

---

9. Bridges and Villemez, "Overeducated Minority Workers"; Holzer and Neumark, "Are Affirmative Action Hires Less Qualified?"; Holzer and Neumark, "Assessing Affirmative Action"; Holzer and Neumark, "What Does Affirmative Action Do?"; Mason, "Race, Culture, and Skill."

are not social scientists and use casual observation to arrive at conclusions.[10] Social scientists have classified theories of racial inequality into three groups: 1) deficiency theory, 2) bias theory, and 3) structural theories. Deficiency theories are subdivided into three groups: 1) cultural deficiency, 2) social deficiency, or 3) biological deficiency.[11] Also researchers have devoted more attention to the problem of investigator bias in race studies than in other areas of research in social science.[12] Nevertheless, social scientists have learned much from the past century, and systematic race studies, when properly conducted, provide us with some of the most telling information about where the nation has been and where the nation is going regarding the race equality issue.

The best principles of social science show that racial inequality has its root cause in bias rather than in the failures of individual Black people, or their deficiency. Because racial inequality is such a volatile issue in the United States, the best social science uses the scientific method to arrive at conclusions and develop basic principles about causation.

Cultural deficiency theories blame racial inequality on the "bad behavior" of individual Blacks rather than group phenomenon. The most familiar example of cultural deficiency was Banfield's *Unheavenly City*, but many others exist today.[13] Social deficiency theories ascribe Black socioeconomic inequality to problems in the social structure of Blacks. The Moynihan Report, published in 1965, is probably the best-known example of a social deficiency theory, but others also are extant.[14]

Biological deficiency theories propound that politico-economic differences between whites and Blacks have their cause in the lower intelligence or higher sexuality of Blacks. In 1989, J. Philippe Rushton, one of the most well-known exponents of biological deficiency, published a paper claiming that susceptibility to AIDS in Africa is based on the genetically driven social behavior of Blacks.[15]

Would that the late Rushton were the only example of biological deficiency, but alas, this literature is always growing.[16] Almost 8 percent of

10. Carson, *One Nation*, 31.

11. Barrera, *Race and Class*, ch. 7.

12. Gould, "Mismeasure by Any Measure"; Van Kleeck, "Foreword."

13. Mead, *Beyond Entitlement*; Steele, *Content of Our Character*; Banfield, *Unheavenly City Revisited*; Sleeper, *Liberal Racism*; McWhorter, *Losing the Race*.

14. D'Souza, *End of Racism*; Meyerson et al., *Alternatives to Racial Preferences*; Moynihan, "Negro Family."

15. Rushton and Bogaert, "Population Differences."

16. Alland, *Race in Mind*; Campbell, Review of *Funding of Scientific Racism*; Herrnstein and Murray, *Bell Curve*.

white Americans in the 2012 GSS openly admit they think racial differences in housing, jobs, and income between whites and Blacks are because Blacks have "less in born [sic] ability to learn."[17] Over 13 percent of Blacks agree with whites.

CNN reported on October 18, 2007, that James Watson, American Nobel laureate and co-discoverer of the DNA double helix, told the *Sunday Times of London* he was "inherently gloomy about the prospect[s] [for] Africa because all our social policies are based on the fact that their intelligence is the same as ours, whereas all the testing says not really."[18] Watson also reportedly said: "There was no reason to believe different races separated by geography should have evolved identically, and that while he hoped everyone was equal, people who have to deal with Black employees find this is not true."[19] Watson apologized for his comments the next day, but that did not protect him from the embarrassing situation of suspension from the Watson School of Biological Sciences at Cold Spring Harbor Laboratory, the school that bore his name.

David Reich is the latest to attempt to ascribe racial differences to biological differences. Strangely, Reich is sharply critical of Watson, even calling him racist.[20] First, Reich considers Africans, Europeans, and Neanderthals as different genetic populations even though little evidence supports this idea. Much of evolutionary genetics is based on a sample of only 147 people from five regions of the world.[21] Determining how often mitochondrial DNA mutates is virtually impossible, so the dates for different populations are pure conjecture.[22] Neanderthals should be considered as modern humans.[23] Second, Reich is different from Watson in that he does not view Blacks as inferior to whites; however, Reich does subscribe to the same type of biological and ideological racism as Watson in stating that human traits are dependent on an individual's human population group.[24]

---

17. T. Smith et al., "General Social Surveys, 1972–2018," mnemonic racdif2.
18. CNN, "Nobel Winner," para. 3.
19. CNN, "Nobel Winner," para. 8.
20. Reich, *Who We Are*, 264.
21. Brown, *In the Beginning*, 319.
22. Barinaga, "African Eve Backers"; Brown, *In the Beginning*, 319; Templeton and Hedges, "Human Origins"; Tierney et al., "Search for Adam and Eve"; *Science News*, "African Eve Gets Lost."
23. Brown, *In the Beginning*, 14; Gish, *Have You Been Brainwashed?*; Gish, *Evolution*, 305; Gore, "Neandertals," 6; Lubenow, *Bones of Contention*, 75–85; Morris and Sherwin, *Fossil Record*, 105–6.
24. Miles, *Racism*.

So how should we prepare for the likelihood that in the coming years, genetic studies will show that behavior or cognitive traits are influenced by genetic variation, and that these traits will differ on average across human populations, both with regard to their average and their variation within populations? Even if we do not yet know what those differences well be, we need to come up with a new way of thinking that can accommodate such differences, rather than deny categorically that difference[s] can exist and so find ourselves caught without a strategy once they are found.[25]

The problem for many is that Reich confuses populations, regions, and geography with something that people call race, which does not exist. Several writers for the *New York Times* commented: "No one objects to use of geography or ancestry as an explanation for population variation in gene distribution. But Africa is a continent. West Africa is a region. Neither is a race."[26] Another said: "As applied to human beings, race is a social grouping. Genetically, there is only one human race."[27] The well-known Black genetic biologist Joseph Graves was reported to have said that "modern genetics show that people cluster in gene groupings that do not necessarily correspond to race or physical appearance."[28]

In contrast, bias theories blame racism, discrimination, segregation, and disparate treatment as the historic and continuing cause for Black inequality. Most of the major civil rights groups supported bias theories.[29] Systems of inequality operating without direct and visible bias from social institutions are a third class of theories known as structural theories. An example of a structural theory would be the poor educational experiences given to Black and Latino inner-city school children who then have poor employment prospects.[30] Social scientists seek to separate ideas based on casual observation from the stronger scientific ideas. Ranking which ideas or theories about the causes for racial inequality are the strongest requires the use of four theory testing tools: timing, parsimony, process, and prediction.

Timing is the first test of a good theory. Logically, one entity cannot be the cause of another if one came after the other. Some have implied that social welfare is responsible for the social and economic differences

25. Reich, *Who We Are*, 265.
26. Mary T. Bassett, in *New York Times*, "Race, Genetics."
27. Alan Goodman, in *New York Times*, "Race, Genetics."
28. Ahuja, "Study the Face Below," para. 6.
29. Kerner, *Kerner Report*.
30. Jaynes and Williams, *Common Destiny*; Orfield and Ashkinaze, *Closing Door*.

between white and Black families.³¹ Before answering, the relevant question is whether this theory is a sound one. Welfare began when FDR signed the Social Security Act on August 14, 1935, which created the program known as Aid to Dependent Children.³² ADC was a Depression-era relief program. See chapter 9 for further discussion of that program. Family income inequality began long before welfare began, however. Almost a century ago, in 1926, a decade before welfare existed, Charles Johnson noted significant income inequality between Black and white families.³³ The test of timing does not lend strong support for a thesis that welfare creates racial inequality, since racial income inequality predated welfare.

Parsimony is the second test of a strong theory. Parsimony in this context means that the starting conditions are simple and easily understood. The strongest theories are the simplest theories. If we have to choose between two arguments, ideas, or theories, the simplest argument wins, with the assumption that all other factors are equal.³⁴ Frequently, when scholars write about racial inequality, they do not state their starting assumptions. All theories have starting assumptions. In the study of race, many begin by assuming that racial prejudice or racial bias are either nonexistent or relatively minor. Neither of these assumptions has ever been supported by a preponderance of evidence. Even the most ardent cultural or social deficiency theorists admit that American slavery created the starting conditions for racial inequality in the United States.³⁵ Parsimony demands that anyone asserting individual Black deficiency as the cause for racial inequality break the chain linking historic causation, slavery, with contemporary causation, individual deficiency.

Deficiency theorists have used many techniques to break the chain of historic causation. Some imply that the Progressive Era, the New Deal, or the Great Society created racial equality, and from that point, all racial groups start on equal footing.³⁶ White denial of the importance of past discrimination is an attempt to create parsimony where little exists.³⁷ Figure 2.1 shows the ratio of Black to white family income from 1880 to 2022.

---

31. Rector, "Welfare Reform," 210. "The onset of the War on Poverty coincided with the disintegration of the low-income family—the Black family in particular. . . . Across the nation, the welfare system has all but destroyed family structure in low-income communities."

32. D. Gordon et al., *Segmented Work*, 253.

33. C. Johnson, *Negro in American Civilization*, 60.

34. Brown, *In the Beginning*, 67; Kramer, "Political Science as Science," 12.

35. Sowell, *Ethnic America*, ch. 8.

36. Mead, *Beyond Entitlement*, 19.

37. Morin, "Distorted Image of Minorities."

From 1880 to 2022, the line is relatively flat and shows little change in over a century of family income inequality. In 1967, the height of the Great Society, Black families made 59 percent of white family income, compared to 63 percent in 2000, a change of less than 5 percent in three decades. In 1880, the ratio of Black to white income was 59 percent, the same as in 2021.[38] Using income inequality as a measure, little has broken the chain of historic racial starting conditions. Parsimony does not lend support to deficiency as a strong theory of racial inequality. It is highly unlikely that Black and white family income equality will reach 100 percent before America becomes mostly non-White before mid-century. The data show stasis, not positive change.

Figure 2.1 Black/White Median Family Income, 1880–2022

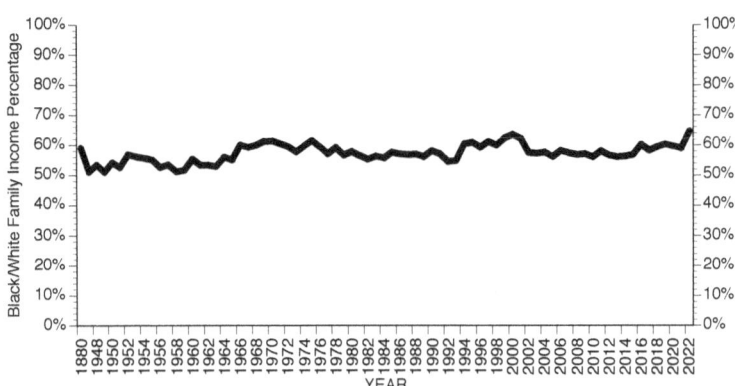

Sources: Current Population Survey Datasets, Annual Social and Economic Supplements. For information on confidentiality protection, sampling error, non-sampling error, and definitions, see U.S. Census Bureau, *Current Population Survey*, table F-5, "Race and Hispanic Origin of Householder—Families by Median and Mean Income: 1947 to 2022." Vedder et al., "Black Exploitation and White Benefits."

Process is the ability to generalize and is the third test of a strong theory. Process in this context means that if two theories are equal in all other respects, the theory that explains more is the stronger theory. For example, if discrimination can explain income inequality, while at the same time accounting for racial healthcare disparities, then that concept strengthens belief in the theory, whereas if discrimination adequately explains racial differences in employment outcomes, but is wholly inadequate to explain inequality in housing, confidence in discrimination as a theory for inequality would decrease. Racial discrimination is a strong theory of inequality not only in explaining inequality in many different areas that impact Blacks but

38. Vedder et al., "Black Exploitation and White Benefits."

also in explaining the impacts that racial inequality has on other non-white racial groups, such as Latinos and American Indians. Deficiency theories lack good generality or process since different traits must be found to explain the disadvantage of each non-white or minority group.

Thomas Sowell, the conservative economist, provides an excellent example of a deficiency theory of racial inequality with weak process. Sowell claimed that "American ethnic groups are too different from one another to be described by any generalization."[39] Then Sowell presented a table of white, Asian, Latino, and Black ethnic groups and what was purported to be their average family incomes. Jews, Japanese, Anglo-Saxons, and Irish all had above-average family incomes. Filipinos, West Indians, Mexicans, and Puerto Ricans had below-average family incomes. Black Americans and American Indians held the two lowest positions.

Sowell writes, "As workers, Blacks had acquired little sense of personal responsibility under slavery. Lack of initiative, evasion of work, half-done work, unpredictable absenteeism, and abuse of tools and equipment were pervasive under slavery, and these patterns did not suddenly disappear with emancipation."[40] Sowell seeks to demonstrate why Black ethnic groups have different family income. He claims that "West Indian" Blacks are far more successful economically than Black Americans, "seriously undermin[ing] the proposition that color is a fatal handicap in the American economy."[41]

Sowell's claims lack the fundamental features of good science, verifiability, and repeatability. Ethnicity data, particularly for whites, is unreliable. Over half of whites in the GSS come from mixed ethnic background or do not know their ethnic background, and as such, direct comparisons are questionable.[42] If "West Indians [are] much more frugal, hard-working, and entrepreneurial,"[43] than are Black Americans, perhaps matching Blacks in the US for their nativity should reveal that: 1) Black incomes should rise in relation to whites; or 2) Black incomes should equal those of whites. Just the opposite happens.

In 2013, average Black individual wages fell $6,178 below wages of whites with the same human capital (age and education) and gender. Matching whether a Black person was born outside the US or is not a US citizen, Black wages fall $6,290 behind those of whites with the same human capital

39. Sowell, *Ethnic America*, 5.
40. Sowell, *Ethnic America*, 200.
41. Sowell, *Ethnic America*, 220.
42. T. Smith et al., "General Social Surveys, 1972–2012," ethnum tabulated with census racial classifications.
43. Sowell, *Ethnic America*, 220.

as Blacks.⁴⁴ That is, a larger wage gap exists between foreign-born Blacks and whites than between American-born Blacks and whites.

Sowell and other cultural deficiency theorists frequently take small subsamples of Blacks, incomes of foreign-born Blacks, or Blacks in the National Basketball Association, for example, and compare them to the larger Black population. Comparing the larger Black population to a small subsample is an attempt to demonstrate that deficient culture, rather than racial discrimination, explains Black disadvantage. Foreign-born, noncitizen Blacks are fewer than 5 percent of all Blacks in the Current Population Survey (CPS) in 2013, and the National Basketball Association is an even smaller subsample.

The late Stanley Lieberson, Harvard sociologist, asserted that America has a hierarchy of race with Blacks on the bottom, followed by Latinos, Asians, and whites at the top.⁴⁵ On considering racial wages matched for human capital, that exact rank ordering is apparent. The CPS in 2013 gives the average white wage as $24,260, with Asians, Latinos, and Blacks down $3,056, $4,119, and $6,290 respectively when controlled for human capital, gender, citizenship status, and nativity.

Prediction helps avoid undesirable and costly outcomes and is the fourth strong theory tool.⁴⁶ In some natural sciences like vaccine development, only near–100 percent accuracy in prediction is acceptable. In social science and medicine, prediction provides for extrapolating or projecting some meaningful information about the population at a higher ratio than the average rate of the phenomena in the population. For example, to predict the nonoccurrence of cancer 99 percent of the time means nothing, since 99 percent of the population does not have cancer.⁴⁷ The "controlled experiment" is considered the most powerful tool in natural science. Professional surveys, using a sufficient number of randomly selected respondents, are one of the most powerful tools in social science. The "audit" or test using two actors or auditors with identical résumés or health symptoms seeking employment or medical treatment is a type of controlled experiment. Predicting the outcome of an audit or test significantly more than 50/50 increases belief or acceptance of the theory.

Most large professional economic surveys, including the GSS, CPS, and MCSUI, show large wage differences between Blacks and whites even when races are matched for human capital, occupation, industry, job tenure,

44. Current Population Survey Datasets, 1962–2013.
45. Lieberson, *Piece of the Pie*, 366.
46. J. Johnson and Joslyn, *Political Science Research Methods*, 18.
47. Tufte, *Data Analysis*, 36–40.

and performance. These results point to racial discrimination rather than Black deficiency as the cause of wage inequality. In addition, Blacks report discrimination in hiring at rates approaching 40 percent, compared to less than 10 percent for whites.[48]

Audits are even more telling. Job and housing audits or tests send Black or white individuals or teams to buy or rent housing or apply for jobs. If the reason Blacks have worse housing or jobs is deficient Black culture, bad culture is controlled or eliminated in the housing or job applications by giving the auditors identical credentials. Frequently the Black auditor is given slightly better credentials.

Theoretically, if racial discrimination is not present, Black and white auditors should be offered jobs or housing at the same rate. Johnny Yinger found that 23.4 percent of the time, Black renters seeking housing were told fewer rental units were available to them than were available to white auditors. Black homebuyers were discriminated against by housing agents 19.44 percent of the time and told fewer units were available to them than were available to whites.[49]

White job seekers are given a job at a rate of 15 percent for white auditors compared to 7 percent for Black auditors, or twice as often. Whites advance further in the interview process at a rate of 20 percent for white auditors to 7 percent for Black auditors, or three times as often.[50] Bertrand and Mullainathan found that applicant résumés with typically white names were 50 percent more likely to be called for an interview than were applicants with Black-sounding names. Since the résumés were identical except for the name, this disputes any claim that the racial differences link solely to skill differences.[51]

Avivi et al. repeated the résumé experiment, but this time they were trying to find out how to target employers who actually discriminate against Blacks. They found that most employers, 53 percent, do not respond to white or Black applicants. However, a minority of employers discriminate intensely, such "that the odds of being called back by a discriminating job are roughly 36 times higher for Whites than equivalent Blacks."[52] Writing on the Avivi et al. study, Miller and Katz reported in the April 8, 2024, online issue of the *New York Times* that not only did Avivi et al. send out

---

48. Coleman, "Racial Discrimination in the Workplace"; Coleman et al., "Are Claims of Discrimination Valid?"
49. Yinger, *Closed Doors*, table 3.1.
50. M. Turner et al., *Opportunities Denied*.
51. Bertrand and Mullainathan, "Are Emily and Brendan More Employable?"
52. Avivi et al., "Adaptive Correspondence Experiments," 44.

eighty thousand résumés, they actually named the companies and their level of discrimination. "Of the 97 companies in the experiment, two stood out as contacting presumed White job applicants significantly more often than presumed Black ones. At fourteen companies, there was little or no difference in how often they called back the presumed White or Black applicants."[53] With nearly one hundred companies tested, only fourteen showed little or no discrimination. America is highly discriminatory when it comes to race, regardless of antidiscrimination law.

Having a strong or a weak theory does not mean that a theory matches the empirical evidence. In addition to the four theory tools discussed (timing, parsimony, process, and prediction), social scientists also have four major empirical tools for examining empirical evidence about the causes for racial inequality: historical analysis, surveys, direct testing, and statistical analysis.

Historical analysis is the oldest of the tools used to evaluate the causes of racial inequality. Historical analysis comprises archival research, historical and contemporary interviews, newspaper searches, government records, and examination of prior scholarly research (historiography), all of which form a mosaic of information about what occurred. Anti-Black thought before and after the Civil War was prominent. Some argued that Blacks had smaller brains, could not stand upright, resembled apes, were ugly, and were generally physically and mentally inferior to whites.[54]

This type of pseudoscientific racism did not end in the nineteenth century and is still active even today.[55] How we know that J. Philippe Rushton is wrong and that racial inequality is not caused by inherent deficiency, biological or otherwise, in Black Americans is that we use good theory.[56] If Blacks were inherently inferior, this condition likely would be permanent. This condition is not the case, however. The contention a century ago that Blacks could not stand upright seems strangely incongruent with today's dominance in some of the most popular professional sports by Blacks. Some commentators have even begun to assert that Blacks are biologically superior.[57]

Before the rise of the African slave trade, Blacks were not considered to be what Shelby Steele called "the most despised race in the human

---

53. C. Miller and Katz, "What Researchers Discovered."
54. Evrie, *White Supremacy*, 3, 99, 100–2, 106, 113.
55. Jacoby and Glauberman, *Bell Curve Debate*, 438–39.
56. Rushton, *Race, Evolution, and Behavior*.
57. Price, "Whatever Happened"; Entine, *Taboo*.

community of races."[58] Despite much of the anti-Black writing of the pre- and post–Civil War period, which attempted to use the Bible to support slavery and anti-miscegenation laws, the biblical record contains no negative descriptions of Africans. Rushton is correct that anti-African writing existed before the Atlantic slave trade,[59] but this writing seems to be the normal, nationalist opposition to those perceived as enemies.

Further, Rushton ignores the many positive descriptions of Africans, as well as most of the evidence that neither Africans nor Black skin were considered deviant. Snowden writes that antiquity had no color line.[60] We know that less than eight hundred years ago Africa had great empires that were so formidable the European tribes had to bargain for trade, just as they do with any other nation. For most of the Atlantic slave trade, the European states had to use internal wars in Africa to secure slaves from the interior because the Europeans did not have the military force to obtain slaves directly from the African interior.

Many people are mesmerized by the military, economic, and political weakness of much of the southern hemisphere (Africa, Latin America) and the power of America, Western Europe, and the northern world. The power imbalance, combined with the racism that developed and spread around the world with the advent of science and the Atlantic slave trade, creates notions of the natural superiority of European Americans.

The ascendancy of America, the North, and the West, however, is a recent phenomenon barely five hundred years old and occurred almost by accident because Western Europe had the calm Atlantic Ocean at its doorstep and was not located at one of the geopolitical hot spots of the day. Europe inherited linguistic, religious, and legal systems from the breakup of the Roman Empire.[61] The rush to Eurocentrism causes many to forget that the European empires unraveled almost as fast as they were made. The northern world lives on a thin technological shell, as Hurricane Katrina demonstrated. Global environmental threats and pandemics could create a situation that rapidly reverses which empires remain dominant.

Even a basic reading of the scientific racism of Rushton is disputed by well-known historical facts. Rushton claims that because of harsh climates, Asians and Europeans had to develop societies that were orderly, had low aggression, and were law keeping. As Leslie points out, a long history of Asian violence exists in the twentieth century, and the Atlantic slave trade

58. Steele, *Content of Our Character*, 44.
59. Rushton, *Race, Evolution, and Behavior*, 15.
60. Snowden: *Blacks in Antiquity*, 169; *Before Color Prejudice*.
61. Abernathy, *Dynamics of Global Dominance*, ch. 2.

cost the lives of millions at sea, not counting those lost in the wars in Africa.[62] In fact, Abernathy asserts that the relatively recent rise of Europe is attributable to the cultures of the European tribes who did not respect the laws and rights of others.[63]

Inherent Black inferiority does not fit with observations of Black behavior. Rather than having bad behavior, Blacks seem to have superior behavior to whites because of the necessity created by their social positions. Blacks outperform whites in many areas once their socioeconomic status is considered, including voting, personal savings, and educational attainment.[64] If Blacks are inherently inferior, the expensive necessity of violence seems unnecessary to repress them.

Horace Bushnell, the nineteenth-century theologian, believed that while the abolition of slavery did pose a serious threat, he saw no reason to oppose abolition, since Blacks would die off because of their indolence and inability to care for themselves.[65] Black Americans did not die off, and a main reason Blacks did not advance as quickly as they might have politico-economically is attributable to the system of unjust laws, court decisions, and Southern terror and violence used to ensure Black subjugation by Rushton's less aggressive white race.

About every twenty or thirty years, a commissioned government or private group of recognized experts completes a major study to assess the state of race relations. These commissioned studies, termed the Great Commissions, differ from normal scholarly works in that the groups who fund them are national groups who put their reputations on the line for objectivity and the best work social science has to offer. The opportunity for individual researcher bias is held to a minimum.

From Charles Johnson's first commissioned study of race in 1930 through the IOM report in 2003, all the Great Commissions, covering almost a century of study, adopt bias and structural theories to explain racial inequality. None finds deficiency theories useful in explaining the phenomena. The unity of these findings is noteworthy.[66] Surveys are scientific in-

---

62. Leslie, "Scientific Racism," 895.

63. Abernathy, *Dynamics of Global Dominance*, ch. 2.

64. For Blacks and voting, relative to socioeconomic status, see ch. 7 in this book. For Blacks and the relationship between educational attainment and socioeconomic background, see Coleman, "African American Popular Wisdom"; Bridges and Villemez, "Overeducated Minority Workers"; Mason, "Race, Culture, and Skill." For Blacks and savings, see Gittleman and Wolff, "Racial Differences"; Ards and Myers, "Color of Money"; Straight, "Survey of Consumer Finances."

65. Bushnell: *God in Christ*; *Census and Slavery*.

66. Jaynes and Williams, *Common Destiny*; C. Johnson, *Negro in American*

struments that ask people what they think or how they feel about a problem or issue. The GSS, CPS, MCSUI, and even the Decennial Census are all survey tools. Most survey tools point not to cultural deficiency but to bias and structural impediments as the cause for racial inequality.

In a study of Chicago employers, many of those employers admitted they discriminated against Black job seekers in the inner city.[67] Also in Chicago, 74 percent of the employers surveyed expressed impressions of Blacks that showed clear racial bias.[68] Certainly the 10–13 percent of whites who openly admit they want segregated neighborhoods and laws against interracial marriage is disturbing.[69] This group of whites is larger than the entire Black population in the US.

One problem with surveys is the difficulty in asking whites about their views, which may include bigotry and/or racial prejudice. Most people today understand that it is not socially acceptable to be outwardly racially prejudiced in public. Determining how much prejudice still remains is a difficult process. Several techniques have been developed. One way is to ask a person to select from a list of general topics that make them angry and see the responses to establish an average of what percentage of the general topics make people angry. Then, researchers can substitute a race topic in the list of topics that make people angry. Depending on the changes in the average number of responses to topics that make people angry, the percentage of people upset by someone's race becomes apparent. This type of research indicates that racial prejudice is prevalent, at least in the South. Forty-two percent of Southern whites and 10 percent of non-Southern whites were angered about a Black family moving in next door.[70]

Comparing questionnaires with direct face-to-face interviews is another way to gauge prejudice. Two researchers found that while over 90 percent of white college students said in a survey they approved of marriage between Blacks and whites, in one-on-one interviews 52 percent expressed reservations.[71] Testing as used here does not refer to statistical testing but job and housing audits. An audit is a test using Black and white males or females. Testers are always the same gender, same height, and with the same physical characteristics. Testers who are handicapped, disabled, or who

---

Civilization; Kerner, *Kerner Report*; Myrdal, *American Dilemma*; Smedley et al., *Unequal Treatment*.

67. Kirschenman and Neckerman, "We'd Love to Hire Them, But."

68. Wilson, *When Work Disappears*, ch. 5.

69. James Davis et al., "General Social Surveys, 1972–2008," variables racseg, racmar.

70. Kuklinski et al., "Racial Prejudice."

71. Bonilla-Silva and Forman, "I Am Not a Racist, But."

have unusual characteristics are not used. The testers are sent out to seek a job, buy a house, or rent an apartment.

If the test is for a job, testers always have nearly identical résumés. Often, the Black tester has a résumé with a slight advantage over the white colleague. If the testers are sent to rent an apartment or buy a house, they earn the same amount of money and have been on the job the same amount of time. The results of audits illustrate that Blacks and whites receive unequal treatment even with identical characteristics (see the discussion on prediction, above, for citations).

Audits have been criticized because in most cases, Blacks and whites are treated the same.[72] The issue is not how many times Blacks do not face discrimination (the rate of discrimination), but the number of times that they receive treatment that is different from whites (the severity of discrimination). Individual Blacks do not experience the rate of discrimination; they experience the severity of discrimination on their lives by differential treatment based on race. Few conservative organizations conduct their own audits and produce evidence of nondiscrimination.

Social scientists use regression or maximum likelihood analysis to match peoples' characteristics to determine which differences between individuals remain. Many technical names represent these techniques, but essentially, all are statistical ways to match characteristics of demography, education, labor force, or politics. Statistical analysis is a way of controlling for culture and deficiency. Matching for human capital, demography, and labor market factors should result in a comparison of people, all of whom want to work, have gone to college, have high income, and live in the same place.

Female headship largely is associated with poverty. The 2013 CPS showed that 39.28 percent of Black families that were female headed were poor, compared with only 10.85 percent of Black married-couple-led families. The rates for white families are 24.46 percent and 4.35 percent, respectively, or about half the rate for Blacks.[73] Black families have far more female heads, and thus Black families tend to be poorer. Forty-four percent of Black families in 2013 were female headed, compared with only 19 percent of white families.

---

72. Heckman, "Detecting Discrimination."
73. Current Population Survey Datasets.

Table 2.1

Female Headedness on Race, Human Capital, Marital Status, Labor Market, and Geography, 2013
Logit Odds Ratios (standard errors in parenthesis)

	Model 1	Model 2	Model 3	Model 4	Model 5
Black	2.94****	2.84****	3.19****	3.05****	3.07****
	(.050)	(.049)	(.063)	(.061)	(.063)
Latino	1.34****	1.20****	1.29****	1.28****	1.30****
	(.022)	(.020)	(.024)	(.024)	(.025)
Asian	1.15****	1.14****	1.21****	1.17****	1.20****
	(.025)	(.025)	(.029)	(.029)	(.030)
Age		.998****	.963****	.965****	.965****
		(.0003)	(.0004)	(.0004)	(.0004)
Education		.956****	.995*	1.03****	1.03****
		(.001)	(.002)	(.002)	(.002)
Married spouse Absent			7.29****	7.41****	7.41****
			(.344)	(.351)	(.351)
Widowed			9.55****	9.60****	9.59****
			(.362)	(.365)	(.365)
Divorced			52.9****	47.9****	48.0****
			(1.76)	(1.60)	(1.61)
Separated			14.1****	14.4****	14.4****
			(.298)	(.305)	(.307)
Employed, Not at Work				1.04	1.04
				(.054)	(.055)
Unemployed				1.24****	1.23****
				(.038)	(.038)
Not in Labor Force				1.10****	1.10****
				(.018)	(.018)
Income				.999****	.999****
				(2.66)	(2.66)
North Central Midwest					.866****
					(.018)
South					.861****
					(.017)
West					.829****
					(.017)

Table 2.1

Female Headedness on Race, Human Capital, Marital Status, Labor Market, and Geography, 2013
Logit Odds Ratios (standard errors in parenthesis)

	Model 1	Model 2	Model 3	Model 4	Model 5
N	155,097	155,097	155,097	155,097	155,097
Pseudo R^2	.0225	.0255	.2058	.2120	.2125
χ^2 (df)	3782.46 (3)	4295.84 (5)	34609.05 (9)	35653.99 (13)	35740.27 (16)

*p=10%; **p=5%; ***p=1%; ****p=<.1%, two-tailed test. Omitted variables: White, married spouse present, employed, northeast. Source: Current Population Survey Datasets.

The next question is whether the causes of Black female headship are: bad Black society (social deficiency), not enough Black men to marry, demographic differences between Black and white women, or other factors. Statistical techniques were performed in table 2.1, matching for different criteria, such as the age, education, and income of the head, the reason for singleness of the head of household, and the employment status, factors that might most logically influence a family to have a female head. Table 2.1 essentially controls for behavior or deficiency.

With controls for race in model 1, Black families are 2.94 times as likely as white families to be female headed. Human capital controls for age and education in model 2 are little changed from model 1. Black families are 2.84 times more likely to be female headed than white families. Models 3 and 4 of table 2.1 add controls for marital and labor force status plus income. The likelihood of Black families being female headed increases to 3.19 and 3.05 respectively. Model 5 adds controls for region.

Regardless of which factors are included, Black families are three times as likely to be female headed. In fact, table 2.1 shows the more Black families match white families, the rate of female headedness tends to increase, not decrease. Even with a family head who has a college degree and an income greater than 75 percent of other people, Black families are still nearly three times (2.86 times) as likely to be female headed.

Human capital and demographic factors make little practical difference in the level of Black female headship. Black female heads earn less money and have less education than white female heads, but Black female heads are older and more often married but separated than are white female heads. Notice also in table 2.1 the class hierarchy of skin color, with Blacks having the highest rate of female headedness, followed by Latinos and Asians in every model.

What causes this higher Black female headship, regardless of age and education, is an important question, as is whether and why these women are alone, what is their employment status, and where they live in the country. Two choices present themselves: 1) all these Black women are more deviant and deficient than white females; or 2) some societal factor influences all Black women.

Black female heads share their race in common. The expectation is that behavior would change based on these demographic and labor market factors, which in turn would impact Black female headship, but Black female headship seems to be constant regardless of the factors that might influence behavior. Higher Black female headship appears to be caused by racial factors that exist in the society, such as the inability of Black women to marry non-Black men, rather than on the individual behaviors of Black women or any deficiency in Black society.[74]

THE HEALTH ISSUE

Health disparities are a topic that frequently evades notice when scholars discuss racial inequality. Health and healthcare are useful, however, in showing basic differences between racial groups. The COVID-19 crisis has raised the issue of health disparities to the very highest level. The Louisiana Department of Health was one of the first to raise the alarm when it announced that as of April 7, 2020, there had been 582 deaths from the coronavirus, 70 percent of which were Black, when Blacks comprised only 32.7 percent of the population of the state.[75] The Department of Health and Human Services Office for Civil Rights in Action issued a warning on March 28, 2020, that healthcare providers were prohibited from making decisions about who should receive care or assessing a person's "relative worth" based on age, race, color, national origin, disability, sex, or religion.[76] The Centers for Disease Control and Prevention reported that 33 percent of those hospitalized nationally with COVID-19 were Black, when Blacks comprise 13.1 percent of the population.[77] Racial disparities and discrimination in the administration of healthcare services are an unfortunate part of race in America.

---

74. Crowder and Tolnay, "New Marriage Squeeze"; Heaton and Jacobson, "Intergroup Marriage."
75. Louisiana Department of Health, "Coronavirus (Covid-19)."
76. HHS Office for Civil Rights in Action, "Civil Rights, HIPAA."
77. Garg et al., "Hospitalization Rates."

Lieberson showed that the starting conditions for Blacks were far worse than those faced by the European immigrant groups, if we use death rates, life expectancy, and infant mortality as basic measures of human well-being. Difficult to realize is that conditions in the American South were worse than those in some of the poorest countries in Europe at the turn of the twentieth century, but this statement is true. Death rates for Blacks were some 30 percent higher, life expectancy 25 percent shorter, and infant mortality sometimes 50 percent higher for Blacks than foreign-born whites.[78]

Much the same situation exists today when we compare basic health and life conditions for Blacks and whites in the US. In some ways, conditions for Blacks mimic those occurring in the Third World. Infant mortality continues to be used by international organizations and scholars as a basic measure of comparative social conditions. By this measure, Blacks continue to lag far behind whites in the US, as well as behind many other nations in the world.

Many nations in the world have lower rates of infant mortality than the US. Countries with socialized medical systems have much lower overall rates of infant mortality. If infant mortality rates are a basic measure of social well-being and equality, then infant mortality rates say a great deal about the wealth of a nation and its social well-being.

Infant mortality rates are measured in the mortality rate per 1,000 live births. Even countries like Cuba (42nd place, rate 4.7) and Serbia (56th place, rate 6.16) do better than the US (57th place, rate 6.17) for infant mortality. Even so, whites in the US rank at 51st place (rate 5.6) while Blacks in the US are at 107th place (rate 13.2), behind Mexico at 103rd place (rate 12.58).[79]

Higher infant mortality rates in the US are not the result of lack of public health spending. The US spends as much or more than many of the nations that outrank it. Sweden (6th place), Norway (3rd place), and Iceland (10th place) spend 7.3, 7.5, and 7.2 percent of their respective GDPs for public health compared with 7.8 percent for the US. Italy (11th place), however, spends only 6.9 percent of its GDP for public health.[80]

Including public and private health expenditures, the US spends more than just about any nation on earth at 16.2 percent of GDP compared to

---

78. Fogel and Engerman, *Time on the Cross*, 125–26; Lieberson, *Piece of the Pie*, 41–47.

79. United States Census Bureau, "Section 2 [2008]"; United States Census Bureau, "Section 2 [2012]," table 116; World Factbook, "Infant Mortality Rate."

80. Readers should not confuse social welfare spending, discussed in ch. 9, with the public and private health expenditures discussed here. Social welfare spending takes in more than just health spending.

BLACK DEFICIENCY THEORY AND COST

Sweden, Norway, Iceland, and Italy at 9.0, 8.8, 9.0, and 8.7 percent respectively, all of whom have lower infant mortality than the US. One has to admire Japan (2nd place, rate 2.13) for spending 8.2 percent of GDP for government-supported healthcare and 9.9 percent of GDP for total spending for health.[81]

Comparing these nations to the US is fair, since all but Norway have lower GDP per capita than the US, and that fact suggests that the US is richer overall and individually. Inequality in the US, however, is far greater.[82]

By almost any measure of health in the United States, equality gaps occur between whites and Blacks. In 2010, Black men live 4.7 years less than white men, when measured from birth. Black women live over 3.3 years less than white women, when measured from birth. Even at sixty-five years of age, Black men can expect to live 1.9 years less than white men, and Black women 1 year less than white women.[83]

Figure 2.2. is an excellent example of what I call the "railroad track effect." Since 1900 life expectancy for Black and white men has increased markedly. The two lines are like railroad tracks. They seem to stretch on endlessly into the distance but never meet or cross; they are parallel. Despite overall improvements for both groups, a constant keeps them from meeting.

Figure 2.2 Life Expectancy at Birth for Males

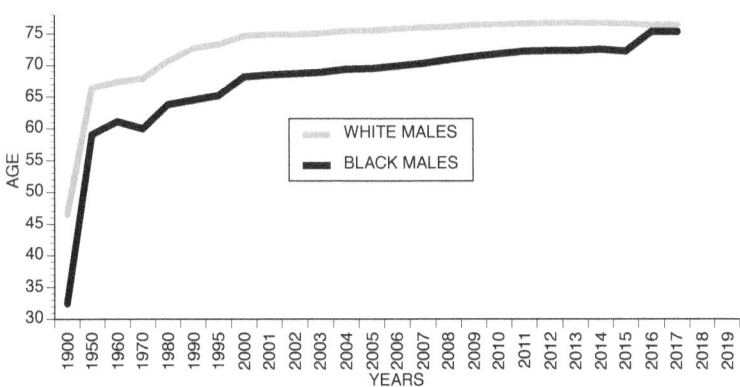

Source: Health, United States—DataFinder. Life expectancy at birth, ages sixty-five and seventy-five, by sex, race, and Hispanic origin: United States, selected years 1900–2019. Excel version (with more data years and standard errors when available),
https://www.cdc.gov/nchs/hus/contents2020-2021.htm#Table-LExpMort.

81. See OECD Data Explorer, s.vv. "Health Expenditure and Financing," for health expenditure since 2000; general government and total expenditure for 2012.

82. World Development Indicators, accessed Dec. 10, 2010.

83. National Center for Health Statistics, *Health, United States, 2014*, table 18.

51

THE COST OF RACIAL EQUALITY

Suggestions that the life expectancy difference results from the different behaviors of white and Black men is unconvincing because behaviors should change over time. From 1900 to 2019 Blacks have moved from the South to the North and back again, changed occupations, increased education, gained civil rights they never had before, and made many advances in income, politics, and employment. These gains are apparent in the steady improvement in life expectancy. What never changes, however, is Black skin, and logic dictates that racial discrimination (access to healthcare, income inequality, environment) is the cause of the racial difference in life expectancy.

Blacks also seem to die at greater rates than do whites. Overall the death rate for Blacks is some 21 percent higher than for whites.[84] Blacks die more from heart disease, cancer, diabetes, and the human immunodeficiency virus (HIV). Compared to whites, Blacks have higher death rates from strokes (43 percent), prostate cancer (139 percent), and breast cancer (40 percent).[85]

Blacks tend to have poorer overall health than do whites in the United States. Twice as many Blacks as whites responded that they had only fair or poor health in 2004. Blacks have serious psychological distress at a rate 10 percent higher than whites. Hypertension and elevated blood pressure, the leading cause of strokes, afflict Blacks at a rate 85 percent higher than whites.[86] In spite of all the concern white females have about their weight, Black females have more problems with being overweight and obese.[87]

To determine that the health disparities between Blacks and whites are not due to bad behavior on the part of Blacks themselves, we match for behavior to see if disparities remain. If disparities remain in populations with similar behavior, the conclusion seems obvious that the difference and cause are racial discrimination.

Dan Buettner published an article in *National Geographic* magazine titled "The Secrets of Long Life." He profiled three groups: the Sardinians of Italy, the Okinawans of Japan, and Seventh-day Adventists of the United States. SDAs were profiled because of their healthy lifestyles.

Buettner points out that Adventists eat nuts and beans; observe the Sabbath; have faith; forbid smoking, as well as the use of alcohol, and biblically unclean food such as pork; and discourage all meat eating and

---

84. National Center for Health Statistics, *Health, United States, 2014*, table 20.

85. National Center for Health Statistics, *Health, United States, 2006*, table 29.

86. National Center for Health Statistics, *Health, United States, 2006*, table 60; table 61; table 69; table 73; table 77; table 63; table 72.

87. Perez and Joiner, "Body Image"; Strigel-Moore et al., "Eating Disorders"; Demarest and Allen, "Body Image." Eating disorders are primarily a white female disease.

caffeinated beverages. The National Institutes of Health funded a twelve-year study of thirty-four thousand California Adventists to see if their health-orientated lifestyle increased their life expectancy and decreased the risk of heart disease and cancer. The study found that Seventh-day Adventists had lower risks for cancer and heart disease and lived from four to ten years longer than the average Californian.

Because SDAs live longer, the National Institute of Health funded an $18 million grant to study what impact lifestyle has on racial differences in health. Black Seventh-day Adventists comprise over 30 percent of the church in the US and generally subscribe to the same health principles as do white SDAs. The healthy lifestyle of Black SDAs seems to improve almost every area of their lives, including life expectancy.[88]

Even this super-health-conscious group of Black SDAs, who live longer than average Blacks, almost match the life expectancy for average whites, and are the oldest living Black men on the planet,[89] cannot match their white SDA counterparts, however. Black male SDAs live almost three years longer than Black men in the US. Black SDA females live almost five years longer than the Black female average in the US. That is, even taking lifestyle into account, a racial health difference still persists. What the cause is becomes the next important question. If genetics is not the cause,[90] and Black SDAs have a healthy lifestyle, only one cause is logical: differences in the treatment people receive based on their race, regardless of their lifestyle.[91]

The racial health differences among Seventh-day Adventists are not the only indicator of racial bias that influences health. The Institute of Medicine (IOM) released its March 20, 2002, study *Unequal Treatment: Confronting Racial and Ethnic Disparities in Health Care*, and created a sensation in the national media with the results. Gwen Ifill, of the *NewsHour* program of the Public Broadcasting System, interviewed two researchers from this

---

88. Fraser, *Diet, Life Expectancy*, 118–21; Fraser et al., "Association Among Health Habits"; Murphy et al., "Mortality Profile."

89. In 1980, Black Americans lived longer than any other population in a Black nation according to the International Database. Blacks SDAs live longer than the Black average in the US.

90. Fraser et al., "Association Among Health Habits," 168. "Currently, there is little evidence that the health disadvantage experienced by Black Americans stems from genetic differences at the population level, and it seems likely that potentially modifiable environmental factors underlie much of this problem."

91. Murphy et al., "Mortality Profile." Amazingly, the Murphy study is the only one which gives life expectancy for Black SDAs. Until the new NIH study of Adventists is completed, no data is available on unique groups of Blacks who are SDAs and vegetarian or vegan.

study who reported that 71 percent of whites got breast cancer screenings compared to only 63 percent for Blacks; for every 100 white patients who received a procedure to clear a blocked heart artery, only 74 Black patients got the procedure; and Blacks were 3.5 times as likely as whites to have a limb amputated for diabetes.

The IOM report was not an original study, but a compilation and synthesis of the results of over one hundred studies covering ten years of considering racial differences in a variety of medical treatments. What seemed to amaze so many was that the racial disparities in treatment remained for the most part even after "adjustment for socioeconomic differences and other healthcare access-related factors."[92] Further, the IOM study found that stereotyping and racial biases all contribute to the unequal treatment that minorities receive. The IOM study went on to say that even though differences remain in the behaviors of minority and nonminority patients in following treatment regimens and delay in seeking care, these differences "are small and have not fully accounted for racial and ethnic disparities in receipt of treatments."[93]

Some have criticized the IOM study for the lack of scientific rigor: "The majority of the studies . . . do not sufficiently control for differences among patients that happened to correlate with race."[94] The lack of adequate controls or sufficient matching is a constant complaint of many who criticize statistical measures of discrimination. Often, however, the same types of statistical measures are accepted as evidence that discrimination does not exist or that racial inequality is due to some lack on the part of Blacks themselves.

For example, the IOM report cites numerous studies showing racial bias by physicians in clinical decision-making.[95] Most of the studies cited are audits or tests of physician responses—that is, actors pose as patients and are filmed describing their health and certain symptoms. The films are then shown to physicians who prescribe treatment. This technique eliminates every difference except race. Frequently the treatment prescribed is different, based on race.

---

92. Smedley et al., *Unequal Treatment*, 5.
93. Smedley et al., *Unequal Treatment*, 7.
94. Satel and Klick, "Institute of Medicine Report," S15.
95. Smedley et al., *Unequal Treatment*, ch. 4.

BLACK DEFICIENCY AND THE CRIME PROBLEM

An issue sometimes considered an internal, endogenous, cultural deficiency in the Black community is criminal behavior, or what is often called "Black-on-Black crime." Certainly, a deficiency theorist might claim, white society does not force Blacks to attack each other. Alvin Poussaint, the well-known Black psychologist, addresses this issue of Black-on-Black violence and connects violence in the Black ghettos directly to white oppression.

> Regrettably, social scientists have cooperated with a system which defines Blacks in negative terms but disguises them in academic jargon. Witness the terms "culturally deprived" and "socially disadvantaged" which are often used to describe Black people. Popularly, we are viewed as emotionally handicapped while Whites masquerade as models of mental health, normalcy and maturity. In fact, it would be more accurate to describe the White racist as abnormal and "deprived." It is currently in vogue to explain Blacks' behavior by labeling it paranoid, but this label would be more appropriate to our oppressors.[96]

Rather than cultural deficiency, Poussaint finds that Blacks have been patient and generous in the face of oppression. Blacks have acted with restraint: "It is clear that Blacks would not have survived one of the most brutal oppressions in history if they did not have a great deal of fortitude, self-love, and sense of self."[97]

Blacks learned violence from white America. America seems to respect violence and often will not respond to the just demands of its citizens unless the citizens are violent. The riots in Los Angeles after the acquittal of white police officers in 1992 in the beating of Rodney King or the civil unrest in Baltimore in 2015 after the death of Freddie Gray in police custody are examples of Black violence in response to government violence. While Black men do not have equal access to legitimate means of advancement in America, whites praise white violence as rugged individualism and supposedly legitimate government action (police brutality) and business (white-collar crime) but condemn Blacks. That is, according to Poussaint, white society benefits from the criminalization of Blacks.

Some costs are more difficult to calculate than others. Besides COVID-19, America is still in the grip of an opioid crisis. The number of deaths from opioid overdoses has increased fivefold since 1999.[98] In 1999,

---

96. Poussaint, *Why Blacks Kill Blacks*, 69–70.
97. Poussaint, *Why Blacks Kill Blacks*, 71.
98. Saloner et al., "Public Health Strategy."

approximately seven thousand people died from opioid use. In 2015, nearly thirty-five thousand died.[99] Drug overdose from opioids, not traffic accidents, is the leading cause of injury death in the United States.[100] No easy way exists to calculate these costs. Calculating a cost for the opioid crisis requires calculating how much a human life is worth. Before costs for the opioid crisis can be calculated, we would first need to know the cause. Strangely, even though Blacks undergo arrest three times as often as whites for drug use, Blacks do not use illicit drugs any more than do whites.[101] In terms of unhealthy lifestyles (use of cigarettes, alcohol, and drugs) Blacks are no worse than whites.[102] Recent reports confirm these earlier findings. Whites in rural areas seem to be taking the greatest hit from the opioid crisis, not Blacks.

> Geographically, the greatest burden of overdoses is in Appalachia, the Southwest, and New England. These realities, combined with rising political attention to rural and low-income White people in the United States, may explain increased interest in addressing opioid overdose in these hard-hit regions. Trends among other affected populations are also concerning. For example, drug overdose mortality among Native Americans has been highly elevated since the inception of the drug overdose crisis in the early 2000s, and the incidence of overdose mortality among African Americans is now rising faster than among other racial/ethnic groups.[103]

The US government estimated the cost in lives of the opioid crisis at $504 billion in 2015. The US government uses a rather complex cost-benefit analysis measurement called the VSL (value of a statistical life).

---

99. Council of Economic Advisers, *Underestimated Cost.*

100. Saloner et al., "Public Health Strategy."

101. In 2005, 64.7 percent of those arrested on drug abuse violations were white and 33.9 percent were Black. Since Blacks are only 12 percent of the population, they are overrepresented in arrests by 300 percent (Crime in the United States 2005, "Persons Arrested," table 43). In April of 2007 the Department of Justice released *Contacts Between Police and the Public, 2005,* which reports that Blacks are no more likely to be stopped by police than are whites but are three times as likely to be searched and twice as likely to be arrested. The report said, "Any of these disparities might be explained by countless other factors and circumstances that were not taken into account in the analysis" (Durose et al., *Contacts,* 5). This statement is not true. Controlling or matching for age, sex, reason for being stopped, and the presence of probable cause for a search or arrest should eliminate racial disparities, unless racial bias on the part of the police is present.

102. National Center for Health Statistics, *Health, United States, 2006.*

103. Saloner et al., "Public Health Strategy," s.vv. "Opioid Overdose Deaths."

"Such valuations are typically based on how individuals trade off wealth for reduced mortality risks." "This [VSL measurement] is over six times larger than the most recently estimated economic cost of the epidemic."[104] Even the government's low estimates of $100 billion for the opioid crisis are substantially higher than President Trump's first-term proposed $5.7 billion border wall to stop illegal entry into the US outside points of entry (POEs) as a solution to the crisis. The Drug Enforcement Administration (DEA) finds that most, 66 percent, of the drugs entering the US are legal controlled prescription drugs in personally owned vehicles (POVs) through POEs as prescriptions.[105] Even most illegal drugs enter the US through POEs in tractor trailers, not illegal and dangerous desert crossings. Rather, the study by the Johns Hopkins Bloomberg School of Public Health lists structural factors (lack of employment opportunity, lack of education, material deprivation, experience of violence, discrimination, and homelessness) as the pull forces driving the opioid crisis.[106] Economically, the opioid crisis is a medium-cost equality program but it is really just another way of saying poverty, wage discrimination, lack of employment, and hopelessness, also medium-cost programs. Border walls are insignificant financially, but in chapter 10 we will see that a border wall can be a major political barrier to the serious fix a problem needs.

RISING INEQUALITY WITH DECLINING PREJUDICE

By some measures, racial prejudice is declining. In 1972, 54 percent of whites opposed interracial marriage.[107] In 2002, only 24 percent of whites opposed interracial marriage. If this measure is a valid indicator of white prejudice, then prejudice is declining. Good reasons persist that seriously question the sincerity of white responses to questions about their own racial bias, but again, we might say that racism and bias are decreasing if we choose to accept the responses of whites at face value.[108]

Conversely, two important measures of inequality rose since the 1960s: female headship for Black women and unemployment for young Black men. In 1962, 13 percent of Black families were headed by women. In 2013, 44 percent of Black families were headed by women. In 1962, 25.86 percent

104. Council of Economic Advisers, *Underestimated Cost*, 3, 1.
105. DEA Strategic Intelligence Section, *2018 National Drug Threat Assessment*.
106. Saloner et al., "Public Health Strategy," 28S.
107. James Davis et al., "General Social Surveys, 1972–2004," variable racmar.
108. Bonilla-Silva and Forman, "I Am Not a Racist, But."

of Black males aged sixteen to nineteen were employed. In 2013, only 16.47 percent of Black males aged sixteen to nineteen were employed.[109]

An important question is how declining race prejudice is associated with rising racial inequality if racial discrimination is the cause of inequality. The answer is simple. If a significant amount of discrimination occurs in the labor market or society generally, and the audit and survey evidence indicates that racial discrimination is widespread, and increasing numbers of Blacks enter the market or social system, a phenomenon can be present with increasing inequality with decreasing bias.

THE BLACK FAMILY DID NOT COLLAPSE ANY MORE THAN THE WHITE FAMILY

The Heritage Foundation has said, "The most important reason for the cessation of progress among Black Americans has been the collapse of the Black family." They go on to state that 85 percent of all poor Black children lived in fatherless families in 1995; a Black child in a female-headed house is five times more likely to be poor than one in a two-parent family; Black births to unmarried mothers rose from 22 percent to 70 percent between 1960 and 1994; and poverty in Black female-headed households has remained almost constant from the 1960s until the 1990s. The Heritage Foundation also claims that welfare is responsible for the social and economic differences between Blacks and whites.[110]

Some of what the Heritage Foundation says is true. In 2013, 68 percent of all poor Black children lived in female-headed households. In 2011, some 67.8 percent of all Black births were to unmarried Black women. In 2013, about 39.2 percent of Black female-headed households were poor. Women headed nearly half (45 percent) of Black families in 2013.[111]

Whether welfare inhibits Black progress relative to whites is the next topic to consider. The answer is an unequivocal no: welfare does not cause or increase Black deficiency. The latest evidence, however, is that welfare does boost whites by forcing the Black poor to subsidize the white poor. A disproportionate number of Blacks and Latinos receive welfare in comparison to their population percentage. Whether this higher ratio is a result of the overgenerous welfare state or whether discrimination creates greater

109. Current Population Survey Datasets, March 1962–2013, variables sexrel and famunit, "_esr."

110. Meyerson et al., *Alternatives to Racial Preferences*; Rector, "Welfare Reform."

111. Current Population Survey Datasets; Shattuck and Kreider, "Social and Economic Characteristics"; United States Census Bureau, "America's Families," table C4.

welfare needs for Black families is an important question to consider and answer.

The same techniques used to answer other questions are useful here: good theory and the tools of social science. Good theory dictates that, as we saw in figure 2.1, family income inequality based on race began long before welfare began. Over one hundred years ago, the ratio of Black to white family income was little changed from its current status.[112] Timing does not support a thesis that welfare creates racial inequality.

Table 2.2 AFDC Status Regressed on Race and Other Factors
Logit Odds Ratios (standard errors in parenthesis)

	Model 1	Model 2	Model 3	Model 4	Model 5	Model 6	Model 7
	Race	Human Capital	Demo-graphic	Labor Market	Discrimination	Assets	Networks
Black	3.57****	3.03****	2.16****	1.92**	1.76**	1.51	1.48
	(.771)	(.667)	(.506)	(.524)	(.498)	(.438)	(.439)
Latino	1.73**	.626*	.563**	.619	.616	.553*	.585*
	(.405)	(.176)	(.164)	(.196)	(.197)	(.177)	(.189)
Asian	.193**	.190**	.229**	.292	.290	.431	.404
	(.142)	(.140)	(.170)	(.224)	(.224)	(.341)	(.325)
Other	2.97*	2.49	1.69	1.43	1.43	1.76	1.92
	(1.95)	(1.67)	(1.20)	(1.11)	(1.14)	(1.39)	(1.54)
Age		.955****	.959****	.971**	.972**	.974**	.971**
		(.008)	(.010)	(.011)	(.011)	(.011)	(.012)
Education (Years)		.813****	.826****	.903***	.904***	.932*	.939
		(.024)	(.026)	(.034)	(.034)	(.036)	(.037)
Number of Children Under 18			1.84****	1.78****	1.81****	1.82****	1.80****
			(.127)	(.147)	(.150)	(.152)	(.152)
Separated			3.26****	2.01*	1.96*	1.71	1.71
			(1.11)	(.761)	(.748)	(.660)	(.668)
Divorced			4.45****	3.78****	3.96****	3.55****	3.63****
			(1.33)	(1.27)	(1.33)	(1.22)	(1.26)
Widowed			4.66***	2.72*	2.84*	2.55	2.75

112. Vedder et al., "Black Exploitation and White Benefits"; Darity and Myers, *Persistent Disparity*, 126.

Table 2.2 AFDC Status Regressed on Race and Other Factors
Logit Odds Ratios (standard errors in parenthesis)

	Model 1	Model 2	Model 3	Model 4	Model 5	Model 6	Model 7
	Race	Human Capital	Demo- graphic	Labor Market	Discrimi- nation	Assets	Networks
Never Married			3.89****	2.72****	2.79****	2.67****	2.62****
			(2.66)	(1.60)	(1.68)	(1.53)	(1.70)
			(1.03)	(.801)	(.827)	(.796)	(.785)
Living with Partner			1.96**	1.50	1.56	1.54	1.44
			(.651)	(.563)	(.588)	(.578)	(.546)
Cit4			.930	1.34	1.34	1.28	1.27
			(.181)	(.303)	(.305)	(.294)	(.295)
Hours Worked				.986	.986	.986	.987
				(.009)	(.009)	(.009)	(.009)
Weeks Worked				.981****	.981****	.983***	.983***
				(.005)	(.005)	(.005)	(.005)
Working Now Full-Time				.325****	.330****	.327****	.335***
				(.112)	(.114)	(.114)	(.118)
Tempo- rarily Laid Off				.716	.723	.649	.673
				(.456)	(.460)	(.412)	(.430)
Sick or Maternity Leave				.233	.244	.239	.196
				(.256)	(.269)	(.264)	(.222)
Unem- ployed				2.05**	2.11**	1.90**	1.78*
				(.635)	(.655)	(.599)	(.567)
Perma- nently Disabled				2.31*	2.39*	2.44*	2.35*
				(1.15)	(1.20)	(1.24)	(1.22)
Home- maker				2.80***	2.78***	2.72**	2.81***
				(1.10)	(1.09)	(1.09)	(1.13)
Student				1.10	1.09	1.07	1.01

Table 2.2 AFDC Status Regressed on Race and Other Factors
Logit Odds Ratios (standard errors in parenthesis)

	Model 1	Model 2	Model 3	Model 4	Model 5	Model 6	Model 7
	Race	Human Capital	Demo-graphic	Labor Market	Discrimination	Assets	Networks
				(.554)	(.554)	(.558)	(.540)
Other Employ				2.00	1.87	2.25	2.36
				(1.85)	(1.77)	(2.22)	(2.43)
Wage				.894****	.893****	.907****	.915***
				(.026)	(.026)	(.027)	(.027)
Discrimination at Work Due to Race					.692	.718	.771
					(.202)	(.210)	(.229)
Denied Raise or Promotion Due to Race					.893	.830	.892
					(.272)	(.255)	(.276)
Denied a Job Due to Race					1.53*	1.50*	1.45*
					(.343)	(.338)	(.332)
Money from Relatives						.788	.756
						(.256)	(.249)
Asset Class						.717****	.715****
						(.063)	(.064)
Networks of People (Number)							.950
							(.126)
Networks of People Who Can Help in Emergency							.895
							(.255)
Networks of People Who Have Jobs							.480****
							(.096)
N	1,801	1,801	1,801	1,801	1,801	1,801	1,801
χ^2	68.22	.1154	243.48	453.63	458.27	478.67	492.36
(df)	4	6	13	24	27	29	32
Pseudo R^2	.0562	.1154	.2006	.3737	.3775	.3943	.4056

Table 2.2 AFDC Status Regressed on Race and Other Factors
Logit Odds Ratios (standard errors in parenthesis)

Model 1	Model 2	Model 3	Model 4	Model 5	Model 6	Model 7
Race	Human Capital	Demographic	Labor Market	Discrimination	Assets	Networks

*p=10%; **p=5%; ***p=1%; ****p=<.1%, two-tailed test. Source: MCSUI (1992–94), Household Survey, Inter-University Consortium for Political and Social Research, Ann Arbor, MI.

Welfare payments are relatively small ($19 billion in 2014 for TANF [see table 9.1] compared to nearly $800 billion in lost income from poverty [see ch. 6]). Such a small government appropriation is unlikely to create the large differences in Black and white family income. That is, the thesis that welfare causes Black deficiency lacks good theoretical support.

Statistical tests can also help answer this question. Table 2.2 uses the MCSUI database for two reasons: 1) MCSUI covers periods before welfare reform when the gap between white and Black AFDC receipt was much higher than today; and 2) MCSUI is one of the few databases with information on racial discrimination, assets, and financial networks, in addition to wages, poverty, and AFDC.

Table 2.2 uses logit odds ratios for simplicity. Table 2.2, model 1, shows that Blacks are 3.57 (357 percent) times as likely as whites are to be on welfare. Latinos are 1.73 times (173 percent) as likely as whites to be on welfare, and Asians are only 19.3 percent as likely as whites are to be on welfare. Factoring in controls for human capital, the likelihood of Blacks to be on welfare, in comparison with whites, drops to a ratio of 3.03 in model 2 of table 2.2. Matching for region, the number of children under eighteen, and marital status, the ratio of Blacks to whites on welfare drops to less than 2 (1.92) (table 2.2, model 3). Adding in labor market characteristics illustrates that the chance that a Black person will be on welfare compared to a white person falls below two times as likely, while the other racial groups are no more likely than a white person to be on welfare (table 2.2, model 4).

Without MCSUI, at this point we would have to stop. But suppose we try to capture labor market discrimination, which in some cases Blacks report at rates four times those of whites and twice those of Latinos. When we add labor market discrimination as a factor (table 2.2, model 5), Blacks are only 1.76 times as likely as whites to be on welfare.

Regarding the greater assets that whites have, even poor whites have more wealth than middle-class Blacks.[113] Also, think about more than monetary assets. Think about what some people call cultural capital. That is, "it's who you know that counts." The ability to pick up the phone and call

---

113. Oliver and Shapiro, *Black Wealth/White Wealth*.

BLACK DEFICIENCY THEORY AND COST

for help, from someone who can help, is more important than most people are willing to admit. If assets and networks for Blacks are matched with the assets and networks of whites, Blacks are no more likely to be on welfare than are whites (table 2.2, models 6 and 7). The ratio for Blacks compared to whites is 1.51 and 1.48 respectively for models 6 and 7, but these ratios are statistically no different from 1:1.[114]

People go on welfare not because they are lazy, but because they are young, have little education, have children, are divorced, separated, or without a partner, have no work or low wages, and have no one to call for help.

Considering Black and white families receiving welfare payments, figure 2.3 shows that in 2013 few Blacks, less than 2 percent, and even fewer whites, receive welfare. Notice that both Black and white welfare rises and falls in unison, and that fact indicates that they are influenced by the same programs, policies, and practices. That is, Blacks do not seem to behave differently than whites in response to welfare payments, although the Black rate is higher than for whites.

Figure 2.3 Race and Receipt of AFDC/TANF Payments

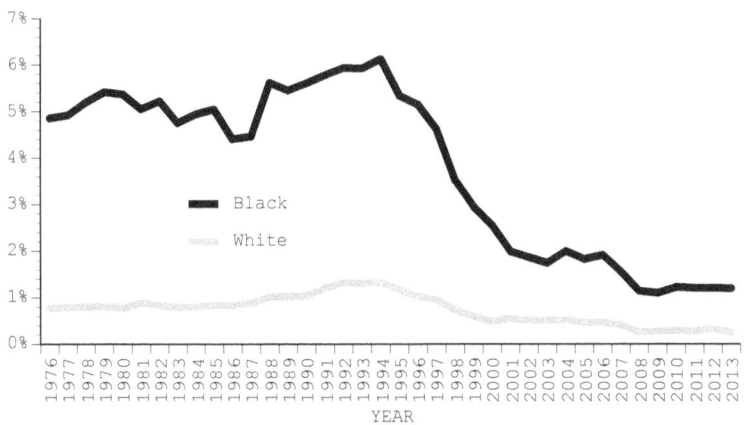

Source: Current Population Survey Datasets, 1962–2013. Washington, DC (machine-readable data files)/conducted by the Bureau of the Census for the Bureau of Labor Statistics. Washington, DC: Bureau of the Census (producer and distributor), 1962–2013. Los Angeles: Unicon Research Corporation (producer and distributor of CPS Utilities), 2013.

Figure 2.4 makes the relationship between Black and white welfare easier to observe. Blacks receive welfare at a rate four to six times that of

---

114. Coleman, "Racial Discrimination in the Workplace," 675; Oliver and Shapiro, *Black Wealth/White Wealth*.

THE COST OF RACIAL EQUALITY

whites. The overall trend however, in Black to white welfare receipt is downward; Blacks are fighting harder than whites to be self-sufficient.

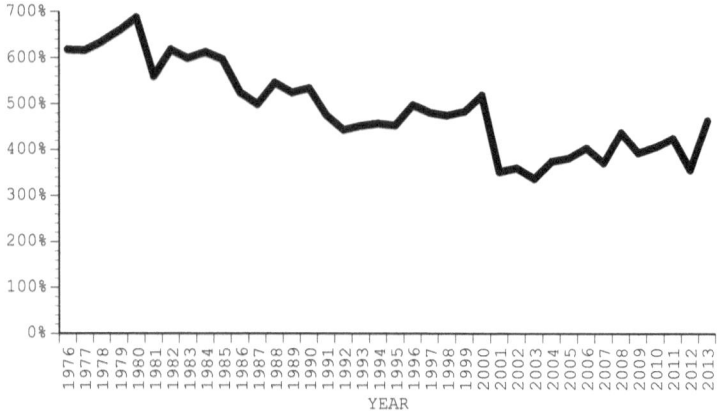

Figure 2.4 Ratio of Blacks to Whites Receiving AFDC/TANF

Source: Current Population Survey Datasets, 1962–2013. Washington, DC (machine-readable data files)/conducted by the Bureau of the Census for the Bureau of Labor Statistics. Washington, DC: Bureau of the Census (producer and distributor), 1962–2013. Los Angeles: Unicon Research Corporation (producer and distributor of CPS Utilities), 2013.

WELFARE REFORMED TO SUBSIDIZE THE WHITE POOR

The Heritage Foundation said the collapse of the Black family was the reason for cessation of Black progress. The Heritage Foundation, however, discussed only Blacks, not whites. This implies that Blacks increasingly in female-headed families are losing ground against whites in stable two-parent families. Neither connotation is true. If white families are collapsing faster than Black families, female headship cannot be the cause of increasing inequality or the cessation of Black progress.

Figure 2.5 shows the percentage of female-headed families by race. The familiar railroad-track pattern is clear to see. Black and white female-headed families increase and decrease in almost perfect synchronization. Welfare reform in 1996 took place during a noticeable decrease in both Black and white female-headed families. Note that the decrease in poverty for female-headed families began before welfare reform in 1996–97.

Figure 2.5 shows the Heritage Foundation is wrong. Poverty in Black, female-headed households has not remained almost constant from the 1960s until the 1990s. There have been ups and downs and constant change in figure 2.5. Economic changes impact Black and white poor families similarly. Claims about the extraordinary pathology of Black female families are false.

Figure 2.5 Female-Headed Families That Are Poor

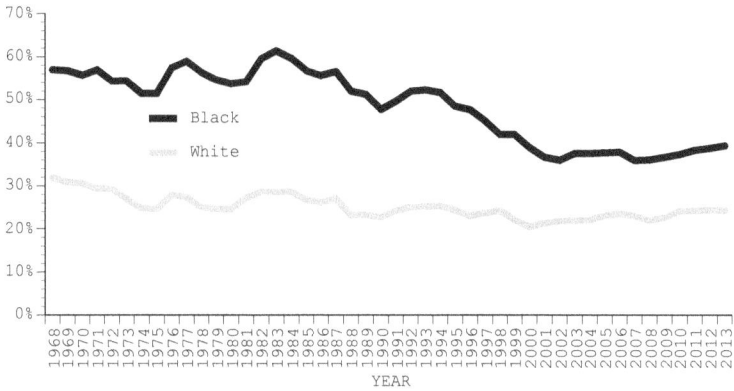

Source: Current Population Survey Datasets, 1962–2013. Washington, DC (machine-readable data files)/conducted by the Bureau of the Census for the Bureau of Labor Statistics. Washington, DC: Bureau of the Census (producer and distributor), 1962–2013. Los Angeles: Unicon Research Corporation (producer and distributor of CPS Utilities), 2013.

Table 2.3 Poverty and AFDC/TANF Status Regressed on Race, Human Capital, Marital Status, Labor Market, and Geography Logit Odds Ratios (standard errors in parenthesis)				
	1976–95		2000–2014	
	Model 1	Model 2	Model 3	Model 4
	POOR	AFDC/TANF	POOR	AFDC/TANF
Black	3.04****	4.61****	2.45****	1.09
	(.019)	(.059)	(.016)	(.068)
Latino	2.61****	2.94****	2.37****	.870**
	(.017)	(.043)	(.015)	(.055)
Asian	2.20****	2.78****	1.73****	.850**
	(.026)	(.069)	(.015)	(.065)
Age	.993****	.973****	.997****	.973****
	(.0001)	(.0004)	(.0001)	(.001)
Education	.940****	.999	.945****	.962****
	(.0006)	(.001)	(.0008)	(.009)

Table 2.3

Poverty and AFDC/TANF Status Regressed on Race, Human Capital, Marital Status, Labor Market, and Geography
Logit Odds Ratios (standard errors in parenthesis)

Wage	.999****	.999****	.999****	.999****
	(9.14)	(1.81)	(4.41)	(2.71)
Number of Children Under 18	1.16****	1.34****	1.17****	1.28****
	(.002)	(.004)	(.002)	(.026)
North Central Midwest	1.12****	.902****	1.06****	1.00
	(.007)	(.012)	(.008)	(.066)
South	1.31****	.465****	1.14****	1.31****
	(.008)	(.006)	(.007)	(.092)
West	1.02****	.674****	.967****	1.00
	(.007)	(.010)	(.007)	(.062)
Employed, Not at Work	1.01	1.17****	.928****	.906
	(.018)	(.055)	(.018)	(.170)
Unemployed	1.63****	3.02****	1.46****	.825**
	(.015)	(.056)	(.014)	(.065)
Not in Labor Force	.786****	2.16****	.723****	.938
	(.004)	(.031)	(.004)	(.057)
Married Spouse Absent	4.32****	3.94****	3.85****	.894
	(.085)	(.159)	(.064)	(.127)
Widowed	6.94****	14.9****	5.32****	1.36****
	(.084)	(.275)	(.071)	(.127)
Divorced	2.61****	1.89****	1.87****	1.57****
	(.021)	(.053)	(.019)	(.185)
Separated	5.39****	14.4****	4.52****	1.30****
	(.046)	(.228)	(.037)	(.093)
Never Married	1.30****	1.05****	1.95****	1.11*
	(.009)	(.016)	(.014)	(.073)
N	2,311,861	1,488,348	2,149,996	
Pseudo R^2	.2470	.2967	.2472	
χ^2 (df)	419,911.22 (18)	129,574.67 (18)	375,810.57 (18)	

*p=10%; **p=5%; ***p=1%; ****p=<.1%, two-tailed test. Omitted variables: White, married spouse present, employed, northeast. Source: Current Population Survey Datasets. Los Angeles: Unicon Research Corporation (producer and distributor of CPS Utilities), 2013.

More than that, in the race against female headedness, Blacks are gaining while whites are fading. Figure 2.6 shows in the late 1970s and early 1980s, Blacks turned the tide in female-headed households and since that time have been making constant progress in comparison with similar white families. That is, the long-term trend in Black to white female headedness is downward.

Figure 2.6 Ratio of Black to White Female Heads Who Are Poor

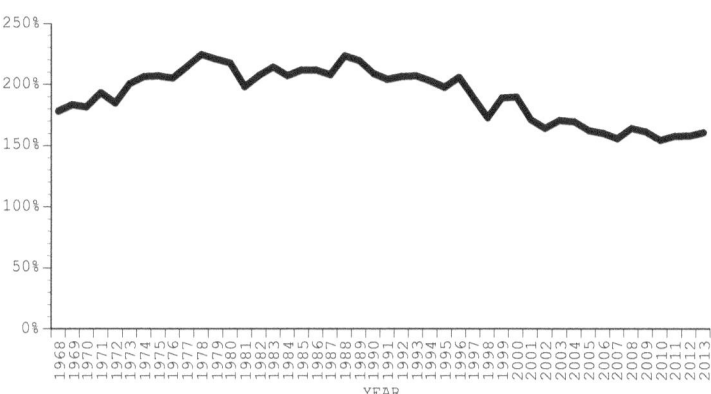

Source: Current Population Survey Datasets, 1962–2013. Washington, DC (machine-readable data files)/conducted by the Bureau of the Census for the Bureau of Labor Statistics. Washington, DC: Bureau of the Census (producer and distributor), 1962–2013. Los Angeles: Unicon Research Corporation (producer and distributor of CPS Utilities), 2013.

Table 2.2 shows that when matched for discrimination, assets, and networks, Blacks do not receive any more welfare than do whites. The higher rate of Black welfare receipt before welfare reform in 1996 was based on real need. This situation is no longer true. Figures 2.3 and 2.4 show that before 1995, the gap between Black and white welfare receipt was much greater than it is today. Even though, in comparison to whites, Black welfare receipt has declined, Black needs have not declined.

Table 2.3 compares Black poverty and welfare receipt before and after welfare reform. Before welfare reform (table 2.3, model 1) Blacks were 3.04 times as likely as whites to have income below poverty when matched for human capital (age, education), wages, number of children, geography, labor force, and marital status. In this same period, however, Blacks were 4.61 times as likely to receive AFDC (table 2.3, model 2). Notice that the discrepancy between comparative poverty and welfare receipt for Blacks is greater than for the other racial groups when comparing models 1 and 2 in table 2.3.

After welfare reform, Blacks are no more likely to receive welfare than are whites, as model 4 of table 2.3 demonstrates. This statistic matches models 6 and 7 of table 2.2. Blacks still are far more likely than are whites to be poor, as in model 3 of table 2.3. The comparative likelihood of poverty for Blacks has changed little, from 3 times as likely to be poor before welfare reform to 2.45 times as likely as are whites to be poor. Even though Blacks are far poorer than are whites, Blacks receive no more welfare than do whites. Welfare under Bill Clinton was reformed so the Black poor could subsidize the white poor.

The compelling story here is that Black families have waged a valiant fight against racial discrimination. Racial discrimination causes much lower family incomes and wages and lower rates of participation in the labor force. Despite all these obstacles, the Black family is gaining on white families with declines in female headedness versus whites. That Blacks are waging this fight alone, with great success and less help from government than whites receive, despite greater Black needs, is a story deserving of further consideration.

RAILROAD TRACKS TO SLAVERY

Most of the empirical evidence demonstrates that our society is rabid with racial discrimination. This discrimination impacts the life chances of Black Americans in ways that whites rarely experience. Deficiency theories claim that racial inequality is the result of some failure or deficit on the part of Black people. The deficit may be individual (cultural), group based (social), or even physical and mental (biological). The solution to racial inequality caused by Black deficiency is somehow to erase the deficit, if this is possible. Programs based on deficiency theory concentrate on fixing Black behavior rather than on white racism.

Any measure of the cultural cost of Black deficiency assumes that a deficiency exists, as does a significant gap between Black culture and society and those in the mainstream. Also, for a cost factor to exist, the deficiency must not be exogenous, that is, not caused by racial discrimination and societal oppression. Thus, the measurement of the costs for Black deficiency are connected intimately with the causes for racial inequality. Because of the problem of exogeneity in Black deficiency, that is, Black deficiency is itself a function of white oppression, bias and structural racism theories have the strongest social science support as the causes for racial inequality. These theories find that racial inequality in America is the result of American slavery and its aftermath: poverty, discrimination, and a hierarchy of American xenophobia toward non-white skin and culture, which persists to this day. Blacks generally are at the bottom of this hierarchy of racism, with other minority and non-white groups in various positions below whites, with the group position often determined by the degree of miscegenation.

Theories about Black deficiency are low cost because the deficiency hypotheses lack strong theoretical foundations. Deficiency theories fail the timing test because Black inequality predates many of the so-called causes for racial inequality, welfare being just one example.

Deficiency theories lack parsimony because they cannot break the chain of historic causation from American slavery. Cultural deficiency theories lack good process or generalizability and cannot explain the racial inequality for Black immigrants to the US. Deficiency theories must find new reasons for the inequality of every non-white racial group. The strongest social science experiments do not support cultural deficiency theories. Statistical wage evidence and audits evince large amounts of racial discrimination in society.

The "railroad-track" patterns date back to slavery. In looking at figure 2.1 for family income, we could draw a line back to 1880, which would include the freedmen (ex-slaves), just fifteen years since slavery. Their income would be 59 percent of the income of whites, and that percentage is similar to what it is today.[115] Family income is not the only railroad track to slavery. Life expectancy is another one that extends nearly that far back. Consider figure 2.2 again. Life expectancy for Black and white men starts in 1900, which would include many of the freedmen. Since slavery, almost no change has taken place in the ratio of Black to white male life expectancy. Racial inequality is a constant that precedes the introduction of welfare, migrations, occupational change, and almost all other variables. We have an almost-constant pattern of inequality based on race that extends back to slavery.

Attempting to fix Black culture and society without major changes in the systems of discrimination that create most if not all of the pathology that we see in poor Black communities exacerbates the problem. As Blacks improve in education, training, and social class, nonetheless they still are far removed from their white peers and further behind than before their personal improvements. This creates justifiable frustration and anger. White resistance and discrimination seem to increase, not decrease, with Black advancement.

---

115. Vedder et al., "Black Exploitation and White Benefits," 130. The 1880 figure for Black income in comparison to white is per capita, not family income.

Any fair reading of the evidence points strongly to racial discrimination as the most serious cause for racial inequality today. The "inherent Black deficiency" thesis has never had a sound basis for support. Welfare has been too small and recent a program to impact much of what makes Blacks unequal, and the collapsing Black family claim applies more to whites than to Blacks. Racism, bias, racialization, discrimination, and institutional and structural impediments, both historic and contemporary, are the cause for inequality between these two racial groups. While Black cultural deficiency has low cultural cost, the same cannot be said for white cultural deficiency. White behavior and cultural belief systems are some of the most erroneous and intransigent, and they carry a high price tag.

Chapter Three

White Cultural Belief Systems
A Glass Half Empty

THE COST OF INCOMPETENCE

Kruger and Dunning, two Cornell University researchers, retell the story of McArthur Wheeler, who robbed two banks in one day. Mr. Wheeler wore no mask and was arrested a short time later after videos of him appeared on the evening news. When shown the clear videos of himself robbing the banks, Mr. Wheeler could not believe that the video cameras had captured his face so clearly. Mr. Wheeler was under the impression that putting lemon juice on his face made him invisible to the video cameras.

Kruger and Dunning used the story of Mr. Wheeler to highlight what they call the "dual burden" of incompetence. The first burden is that lack of knowledge leads to bad decisions. The second burden is that incompetence robs people of the ability to recognize bad decisions and thus improve. The solution to incompetence is education and training—what Kruger and Dunning term "skill improvement." Strangely, skill improvement allows people to recognize the limits of their skill. As students learn, they know more about what they do not know.[1]

The best social science evidence shows that many whites are racially incompetent. White racial incompetence has a dual cost. The first cost is that whites reach erroneous conclusions about Blacks and the politico-economics of race. The second cost, which is more expensive, is that the ability of whites to correct their incompetence is limited because they are unaware of their racial incompetence. These factors create a high cost of changing white cultural beliefs.

1. Kruger and Dunning, "Unskilled and Unaware of It."

Political systems build in many protections against this type of dual burden of racial incompetence, but often these systems fail. In politics, gross prejudice can destroy the system of checks and balances. The Dred Scott case in 1856 was one such example. A Catholic Supreme Court chief justice, who believed slavery was evil and who had freed the slaves he had inherited before he came to the Supreme Court, nevertheless ruled that Blacks had no rights that the white man was bound to respect.[2] The economic system was politically dependent on the labor of Black slaves. The executive branch feared disruption and bent to the will of the South. The legislature supported the popular will, and the courts responded to the culture of the times. Not even a system of checks and balances can control that level of political incompetence.

The costs of building a society on faulty information are well known. The repression of physical science by the church before the Enlightenment in Europe; the fear and distrust in the US spread by the communist scares of the 1950s; and the threats against those seeking equal rights for workers, women or Blacks in the '50s and '60s all are examples of cultural costs from incompetence.

In 1911, one of the most respected names in the information science of the times, the *Encyclopaedia Britannica*, stated that Blacks were inferior to whites. While Black children seemed to be full of intelligence, as Blacks aged, they became dull, lethargic, and indolent, because unlike whites, the cranial sutures of Black brains were constricted, claimed the *Britannica*.[3] Writing nearly one hundred years before, Thomas Jefferson also found that Blacks were mentally inferior to whites, and he even accounted for environmental factors. Jefferson noted how much smarter Mulattoes were compared to full-blooded Blacks, and the implication was that the white racial breeding improved the Black race.[4]

Today, most would find it remarkable that both Thomas Jefferson and the *Encyclopaedia Britannica* could observe so clearly the effects of oppression and racism on adult Blacks but could not recognize their own bias. Adolf Hitler built his ideas of the master race from the American race science called eugenics.[5] This bad information helped fuel the Holocaust and the terror of Jim Crow. While such ideas as a master race have long since earned their repudiation, the fountains from which these ideas sprang still exist. Pervasive racial inequality, segregation, and racial isolation, combined with political control of ideas, may still lead to the dual burden of racial incompetence.

2. Schumacher et al., "Roger B. Taney."
3. Jacoby and Glauberman, *Bell Curve Debate*, 438.
4. Weyl and Marina, *American Statesmen*, 87–88.
5. E. Black, *War Against the Weak*, ch. 15.

Frequently, the gap between white ideas and those of Blacks are at such variance; both cannot be right. In his last book, MLK Jr. said, "The Negro on a mass scale is working vigorously to over-come his deficiencies and his maladjustments. . . . Whites, it must frankly be said, are not putting in a similar mass effort to re-educate themselves out of their racial ignorance. It is an aspect of their sense of superiority that the white people of America believe they have so little to learn."[6] Racial incompetence could compound American political polarization at a time when racial and political unity are necessary. Severe ethnic and racial polarization can lead to race war.

White cultural belief systems carry high cultural reeducation costs. The solution to racial incompetence is skill improvement, that is, education and training in the social science of race. Citizens, but particularly whites, must have their erroneous ideas exposed for what they are—racial incompetence. White belief systems must be challenged by the best social science available. These reeducation programs will need to be extensive, expensive, and rapid to avoid continued racial polarization.

Several rationales may explain why whites so often suffer from racial incompetence, and the costs are high. First, whites seem not to understand the difference between absolute, relative, and strategic improvement in the conditions of Black life. Second, whites are among the most spatially isolated of all racial groups in the US. Third, the length of time these erroneous ideas have been held demonstrates that they are deeply ingrained and will not change easily. Fourth, the number of areas in which white racial ideas depart from what good social science has determined to be correct is large and growing.

Last, the leadership institutions we normally expect to look to for change show that these erroneous ideas control even the leading social indicators, namely, K–12 school integration, the moral leadership of the church, the eyes of the media, elite academic institutions, and the important counter-majoritarian institution of the law and the courts. White cultural belief systems are not confined only to ideas, opinions, and beliefs held by the white public. White cultural belief systems also include the writings and arguments of scholars who feed faulty information to the white populous.

STRATEGIC IMPROVEMENT

Often-outmoded social science models are the basis for classification of the conditions of Black life. Comparing Blacks to their ancestors during slavery or Jim Crow has little meaning in the world of today. Even comparing Blacks to contemporary whites can be misleading. As we near a future where whites are no longer a majority, when a majority of the nation is

---

6. King, *Where Do We Go from Here*, 9.

comprised of peoples of color (Blacks, Latinos, Asians, and American Indians, often called a majority minority), any large, socioeconomic racial gaps could prove disastrous.

Racial progress can be measured in three ways. Absolute improvement compares Blacks to their own historic past. Measures of absolute improvements for Blacks are a favorite pastime of conservative think tanks. Few people would consider this measurement an important one, since few people feel they are well off simply because one hundred years ago their great-great-grandparents had less. Few people compare themselves to what they had even ten or twenty years ago.[7]

Figure 3.1 is an example of absolute improvement. Figure 3.1 shows the percentage of persons over twenty-five with a bachelor's degree or higher. These numbers have been rising so rapidly that some researchers have difficulty keeping up with the changes. In 1990, only 26 percent, 13 percent, and 8 percent of whites, Blacks, and Latinos, respectively, had a bachelor degree or more. In 2012, the figures were 39 percent, 23 percent, and 12 percent for whites, Blacks, and Latinos who possess a baccalaureate degree or more. The latest data shows that in 2022, 41 percent of whites possess at least a baccalaureate degree, compared to 27 percent and 20 percent for Blacks and Latinos respectively. In absolute terms, whites, Blacks, and Latinos have been making strong gains in higher education.

Figure 3.1 Persons Aged 25 and Over with Bachelor's Degree or Higher

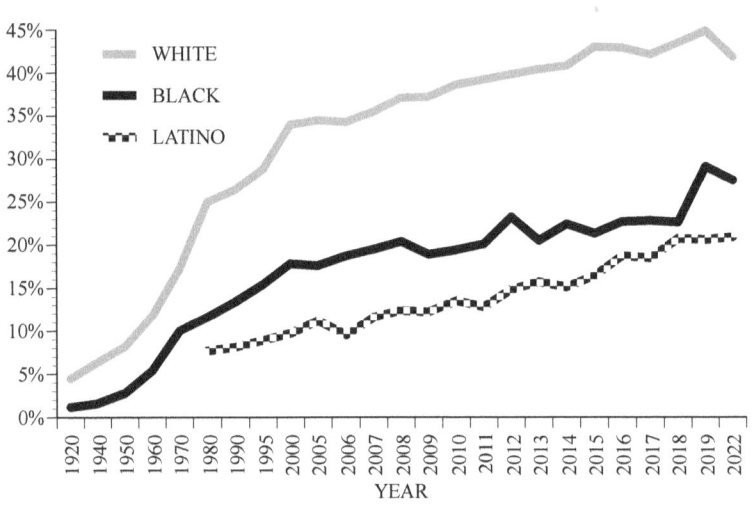

Sources: United States Census Bureau: "1960 Census"; Current Population Reports, series P-20, various years; Current Population Survey Datasets, Annual Social and Economic Supplement, 1970–2019; "2022 Annual Social and Economic Supplements," table 3.

7. Meyerson et al., *Alternatives to Racial Preferences*.

Relative improvement compares Blacks to whites over time or in a contemporary setting. This comparison has real meaning, and relative comparisons are used in this book. But figure 3.2 tells a different story than figure 3.1. In figure 3.2 the ratio of Black baccalaureate or more completion to white baccalaureate or more completion has been nearly flat since 1960 at 45 percent till 2018 at 51 percent. In 2022, the Black to white baccalaureate or more completion rate is only 65 percent. And the road forward has been anything but steady. In 2009, 2013, and 2015, the Black to white baccalaureate or more completion rate went down, not up, and there have been other ups and downs along the way.

Figure 3.2 also compares Latino to white baccalaureate or more completion since 1980. In 1980, Latinos' baccalaureate or more completion rate was only 30 percent that of whites. In 2022, after nearly half a century of trying, Latinos have clawed their way up to 50 percent of the white rate. This is an ominous sign for the fastest-growing minority group in America. Even relative improvement fails, however, to consider future goals or targets that must be reached to achieve a desired end.[8]

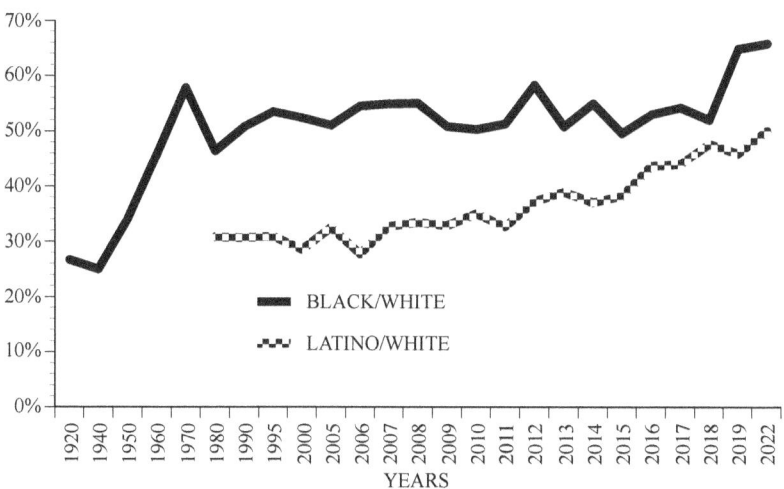

Figure 3.2 Ratio of Persons Aged 25 and Over with Bachelor's Degree or Higher

Sources: United States Census Bureau: "1960 Census"; Current Population Reports, series P-20, various years; Current Population Survey Datasets, Annual Social and Economic Supplement, 1970–2019; "2022 Annual Social and Economic Supplements," table 3.

8. Bobo and Charles, "Race in the American Mind."

Strategic improvement or equality compares racial progress to an important goal or milestone that must be reached for continued success. America is seriously lacking in this category.[9] Low- or no-cost equality, equality which is only procedural or symbolic, assumes that no crises are on the horizon that would require substantive racial equality. This viewpoint is a serious mistake. Absolute and relative improvement can increase incrementally almost indefinitely and never reach substantive equality or the strategic goals necessary to avert a crisis.

Given what may need to take place to adapt to the growing ratio of Blacks, Latinos, and other minorities, we could become less equal. Two books with similar titles, *The Coming Race War* and *The Coming Race War in America*, indicate the urgency of the need for strategic equality.[10] Martin Luther King Jr. captured the distinctions between "improvement" models when he said that whites view equality as a loose expression for "improvement."[11] As astounding as the increase in college education has been for American's largest minority racial group and Latinos, strategically, little progress has occurred for the last forty years. Figure 3.2 illustrates little or no progress in educational equality between whites, Blacks, and Latinos. In 1970, the ratio of Black to white baccalaureate possession was 57 percent. In 2022, the ratio of Black to white baccalaureate possession was 65 percent. This is not an impressive increase given the nearly half a century it took to reach it.

At the rates Blacks and Latinos are playing catchup in higher education, by 2040, when America becomes mostly peoples of color, Latinos and Blacks will still lag substantially behind whites. Figure 3.3 shows that progress is not steady or certain. With non-whites having numerical and voting majorities, any substantial differences in major measures of equality could create serious problems with doing business as usual. The safest route to equality in figure 3.3 is to plot a line from where we are now in possession of a baccalaureate for peoples of color and where we want to be in 2040. The gap between the safest equality route and where we are at any given point is called the strategic equality gap. As late as 2024, this gap was widening, not diminishing, thus, strategically speaking we are going backward if equality is measured by having a baccalaureate degree or more. If the next twenty years is a repeat of the last twenty years in figure 3.3, we will be further away from equality than when we started.

---

9. Coleman, "Strategic Equality."
10. Delgado, *Coming Race War*; Rowan, *Coming Race War in America*.
11. King, *Where Do We Go from Here*.

Figure 3.3 Safest Equality Route and Strategic Equality Gap for Baccalaureate or More Completion Rate

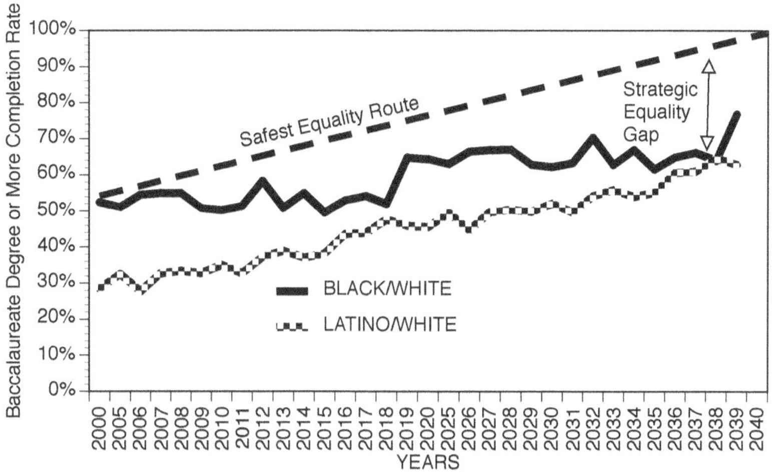

Sources: United States Census Bureau: "1960 Census"; Current Population Reports, series P-20, various years; Current Population Survey Datasets, Annual Social and Economic Supplement, 1970–2019. This table was prepared Oct. 2019.

SPATIAL ISOLATION

The cultural cost to educate whites out of their racial incompetence will be high because whites are so difficult to reach physically, spatially, and logistically. Some whites have built a wall around themselves and the rest of the nation, and they give little indication that the walls are getting lower. Whites are among the most spatially isolated groups, which cuts them off from information flows from the future majority minority.

Table 3.1 is recent data from the Census Bureau on residential segregation for Blacks. The dissimilarity index is like the Gini coefficient. A value of zero indicates total integration; a value of one indicates total segregation. Another way of describing the dissimilarity index is the percent of Blacks or whites who would have to move to achieve perfect residential integration.

Notice how high residential segregation remains in the largest American cities. In New York 81 percent of Blacks would have to move, in Los Angeles 66 percent, in Chicago 80 percent. Even the lowest values are near .4 when .6 is considered high, and the most segregated cities have almost total segregation in housing. The average residential segregation in these forty-three cities has dropped from .72 to .63 in twenty years. Compared to the late nineteenth and early twentieth centuries, cities are becoming more segregated.[12] We do not like to live together.

Table 3.1
Residential Segregation for Blacks or African Americans in Large Metropolitan Areas: 1980, 1990, and 2000, Dissimilarity Index

MSA/PMSA Name	1980	1990	2000	2000 Rank
Detroit, MI PMSA	0.874	0.874	0.846	1
Milwaukee-Waukesha, WI PMSA	0.839	0.826	0.818	2
New York, NY PMSA	0.812	0.813	0.81	3
Newark, NJ PMSA	0.827	0.825	0.801	4
Chicago, IL PMSA	0.878	0.838	0.797	5
Cleveland-Lorain-Elyria, OH PMSA	0.854	0.824	0.768	6
Buffalo-Niagara Falls, NY MSA	0.801	0.8	0.766	7
Cincinnati, OH-KY-IN PMSA	0.781	0.761	0.739	8
Saint Louis, MO-IL MSA	0.817	0.769	0.731	9
Nassau-Suffolk, NY PMSA	0.767	0.761	0.73	10
Bergen-Passaic, NJ PMSA	0.803	0.768	0.723	11
Philadelphia, PA-NJ PMSA	0.781	0.768	0.72	12
Indianapolis, IN MSA	0.788	0.746	0.704	13
Miami, FL PMSA	0.785	0.69	0.694	14
Kansas City, MO-KS MSA	0.773	0.725	0.688	15
New Orleans, LA MSA	0.698	0.679	0.684	16
Baltimore, MD PMSA	0.744	0.713	0.675	17
Pittsburgh, PA MSA	0.725	0.707	0.671	18
Los Angeles-Long Beach, CA PMSA	0.808	0.728	0.664	19
Houston, TX PMSA	0.754	0.664	0.663	20
Rochester, NY MSA	0.677	0.672	0.661	21
Boston, MA-NH PMSA	0.763	0.693	0.658	22
Atlanta, GA MSA	0.737	0.671	0.645	23
Hartford, CT MSA	0.712	0.696	0.644	24
Tampa-St. Petersburg-Clearwater, FL MSA	0.781	0.693	0.629	25
Washington, DC-MD-VA-WV PMSA	0.687	0.65	0.625	26
Oakland, CA PMSA	0.739	0.678	0.618	27
Columbus, OH MSA	0.729	0.673	0.616	28
Fort Lauderdale, FL PMSA	0.836	0.683	0.608	29
Denver, CO PMSA	0.689	0.64	0.605	30

12. Carr and Kutty, *Segregation*, 3–10.

Table 3.1
Residential Segregation for Blacks or African Americans in Large Metropolitan Areas: 1980, 1990, and 2000, Dissimilarity Index

MSA/PMSA Name	1980	1990	2000	2000 Rank
San Francisco, CA PMSA	0.675	0.638	0.6	31
Providence-Fall River-Warwick, RI-MA MSA	0.727	0.664	0.6	32
Dallas, TX PMSA	0.771	0.625	0.587	33
Minneapolis-St. Paul, MN-WI MSA	0.677	0.622	0.576	34
San Diego, CA MSA	0.643	0.579	0.535	35
San Antonio, TX MSA	0.613	0.543	0.492	36
Seattle-Bellevue-Everett, WA PMSA	0.671	0.559	0.489	37
Portland-Vancouver, OR-WA PMSA	0.686	0.63	0.464	38
Norfolk-Virginia Beach-Newport News, VA-NC MSA	0.595	0.494	0.46	39
Riverside-San Bernardino, CA PMSA	0.526	0.439	0.449	40
Phoenix-Mesa, AZ MSA	0.613	0.503	0.433	41
San Jose, CA PMSA	0.478	0.43	0.399	42
Orange County, CA PMSA	0.447	0.382	0.371	43

Source: United States Census Bureau, "Housing Patterns Tables," s.vv. "Black or African Americans: Residential Segregation in Large Metropolitan Areas: 1980, 1990, and 2000," table 5.4.

Generally residential segregation calls to mind discrimination against Blacks or Latinos. The impact that residential segregation has on whites has serious implications for the future of America, however. Logan and Stults capture the seriousness of this situation by pointing out that before 2020, whites will be a minority of the children of this nation.[13] Whites already are a minority of the babies born. These white children will grow up in communities that are racially different from the neighborhoods of the typical American, who will be an Asian, Latino, or Black person.

Figure 3.4 shows that whites live in the least diverse neighborhoods. Only Asians live in neighborhoods where their own racial group is not the plurality. Asians live in places that are only 22 percent Asian but 49 percent white. Blacks live in communities that are 45 percent Black. Latinos live in neighborhoods that are 35 percent Latino. Whites, however, live in neighborhoods that are 75 percent white. While this number is down from the 88 percent white in 1980, 75 percent homogeneity is still high compared to the other racial groups.

13. Logan and Stults, *Persistence of Segregation*, 2.

Figure 3.4 Diversity in Neighborhoods by Race

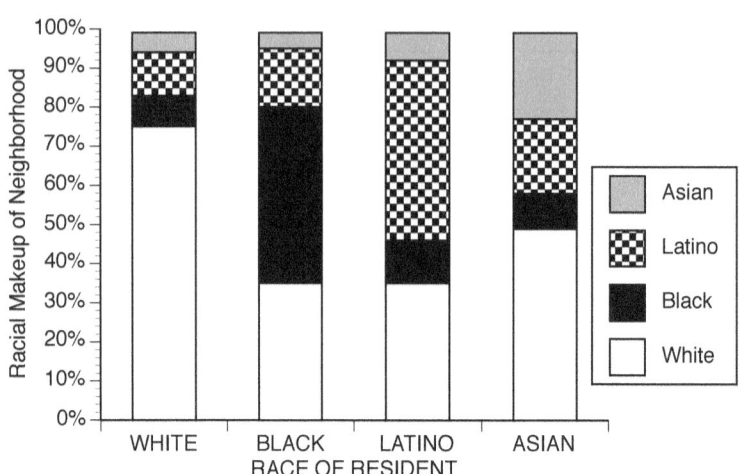

Source: Logan and Stults, *Persistence of Segregation*.

LONG-TERM DISCONNECTION

The length of time erroneous ideas have been held, about the causes of racial inequality, the lack of need for federal backing of school integration, and the real economic conditions for Blacks, demonstrates white ideas are deeply ingrained and will not be easily changed. Whites have never believed that racial inequality is owed primarily to discrimination, not even at the height of the civil rights movement.[14]

The GSS asked respondents if worsened housing, jobs, and income of Blacks were owed to discrimination. The questioning began in 1977 and has continued until the latest GSS. Black responses consistently have affirmed that racial inequality is fundamentally an issue of racial discrimination.

For whites, the highest rate of affirmation for discrimination as the cause of racial inequality was in 1977 when 41 percent of whites responded yes. Nearly 80 percent of Blacks in 1985 agreed that racial discrimination causes racial inequality.[15] By 2018, only a third of whites, compared with 60 percent of Blacks, thought that racial discrimination causes racial

---

14. See Gallup poll data in ch. 2.
15. T. Smith et al., "General Social Surveys, 1972–2018," mnemonics race and racdif1.

inequality.[16] Nearly fifty years of white denial of the reality of racial discrimination will not be easily changed.

Strong opposition to government-sponsored school integration is another area of long-term white racial denial. For decades the evidence has shown that separation is inherently unequal. (See the ch. 8 section on "Why Segregation Is Inherently Unequal" for further discussion.) Nevertheless, in 1962, less than a decade after the *Brown v. Board of Education* decision in 1954, and after the better part of a century of government-sponsored racial segregation, not even half of whites thought that the federal government should be involved in seeing "that White and Colored children are allowed to go to the same schools."[17]

The Gallup poll never asked only whites if they supported the *Brown* decision prior to the 1960s.[18] In 1962, the NES showed that only 45 percent of whites supported national-sponsored school integration. Given the poor record of state support for school integration, lack of support for a national program is tantamount to no support at all.[19]

White support for national-sponsored school integration has generally dropped since the 1960s. By 1968, only 33 percent of whites were in support; in 1976, only 18 percent of whites backed national support for K–12 school integration. In 2000, the last year NES asked a question on school integration, only 29 percent of whites supported the involvement of the government in Washington in "White and Colored children going to school together."[20] White opposition continues at a time when the most recent data show that the majority of Black students attend mostly minority schools, occupied by mostly poverty-stricken children.[21] The cultural cost of changing white ideas, if they can be changed at all, will be very high.

For almost a decade between 1994 and 2002 the General Social Survey asked respondents: "In the past few years, do you think conditions for Black people have improved, gotten worse, or stayed about the same?" Similar to the results found by Richard Morin and others, whites are generally far more optimistic about Black prospects than are Blacks themselves.[22]

16. T. Smith et al., "General Social Surveys, 1972–2018," mnemonics racecen and racdif1.

17. Time Series Cumulative Data File, variable VCF0816.

18. Gallup, *Gallup Poll*, vols. 2–3.

19. Orfield, *Must We Bus?*; Rosenberg, *Hollow Hope*; Bell, *Race, Racism, and American Law*, ch. 3.

20. Time Series Cumulative Data File, variable VCF0816.

21. Orfield: *Schools More Separate*; *Reviving the Goal*.

22. T. Smith et al., "General Social Surveys, 1972–2012," variable blksimp; Morin, "Distorted Image of Minorities."

In 1994, 58 percent of whites thought that conditions were improving for Blacks. This view was the most pessimistic whites have expressed during the time GSS asked the question. In 1996, 64 percent of whites thought situations were improving for Blacks. By 1998, the percentage of whites who were positive about Black prospects had climbed to 70 percent and remained high in 2000, at 67.5 percent, and 2002, at 69 percent.

Black optimism steadily rose between 1994 and 2002, yet Blacks have been far less positive about their own prospects than whites. In 1994 and 1996, only a third of Blacks thought conditions were improving for them. By 1998, 42 percent of Blacks thought that conditions for Blacks had improved. In 2000 and 2002, respectively, 51 percent and 58 percent of Blacks thought situations for Blacks were improving. The year 2002 was the last year the GSS asked a question about improving conditions for Blacks.

White optimism consistently outpacing that of Blacks is not the only issue. White optimism at the end of the Clinton years came at a time when non-white male and female wages were on a sharp decline in comparison to white wages in figures 3.5 and 3.6 below. Little reason for optimism existed.

BROAD AND DEEP

The number of areas in which white racial ideas depart from what social science has determined to be correct is large and growing and includes criminal justice, healthcare, wage inequality, and civil rights, among others. Peffley and Hurwitz stunned many social scientists with evidence of what many had long suspected: that white views of the criminal justice system were severely distorted.[23] Peffley and Hurwitz used three sources of information: 1) statistical evidence of racial bias in the criminal justice system, 2) personal experiences of individuals, and 3) individual perceptions of racial bias in neighborhoods.

In summarizing the social science evidence of racial bias against Blacks, Peffley and Hurwitz state the "evidence points to a justice system that is not only riddled with racial bias but that also defies any facile characterization."[24] Blacks are more likely to be prosecuted than are whites for similar crimes; Blacks are disproportionately sentenced to prison than are whites; three out of two hundred young whites were incarcerated in 2000 compared to one in nine for young Blacks. "By the time they reach

---

23. Peffley and Hurwitz: "Persuasion and Resistance"; *Justice in America*.
24. Peffley and Hurwitz, *Justice in America*, 28.

their mid-thirties, an astonishing 60 percent of Black high school dropouts are prisoners or ex-convicts, versus 11 percent for White dropouts."[25]

Claims of racial bias in the criminal justice system have divided scholars for many years, with some claiming that higher criminality among Blacks causes the racial differences in treatment. Whether controlling for "legally relevant variables, such as a prior criminal record," removes the racial differences is the central question.[26]

Peffley and Hurwitz conclude that racial differences in treatment remain even after controlling for legally relevant variables. There is a higher probability of execution in murdering a white person than in murdering a Black person.[27] Police use more force when they interact with Black citizens than white citizens.[28] In their cars, Blacks are more often stopped than whites, even after location, demeanor of motorist, and other factors are taken into consideration.[29] Black juveniles receive more punitive treatment at almost every stage of the criminal justice system, from initial intake to placement in detention centers.[30]

Some of the discrepancies between Black and white treatment by the criminal justice system are so wide as to make control variables almost irrelevant. Seventy-five percent of the motorists on a section of Interstate 95 were white, while 73 percent of those searched were Black. In one city Black youth were only 35 percent of the youth population, but were 77 percent of those who were brought to secure detention. Crack cocaine is a cheaper form of cocaine used primarily by Blacks, compared to powered cocaine, used mainly by whites. Federal drug law mandates a five-year prison term for 1 gram (1/3 of an ounce) of crack cocaine compared to 100 grams (3.5 ounces) of powdered cocaine, even though both forms have the same chemical power.[31]

Against the realities of racially discriminatory treatment, only 25 percent of whites say racial profiling is a serious problem, compared to 75 percent of Blacks. Only 12 percent of whites say harsher court sentences for Blacks is a serious problem, compared to nearly 70 percent for Blacks. Greater concern by the police for crimes against whites than crimes against

---

25. Peffley and Hurwitz, *Justice in America*, 30.
26. Peffley and Hurwitz, *Justice in America*, 32.
27. Keil and Vito, "Race and the Death Penalty"; Paternoster, "Prosecutorial Discretion."
28. Jacobs and O'Brien, "Determinants of Deadly Force."
29. D. Harris, *Driving While Black*; MacDonald, "Analytic Methods."
30. Peffley and Hurwitz, *Justice in America*, 34.
31. Peffley and Hurwitz, *Justice in America*, 35–36.

Blacks is a serious problem for only 12 percent of whites, compared to 65 percent of Blacks.[32]

Peffley and Hurwitz used a list-type experiment popularized by Kuklinski and Sniderman to examine the degree to which Black and white views toward the death penalty were influenced by racial bias.[33] Respondents were first asked if they supported or opposed the death penalty. Next, respondents were told that some say the death penalty unfairly targets Blacks and then asked if they supported or opposed the death penalty. Finally, respondents were told that some say the death penalty executes too many innocent people and then asked if they supported or opposed the death penalty.

Black respondents answered in a predictable fashion. Fifty percent supported the death penalty in the first question. When presented with information that Blacks are unfairly targeted, Black support for the death penalty dropped to only 37 percent. Finally, when Black respondents were told that the death penalty is used against innocent people, Black support for the death penalty dropped to 33 percent.

White respondents' support for the death penalty was 65 percent in the first question. White support for the death penalty increased to 77 percent when they were presented with information that the death penalty unfairly targets Blacks. The possibility of the execution of innocent people made no difference to white respondents.[34] The criminal justice system treats Blacks and whites differently in similar circumstances. Blacks understand this. Whites clearly do not.

Chapter 2 used the IOM study of differences in healthcare treatment to challenge the claim that differences in Black and white health originate in deficient Black behavior. The IOM study found that even though differences occur in how Blacks and whites sought healthcare, these differences were "small and have not fully accounted for racial and ethnic disparities in receipt of treatments."[35]

What was not mentioned in chapter 2 was the differences in what whites and Blacks think about the equality of racial healthcare treatment. Writing in the July 11, 2001, issue of the *Washington Post*, journalist Richard Morin reported on a national poll of Americans' views of policy issues, including healthcare. Sixty-one percent of whites say the average Black person has equal or better access to healthcare than the average white person. The reality is that Blacks are nearly twice as likely to be without health insurance

32. Peffley and Hurwitz, *Justice in America*, 43.
33. Kuklinski et al., "Racial Prejudice."
34. Peffley and Hurwitz, *Justice in America*, 158–59.
35. Smedley et al., *Unequal Treatment*, 7.

as are whites.[36] Healthcare for Blacks is poor, but not as poor as for Latinos. In 1996, 24 percent of Blacks were uninsured compared to only 15 percent for whites. In that same year, 36 percent of Latinos were uninsured.[37]

White misperceptions of racial equality involved more than just criminal justice. White misperceptions extend to many other areas, including healthcare. The Affordable Care Act, commonly called "Obamacare," was signed into law on March 23, 2010. The Census Bureau estimated in 2012 that those uninsured by race were 11 percent, 19 percent, and 29 percent for whites, Blacks, and Latinos respectively.[38] In 2016, the rates for those uninsured by race were 6.3 percent, 10.5 percent, and 16 percent for whites (not Hispanic), Blacks, and Latinos respectively.[39] So far the act has reduced the rates of the uninsured but has not reduced healthcare insurance inequality. Relatively speaking, healthcare inequality has gone nowhere. Strategically, matters are declining because Blacks and Latinos continue to lag far behind whites in healthcare as white population ratios decline.

Why white perceptions of race and healthcare differ so much from reality is a pertinent question. Morin says, "The sources of these misperceptions remain elusive." As for cost, white "mistaken beliefs represent formidable obstacles to any government effort to equalize the social and economic standing of the races."[40] In the same report by Richard Morin, in the July 11, 2001, issue of the *Washington Post*, most whites in a national survey reported that "Blacks are pretty much equal in terms of income and other things these days. It is good that the bad days are past and Blacks have come up."[41] Few ideas, such as economic racial equality, could be further from the truth.

THE HIGH COST OF EXPERTISE

High cost for white cultural belief systems comes not only from the white public. Experts who feed ideas and misinformation to the public also contribute to belief system cost when the ideas do not fit the empirical evidence. The problem with experts is that the public rarely has the skill or

---

36. Morin, "Misperceptions."
37. Lillie-Blanton et al., "Site of Medical Care," 22.
38. DeNavas-Walt et al., *Income, Poverty: 2012*, s.vv. "People Without Health Insurance Coverage by Race and Hispanic Origin Using 2- and 3- Year Averages: 2009–2010 and 2011–2012."
39. Barnett and Berchick, "Current Population Reports."
40. Morin, "Misperceptions," paras. 30, 4.
41. Morin, "Misperceptions," para. 7.

information to challenge the statements made by experts. To challenge an expert, an expert will be helpful. Experts usually do not give patently false information. The problems arise when technically correct general information is misapplied to a specific situation. I am not certain to what degree misinformation by experts colors the cultural beliefs of the white general public. Experts may, however, exert greater influence on policy makers who read their studies. White conservative expertise has high cultural cost because such information strays so markedly from the best social science evidence on race and equality.

Sowell asserts that affirmative action is, at best, unnecessary because Black occupational advances (in professional and technical occupations) came decades before any civil rights laws or affirmative action. Sowell claims that occupational advances after passage of the 1964 Civil Rights Act "represented no acceleration in trends that had been going on for many years."[42] The implication here is that the civil rights movement had little if any impact on the economic position of Blacks.

Stephan and Abigail Thernstrom characterize affirmative action as "a policy that in 1996 was still being pursued and strenuously defended as absolutely necessary for further Black progress only 'worked' in the South, and ceased to be effective more than twenty years ago."[43]

Three ways to measure the impact of affirmative action are effective: occupational increases, wage increases, or employment increases. All these criteria must be analyzed as ratios, that is, compared to whites, but not presented, as Sowell does, as absolute Black advances in occupations, which do not necessarily show advances relative to whites.

In addition, we must ask whether we are measuring the impact of civil rights policy, civil rights enforcement, affirmative action policy, or affirmative action enforcement. Civil rights and affirmative action are notorious for being under enforced. Lack of enforcement does not necessarily mean the policies themselves would be ineffective.

Nearly all the older studies show that affirmative action is associated with increased employment for Black workers and increased occupational levels. Most of these older studies (table 5.1) examined the impact of having a government contract on the racial makeup of firms using data supplied by the EEOC.[44]

42. Sowell, *Civil Rights*, 49.
43. Thernstrom and Thernstrom, *America in Black and White*, 450.
44. Ashenfelter and Heckman, "Measuring the Effects"; Burman, "Economics of Discrimination"; Heckman and Wolpin, "Does the Contract Compliance Program Work?"; Leonard, "Antidiscrimination or Reverse Discrimination"; Leonard, "Employment and Occupational Advance"; J. Smith and Welch, "Affirmative Action."

Generally these older studies found that a government contract is associated with higher ratios of Black male workers. Women, both Black and white, seem almost unaffected. A government contract is also associated with higher ratios of white male workers, probably because of the need for supervisors with the possession of a government contract.[45]

A government contract is used as a proxy for affirmative action because government contractors with contracts of $50,000 or more are required to comply with President Johnson's Executive Order 11246, identify underutilization of minorities and women, and establish goals and timetables for correction.

Possession of a government contract does not mean that firms actively pursue affirmative action or that sanctions are enforced. Nevertheless, using data from 1997 shows that firms with a government contract have higher ratios of Black men; a government contract has almost no impact on Black women; government contractors have higher ratios of white men and a lower percentage of white females.[46] One constant in studies of the effectiveness of affirmative action is that affirmative action in employment results in increased percentages of Black men.[47]

Table 3.2
Affirmative Action (AA) and Non-Affirmative Action (N-AA) Firms by Race, Gender, and Occupation of Workers

Occupation						
	Males					
	White		Black		Latino	
	AA	N-AA	AA	N-AA	AA	N-AA
Officials and Managers	8.03%	6.39%	0.36%	0.29%	6.10%	7.01%
Professionals	6.15%	3.39%	0.32%	0.19%	5.31%	6.06%
Technicians	3.10%	1.73%	0.28%	0.16%	0.00%	0.00%
Sales	5.18%	6.37%	0.66%	0.93%	0.00%	0.00%
Office and Clerical	2.01%	1.66%	0.39%	0.28%	0.10%	0.07%
Craft	6.69%	3.50%	0.69%	0.35%	0.33%	0.24%
Operatives	7.61%	5.01%	1.66%	1.01%	0.10%	0.07%
Laborers	2.79%	2.87%	0.89%	0.83%	0.12%	0.32%
Service	2.25%	4.34%	0.97%	1.57%	0.37%	0.29%
Total	43.81%	35.24%	6.21%	5.62%	12.42%	14.07%

45. Goldstein and Smith, "Estimated Impact."
46. Coleman, "Contesting the Magic."
47. Herring and Collins, "Retreat from Equal Opportunity?"; Holzer and Neumark, "What Does Affirmative Action Do?"

THE COST OF RACIAL EQUALITY

Number of Firms	116,024	91,727	116,030	91,728	115,919	91,644	
			Females				
	White		Black		Latina		
	AA	N-AA	AA	N-AA	AA	N-AA	
Officials and Managers	3.31%	3.10%	0.28%	0.23%	0.04%	0.03%	
Professionals	4.51%	4.02%	0.46%	0.38%	0.20%	0.15%	
Technicians	1.54%	1.52%	0.28%	0.25%	0.07%	0.10%	
Sales	4.43%	9.60%	0.81%	1.83%	0.18%	0.26%	
Office and Clerical	10.12%	8.92%	1.67%	1.21%	1.50%	1.53%	
Craft	0.66%	0.83%	0.13%	0.12%	1.31%	1.33%	
Operatives	2.51%	2.04%	0.78%	0.54%	0.00%	0.00%	
Laborers	1.26%	1.52%	0.41%	0.41%	0.00%	0.00%	
Service	3.11%	7.26%	1.31%	2.08%	0.02%	0.01%	
Total	28.13%	35.70%	5.84%	6.81%	3.27%	3.38%	
Number of Firms	116,023	91725	116,032	91,728	116,013	91,722	

Affirmative action firms are those with a government contract valued at $50,000 or more, which requires that they comply with Executive Order 11246, mandating goals and timetables for minority hiring. Source: EEOC, 1997.

Table 3.2 separates firms by race, gender, occupation, and affirmative action status for 1997. The year 1997 is an important year because it occurred immediately after the *Adarand Constructors* case in 1995. The Supreme Court ruled that even federal government affirmative action programs would be subject to strict scrutiny and had to satisfy some important governmental interest and be narrowly tailored to pass constitutional muster. If affirmative action were going to fail, that should show up in 1997, the first year the government could adjust its contracting to comply with Supreme Court mandates.[48]

Table 3.2 demonstrates that government contractor status certainly helps white and Black males. The average percentage of white males in affirmative action firms in 1997 was 43 percent compared to only 35 percent for non-affirmative action firms. The average percent of Black men in affirmative action firms is 6, compared to 5 for non-affirmative action firms. None of the other race and gender groups (white females, Latinos, Black females, Latinas) have higher representation in affirmative action firms. Table 3.2 results match almost exactly the results of the early studies from the 1960s about the impact of affirmative action and gains for Black and white males, with little impact on other groups.

48. *Adarand v. Peña*.

WHITE CULTURAL BELIEF SYSTEMS

Regression analysis is useful in understanding the impact of affirmative action by region. In the non-South (table 3.3), affirmative action firms have on average .6 percent more Black male workers. In the South, however, affirmative action firms have on average 1.2 percent more Black male workers. As late as 1997, then, affirmative action clearly still works, and it works in the non-South and the South. Since most Blacks live in the South, the greater impact in that region is important. As in other studies involving government contractor status, white males gain the most in table 3.3. Government contractors tend to have almost 5 percent more white males in the non-South, and 4 percent more white males in the South.

Table 3.3
Male Employment on Government Contractor Status
(Tobit Coefficients, standard errors in parenthesis)

	Black Males in the Non-South	Black Males in the South	White Males in the Non-South	White Males in the South
Government Contract	.006**** (.0005)	.012**** (.0009)	.049**** (.001)	.039**** (.001)
Total Employment	.000007**** (.0000004)	.000003**** (.000001)	-.00001**** (.000001)	-.00001**** (.000001)
Unionization	.00008**** (.00003)	.0005**** (.00005)	.0009**** (.00007)	.001**** (.00009)
Blue Collar	.053**** (.001)	.129**** (.001)	.126**** (.002)	.067**** (.003)
Concentration	.016**** (.001)	-.0008 (.002)	-.055**** (.003)	-.055**** (.004)
Industrial Sector	Yes	Yes	Yes	Yes
State	Yes	Yes	Yes	Yes
State*Metro Area	Yes	Yes	Yes	Yes
Constant	-.113**** (.009)	-.006 (.017)	.274**** (.021)	.355**** (.031)
N (Firms)	102,291	59,552	102,291	59,552
χ^2 (df)	22246.97 (79)	15235.08 (45)	41343.31 (79)	18092.90 (45)

*p=10%; **p=5%; ***p=1%; ****p=<.1%, two-tailed test. Source: EEOC confidential files, 1997.

Affirmative action (the possession of a government contract) is not related to Black female employment in any region in table 3.4. The white female employment ratio is greatest in firms without government contracts.

Claiming that Black occupational advances came before the age of affirmative action is different from saying that affirmative action does not work. Blacks, as with whites, unquestionably were making occupational advances prior to the heyday of the civil rights movement. This advance owed mostly to the decline in farming occupations and the movement of Blacks from rural areas to the cities and from the South to the North.

Table 3.4
Female Employment on Government Contractor Status
(Tobit Coefficients, standard errors in parenthesis)

	Black Females in the Non-South	Black Females in the South	White Females in the Non-South	White Females in the South
Government Contract	.0008 (.0007)	.0003 (.001)	-.047**** (.001)	-.042**** (.001)
Total Employment	.00001**** (.0000006)	.00002**** (.000001)	.000006**** (.000001)	.00001**** (.000001)
Unionization	.0001**** (.00004)	-.0001*** (.00007)	-.0005**** (.00007)	-.001**** (.002)
Blue Collar	-.038**** (.001)	-.033**** (.002)	-.238**** (.002)	-.235**** (.002)
Concentration	.047**** (.001)	.059**** (.003)	-.014 (.034)	.432**** (.027)
Industrial Sector	Yes	Yes	Yes	Yes
State	Yes	Yes	Yes	Yes
State*Metro Area	Yes	Yes	Yes	Yes
Constant	-.147**** (.013)	-.0005 (.023)	.411**** (.020)	.432**** (.027)
N (Firms)	102,291	59,552	102,291	59,552
χ^2 (df)	25698.12 (79)	12893.81 (45)	46191.28 (79)	25150.09 (45)

*p=10%; **p=5%; ***p=1%; ****p=<.1%, two-tailed test. Source: EEOC confidential files, 1997.

Between 1940 and 2000, a sharp drop occurred in farm occupations for both Black and white men. In 1940, 21 percent of white men and 41 percent of Black men were in farming, forestry, and fishing. By 1950, the percentages were 14 percent and 24 percent respectively, and by 1960, 8 percent and 11 percent.[49]

---

49. Current Population Survey Datasets; Department of Commerce, *Occupations* [1920 census]; U.S. Department of Commerce, *Occupations* [1930 census]; United States Department of Commerce, *Labor Force* [1940 census]; U.S. Department of Commerce, *Employment and Personal Characteristics* [1950 census]; United States Census Bureau, "1960 Census"; U.S. Department of Commerce, *Subject Reports* [1970 census]; U.S. Department of Commerce, *Subject Reports* [1980 census]; U.S. Department of Commerce, *1990 Census of Population*.

Where these workers were going is a relevant question. Almost all of the other occupations for men grew and absorbed these workers. Black men outpaced white men in precision production and craft occupations and as machine operators from 1940 to 1950. Black men have not made many such gains over white men in executive, administrative, and managerial occupations prior to the 1990s.

Before the age of civil rights, Black females worked primarily cleaning the homes of whites. In 1940, 60 percent of Black women were employed in private households, compared to only 11 percent of white women, who generally worked as secretaries in administration and sales (33 percent). By 1950, the percentage of Black women in private household occupations was still high at 42 percent but began to decline sharply between 1960 and 1970, when it reached 18 percent. Black females began to advance more than white females in the administrative area only in the 1960s.

Thomas Sowell and the Thernstroms' statement is misleading that occupational advances in professional and technical occupations came decades before any civil rights laws or affirmative action. Most of the occupational advances for Blacks in professional and technical occupations relative to whites came in the decade of the 1950s, 1960s, and 1970s. These advances were not before civil rights laws or affirmative action. The Fair Employment Practice Committee began in the 1940s, and the civil rights movement was well underway in the 1950s. The movement was inspired by the returning WWII veterans, the *Brown* decision, the murder of Emmett Till, and the Montgomery bus boycott.

Sowell's claim that the 1964 CRA did not coincide with any acceleration of Black occupational advances is not supported by the evidence. Figures 4.2 and 4.3 in chapter 4 show the rapid occupational changes for Blacks in the construction industry with the government-sponsored "Philadelphia Plan" during this period. Similar rapid gains accrued in wages for Blacks relative to whites following passage of the Civil Rights Act of 1964.

Figure 3.5 shows the ratio of non-white male to white incomes from 1948 to 2013 for full-time workers and for all workers. Notice the dramatic increases from 55 percent of white male income to 62 percent of white male income between the years 1959 and 1968. For all non-white male workers, this increase certainly represented an acceleration of the trend from 1948 to 1958. Before the 1960s, non-white males' incomes were stagnating, even with the post-WWII boom in full swing. The civil rights movement changed this trend. The data from some of the most conservative economists support the rapid rise in the ratio of non-white to white male earnings during the civil rights years.[50]

50. Welch, "Affirmative Action," 184–85.

THE COST OF RACIAL EQUALITY

Figure 3.5 Income Ratios for Non-White Male Workers as a Percentage of White Male Workers

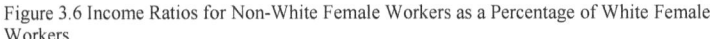

Sources: 1948–87: U.S. Department of Commerce, *Money Income of Households: 1987*, table 29. 1988–2013: Current Population Survey Datasets, 1988–2013. Washington, DC (machine-readable data files)/conducted by the Bureau of the Census for the Bureau of Labor Statistics. Washington, DC: Bureau of the Census (producer and distributor), 1988–2013. Los Angeles: Unicon Research Corporation (producer and distributor of CPS Utilities), 2013. Author's computations.

Figure 3.6 compares non-white female to white female income for the years 1948 to 2013. Notice the differences between figures 3.6 and 3.5 for non-white male income. Non-white females nearly reached parity with white female income in the late 1970s and early 1980s because gender tends to compress all female income, regardless of race.

Figure 3.6 Income Ratios for Non-White Female Workers as a Percentage of White Female Workers

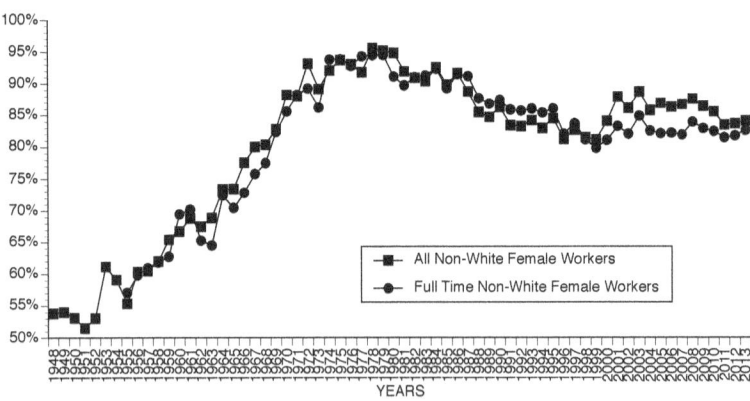

Sources: 1948–87: U.S. Department of Commerce, *Money Income of Households: 1987*, table 29. 1988–2013: Current Population Survey Datasets, 1988–2013. Washington, DC (machine-readable data files)/conducted by the Bureau of the Census for the Bureau of Labor Statistics. Washington, DC: Bureau of the Census (producer and distributor), 1988–2013. Los Angeles: Unicon Research Corporation (producer and distributor of CPS Utilities), 2013. Author's computations.

WHITE CULTURAL BELIEF SYSTEMS

Nevertheless, a similar pattern emerges for non-white females as for non-white males. Prior to the mid-1950s, non-white female incomes were not showing much improvement against their white female counterparts. In the mid-1950s, however, approximately at the time of the *Brown v. Board of Education* decision, a rapid rise occurred from 1954 until the beginning of the Reagan/Bush years in the early 1980s. See figure 3.6.

Sowell uses sleight of hand with words and numbers. First, occupational gains are different from income gains. Second, occupational gains for minorities, while different from income, did not precede the modern civil rights movement. Apart from the decline in farming occupations for white and Black men, the main occupational advances for Blacks did not precede the civil rights years. Third, while a rapid acceleration in occupations for Blacks and other non-white groups associated with the civil rights movement might not have occurred, rapid gains did take place that were associated with the civil rights movement for Black and non-white incomes.

Equally clear in figures 3.5 and 3.6 is the lack of progress beginning with the Reagan/Bush years in the early 1980s. The empirical evidence does not support Sowell's implication that the civil rights movement represented no acceleration of Black income advances. On the contrary, the Reagan/Bush years were the beginning of the end of the sharp gains for Blacks and non-whites. Strange the Thernstroms and Sowell did not mention this fact. Occupational advances for Blacks continue to this day. The same cannot be said for income advances.

NO HOPE IN SIGHT

White cultural beliefs are a glass half empty because the prospect for improvement or change is bleak. The leadership institutions that normally would look to future changes in ideas show that even they are controlled by erroneous white cultural beliefs.

K–12 schooling, the moral leadership of the churches, the eyes of the media, and the important counter-majoritarian institution of the law and courts are what many consider to be the leading social institutions, those institutions that point toward what we are becoming or want to become, not what we are now or where we have been.[51] Our children, churches, media, and courts are the future. If they cannot help us, little hope is imaginable.

K–12 schools reached a low for segregation in the 1980s, but they have never been desegregated in the sense that Black and Latino children go to schools with mostly white children. In 1988, 43.5 percent of Black children

---

51. Gallup: *Most Segregated Hour; Most Segregated Hour, Part 2.*

in the South attended mostly white schools. This is the highest degree of K–12 racial integration achieved in the history of the South, and the South is the most racially integrated region of the country.[52] In 1991, 33.5 percent of Black school children were in schools with 90–100 percent minority students. In 2006, 38.5 percent of Black students were in such schools. Schools are becoming more, not less, segregated. Chapter 9 shows that as of 2018, the situation has not improved. This situation is not good for the future.[53]

The church should be the most integrated. Almost 80 percent of the US is Christian, and one of the founding principles of Jesus was nondiscrimination. Jesus's principles of inclusiveness, however, have little impact on the church in the US. Only 2 percent of the Catholic Church, the largest Christian denomination in the US, is Black. The largest Protestant denomination in the US, the Southern Baptist Convention, is less than 1 percent Black.

Only 2 percent of the membership of the historically Black Protestant churches are white. Only 2 percent of the mainline Protestant churches are Black. Gallup poll information shows that while many Blacks worship in white churches, almost no whites worship in Black churches. Martin Luther King Jr. said that Sunday morning was America's most segregated hour, and this fact of life still seems to be true.[54]

An independent and free media is one of the founding principles of the US. The First Amendment to the US Constitution prohibits the Congress from making any laws "abridging the freedom of speech, or of the press." The Constitution says nothing about diversity in the press or the media, but the 1964 CRA prohibits discrimination in employment for race or color. If the media is America's eyes and ears, we would expect diversity here.

The Screen Actors Guild reports that in 2008 72.5 percent of roles in television and theaters went to whites, 13.3 percent went to Blacks, and 6.4 percent went to Latinos. For leading roles, 76 percent were white, 11.8 percent Black, and 5.2 percent Latino. The white population of the US in 2010 was 72.4 percent. The sharp underrepresentation of Latinos, the fastest-growing minority group, is troubling. Whites are overrepresented in leading roles in television and theaters.[55] A recent study from the University of Southern California of six hundred popular films found that whites

---

52. Orfield, *Schools More Separate*, 29, 36–37.

53. Orfield, *Reviving the Goal*, 11–13.

54. Gallup, *Most Segregated Hour*; Gallup, *Most Segregated Hour, Part 2*; P. Jones, *Southern Baptist Congregations Today*; Pew Research Center, *U.S. Religious Landscape Survey*; Score and Score, *Martin's Lament*.

55. Screen Actors Guild, "2007 & 2008 Casting Data Reports."

have been consistently overrepresented in films between 2007 and 2013. "Hispanics clearly are the most underserved racial/ethnic group by the film industry."[56]

America's entertainment media is disproportionately white, but newsrooms fall far short of the entertainment media. In 2014, the American Society of Newsroom Editors reported that only 13.34 percent of employees for all daily newspapers were minority. Of the 8,991 daily newspaper supervisors, 376 were Black, 330 Latino, and 219 Asian. Over 30 percent of the US is non-white.[57]

The purpose of lifetime tenure for federal judges and academic tenure for professors supposedly is to assure independence and advance the search for knowledge and truth. If the courts do not reflect what America is racially, they cannot be impartial. Courts that merely reflect white cultural beliefs are not democratic or just. The courts and the justice system may be the most important social institutions in avoiding a racial crisis because they have the ability and often the duty to be counter-majoritarian.

The ratio of Black lawyers, judges, and prosecutors is also low. Between 2003 and 2013, the ratio of Black lawyers, judges, and magistrates oscillated between a low of 3.74 percent in 2007 to a high of 6.63 percent in 2011. In 2013, 5.2 percent of the nation's lawyers, judges, and magistrates were Black. Similar rates apply for Latinos.[58] The trend is not upward.

Only 8 percent of federal prosecutors are Black.[59] An accurate count of the ratio of Black federal judges is difficult to determine. The Federal Judicial Center lists a total of 1,760 federal judges and magistrates. The Federal Judicial Center lists 203 Black judges; some of those listed are deceased.

Debra Cassens Weiss, on May 30, 2014, in the *American Bar Association Journal* reported that only 1.9 percent of partners at large law firms are Black.[60] Of the nation's one hundred largest law firms, many had no Black partners at all. Large law firms are frequently the best route to a top-level or federal judicial appointment. Regarding diversity, if the courts are the future of America, the future is not bright.

---

56. S. Smith et al., "Race/Ethnicity in 600 Popular Films," 3.
57. News Leaders Association, "Minority Employment in Daily Newspapers."
58. Current Population Survey Datasets.
59. Weatherspoon, "Status of African American Males."
60. Weiss, "Only 3 Percent."

WHY A RISING TIDE CANNOT HELP

Suppose white cultural beliefs are correct. What if the American economy is the answer in terms of equality, as some have surmised. In 1963, at the dedication of the Greers Ferry Dam, President Kennedy said, "A rising tide lifts all the boats and as Arkansas becomes more prosperous so does the United States." Given government spending on the Great Society and the military in the 1960s, most people believed, or behaved as if they believed, the post-WWII boom would continue forever. It could not.[61]

Richard Epstein claims that market competition is sufficient to protect Black rights with no need for affirmative action.[62] President Obama voiced similar beliefs about the ability of a strong economy to create some sort of equality. At his 100th-day press briefing on April 29, 2009, President Obama was asked about what he was doing to help Blacks, who were disproportionately affected by the Great Recession. He responded: "So my general approach is that if the economy is strong, that will lift all boats, as long as it is also supported by, for example, strategies around college affordability and job training; tax cuts for working families, as opposed to the wealthiest, that level the playing field and ensure bottom-up economic growth."[63]

Little evidence supports claims that Black versus white inequality is altered significantly by economic cycles or programs designed to stimulate overall economic growth absent programs specifically targeted to address racial inequality.

Figure 3.7 shows the Black and white male unemployment rates since 1972. Notice that Black unemployment is more than double that of white male unemployment. Black and white male unemployment parallel each other like railroad tracks that never meet. They go up and down together, indicating the same forces influence them.

During the Great Depression of the 1930s, the national unemployment rate reached nearly 25 percent. Black unemployment rates approached those levels during the recessions of the early 1980s, the Great Recession of 2008–9, and the COVID-19 pandemic.

Overlaid on figure 3.7 is the Black to white male unemployment ratio. The straight line at 220 percent in figure 3.7 shows the ratio of Black to white male unemployment as a measure of equality has not shifted much in nearly half a century. In February of 1972 the Black unemployment ratio was 2.2 times (220 percent) that of white males. In December of 2021,

---

61. Kennedy, "Remarks in Heber Springs," para. 11.
62. Epstein, *Forbidden Grounds*.
63. Obama, "100th Day Press Briefing."

the Black unemployment ratio was 2.2 times that of white men. Whether male unemployment goes up or down, the ratio of Black to white male unemployment is nearly constant over this nearly fifty-year span. No rising tide here.

Figure 3.7 Black and White Male Monthly Unemployment Rate and Ratio, 1972–2022

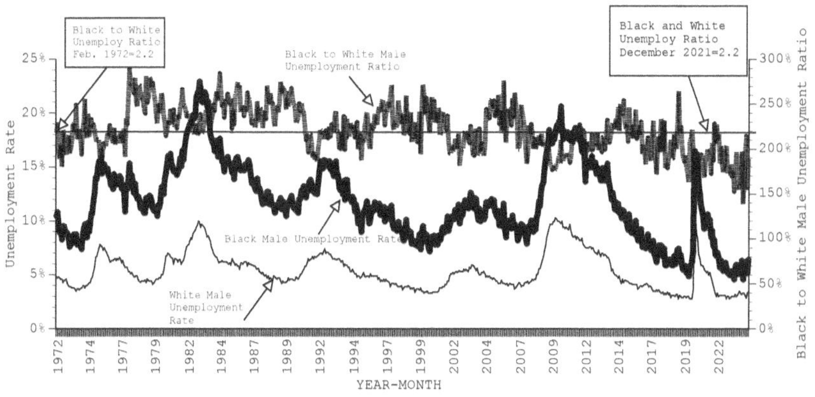

Source: BLS Data Finder 1.1, sixteen years and over Black and white males.

During the booming Reagan military buildup, 1981–88, unemployment dropped in figure 3.7, yet the ratio of Black to white unemployment was nearly constant. The high-growth Clinton years of the 1990s saw Black to white inequality increase as the ratio of Black to white unemployment rose, even as the unemployment rate dropped. The Obama years stand out as a classic time of a strengthening job market for Black and white men, and also steady or growing inequality in figure 3.7.

THE VICIOUS CIRCLE

White racial incompetence carries a dual burden. First, whites' ideas about racial equality have little in common with what the best social science indicates as correct. Second, the prospects for ending white racial incompetence are dim.

The solution to any type of incompetence is education, training, and skill improvement. The reeducation necessary to affect white cultural beliefs positively or their erroneous ideas will be very expensive. High costs are involved because the extent of biased white thinking is great. In addition, K–12 education, the church, the media, the law and courts, the social institutions most relied on for correction of cultural bias, are also highly segregated racially.

In discussing the implications of *The 1968 Report of the National Advisory Commission on Civil Disorder*, popularly known as the Kerner Report, Tom Wicker, in his twenty-year reappraisal, said the intractable problem was that racial inequality is primarily a function of white racial bias, discrimination, prejudice, and misinformation, and yet the solution to racial inequality rests largely with white largess. This creates a type of death spiral that Wicker called "a vicious circle."[64]

The problem is not just that whites have never believed, not even at the height of the civil rights movement, that white racial discrimination was the major problem with racial inequality in America or that white ideas about conditions for Blacks long have been held. The problem is that the white population is not positioned well to manage effectively the rapidly changing nature of the American population, electorate, and labor force, as all of these groups become mostly Black, Latino, and minority. The existing cultural belief systems likely will inhibit the ability to understand the seriousness of the problem of racial inequality and craft solutions.

THE NEW ANTI-STRUCTURALISM

Given the clear evidence that racial inequality is not caused by biological, cultural, or social deficiencies in peoples of color, the new white backlash against the findings that bias and structural theories of inequality have the most scientific support requires answers as to why this resistance to bias and structural theory is new and why resistance to accepting bias and structural theories of racial inequality come now in the post–civil rights era. America has thrived on racial inequality theories that support white biological, cultural, and social superiority. From Thomas Jefferson in the eighteenth century to the *Encyclopaedia Britannica* in the early twentieth century, theories of Black inferiority have held sway. The Great Commissions have fought hard to counter these erroneous ideas but it seems to no avail. Since the 1970s and our ability to measure with surveys, most whites have not accepted bias or structural theories for racial inequality. In the year 1977, 58.92 percent of whites believe that the worse jobs, income, and housing that Black people have are not due to discrimination. In the year 2000, 66.62 percent of whites did not believe that racial inequality is caused by racial discrimination. In 2018, 57.90 percent of whites did not believe that racial inequality is caused by racial discrimination. White rejection of

64. Wicker, "Introduction to the 1988 Edition," xii.

a bias theory for racial inequality has been consistent for half a century and does not seem to be in decline.⁶⁵ And while whites have clearly rejected biological deficiency as the cause for racial inequality, they lean heavily toward cultural deficiency as the cause. Ninety-four percent of whites in 2018 rejected the idea that the worse incomes, jobs, and housing of Blacks are due to less inborn ability. This rejection of biological deficiency by whites as the reason for racial inequality is a good sign.⁶⁶

The problem is that whites have never been able to fully let go of the idea that Blacks as individuals lack cultural development. Whites' firm rejection of both biological deficiency on the one hand and bias and structural theories for inequality on the other in the postwar period have left them with little room to maneuver, making them extremely vulnerable to cultural and social deficiency theory. In 1977, two-thirds (66 percent) of whites believed racial inequality was due to a lack of willpower on the part of Blacks.⁶⁷ This is cultural deficiency. By the year 2000, over half of whites (50.57 percent) accepted lack of willpower on the part of Blacks as the reason for racial inequality. Whites have slowly relinquished their cultural deficiency biases about Blacks, with the rate of cultural deficiency ideas dropping to 36.04 percent in 2018, the lowest rate ever measured. Nevertheless, whites have not accepted bias and structural theories for racial inequality, leaving them in a never-never land. The reasons behind white fictional ideas are complex and require more research, but one result of these ideas, combined with white spatial isolation, may be that whites are easily duped into accepting fictional, unscientific, and erroneous ideas about Blacks.

Even though anti-Black racism and bias have been with America since the beginning, this new revolt against the findings of all five of the Great Commissions that racial inequality is indeed caused by white bias and the resulting structural impediments is different from the past in that white-controlled legislatures are attempting to enshrine these false ideas into law. America has never hesitated to tell its citizens how to act toward Blacks. The new anti-structuralism is attempting to tell citizens how to think about Blacks, peoples of color, and the history of race and racial theory. Widespread anti-Black ideas not only harm whites by creating a false sense of white superiority, but bad social science also creates a false sense of inferiority in the minds of Blacks, particularly Black children.

On April 19, 2021, the Department of Education solicited comments for "Proposed Priorities—American History and Civics Education." The

---

65. T. Smith et al., "General Social Surveys, 1972–2018," mnemonic racedif1.
66. T. Smith et al., "General Social Surveys, 1972–2018," mnemonic racedif2.
67. T. Smith et al., "General Social Surveys, 1972–2018," mnemonics race, racedif4.

THE COST OF RACIAL EQUALITY

proposal stated its purpose was to "Incorporate Racially, Ethnically, Culturally, and Linguistically Diverse Perspectives into Teaching and Learning" and that "our country faces converging economic, health, and climate crises that have exposed and exacerbated inequities, while a historic movement for justice has highlighted the unbearable human costs of systemic racism. Our Nation deserves an ambitious whole-of-government equity agenda that matches the scale of the opportunities and challenges that we face."[68] Further,

> American History and Civics Education programs can play an important role in this critical effort by supporting teaching and learning that reflects the breadth and depth of our Nation's diverse history and the vital role of diversity in our Nation's democracy. For example, there is growing acknowledgement of the importance of including, in the teaching and learning of our country's history, both the consequences of slavery, and the significant contributions of Black Americans to our society. This acknowledgement is reflected, for example, in the *New York Times*' landmark "1619 Project" and in the resources of the Smithsonian's National Museum of African American History.
> Accordingly, schools across the country are working to incorporate anti-racist practices into teaching and learning. As the scholar Ibram X. Kendi has expressed, "[a]n antiracist idea is any idea that suggests the racial groups are equals in all their apparent differences—that there is nothing right or wrong with any racial group. Antiracist ideas argue that racist policies are the cause of racial inequities." It is critical that the teaching of American history and civics creates learning experiences that validate and reflect the diversity, identities, histories, contributions, and experiences of all students.[69]

The Department of Education proposed to offer priority to grant projects that "take into account systemic marginalization, biases, inequities, and discriminatory policy and practice in American history."[70] The Biden Administration proposed that bias and structural theories of racial inequality be given priority in K-12 education, a clear rejection not only of the deficiency theories formerly held by most whites, but also of the Turner and Beard view of American exceptionalism and that racism and slavery were inconsequential aspects of American history.[71] Turner and Beard were con-

68. Ryder, "Proposed Priorities," 20349.
69. Ryder, "Proposed Priorities," 20349; quoting Executive Order 13985.
70. Ryder, "Proposed Priorities," 20349.
71. F. Turner, *Frontier in American History*; Beard, *Economic Interpretation*.

sidered the fathers of modern American history and their views dominated K–12 text books for most of the twentieth century.[72] Soon after the Department of Education's "Proposed Priorities—American History and Civics Education" was issued, many Republican-controlled state legislatures began to propose and enact new educational mandates for how American history and social studies are to be taught in grade schools and high schools.[73] Many of these state laws, resolutions, and proposals specifically banned "the 1619 Project . . . an ongoing initiative from the *New York Times Magazine* that began in August 2019, the 400th anniversary of the beginning of American slavery. It aims to reframe the country's history by placing the consequences of slavery and the contributions of [B]lack Americans at the very center of our national narrative."[74]

Florida is an example of a state opposed to the Department of Education's proposed policy. The Florida State Board of Education issued a rule mandating that

> instruction on the required topics must be factual and objective, and may not suppress or distort significant historical events, such as the Holocaust, slavery, the Civil War and Reconstruction, the civil rights movement and the contributions of women, African American and Hispanic people to our country, as already provided. . . . Examples of theories that distort historical events and are inconsistent with State Board approved standards include the denial or minimization of the Holocaust, and the teaching of Critical Race Theory, meaning the theory that racism is not merely the product of prejudice, but that racism is embedded in American society and its legal systems in order to uphold the supremacy of White persons. Instruction may not utilize material from the 1619 Project and may not define American history as something other than the creation of a new nation based largely on universal principles stated in the Declaration of Independence.[75]

Some eleven states are expanding their curricula in response to the Department of Education's proposal. California's State Board of Education issued a model curriculum for ethnic studies that will be mandated for all

---

72. Lynd, *Class Conflict*, pt. 2, "Slavery."
73. Stout and LeMee, "Efforts to Restrict Teaching."
74. Silverstein, "Why We Published the 1619 Project," para. 4. See also 1619 Project.
75. Schwartz, "Where Critical Race Theory"; Department of Education, "Required Instruction," s.vv. "Change 6A-1.094124" (June 14, 2021).

students.[76] "This model curriculum is a step toward rectifying omission of the experiences and cultures of communities within California. Ethnic studies courses address institutionalized systems of advantage, and address the causes of racism and other forms of bigotry including, but not limited to, anti-Blackness, anti-Indigeneity, xenophobia, antisemitism, and Islamophobia within our culture and governmental policies."[77] However, twenty-eight states have proposed restrictions or actually passed laws or resolutions against the Department of Education's "Proposed Priorities— American History and Civics Education."[78] In many ways a second civil war, where peoples of color and their white allies battle for political, social, and cultural control of the nation, envisioned by Delgado and Rowan, is already underway.[79]

76. Stout and LeMee, "Efforts to Restrict Teaching."
77. California Department of Education, *Ethnic Studies Model Curriculum*, 3–4.
78. Stout and LeMee, "Efforts to Restrict Teaching."
79. Delgado, *Coming Race War*; Rowan, *Coming Race War in America*.

Chapter Four

The Costs of the Law

MARTIN LUTHER KING JR. was not speaking metaphorically when he said, "The practical cost of change for the nation up to this point has been cheap. The limited reforms have been obtained at bargain rates. There are no expenses, and no taxes are required, for Negroes to share lunch counters, libraries, parks, hotels, and other facilities with whites."[1] In some sense, the costs for the law involve all the costs in table 1 because the law forms the basis for all racial inequality in the US. Using that schema becomes unwieldy, however. The main costs of equality before the law are the perceived political costs in the courts and cultural costs for individual whites. Richard A. Posner, a former chief judge in the federal court system, appointed by a Republican president, has said: "Viewed realistically, the Supreme Court, at least most of the time, when it is deciding constitutional cases is a political organ." Posner warned of the danger of substituting the ideas of elites, in the form of judges, for the will of the people. Posner used the example of Adolf Hitler's boast that he was a better representative of the German people than any elected official was. Using elites as a substitute for the will of the people is called: "the Führer principle."[2] America's courts are dominated by elite white judges making decisions about a future majority minority of which they are not a part.[3] This condition could be dangerous for a nation becoming a majority minority.

At the federal level, the political connection to the law is indirect; judges are appointed, not elected. Most of the social costs involving changes in group behavior, regarding racial equality, are already the law: school

1. King, *Where Do We Go from Here*, 5.
2. Posner, "Political Court," 34.
3. Weatherspoon, "Status of African American Males."

integration, antidiscrimination in employment, voting. Few people would say that school segregation, job discrimination, and racially restricted voting are just and fair. This chapter will show that few if any negative economic costs are involved in achieving racial equality or in moving Blacks to the higher occupational levels their skill and training deserve. The major economic costs for racial inequality come from maintaining non-meritorious white privileges. For 188 years of the nation's 245-year history, from the founding of the nation in 1776 to the signing of the 1964 CRA on July 2, 1964, America has been officially anti-Black, the short Reconstruction period excepted. Race neutrality in such a system is a dangerous legal fiction propagated and promulgated largely by the courts. The overwhelming weight of the evidence shows that racial bias, prejudice, and even bigotry are endemic in the US. Even though racial discrimination against peoples of color in many domains is against the law, these laws lack serious enforcement. Failure to engage in some sort of restitution, balancing, or recognition of the greater difficulties peoples of color have in securing jobs, housing, education, respect, and even freedom from police abuse, simply because of their race, results in massive non-meritorious advantages to whites at best and white supremacy at worst. The courts are creating a situation in which only constitutional change or abolishment can resolve the situation.

King was correct that no dollar expenses or taxes were necessary to end Jim Crow or to use the law to create substantive economic equality. Even social costs for legal changes are low, since many of the legal issues involved (voting rights, antidiscrimination, diversity) already are established law or policy and lack only sufficient enforcement. Intrinsic political costs are changes a political party makes in its fundamental ideology or in supporting a particular equality program. Intrinsic political costs are low, since in the past both Democrats and Republicans have supported substantive racial equality. Still, costs to the law are apparent.

In the political environment of today, the perception is real that any concessions to Black rights in the law are an affront to white rights. The perceived political costs generally apply to the courts, while cultural costs apply to anti-affirmative action attitudes by individual whites, including judges. Surveys of the radically different voting patterns and ideas of Blacks and whites toward affirmative action and anti-affirmative action laws show that the cultural costs of changing individual white ideas about racial equality and the law are high. This chapter traces these high cultural and perceived political costs while showing the low economic costs involved in creating racial equality in the law.

Few people, white or Black, can imagine another civil war. The desire to maintain the racial inequality laid by the founders does not ensure that our democracy will continue. Rather, using the law to support inequality goes far toward ensuring that racial inequality will not find a remedy via normal constitutional channels. Changing the legal system to operate in the interests of equality for all, so that the law can facilitate the changes necessary for the majority minority of the future in America, should be the goal, if racial equality is to be attained. Chapter 1 defined cultural costs as the effort involved in changing individual behaviors and thinking to match some standard of acceptable behavior that fits some type of politico-economic reality. The racially neutral standard imagined by the courts does not fit the reality of America's history or present condition; thus, the cultural costs for the courts are high. Perceived political costs were defined as those costs that a political party pays in lost votes or influence by supporting a particular program. The political fight to control the courts, even by unconstitutional means, shows the perceived political costs of the law are also high.

THE DANGEROUS CONTEMPORARY LEGAL PERIOD

Five legal issues show the high perceived political and cultural costs of the law, three in the contemporary period and two more long term and historical: 1) the refusal of the 2016 GOP-controlled US Senate to vote on Barack Obama's replacement for Antonin Scalia and the rapid appointment of Amy Coney Barrett, a mere eight days before the election of a new Democratic president; 2) the 2013 and 2016 affirmative action cases *Fisher v. University of Texas* (*Fisher I* and *II*); 3) the 2014 Michigan affirmative action case; 4) the history of non-meritorious white affirmative action; and 5) the history of meritorious Black affirmative action, which includes the infamous Philadelphia Plan. The Philadelphia Plan in the construction trades was as close as the nation ever came to proportional quotas. If no costs are found in the Philadelphia Plan for the claimed less qualified Black workers, we can be fairly sure no such costs exist.

After Antonin Scalia, who was one of the most anti–affirmative action judges in modern history, died on February 13, 2016, President Obama, on March 16, 2016, nominated Merrick Garland to take Scalia's place. Garland was a Harvard-educated, white Jewish lawyer raised in Chicago, and chief judge of the US Court of Appeals for the District of Columbia.[4] Most people considered Garland to be a moderate, and he had been supported by Republicans before. On the day of the nomination, Senate Majority Leader Mitch McConnell stated the nomination would not be considered, and it was not. Almost a year later, 294 days, the nomination expired when the

4. J. Jones, "Merrick Garland"; Tillman, "Obama Nominates Merrick Garland."

new 115th Congress took office on January 3, 2017. Prior to the Garland nomination, the longest time the Senate had taken to consider a candidate was 125 days.

JoLissa Jones, writing in the *Thurgood Marshall Law Review* out of Texas Southern University, finds that while the Senate is not legally required to hold a vote on a nominee, to let a nomination languish is an abdication of their responsibility as elected officials and ultimately harms the nation.[5] Theoretically, the Senate could refuse to act on any nomination put forward by the president for the entirety of his term, simply for partisan reasons. No government could function long in this manner. Jones recommends a change to Senate rules that require a vote on a nominee before the session expires.

The Senate has decided not to act on a nomination in the past when a president has only weeks left in office.[6] To refuse even to vote on a nomination by a president, with almost a year left in his term, is a more harsh brand of racial, partisan politics. Liberal Justice Ruth Bader Ginsburg's death on September 18, 2020, just weeks before the presidential election, and the confirmation of Amy Coney Barrett as a conservative replacement for Ginsburg on October 26, 2020, just eight days before the election of Joe Biden, by many of the same GOP senators who refused an Obama appointment, indicts brutal fighting for political and racial control of the courts and the law. The political costs are perceived to be extremely high for those involved in this struggle. In January of 2021 Garland was nominated by President Biden to be the eighty-sixth attorney general of the United States and confirmed in March of 2021 by the United States Senate by a vote of seventy to thirty.

The right decision for the wrong reason is the best way to describe the final 4–3 decision in *Fisher v. University of Texas* in 2016 (*Fisher II*). The Supreme Court held in *Fisher II* that the affirmative action program at the University of Texas at Austin was constitutionally permissible because the university had demonstrated a compelling government interest in maintaining a diverse student body and the narrowly tailored race-conscious plan met that interest. Further, while a university bears a heavy burden to show that race-neutral admissions criteria are not sufficient to achieve diversity, evidence about the increase in admissions of peoples of color using the university's race-conscious program was sufficient to show the program had a meaningful impact on diversity. Narrow tailoring does not require

5. J. Jones, "Merrick Garland."
6. "[In 1853] President Millard Fillmore nominated William C. Micou in the last two weeks of his presidency, and Congress thought it would be best to leave the seat on the bench vacant" (J. Jones, "Merrick Garland," 10).

that the university exhaust every imaginable race-neutral alternative. However, the court should have decided that the affirmative action plan was constitutional because Texas had a well-known history of racial discrimination in higher education, the nation must rid itself of all vestiges of racial inequality as quickly as possible, and given the horrible history of racial oppression and genocide, with the full support of the courts, race neutrality is an outmoded myth and a dangerous legal fiction that gives rise to notions of white superiority.

Fisher v. University of Texas (2013) was another of too many examples of the classic American dilemma and harm to the nation by the courts.[7] I have stated elsewhere that "the facts of the case follow a familiar pattern: a white female denied admission to a prestigious predominantly white university with a well-known history of racial discrimination which is, however, not part of the case record."[8]

> The University of Texas at Austin ... uses an undergraduate admissions system containing two components. First, as required by the State's Top Ten Percent Law, it offers admission to any students who graduate from a Texas high school in the top 10% of their class. It then fills the remainder of its incoming freshman class, some 25%, by combining an applicant's "Academic Index"—the student's SAT score and high school academic performance—with the applicant's "Personal Achievement Index," a holistic review containing numerous factors, including race. The University adopted its current admissions process in 2004, after a year-long study of its admissions process ... led it to conclude that its prior race-neutral system did not reach its goal of providing the educational benefits of diversity to its undergraduate students. Petitioner Abigail Fisher, who was not in the top 10% of her high school class, was denied admission to the University's 2008 freshman class. She filed suit, alleging that the University's consideration of race as part of its holistic-review process disadvantaged her and other Caucasian applicants, in violation of the Equal Protection Clause.[9]

The University of Texas, like most state universities in the South, denied admission to anyone who was Black until they were sued and forced to open their doors. After the civil rights movement, racial mixing to increase the education experience of mainly white campuses became popular. This

7. *Fisher I.*
8. Coleman, "Strategic Equality," 33–34, referring to *Sweatt v. Painter*, with a description of the admission formulas.
9. *Fisher II*, 2202.

racial mixing of relatively small numbers of highly qualified Blacks on white campuses now has the title of diversity. The state of Texas is 11.8 percent Black while the prestigious flagship campus of the University of Texas at Austin was only 4 percent Black in 2011 and was still only 6.8 percent Black by the time of *Fisher II* in 2016.[10]

Diversity is not remedial, nor is it an attempt to ameliorate the sins of the Jim Crow era or assist in creating a system of equality, so that a flagship campus mirrors the Black population ratio. Remedies like proportional quotas, back pay, hiring, and admission into college, graduate schools, or professional schools for Blacks are usually used for disparate (racially biased) treatment. Hiring only whites for certain jobs or accepting only whites into certain schools today is a violation of law. Disparate treatment remedies should address a range of offences beyond blatant racial discrimination and "an open invidious purpose."[11] Disparate treatment remedies should also be available as a solution for racial imbalances so profound as to threaten the democratic foundations of the nation.

Disparate impact means treating Blacks differently because of their group membership, while using a proxy for race, such as a dubious test score, educational credential, or zoning laws. Disparate impact, like disparate treatment, is a violation of the law in many circumstances and may encompass a range of remedies. The most famous case in this area is *Griggs v. Duke Power* in 1971. Prior to the effective date of the 1964 Civil Rights Act, Duke Power Company had openly and actively discriminated against Black workers by restricting them to the lowest-paying department—the labor department—regardless of their education. On July 2, 1965, the day that the 1964 Civil Rights Act became effective, Duke Power Company began requiring that applicants have a high school diploma and achieve satisfactory scores on two aptitude tests, and a satisfactory score was determined by the average score of a high school graduate. All but one of the Black employees lacked a high school diploma. Whites without a high school diploma, who were allowed in higher-paying departments prior to the education and test requirements, were allowed to keep their positions.

In *Griggs v. Duke Power*, Chief Justice Warren E. Burger ruled that disparate impact may also be a violation of the law when "practices, procedures, or tests neutral on their face, and even neutral in terms of intent, cannot be maintained if they operate to 'freeze' the status quo of prior discriminatory employment practices."[12] Most of the struggles at the Supreme Court have concerned applying these standards: disparate treatment,

10. *Chronicle of Higher Education*: "Diversity in Academe"; "Almanac Issue."
11. *Coalition v. Regents*, 338.
12. *Griggs v. Duke Power*, 429.

disparate impact, and diversity to whites, a group they should never have been intended to serve.

Diversity seeks to improve the educational environment only by racial mixing. The Supreme Court has ruled that racial diversity satisfies the strict scrutiny standard of judicial review of state-sponsored racial classifications if the purpose meets a compelling government interest and the program planners narrowly tailored it to meet that interest.[13]

In seeking to implement racial diversity on campus, universities may consider race as one of many factors but may not set up strict numerical quotas to ensure particular ratios.[14] Following these Supreme Court dictates, the University of Texas at Austin set up a diversity program that considered race as one of many factors. Something went wrong, nonetheless. In *Fisher I*, a 7–1 majority of the Supreme Court ruled lower courts must evaluate the plan and determine its necessity in considering race to achieve diversity, rather than merely accepting the claims of the university.[15]

Justice Ginsburg was the only dissenting justice in the 2013 *Fisher I* case. She said:

> Only an ostrich could regard the supposedly neutral alternatives as race unconscious. . . . The percentage plan in Texas was adopted with racially segregated neighborhoods and schools front and center stage. . . . Race consciousness, not blindness to race, drives such plans. . . . I have several times explained why government actors, including state universities, need not be blind to the lingering effects of "an overtly discriminatory past," the legacy of "centuries of law-sanctioned inequality."[16]

Justice Ginsburg understood that race neutrality, after nearly four hundred years of Black slavery, subjugation, discrimination, and inequality, was a practical impossibility. In the context of the history of the state of Texas, the University of Texas, and the US, race neutrality can mean only continued white supremacy and advantage. Most whites do not seem to accept the idea that "race neutrality" is white supremacy by another name. Whites rather seem to believe, as Cheryl I. Harris and Kimberly West-Faulcon have noted, "discrimination [is] any anti-discrimination remedy that displaces the expectations of Whites with regard to the racial status quo."[17]

13. *Grutter v. Bollinger*.
14. *Regents v. Bakke*; *Hopwood v. Texas*.
15. *Fisher I*, 2420.
16. *Fisher I*, 2433.
17. C. Harris and West-Faulcon, "Reading Ricci," 117. See also Haney-López, "Intentional Blindness."

Most Blacks, however, seem to understand that to leave the current system of white advantages in place is to create a nation with a permanent racial caste. White advantages did not occur in a race-neutral system. White advantage took place over centuries of open and legal racial oppression. Michigan Proposition 2 in 2006 made this racial difference of opinion clear. Differing racial voting patterns on the laws of racial equality are at the heart of the high cultural cost of the law. After the 2003 Supreme Court ruling in *Grutter v. Bollinger*, that affirmative action for purposes of diversity in university admissions was constitutional if the program met a compelling governmental interest and was narrowly tailored to meet that interest, opponents organized a petition to amend the Michigan Constitution to prohibit all "preferential treatment to any individual or group on the basis of race, sex, color, ethnicity, or national origin in the operation of public employment, public education, or public contracting."[18] The amendment passed with 64 percent of whites supporting and 86 percent of Blacks opposing.[19] Michigan is 78.9 percent white, 14.2 percent Black, and 4.4 percent Latino. The flagship campus at Ann Arbor, Michigan, is only 6 percent Black.[20] In effect, whites were using their majority position to make permanent certain advantages in education and employment, contracting a constitutional right in Michigan.

On November 8, 2006, a civil rights group called Coalition to Defend Affirmative Action, Integration, and Immigration Rights and Fight for Equality by Any Means Necessary (BAMN) sued the governor of the state of Michigan, the attorney general of Michigan, and the regents and boards of trustees of the major universities of the state. "Coalition" claimed that Proposition 2 violated the equal protection clause of the Fourteenth Amendment to the US Constitution as applied to public colleges and universities.

Coalition argued that Proposition 2 violated the Fourteenth Amendment because it restricted Blacks to changing the state constitution as the only means by which they could implement affirmative action policies concerning their race. Given the racial makeup of the state of Michigan, such a change would be impossible. Groups seeking alumni, athletic, regional, class, or grade-based admissions could use lesser means, such as petitioning university officials.

The federal district court found Proposition 2 to be constitutional. The United States Court of Appeals for the Sixth Circuit reversed the district

---

18. Michigan Constitution, art. 1, §26 (West).
19. America Votes 2006, s.vv. "Ballot Measures: Michigan Proposition 2: Exit Poll."
20. *Chronicle of Higher Education*: "Diversity in Academe"; "Almanac Issue."

court and found Proposition 2 an unconstitutional violation of equal protection. Judge Cole, writing for the Sixth Circuit, said:

> A student seeking to have her family's alumni connections considered in her application to one of Michigan's esteemed public universities could do one of four things to have the school adopt a legacy-conscious admissions policy: she could lobby the admissions committee, she could petition the leadership of the university, she could seek to influence the school's governing board, or, as a measure of last resort, she could initiate a statewide campaign to alter the state's constitution. The same cannot be said for a black student seeking the adoption of a constitutionally permissible race-conscious admissions policy. That student could do only one thing to effect change: she could attempt to amend the Michigan Constitution—a lengthy, expensive, and arduous process—to repeal the consequences of Proposal 2. The existence of such a comparative structural burden undermines the Equal Protection Clause's guarantee that all citizens ought to have equal access to the tools of political change.[21]

On March 25, 2013, the Supreme Court agreed to hear the case of *Schuette v. Coalition to Defend Affirmative Action*. The Supreme Court, in a 6–2 ruling, reversed the circuit court, holding the case was not about the constitutionality of race-based admissions, but about who may decide and in what manner such decisions may occur. The federal courts have no authority to dictate to a state how to make decisions to approve or prohibit racial references.

One day the majority opinion in the *Coalition* case may be ignored, and only the dissent will be cited, as occurred in the case of *Plessy v. Ferguson*. In *Coalition*, Justice Ginsburg joined Justice Sotomayor in dissent:

> We are fortunate to live in a democratic society. But without checks, democratically approved legislation can oppress minority groups. For that reason, our Constitution places limits on what a majority of the people may do. This case implicates one such limit: the guarantee of equal protection of the laws. Although that guarantee is traditionally understood to prohibit intentional discrimination under existing laws, equal protection does not end there. Another fundamental strand of our equal protection jurisprudence focuses on process, securing to all citizens the right to participate meaningfully and equally in self-government. That right is the bedrock of our democracy, for it preserves all other rights.

21. *Coalition v. Regents*, 470.

THE COST OF RACIAL EQUALITY

> Yet to know the history of our Nation is to understand its long and lamentable record of stymieing the right of racial minorities to participate in the political process. At first, the majority acted with an open, invidious purpose. Notwithstanding the command of the Fifteenth Amendment, certain States shut racial minorities out of the political process altogether by withholding the right to vote. This Court intervened to preserve that right. The majority tried again, replacing outright bans on voting with literacy tests, good character requirements, poll taxes, and gerrymandering. The Court was not fooled; it invalidated those measures, too. The majority persisted. This time, although it allowed the minority access to the political process, the majority changed the ground rules of the process so as to make it more difficult for the minority, and the minority alone, to obtain policies designed to foster racial integration. Although these political restructurings may not have been discriminatory in purpose, the Court reaffirmed the right of minority members of our society to participate meaningfully and equally in the political process.
>
> This case involves this last chapter of discrimination: A majority of the Michigan electorate changed the basic rules of the political process in that State in a manner that uniquely disadvantaged racial minorities.[22]

In *Coalition*, the Supreme Court put itself in the position of creating the conditions for anarchy by making substantive racial equality legally almost impossible. This disconnect between white attitudes and those of Blacks could become intolerable as the nation becomes mostly non-white.

Riots, tanks, burned tires and cars with bodies lying in the streets can happen in the US. Disrespect for law is dangerous in any society but particularly for democracies. Totalitarian states do not expect the populous to respect the laws, but rather only to obey them. Any disobedience in oppressive regimes can be punished severely. In addition, a repressive state can control information flows, movement, and organizing to a great extent. Oftentimes, physical and violent repression by authorities generates massive disrespect for the laws that are used to control the masses.

Use of the law to maintain white privileges, or using the law simply as an extension of white cultural power, risks two violations: 1) promotion, protection, and elevation of workers with non-meritorious white racial phenotypes; and 2) alienation of the future majority of the non-white workforce. Americans are accustomed to watching nations tear themselves apart with

---

22. *Schuette v. Coalition*, 337–38.

government corruption, greed, and widespread contempt for principles of justice. Perusing the front page of the *New York Times* on any given day brings multiple examples: riots in the streets of Bangladesh, military takeovers in Myanmar, African contempt for the International Criminal Court at the Hague for racial bias in the court's choice of which countries' leaders to prosecute, the struggles as Egypt seeks to recreate a government of some sort, South African Blacks who control the vote but not the economy, and North Korean power struggles. A Ukrainian type of political and ethnic divide is the type of ethno-political polarization that can defeat democracy.

Some may think such politico-ethnic crisis can never happen in America, but our own nation has been rocked with massive discord before. People are still living who remember the riots that took place at the University of Mississippi in 1962 when James Meredith was admitted as the first Black student. President Kennedy's response was that no mob, however boisterous or unruly, would be allowed to oppose the law. Similar mobs opposed the integration of the Boston public schools in the 1970s and the certification of Biden as president in 2021. Social discord that threatens the democratic foundations of the nation can happen again.

Given the refusal of the Senate to consider Obama's Supreme Court nominee, and the subsequent Trump appointments of Neil Gorsuch, Brett M. Kavanaugh, and Amy Coney Barrett, it was clear to many that the new Court would not again approve an affirmative action plan like that of *Fisher II*. We did not have to wait long to find the answer to this question. In 2014, Students for Fair Admissions (SFFA) filed a lawsuit against Harvard University in which SFFA alleged that Harvard's admissions standards discriminated against Asian American undergraduate applicants. Harvard admits only 1,600 undergrads each year out of 35,000 applicants. Harvard has a six-step admission process: 1) pre-application recruitment, 2) submission of the application, 3) first read of applications, 4) admissions officer and alumni interviews, 5) subcommittee meetings of admissions officers for recommendation to the full committee, 6) full committee final decisions.

Harvard also has a system of plus factors called tips, which may be considered at any time after step 3 in the process. These tip factors include, but are not limited to: "outstanding and unusual intellectual ability, unusually appealing personal qualities, outstanding capacity for leadership, creative ability, athletic ability, legacy status, and geographic, ethnic, or economic factors."[23] Harvard "admits that race can be considered during the 'first read' of application materials at Harvard only when assigning an applicant's overall rating. [Harvard] also admits that an applicant's race can

---

23. *Students for Fair Admissions v. Harvard*, 170.

be considered in both subcommittee and full committee meetings. Harvard denies that race is considered in assigning an applicant's personal rating during the 'first read.'"[24]

The Federal District Court for Massachusetts ruled in favor of Harvard as did the Court of Appeals for the First Circuit, holding, after a lengthy opinion, that the "university's undergraduate admissions policy was narrowly tailored to its substantial interest in student body diversity and, thus, did not violate Title VI of Civil Rights Act" and that the "university considered race-neutral alternatives before adopting admissions policy and legitimately concluded they were not workable."[25] Under the current Harvard admission system, the white, Black, Latino, and Asian admits are 40 percent, 14 percent, 24 percent, and 14 percent respectively. Under a facially race-blind system, the white, Black, Latino, and Asian percentages would be 33 percent, 10 percent, 31 percent, and 19 percent respectively.[26] On March 1, 2021, SFFA appealed to the US Supreme Court, and on January 24, 2021, the US Supreme Court granted certiorari with a consolidated case from North Carolina. From the start this was not a good sign, as Harvard-type plans have passed strict scrutiny muster since at least *Grutter v. Bollinger* in 2003. A 6–3 decision opposing Harvard and the University of North Carolina with Roberts, Kavanaugh, Thomas, Barrett, Gorsuch, and Alito in the majority was not difficult to imagine as Roberts, Thomas, and Alito had never supported an affirmative action case, and Gorsuch, Kavanaugh, and Barrett, three Trump appointees, were unknown quantities at the time.

Therefore, it was not a real surprise when *Students for Fair Admissions v. Harvard* came down as a 6–3 majority with Justices Roberts, Kavanaugh, Thomas, Barrett, Gorsuch, and Alito in the majority and Justices Sotomayor, Kagan, and Jackson in the dissent. As with most of the anti-affirmative action in postsecondary education cases, the majority holding is not particularly enlightening. Chief Justice Roberts, writing for the majority, held that

> respondents have fallen short of satisfying that burden [of a compelling governmental interest]. First, the interests they view as compelling cannot be subjected to meaningful judicial review. Harvard identifies the following educational benefits that it is pursuing: (1) "training future leaders in the public and private sectors"; (2) preparing graduates to "adapt to an increasingly pluralistic society"; (3) "better educating its students through diversity"; and (4) "producing new knowledge

24. *Students for Fair Admissions v. Harvard*, 170.
25. *Students for Fair Admissions v. Harvard*, 170.
26. *Students for Fair Admissions v. Harvard*, 193.

stemming from diverse outlooks." . . . UNC points to similar benefits, namely, "(1) promoting the robust exchange of ideas; (2) broadening and refining understanding; (3) fostering innovation and problem-solving; (4) preparing engaged and productive citizens and leaders; [and] (5) enhancing appreciation, respect, and empathy, cross-racial understanding, and breaking down stereotypes." Although these are commendable goals, they are not sufficiently coherent for purposes of strict scrutiny. At the outset, it is unclear how courts are supposed to measure any of these goals.[27]

One wonders if avoiding a race war, civil war, race riots, and civil unrest would be a compelling enough interest for Roberts. Before the middle of this century, most of the wealth will be in the hands of a distinct and undeserving white minority. That threat may change the Supreme Court's mind.

Just as with *Brown v. Board of Education*, which was seen by many as a vindication of Justice John Marshall Harlan's dissent in *Plessy v. Ferguson*,[28] I predict that one day, the dissent, not the majority in *Students for Fair Admissions*, will be cited as the only logical solution for a nation torn asunder by racial injustice. Justice Sotomayor captured the relationship between racial inclusiveness, democracy, and social unity when she said:

> More broadly, inclusive institutions that are "visibly open to talented and qualified individuals of every race and ethnicity" instill public confidence in the "legitimacy" and "integrity" of those institutions and the diverse set of graduates that they cultivate. . . . That is particularly true in the context of higher education, where colleges and universities play a critical role in "maintaining the fabric of society" and serve as "the training ground for a large number of our Nation's leaders." . . . It is thus an objective of the highest order, a "compelling interest" indeed, that universities pursue the benefits of racial diversity and ensure that "the diffusion of knowledge and opportunity" is available to students of all races.
>
> This compelling interest in student body diversity is grounded not only in the Court's equal protection jurisprudence but also in principles of "academic freedom," which "long [have] been viewed as a special concern of the First Amendment." In light of "the important purpose of public education and the expansive freedoms of speech and thought associated with the university environment," this Court's precedents

27. *Students for Fair Admissions v. Harvard*, 209–10.
28. NCC Staff, "Looking Back."

recognize the imperative nature of diverse student bodies on American college campuses. Consistent with the First Amendment, student body diversity allows universities to promote "th[e] robust exchange of ideas which discovers truth out of a multitude of tongues [rather] than through any kind of authoritative selection."[29]

Justice Ketanji Onyika Brown Jackson is the first Black woman to sit on the US Supreme Court. She was appointed by President Biden and replaced Stephen Breyer. In *Students for Fair Admissions v. Harvard*, Jackson wrote, "Gulf-sized race-based gaps exist with respect to the health, wealth, and well-being of American citizens. They were created in the distant past, but have indisputably been passed down to the present day through the generations. Every moment these gaps persist is a moment in which this great country falls short of actualizing one of its foundational principles—the 'self-evident' truth that all of us are created equal."[30]

The decision in *Students for Fair Admissions v. Harvard* is little more than court packing by the Republican Party. Biden recognized the injustices by the GOP-controlled Senate in denying Obama's Supreme Court appointments. Thus, on April 9, 2021, President Joseph Biden issued an Executive Order on the Establishment of the Presidential Commission on the Supreme Court of the United States (SCOTUS Report) to "produce a report for the President that includes the following: (i) An account of the contemporary commentary and debate about the role and operation of the Supreme Court in our constitutional system and about the functioning of the constitutional process by which the President nominates and, by and with the advice and consent of the Senate, appoints Justices to the Supreme Court; (ii) The historical background of other periods in the Nation's history when the Supreme Court's role and the nominations and advice-and-consent process were subject to critical assessment and prompted proposals for reform."[31] The Supreme Court's granting of certiorari in the SFFA cases would seem to increase the pressure from progressive Democrats to expand the Supreme Court to counter the Trump appointments and the blocking of the Garland nomination, which would in turn increase the perceived political costs of the laws. However, the final SCOTUS Report issued in December of 2021 officially took no position on Supreme Court expansion even after showing the US has nearly the lowest number of judges for constitutional courts among comparable nations. One can only guess the

---

29. *Students for Fair Admissions v. Harvard*, 332–33.
30. *Students for Fair Admissions v. Harvard*, 384.
31. Biden, "Executive Order," paras. 6–8.

reason for the weakness of the SCOTUS Report was the current political stalemate in the US Senate and the unlikely possibility such proposals could be enacted. The SCOTUS Report also noted the sizable majorities of the general public opposing court expansion.

THE DIZZYING COST OF RACE NEUTRALITY

Respect for the rulings of courts is based on public consideration that such rulings represent more than just the political will of those in power. Using the courts and court rulings as a cultural weapon means that the opposition, or those whom the courts oppress, will in all likelihood use the courts the same way if they ever come to power. The federal courts provided the foundation for many of the Civil Rights victories and the ending of the Jim Crow system in cases such as *Brown v. Board of Education* (1954), which found segregated schools inherently unequal; *Griggs v. Duke Power* (1971), which gave support for the concept of societal discrimination; *Steelworkers v. Weber* (1979), which supported voluntary affirmative action in employment; and *Grutter v. Bollinger* (2003), which supported racial diversity in higher education. A majority peoples-of-color nation with white cultural courts and laws would not offer stability. Many writers have warned of this danger.[32] Courts dominated by white elites and making rulings from white cultural perspectives are dangerously high cultural costs.

By refusing to support large-scale government intervention to eliminate the systematic deprivation Black students and workers face, whites are inadvertently ensuring high-cost cultural polarization. When the legal system stamps white ideas with the seal of approval as just and fair, the law becomes culturally polarized and unable to respond quickly to the coming new majority minority.

The solution to a possible breakdown of our legal system is to understand which costs whites are choosing and at what level or price. Understanding all of the forces at play is no easy task. Legal scholars must understand that when affirmative action is defined generically, it applies more to whites than to Blacks. The public must also understand that the most careful analysis of the record shows that one of the strongest Black affirmative action programs, the "Philadelphia Plan," was fully merit based. Whites have little to fear from low-cost, merit-based Black equality and

---

32. Müller, *Hitler's Justice*; Cose, *Rage of a Privileged Class*; Feagin and Sikes, *Living with Racism*; P. Harris, *Black Rage Confronts the Law*; Winant, "Dictatorship"; B. Wright, *Black Robes, White Justice*; King, "Letter from Birmingham Jail"; Ransom, "Race Problem in a Christian State"; Leiter and Leiter, *Affirmative Action*, 232.

much to fear from white expectations of maintaining the racial status quo. Little indicates that Blacks, the largest racial group of the future peoples-of-color majority, are asking for high-cost economic equality such as reparations. If low-cost, merit-based economic equality programs are ignored or abandoned, however, as the courts have done, the demands for high-cost programs seem certain.

A NATION FOUNDED ON WHITE AFFIRMATIVE ACTION

The US Constitution, early Supreme Court cases, and the American story have their roots in white supremacy. The difficulty of changing the impact of these early legal concepts is what makes the cultural cost of the law so high. The US Constitution does not mention the words "slave" or "slavery" until the Thirteenth Amendment, which forbids slavery and was ratified on December 6, 1865. However, the issue of race and the assumption that America was a white person's country are clear in the document.

Article I, section 2, allows slaves to be counted for legislative apportionment purposes. Article I, section 8, gives Congress power to suppress insurrections, which would include slave revolts. Section 9 of Article I, referring to slaves without using the words, allows the "importation of such persons as any of the States now existing shall think proper to admit," until the year 1808. Article IV ensures that escaped slaves cannot take advantage of different laws in states that had prohibited slavery. Article V prohibits amendments to any of the sections of the Constitution allowing the import of slaves until after 1808.

The Civil War amendments (Thirteenth, Fourteenth, and Fifteenth) prohibited slavery and gave ex-slaves citizenship and rights under the law, including the right to vote. The disastrous Supreme Court decisions following the collapse of Reconstruction, however, almost obliterated the ability of these laws to help Blacks achieve their rights.

In *Strauder v. West Virginia* (1879), the Supreme Court held that Blacks could not be excluded from serving on juries simply because they were Black, but the court essentially wrote a model script for how states could exclude Blacks, in accord with accepted constitutional principles, when it said that states could limit jury service "to males, to freeholders, to citizens, to persons within certain ages, or to persons having educational qualifications. We do not believe the Fourteenth Amendment was ever intended to prohibit this."[33]

33. *Strauder v. West Virginia.*

In the *Civil Rights Cases* (1883) the Supreme Court held that the Civil Rights Act of 1875 was unconstitutional. The Civil Rights Act of 1875 was one of the strongest antidiscrimination laws ever enacted and gave Blacks "full and equal enjoyment of the accommodations, advantages, facilities, and privileges of inns, public conveyances on land or water, theaters, and other places of public amusement."[34]

The Civil Rights Act of 1875 also levied civil fines of $500 (almost $10,000 in the economy of today) to be paid to the person suffering the discrimination and criminal fines of $500–1,000 to anyone who violated these rights. In the *Civil Rights Cases* the Supreme Court held that the Fourteenth Amendment of the Constitution applied only to the official actions of state and local governments, not the actions of individuals. *Plessy v. Ferguson* (1896) held that racial separation was permissible action by states as long as equal facilities were provided. The better part of a century lapsed before the nation learned that "separation is inherently unequal" in *Brown v. Board of Education* (1954).

From the founding of the nation and before, processes set in motion concepts of white supremacy that are still strong. After the end of slavery, the abolitionist movement, and Reconstruction (1865–90s), the idea that the United States was founded on a compromise with slavery and the acceptance of Black oppression had to wait until the rise of Black studies programs in the 1960s became popular.

The two fathers of modern American history essentially wrote slavery out of the center of study.[35] Frederick Jackson Turner (1861–1932) and Charles Austin Beard (1874–1948) were leading scholars at Harvard and Columbia Universities, respectively.[36] Both of these men influenced generations of American historians, and Turner and Beard's work in the early twentieth century set the tone for the idea that slavery was not the cause of the Civil War nor the basis for the founding of the nation. Beard says relatively little about slavery: the South feared slave revolt; economic interests were paramount; the border states already had too many slaves and did not want the price of slaves to drop with excessive importation. The moral contradictions of a slave-holding democracy receive little mention.

Turner says, "When American history comes to be rightly viewed it will be seen that the slavery question is an incident."[37] Slavery was "unimportant," though not unknown as the US expanded west toward the

---

34. Civil Rights Act, pt. 3.
35. Lynd, *Class Conflict*, pt. 2, "Slavery."
36. F. Turner, *Frontier in American History*; Beard, *Economic Interpretation*.
37. F. Turner, *Frontier in American History*, 24.

Mississippi River, claims Turner.[38] According to him, the most important feature of slavery was that it showed the greatness of the nation that ended it.[39]

Many scholars today disagree with Turner and recognize that slavery and racial caste were in some sense the founding principles of the United States.[40] Nevertheless, most textbooks on American government do not regard slavery and Black subjugation as fundamental issues in the founding of the nation. How often slavery appears as a discussion in the text reflects this view, as does how early in the textbook the discussion of America's slave history begins. Whether race and racism are viewed as just one of many historical issues or as the fundamental nature of American politics may also be determined by how Black civil rights are treated in the text. Whether race and racism are grouped with other equality issues (gender, poverty, physical disability, sexual preference), in the now-obligatory chapter on civil rights that such books must have, or presented early on as a singular factor in the shaping of the nation, often determines how the author views Black subjugation's relationship to the nation's character. However, a number of textbooks now are writing slavery and Black oppression back into the center of US history and political science.[41]

The US Constitution and early Supreme Court cases delineate two forms of affirmative action: one white and one Black. Affirmative action for Blacks and other minorities as practiced in contemporary America denotes programs and policies of governments, governmental units, nonprofits, and private industry that are designed to bring about either passive nondiscrimination toward peoples of color or marginally and incrementally increase the ratios of these traditionally underrepresented groups.

Generic affirmative action is the operation of governments, institutions, and business to advance the interests of particular racial groups. If we define affirmative action generically, most affirmative action applies to whites, not Blacks. Terms such as "preferences," "group rights," "favored groups" historically apply more to whites than to Blacks.

38. F. Turner, *Frontier in American History*, 98.
39. F. Turner, *Frontier in American History*, 256.
40. Blumrosen and Blumrosen, *Slave Nation*; Drinnon, *Facing West*, 332; Du Bois, *Suppression of the African Slave-Trade*, 53–69; Goldstone, *Dark Bargain*; Horsman, *Race and Manifest Destiny*, 1; Leiter and Leiter, *Affirmative Action*, 24; Morone, "Race and Inequality."
41. Greenberg and Page, *Struggle for Democracy*; McClain and Tauber, *American Government in Black and White*.

THE COTTON KINGDOM

The economic importance of slave labor for cotton production made anti-Black laws culturally acceptable to whites in the antebellum era. This acceptance of Black deprivation continues in modern scholarship. Slavery was America's first affirmative action program. Slavery was not Black affirmative action, however, but rather was the first affirmative action program for whites. Slavery created unprecedented opportunities for whites by expanding the American economy of which generally only whites could take advantage. Even some of those people who see slavery as a relatively benign institution recognize the tremendous boon of slavery for the US. Fogel and Engerman shocked the academic world with their 1974 book claiming that since slavery was economically efficient, slaves were treated relatively well. They make a case that the American South grew rich primarily from cotton and slavery.[42] Even Fogel and Engerman's detractors agree that the worldwide demand for cotton from 1825 to 1860 drove the economic engine of the South, as well as American factories in the North.[43]

Few are aware that by 1860, the US economy was larger than that of Great Britain, then the superpower of the world.[44] Cotton and slavery were the most important parts of the US economy.[45] It may be impossible to understand fully the antebellum Southern economy and just how much of a king cotton was, but by most measures nothing in the economic picture was as lucrative as cotton production. Twenty years after the Civil War, when slavery no longer existed, the book value of capital in cotton manufacturing was larger than any other single component in manufacturing, except for iron and steel, which cotton nearly equaled.[46] Those living in the 1850s said openly that the entire US economy and balance of payments depended on cotton because most of what was grown agriculturally in the US was also consumed in the US. Cotton was almost the sole exception to that rule.[47] The income from cotton created the rapid expansion of the US economy in the 1830s, which in turn allowed the Northeast to industrialize, improve transportation, and open the West.[48]

---

42. Fogel and Engerman, *Time on the Cross*, 247–51.
43. G. Wright, "Prosperity, Progress, and American Slavery."
44. Krasner, "State Power," 336.
45. B. Moore, *Social Origins*, 116.
46. U.S. Department of Commerce, *Historical Statistics, Part 2*, 684. Total manufacturing capital was $2.718 billion, of which $246 million was in cotton manufacturing.
47. Bruchey, *Cotton*, 73–75.
48. North, *Economic Growth*, 69–70; Bruchey, *Cotton*, 2–3.

THE ONE-DROP RULE AND THE LEGAL CONSTRUCTION OF WHITENESS

Legal whiteness is part of the perceived political and cultural cost of American law. The legal creation of whiteness was the first formal affirmative action law. Informally, the early colonial laws that determined the race of a newborn child by defining which children were not white are known as the "one-drop rules"—that is, any known or traceable Black ancestry makes a person Black, and not white. The courts did not assess what whiteness is because whiteness is thought to be universal and thus invisible. Rather, courts see what defiles whiteness, and what they saw destroying white racial purity was Blackness.[49]

"One-drop" anti-miscegenation laws were numerous in the South, West, Midwest, and border states. At the peak (1913–48), more states had the one-drop laws than not. In the lower forty-eight states, only Washington, North and South Dakota, Wisconsin, New Mexico, New York, New Hampshire, Vermont, and Connecticut never had one-drop laws either as colonies or states.[50]

Table 4.1
Race and Immigration into the US, 1820–2000

Year	Total Immigration	Europe	Canada	Not Specified	Africa	Europe and Canada*	African
1820	8,385	7,690	209	300.00	1	97.78%	0.01%
1821–30	143,439	98,797	2,277	33,030.00	16	93.49%	0.01%
1831–40	599,125	495,681	13,624	69,902.00	54	96.68%	0.01%
1841–50	1,713,251	1,597,442	41,723	53,115.00	55	98.78%	0.00%
1851–60	2,598,214	2,452,577	59,309	29,011.00	210	97.79%	0.01%
1861–70	2,314,824	2,065,141	153,878	17,791.00	312	96.63%	0.01%
1871–80	2,812,191	2,271,925	383,640	790.00	358	94.46%	0.01%

49. "There exists a tendency among Whites not to see themselves in racial terms" (López, *White by Law*, 23). "In any nation, not only the United States, the citizens who are members of the dominant culture will not have a collective definition beyond the national identity nor a sense of having a culture. Only those cultures that are different from and marginal to the national norm will be marked as 'cultures.' In the United States, White culture is co-constructed with American culture and, by virtue of saturating everyday life, is taken for granted and culturally invisible. Only African and Americans, Latinos, Asian Americans, and other minorities are represented as having culture" (Perry, *Shades of White*, 96).

50. Wallenstein, *Tell the Court*; D. Fowler, *Northern Attitudes*.

Table 4.1

Race and Immigration into the US, 1820-2000

Year	Total Immigration	Europe	Canada	Not Specified	Africa	Europe and Canada*	African
1881-90	5,246,613	4,735,484	393,304	789.00	857	97.77%	0.02%
1891-00	3,687,564	3,555,352	3,311	14,063.00	350	96.89%	0.01%
1901-10	8,795,386	8,056,040	179,226	33,523.00	7,368	94.01%	0.08%
1911-20	5,735,811	4,321,887	742,185	1,147.00	8,443	88.31%	0.15%
1921-30	4,107,209	2,463,194	924,515	228.00	6,286	82.49%	0.15%
1931-40	528,431	347,566	108,527		1,750	86.31%	0.33%
1941-50	1,035,039	621,147	171,718	142.00	7,367	76.62%	0.71%
1951-60	2,515,479	1,325,727	377,952	12,491.00	14,092	68.22%	0.56%
1961-70	3,321,677	1,123,492	413,310	93.00	28,954	46.27%	0.87%
1971-80	4,493,314	800,368	169,939	12.00	80,779	21.59%	1.80%
1981-90	7,338,062	761,550	156,938	1,032.00	176,893	12.53%	2.41%
1991-20	9,095,417	1,359,737	191,987	42,418	354,939	17.06%	3.90%

*Includes those not specified. Source: U.S. Department of Justice, *2001 Statistical Yearbook*, 19, table 2.

The United States thus has worked very consciously and deliberately to keep America white and make sure America worked for the benefits of whites. From the first naturalization act in 1790, and for 150 years thereafter until 1952, naturalization has been based on whiteness.[51] This act assured that, other than non-whites born in the US, all population growth from immigration would be white. The original 1790 naturalization act and the ones that followed were directly responsible for the explosion of European groups who flooded into the Northern US to fill labor demands, while Blacks were captive in the South.

Only after the Civil War did immigration open to Blacks. An act to amend the naturalization laws and to punish crimes against the same, and for other purposes, of July 14, 1870, 16 Stat. 254, 256, section 7, was in response to the Civil War and provided "that the naturalization laws are hereby extended to aliens of African nativity and to persons of African

---

51. "Be it enacted by the Senate and House of Representatives of the United States of America in Congress assembled, That any alien, being a free White person, who shall have resided within the limits and under the jurisdiction of the United States for the term of two years, may be admitted to become a citizen thereof, on application to any common law court of record, in any one of the states wherein he shall have resided for the term of one year at least" (An Act to Establish Uniform Rule of Naturalization, Mar. 26, 1790, 1 Stat. 103; repealed by act of Jan. 29, 1795, ch. 20).

descent." Prior to 1930, however, the annual immigration of persons from Africa was less than one-tenth of 1 percent of the total of US immigration.[52]

Table 4.2

US Immigration by Area, 2017

	Area Population[1]	World Population[2]	Immigration Total[3]	Immigration by Area[3]	Area Ratio of World Population	Area Immigration Ratio of Total Immigration
Africa	1,308,064,195	7,547,858,925	1,127,167	116,667	17.3%	10.4%
Asia*	4,601,371,198	7,547,858,925	1,127,167	404,371	61.0%	35.9%
Latin America and Caribbean**	648,120,957	7,547,858,925	1,127,167	471,207	8.6%	41.8%
Europe	747,182,751	7,547,858,925	1,127,167	89,706	9.9%	8.0%
Oceania	42,128,035	7,547,858,925	1,127,167	5.986	0.6%	0.0%
Canada and Newfoundland	37,538,594	7,547,858,925	1,127,167	18,469	0.5%	1.6%

*Includes the Near East. **Americas minus Canada and Newfoundland. Sources: 1. Regions in the World, accessed Nov. 18, 2019. 2. Current World Population, accessed Nov. 18, 2019. 3. Office of Immigration Statistics, *2017 Yearbook of Immigration Statistics*.

Table 4.1 shows that the impact of white affirmative action in naturalization has been, and continues to be, profound. From 1820 until 1940, Europe has had immigration and naturalization quotas approaching 100 percent in most decades. Only after 1980 did European immigration drop to European world population percentages—around 12 percent. Even though laws in 1870 allowed Africans to enter the US as naturalized citizens, the ratios remained below single digits until 1970 in table 4.1. This is difficult to imagine. Even today African immigration is underrepresented in table 4.2. Africa represents over 17 percent of world population but only 10 percent of immigration. Europe is 9 percent of world population and 8 percent of US immigration. America still seems to fear Blackness.

52. U.S. Department of Justice, *1998 Statistical Yearbook*.

CONTEMPORARY WHITE AFFIRMATIVE ACTION PROGRAMS

White affirmative action adds cultural cost to the law because the future majority minority know the difference between genuine merit and white cultural substitutes for merit. In the inaugural address for the Barbara Jordan Lecture Series at Penn State University on October 4, 2004, Lani Guinier, the first tenured Black female law professor at Harvard, said that the SAT serves to launder wealth by turning the socioeconomic status of parents and grandparents into merit. She also said that the SAT is a gift from the poor to the wealthy because while the poor also pay taxes, they do not get the benefits of attending elite public institutions that are open only to those with supposed merit.

Aptitude tests, spurious education requirements, and anything that bears little relation to job performance, but which is highly correlated with socioeconomic status, tends to operate as white affirmative action. For example, most people would not be surprised to learn that they have more education than the duties on their job require to perform the job effectively. We know that generally whites have more education than Blacks. Given the jobs that whites and Blacks have, however, Blacks are more overqualified by education than are whites.[53] If employers demand educational requirements that are not substantially related to job performance, such requirements thus advantage those who can obtain such credentials.

Tony Perry writes in the December 4, 2002, *Los Angeles Times* about the well-known Black poet Quincy Troupe, who became poet laureate of California before it was discovered he did not have a bachelor degree, which he claimed to have. Also, Zak Sos and Richard Davis reported on CNN on April 27, 2007, that Marilee Jones, the white female dean of admissions at MIT, resigned, after receiving two of the highest awards in the university, when it became clear that she did not have a bachelor degree, which she also claimed to have.

Both individuals reportedly lied about their credentials, but both were excellent at their crafts. Whether these talented and skilled individuals ever would have had the opportunity to pursue their occupations, if it were known from the start they had no academic degrees, is uncertain. The lack of a degree did not hinder their performance. The two cases highlight the pressure to have academic credentials, which are generally a boon for whites.

---

53. Bridges and Villemez, "Overeducated Minority Workers."

The "race norming" discussion of the late 1980s and 1990s concerned the battle of white affirmative action versus Black affirmative action. State employment agencies used the General Aptitude and Test Battery (GATBY) to assign workers to jobs. Extensive use of the test revealed that whites scored higher on the test than Blacks, but the higher test score was unmatched with on-the-job performance. Lower-scoring Blacks performed equally or better than higher-scoring whites. To assign applicants to jobs on the basis of raw scores had an inverse relation to on-the-job performance as concerned Black versus white workers. To correct for the imbalance of the test, agencies would "norm" the scores, and assign Blacks with lower scores but equal performance to the same jobs as whites with higher scores. This "race norming" was outlawed by the 1991 Civil Rights Act. To continue to use a test that favors white test takers who have lower job performance, however, is a bold form of white, non-meritorious, preference.

Operations of governments, institutions, and business work in many ways to advance the interests of whites. These operations are invisible because society takes such actions for granted. Higher wages, freedom from police abuse, far lower arrest rates for drug use, greater home equity in white neighborhoods, and the assumption that skin color will work for whites rather than against them are but a few examples.[54]

Contemporary white privilege programs are not only those currently in operation, but past programs having contemporary effects. Oliver, Shapiro, and Katznelson spend considerable time tracing the history of the most well-known programs used to further white social, economic, and political interest.[55]

Social security excluded the two most common Black occupations (domestic workers and agriculture); Welfare programs disproportionately excluded Black women and children; and the federal housing authority not only refused to approve loans in Black or even mixed areas, but also the FHA wrote model restrictive covenants for white homeowners to keep Blacks and Jews out of white neighborhoods. The GI Bill was universal in its language but racially biased in application. Many WWII veterans went to college on the GI Bill, but because the bill was administered at the state level, Black GIs in the South, where most lived, were limited to underfunded, understaffed, and overcrowded Black institutions.

Nepotism, giving jobs and positions to relatives and friends, is a strange concept. Nepotism is illegal in the public domain while at the same

---

54. McIntosh, *White Privilege and Male Privilege*.

55. Oliver and Shapiro, *Black Wealth/White Wealth*; Katznelson, *When Affirmative Action Was White*.

time it is praised, even lauded, in private business. Coons et al. see nepotism operating in unequal school funding and write there is "no graver threat to the capitalist system than the present cyclical replacement of the fittest of one generation by their artificially advantaged offspring."[56] Nepotism in business and rich school districts tends to advantage people who have no special claim to talent other than that their parents were wealthy. No one can be sure of the degree of nepotism in business, but certainly the disproportionately low level of Black business assures that nepotism, which is anti-meritorious by definition, almost always works in favor of whites.[57]

BLACK AFFIRMATIVE ACTION

Black affirmative action is a recent innovation, and the court cases are demonstrating that Black affirmative action may be fleeting and temporary. The evidence shows that, unlike white affirmative action, Black affirmative action is merit based and therefore, at worst, economically costless to whites and, at best, an economic benefit to whites and the entire nation.

Free Black labor was the first affirmative action program in America for Blacks. On the eve of the Civil War, five million Blacks lived in the United States, and about 11 percent of them were free. Ninety-two percent of Blacks lived in the South, and few of them were free. In 1860, half of all free Blacks lived in the North, where only 7 percent of Blacks lived. In the antebellum US, freedom was a Northern proposition. Berlin makes clear that three groups of free Blacks existed: those in the North, in the upper South, and in the deep South.[58]

Many Blacks in the North were freed by the fervor of liberty that impacted many whites during the War of Independence from Britain. The need for Blacks to fight in the war forced some colonialists to offer liberty to Blacks in exchange for service in the Army. Laws in many of the Northern states freed Blacks as they reached certain ages. Because Northern freedom was nearly universal, most free Blacks in the North were not mixed race people. That is, freedom for Blacks in the North was not based on white ancestry, as it frequently was in the South. Most Blacks in the North thus

---

56. Coons et al., *Private Wealth*, 412.

57. Bergmann, *In Defense of Affirmative Action*, ch. 6; Skrentny, *Ironies of Affirmative Action*, 50–53, "Are preferences based on ascribed traits forbidden? The case of nepotism."

58. U.S. Department of Commerce, *Historical Statistics, Part 1*; Berlin, "Structure of the Free Negro Caste."

were dark skinned, and not skilled or educated, which tended to keep them at the bottom of the economic structure.

Free Blacks in the North faced many of the same problems all Blacks were to face after the end of the Civil War, including white hatred and segregation, second-class status, and menial work. America's preference for native white labor or even immigrant white labor from Irish and German groups pushed out many Black skilled workers.

In several Northern states the adoption of universal suffrage for white men was accompanied by disfranchisement of Blacks. Often those who opposed expanding the electorate used voting rights for Blacks to demonstrate the dangers of universal suffrage.[59] The plight of Blacks in the antebellum North might well be called the Jim Crow North, because free Blacks faced repression in every area, just as they did in the antebellum South and after the collapse of Reconstruction. Free Blacks in the North had segregated and poorer-quality schools, dilapidated and segregated housing, discrimination and hostility wherever they went. Twenty years before the Civil War, most Blacks in the North had lost the right to vote, and Alexis de Tocqueville noted in 1850 that racial bigotry was stronger in the North than in the South.[60]

One advantage of rigid racial segregation was that Blacks formed their own churches and associations that advocated for the end of slavery. Many of these free Blacks, including David Walker, Richard Allen, and Frederick Douglass, wrote some of the most stirring and fervent anti-slavery appeals and formed prominent organizations. These Black-owned organizations still form the most important centers for Black advancement and development. The prewar free Blacks in the South were also the Black leaders during the Reconstruction period. Almost half of the Blacks who served in Congress from 1869 to 1900 had been free before the war, even though this number represented only 11 percent of all Blacks. One difference between free Blacks in the North and in the South was that Northern Blacks constituted one class, with few mixed-race members. Free Blacks in the South, particularly the Deep South, were frequently of mixed race and did not always identify with the anti-slavery cause.[61] The many appeals to virtue and temperance from Black leaders illustrates the desire of free Blacks to make good use of their new status in the North and to be exemplary citizens.[62] Free Blacks, however, witnessed the same impediment of united white

---

59. Litwack, *North of Slavery*, 75.

60. Tocqueville, *Democracy in America*, 343, 357.

61. Berlin, "Structure of the Free Negro Caste"; Fireside, *Separate and Unequal*, ch. 4.

62. Sernett, *African American Religious History*, sec. 3, "Black Churches."

opposition to equality that Blacks faced during and after Reconstruction and in the civil rights era.

Reconstruction was the second affirmative action program for Blacks in America. The Emancipation Proclamation freed almost no one. Some scholars believe that Lincoln's purpose was to keep Blacks enslaved until they all could be deported to Africa. Most Blacks were freed either by escape or the advancing Union troops.[63] The period that followed the Civil War known as Reconstruction saw the greatest advances Blacks would make in the United States for almost one hundred years, until the 1970s. The Bureau of Refugees, Freedmen, and Abandoned Lands that was established in 1865 and seated in the War Department came to be called simply the Freedmen's Bureau. The Freedmen's Bureau was a full social service agency that ran schools, legalized marriages, negotiated labor contracts for former slaves, and helped them become taxpayers, voters, landowners, and businesspeople.

Reconstruction saw the founding of many of the most famous, historically Black colleges and universities, including Howard University in Washington, DC; Fisk University in Nashville, Tennessee; Morgan College (Morgan State University) in Baltimore, Maryland; and Morehouse College in Atlanta, Georgia. Blacks became the majority of eligible voters in South Carolina, Florida, Mississippi, and Louisiana, even though they never became voting majorities in any state.[64] Between 1868 and 1901, Blacks elected two US senators from Mississippi and more than twenty Black Congressmen from eight of twelve states of the former Confederacy.[65]

Compared to other states, South Carolina had the greatest representation of Blacks in government during the Reconstruction period. Most Black politicians in South Carolina were Mulattoes, who had been free before the war and literate; thus they were exceptions. Nevertheless, Blacks were 60 percent of the postwar constitutional convention in South Carolina, and 57 percent of those Blacks had been slaves. Alonzo J. Ransier, a free Mulatto, was lieutenant governor of South Carolina 1870–72. Even more remarkable were Abraham Smith, a former Black slave who worked as a sexton before the war but was literate and served in the South Carolina House 1868–70, and John Vanderpool, also a Black slave who was a common field hand before the war but nonetheless was literate and served in the South Carolina House 1872–74.[66]

63. Bennett, *Forced into Glory*; Foner, *Fiery Trial*, 240–41, 306–8.
64. Horton and Horton, *Hard Road to Freedom*, 185.
65. Barker and Jones, *African Americans*, 241.
66. Hine, "Black Politicians."

THE COST OF RACIAL EQUALITY

The new state constitution in South Carolina in 1868 outlawed racial discrimination in voting, schools, and the state militia. This constitution ended property requirements for voting or office holding and imprisonment for debt.[67]

Reconstruction is an example of Black affirmative action, or special action, associated with the unique position of the freedmen and women. The freedmen's circumstances necessitated the creation of substantive, not merely procedurally equal, citizenship.[68] Reconstruction and the civil rights movement, often called the Second Reconstruction, departed radically from white cultural concepts of race neutrality and maintenance of the status quo in the face of massive racial inequality.

The federal Civil Rights Acts, state laws, and constitutions of the Reconstruction era recognized that to free Blacks from slavery and provide no positive tools for their advancement provided neither freedom nor equal citizenship. Shortly after the Civil War ended, the Southern states began to pass Black codes and special vagrancy laws designed to limit the rights of the freedmen to resist labor on the plantations.

The Civil Rights Act (CRA) of 1866 purported to stop such restrictions against Blacks. Three major provisions were included: 1) all persons born or naturalized in the US were citizens and had equal rights to make and enforce contracts, sue, and convey property, as are enjoyed by white citizens; 2) provided civil penalties for violations; and 3) placed jurisdiction for violations exclusively in the federal district courts, to eliminate the racial bias so obvious in the Southern state courts.

The Civil Rights Act of 1866 passed despite a presidential veto by Andrew Johnson. Lingering doubts remained, however, as to whether the Civil Rights Act of 1866 had the power to make Blacks citizens. Also the 1866 CRA act targeted only discriminatory state laws, when newly freed Blacks faced many acts of private violence and discrimination from whites. Additional steps had to be taken.[69]

The Fourteenth and Fifteenth Amendments to the US Constitution, ratified July 9, 1868, and February 3, 1870, respectively, were to rectify the weaknesses of the 1866 CRA and circumvent presidential vetoes. The 1870 CRA (passed May 31, 1870) required that all citizens have the equal right to vote without distinction of race or previous condition of servitude. Also the amendments to the 1870 CRA contained penalties and anti-Klan provisions.

67. Horton and Horton, *Hard Road to Freedom*, 186.
68. Leiter and Leiter, *Affirmative Action*, 23–25.
69. Foner, *Reconstruction*, 244–45.

The CRA of 1871 (April 20, 1871) made it a federal crime to oppose by force the execution of the laws of the US with the intent to deny citizens the equal protection of the laws. The 1875 CRA differed from the other Civil Rights Acts in that it prohibited the action of individual persons, regardless of whether they were acting under cover of state law. The 1875 CRA was declared unconstitutional by the *Civil Rights Cases* (1883) with the still dubious claim that the Fourteenth Amendment to the Constitution applied only to the actions of the states, not to individuals.

While Southern Blacks, with the aid of Southern whites loyal to the Union and transplanted Northern white Republicans, ruled the South for a generation, eventually Reconstruction collapsed. Many reasons suggest how it was possible, with three constitutional amendments and a plethora of Civil Rights acts, that Blacks still could not be protected in the South. The failure to redistribute land to Blacks in an agricultural economy was devastating, as was the removal of federal troops, which exposed Blacks to Southern terror. Some suggest that the white Republicans' problem was that they never trusted the federal government as an institution, and thus the special case of Blacks, who needed the strong arm of federal law to protect their voting franchise, was never fully understood.[70] That is, Northern whites vastly underestimated their own bias and the vituperative nature of Southern white hatred.

Reconstruction seems to have ended with the Compromise of 1877 when the Republican presidential candidate Rutherford B. Hayes was awarded the presidency over Democratic candidate Samuel J. Tilden. The Southern Democrats in the US Senate agreed not to filibuster the report of the special electoral commission if the Republicans would remove federal troops and invest in Southern industrial development. Federal troops were removed from the last three Southern states (Louisiana, South Carolina, and Florida) in April of 1877.

WAGNER TO JFK: THE COST OF DELAY

Racial explosions of the 1960s are directly traceable to the failure to enforce the Civil Rights laws of the nineteenth century. This failure cost the nation dearly in international respect, Black loyalty, and racial unity. Reconstruction did not end completely until 1901, when George H. Wilson, the last Black Congressman from the South, was put out of office and replaced by a Southern racist. No Blacks would appear on the congressional stage from the South for over seventy years. This period saw some of the worst

70. Richardson, *Death of Reconstruction*, ch. 2.

atrocities against Blacks. In some years one lynching occurred every other day in the South.[71] The slaughter of Blacks in the South caused the famous bishop of the African Methodist Episcopal Church, Henry McNeal Turner, to advocate immigration of Black Americans to Africa.[72]

This type of terror, combined with unjust laws, depressions, the decline of cotton, and loss of the voting franchise, almost forced Blacks to leave the South. This period (1900-1950) is known as the Great Migration, an era when Blacks moved to the North and West. Not only did geographic changes occur, but Blacks also began to leave agriculture for manufacturing and move from rural areas to the cities. As Blacks centered in Chicago and New York, they began to amass the voting power they had lost in the South.

The elimination of the Black vote created a situation in which both major parties vied to be the most anti-Black in an effort to attract white Southern voters. The Great Depression and business failures created a strong incentive for Congress to make laws protecting the rights of workers. Senator Robert F. Wagner (D-NY, 1927-49) gained passage of the National Labor Relations Act, popularly known as the Wagner Act, in 1935. Prior to the Wagner Act, businesses sought action via the courts to enjoin workers from striking and interfering with the "property rights" of business owners to conduct business.[73] The Wagner Act was the first federal law to grant positive protections for the right to organize.

Among the provisions of the Wagner Act were the right to organize, definitions of unfair labor practices, and the creation of the National Labor Relations Board (NLRB). The NLRB had the power, upon a finding of fact of an unfair labor practice, to issue a cease and desist order and require a firm "to take such affirmative action, including reinstatement of employees with or without back pay, as will effectuate the policies of the Act."[74] The term "affirmative action" in the Wagner Act indicates more than simply ceasing and desisting from the unfair labor practice: the object is to make the offended party whole.

In an ironic twist, the ability of unions to organize and receive affirmative action for unfair labor practices was signed into law over the strenuous objections of the two major Black civil rights groups: the NAACP and the Urban League. Both groups objected that the racially discriminatory practices of unions would become virtually legal, since a union to which a majority of the workers belonged had exclusive bargaining rights. These

71. Koslow, *African American Desk Reference*, 316.
72. H. Turner, "Emigration to Africa."
73. Millis and Brown, *From the Wagner Act to Taft-Hartley*, ch. 1.
74. National Archives, "National Labor Relations Act," sec. 10c.

"closed shops" could eliminate Black workers from the job site by not allowing them in the union. The Wagner Act protected white workers as a class while it allowed continued discrimination against Black workers as a class. The first use of the term "affirmative action," thus, was reserved almost exclusively for whites with the tremendous support of the white working class.[75] This same fear of losing the white Southern vote prevented FDR from supporting anti-lynching legislation as the US entered WWII.

The claim can be made that Black affirmative action in the twentieth century began with A. Phillip Randolph and the original March on Washington movement in 1940, designed to halt the exclusion of Blacks from the defense industries. This movement served as the impetus for the Fair Employment Practice Committee (FEPC), which Franklin Roosevelt instituted to forestall a Black protest large enough to interfere with the war effort.

Randolph proposed the march for the specific purpose of protesting discrimination in defense industries. He stated that Negroes wanted "to exact their rights in National Defense employment and the armed forces of the country."[76] Executive Order 8802 "barred discrimination in the employment of workers in defense industries or government because of race, creed, color, or national origin and stated that it is the duty of employers and of labor organizations . . . to provide for the full and equitable participation of all workers in defense industries." Two years later Roosevelt issued Order 9346, which prohibited discrimination in federal agencies, and mandated nondiscrimination clauses in all government contracts. The administration of both orders was given to the FEPC. Neither of these orders had sanctions, and neither stopped employment discrimination in defense industries or any other industries. Some effects were beneficial. Following Roosevelt's orders, twenty-six states passed similar laws prohibiting discrimination in state government employment and established their own FEPCs.[77]

Eisenhower believed that his support from Black voters was decreasing. This decline could have occurred because Eisenhower did not pass any civil rights legislation during his first term. In an effort to increase his Negro voter base, Eisenhower created his own FEPC and placed Vice President Nixon in charge of the effort. Eisenhower's Executive Order 10557 even required that contractors post public notices of nondiscrimination. The results of these efforts were nearly double the Black votes for Eisenhower in 1956 (36 percent of Blacks voting for the GOP) over 1952 (19 percent of Blacks voting for the GOP). See table 7.3.

75. Hill: *Black Labor*, 105–6; "Black Labor."
76. Ruchames, *Race, Jobs and Politics*, 17.
77. Belz, *Equality Transformed*, 14.

THE COST OF RACIAL EQUALITY

President Eisenhower passed two civil rights acts in his second term. The CRA of 1957 established the Commission on Civil Rights, which was empowered to "investigate allegations . . . that certain citizens of the United States are being deprived of their right to vote . . . by reason of their color, race, religion, or national origin; . . . study and collect information concerning legal developments constituting a denial of equal protection of the laws."[78] The 1957 CRA also created the assistant attorney general for civil rights in the Justice Department.

The CRA of 1960 had three main tasks: 1) prosecuting those who fled in interstate commerce to avoid prosecution for blowing up or burning down a Black church, which had become a problem after the Montgomery bus boycott and was made a federal offense; 2) election officers had to maintain records of voting applications and registrations for twenty-two months; and 3) children of Black service people were allowed to have free federal education if the local schools were not open to Black children because of Jim Crow laws.

The appointment of Richard Nixon as head of the FEPC was significant in that it gave later–President Nixon a great deal of experience with equal employment and affirmative action, and it placed the issues high on the agenda of any future president who sought the Black vote. And President Kennedy, as it turned out, needed the Black vote.

Timidity might be the one word to describe the Kennedy Administration when talking specifically about affirmative action or civil rights generally. Kennedy had two voter problems: first, Kennedy was Catholic, and his religion always was an issue, particularly in the South;[79] second, Kennedy won the White House by two-tenths of 1 percent (0.2 percent) of the popular vote, with Blacks comprising just 6.95 percent of his voter base (table 7.1). As critical as Black votes were, Kennedy could not afford to lose white votes in the South either.[80] The reason for so few Black votes was that even in 1960 most Blacks could not vote because of the Jim Crow system in the South. This situation was to change by the 1968 election.

During the campaign JFK had promised to support Black civil rights and to end discrimination in federal housing with "the stroke of a pen." Also, he had played a critical part in securing the release of Martin Luther King Jr. from a transfer from the local jail to the state prison on minor traffic charges in Atlanta, Georgia. MLK Jr. was in danger of murder while in transit in a police car on the back roads of Georgia. Kennedy's intervention and

---

78. Civil Rights Act of 1957, sec. 104.
79. Donaldson, *First Modern Campaign*, 57–58.
80. Donaldson, *First Modern Campaign*, 78.

subsequent release of MLK Jr. caused "Daddy King" (Martin Luther King Sr.), a lifelong Republican who disliked Catholics and already had publicly endorsed Richard Nixon, to say: "I've got a suitcase of votes and I'm going to take them to Mr. Kennedy and dump them in his lap."[81] Kennedy won 74 percent of the Black vote in 1960, up 10 percent for the Democrats from 1956 (table 7.3).

Once in office Kennedy failed to pass a civil rights bill. Rather, he issued Executive Order 10925 as a substitute to appease civil rights groups. Executive Order 10925 had four major parts: first, it established the President's Committee on Equal Employment Opportunity, which was to investigate cases of employment discrimination in the government and with government contractors, to publish the names of violators, and to recommend action to the department of justice; second, prohibitions on discrimination in federal employment were reaffirmed; third, government contractors were required to "take affirmative action to ensure that applicants are employed, and that employees are treated . . . without regard to their race, creed, color, or national origin"; and fourth, labor unions working on government contracts were required to comply with the executive order.

Vice President Lyndon Johnson was in charge of the new FEPC, called the President's Committee on Equal Employment Opportunity. The crisis of violence against Blacks in Birmingham, Alabama, and the South forced Kennedy to take action and draft a civil rights bill in 1963.[82]

JFK's bill, the CRA of 1963, came before the House on June 20, 1963, as HR 7152. The original bill from the White House addressed discrimination in voting, public accommodations (hotels, stores, etc.), public education, and federally funded programs. Kennedy's bill also created the Commission on Equal Employment Opportunity, which later became the EEOC. Kennedy's draft, however, did not contain a section making discrimination in employment illegal.

While the House debated HR 7152, MLK Jr. delivered his "I Have a Dream" speech, during the March on Washington on August 28, 1963, arguably the greatest speech of the twentieth century. Two weeks later on Sunday, September 15, four young Black girls were killed in the bombing of the Sixteenth Street Baptist Church in Birmingham, Alabama. Just eight weeks later, Kennedy was assassinated. Suddenly, Black civil rights was the nation's first priority.

---

81. D. Lewis, *King*, 129.
82. Branch, *Parting the Waters*, 807–8; Graham, *Civil Rights Era*, 70.

LBJ, THE CIVIL RIGHTS ACT OF 1964, AND GOVERNMENT CONTRACTORS

The history of the passage of the 1964 CRA is thrilling reading.[83] The haste to pass the bill explains to some degree why so much confusion exists about whether the intent of this seminal civil rights legislation was to end legal discrimination and Jim Crow without any further government-sponsored efforts, and leaving existing inequalities in place, or to complete the work of the First Reconstruction by bringing Blacks to substantive equality. The legislative record seems to show that both outcomes were intended. Opponents hoped the act would do little or nothing to change the basic economic positions of the races, other than to eliminate blatant discrimination. Supporters hoped that the end of legal discrimination would allow Blacks to rise in accord with the myths surrounding the advances of the white European migrants.[84]

The Civil Rights Act of 1964 (codified as 42 U.S.C. § 2000e-2) prohibits official discrimination on the basis of race, color, religion, or gender, and it makes it an unlawful employment practice "to fail or refuse to hire or to discharge any individual, or otherwise to discriminate against any individual with respect to his compensation, terms, conditions, or privileges of employment, because of such individual's race, color, religion, sex, or national origin."

The enforcement provisions of the Civil Rights Act of 1964 (42 U.S.C. § 2000e-5[g] [1]) mandate that if a business is found to have discriminated against people in violation of the act, a court may order "affirmative action." The affirmative action may include reinstatement or hiring of employees, with or without back pay (payable by the employer, employment agency, or labor organization, as the case may be, responsible for the unlawful employment practice), or any other equitable relief as the court may deem appropriate.

On September 28, 1965, President Johnson issued Executive Order 11246, which prohibited discrimination in federal employment on the basis of race, creed, color, or national origin, and mandated that federal contractors also practice nondiscrimination. President Johnson amended Executive Order 11246 in 1967 to also prohibit sex discrimination. Executive Order 11246 may be the most famous of the affirmative action executive orders,

---

83. Branch: *Parting the Waters*; *Pillar of Fire*; *At Canaan's Edge*; Muse, *American Negro Revolution*.

84. Lieberson, *Piece of the Pie*; Steinberg, *Ethnic Myth*. See the discussion earlier in this chapter about why the social advancement of European immigrants is generally mythical.

and was fully in force for nearly sixty years until President Trump rescinded it on January 21, 2025 and replaced it with Executive Order 14173. Trump's Executive Order 14173 claims that "diversity, equity, and inclusion (DEI) or diversity, equity, inclusion, and accessibility (DEIA) . . . violate the civil-rights laws of this Nation." Trump's Executive Order 14173 claims that DEI and DEIA are "dangerous, demeaning, and immoral." Given what we learned in chapter 3 on white views, that the least-informed whites believe they suffer more from discrimination than Blacks, Trump's executive order is fully in line with those views. However, neither white views nor Executive Order 14173 are in line with social science reality. It is difficult to grasp the Executive Order 14173 claim that making buildings accessible to the disabled is "dangerous, demeaning, and immoral." For sixty years presidents from the most liberal to the most conservative supported Executive Order 11246, but no longer, on the cusp of America becoming mostly non-white. This is the type of madness that destroys nations and creates race war.

THE PHILADELPHIA PLAN AND THE COST OF THE LAW

Beginning with the congressional debates over the 1964 Civil Rights Act, opponents of affirmative action recognized that any demand that Blacks have employment or occupational numbers even closely parallel to their population percentage would be costly to whites, who were and are substantially overrepresented in high-paying occupations and in employment.[85]

The Philadelphia Plan, more than any other part of affirmative action, has been described as the implementation of quota systems in America.[86] The Philadelphia Plan was strong medicine for one of the most segregated occupations in the country, the construction crafts. The Philadelphia Plan dramatically changed the racial face of the construction job site. Even the much-maligned Philadelphia Plan, however, never even came close to proportional representation of Blacks as craftsman on the construction site.

Richard Nixon amended Executive Order 11246 by Executive Order 11478, continuing the earlier mandate for nondiscrimination in the federal government and requiring federal agencies to have "affirmative action

---

85. *Congressional Record* 110, pt. 11, 88th Congress, 2nd session: June 9, 1964, 13076–78, 13080; June 19, 1964, 14511.

86. Roberts and Stratton, *New Color Line*, 102–4. No less a scholar than Hugh Davis Graham says: "From the office of Federal Contract Compliance . . . came rules requiring rough proportional representation of minorities in construction employment" ("Civil Rights Policy," 203).

programs for equal employment opportunity." Executive Order 11478 has since been amended to forbid not only discrimination based on race, color, religion, sex, and national origin but also on handicap, age, sexual orientation, and parental status.[87] President Nixon was not the inventor of Black affirmative action, but because of two programs he started and expanded, he receives popular credit as the originator of contemporary Black affirmative action.

First, Nixon created the Office of Minority Business Enterprise in the Department of Commerce, which came to be popularly known as "Black capitalism."[88] The purpose of the program was for the "establishment, preservation and strengthening of minority business enterprise." As of 2025, the renamed Minority Business Development Agency still exists in the Department of Commerce.

Second, the "Philadelphia Plan," which set numerical quotas for Blacks in the construction trades for federal contractors, also is associated with Nixon, although Nixon did not initiate the plan. The construction industry was notorious for discriminatory hiring practices. Blacks were generally hired only as laborers, the lowest-paid construction occupation, and rarely as skilled tradesmen (carpenters, brick masons, electricians, plumbers, etc.), who earned the highest wages.

Since the early 1960s CORE and other groups had been protesting against discriminatory employers. Many Blacks and civil rights groups complained that the Johnson Administration was too slow to attack job discrimination after passage of the 1964 Civil Rights Act.[89] The highly paid and segregated construction trades in Chicago and Philadelphia were the focus of these demonstrations. In 1963, the Philadelphia CORE chapter challenged the bigotry of the city and the construction trades, which were supported by city contracts.[90]

Edward C. Sylvester, a Black administrator in charge of OFCC, ordered contractors in St. Louis, San Francisco, Cleveland, Chicago, and Philadelphia to submit affirmative action plans stating how many minorities would be hired. First, contractors were asked if they complied with federal laws

---

87. President Carter added handicap and age (Executive Order 12106, 44 Fed. Reg. 1053 [1978]). President Clinton added sexual orientation (Executive Order 13087, 63 Fed. Reg. 30097 [1998]) and parental status (Executive Order 13152, 65 Fed. Reg. 26115 [2000]).

88. Executive Order 11458, 34 Fed. Reg. 4937 (1969) established the Office of Minority Business Enterprise and Executive Order 11625, 36 Fed. Reg. 19967 (1971) defined what a minority business was.

89. Fletcher, *Silent Sell-Out*, 57.

90. Meier and Rudwick, *CORE*, 192.

against segregated facilities. The purpose of this question was to receive assurances that the government would later challenge when they began investigating the skilled trades, which were almost totally segregated. Second, after the low bidder was selected, but before the contract was awarded, the contractor would be asked to submit a plan for the numbers of minorities that would be hired. No firm numbers were set, to avoid the charge that the federal government was demanding "quotas" in hiring. Third, the low bidder was than checked for compliance with his own hiring plan. The award was withheld until the bidder complied. The bidder had the responsibility of interacting with the craft unions.

When Nixon became president, he named a Black man, Arthur Fletcher, as assistant secretary of labor in charge of enforcing equal opportunity. The Philadelphia Plan was revised in 1969 to set exact percentages that were far below population parity. That is, if a quota is a specific percentage of a racial group, these were quotas, but these specified percentages were lower than the ratio of Blacks in the population or even in the construction industry. OFCC set escalating goals from 5 percent to 22 percent over a five-year period, beginning in 1970 in the skilled construction trades. Some of the construction trades in Philadelphia had percentages as low as half a percent in a city that was 30 percent Black.[91]

Nixon's labor secretary, George P. Shultz, seemed unsupportive of OFCC, although Shultz had been responsible for adopting Johnson's plan for the skilled trades in Philadelphia and other cities. Shultz had issued an order, order number 4, which required "the rate of minority applicants recruited should approximate or equal the ratio of minorities to the applicant population in each location."[92] Under political pressure not to set rigid percentages, Shultz revised this order in February of 1970 and required affirmative action compliance when there were "fewer minorities in a particular job class than would reasonably be expected by their availability."[93]

Shultz warned contractors that if they did not comply with this "hometown plan," the quota-type Philadelphia Plan of the original order number 4 would be implemented. Revised order number 4, which came to be known as the "Hometown Plan," stressed goals and timetables but not fixed and escalating percentages.[94] In January 1970 and October 1971, the Supreme Court declined to hear two cases in which lower courts had upheld the right of the government to refuse to award a contract to the low bidder

91. Graham, *Civil Rights Era*.
92. Graham, *Civil Rights Era*, 342.
93. Graham, *Civil Rights Era*, 343.
94. Graham, *Civil Rights Era*, 542n102.

whose affirmative action plan failed OFCC requirements, and in doing so the court left those requirements in place.[95]

Shortly after the victories of OFCC, Arthur Fletcher resigned as assistant secretary of labor. Fletcher regarded the change from order number 4 to revised order number 4 as a "sell-out" of Blacks to the craft unions.[96] The Philadelphia Plan perhaps was as close as the US government has yet come to proportional representation in employment or quotas, and that was not close at all.

Analysis of the Philadelphia Plan is a good overview of the perceived political and cultural costs of the law. An empirical evaluation of the Philadelphia Plan answers a host of questions about racial equality and merit: 1) whether racial occupational disparities existed; 2) if racial discrimination caused these disparities; 3) whether the affirmative action program changed the nature of Black occupational distribution—that is, whether affirmative action worked; 4) whether the Blacks who were hired were unqualified or less qualified than whites; and 5) whether the Philadelphia Plan was a quota.

Most people who work in construction work either as unskilled laborers or skilled tradesman. The skilled trades or crafts earn far more than do laborers. Between 1963 and 2001, most white men have been concentrated in the higher-paying craft occupations. Between 50 percent and 60 percent of whites in construction work in the crafts. Only about 10 percent of whites in construction work in the lower-paying labor positions.

Philadelphia was much like the rest of the nation for whites in figure 4.1. Between 30 and 50 percent of whites in construction work in the skilled crafts, while only 10–25 percent work as laborers, with the corresponding lower wages. Indeed, seeing a white man working as a common laborer in the 1960s in Philadelphia must have been a rarity.

95. Weiner v. Cuyahoga Community College; Contractors Ass'n of Eastern Pa v. Secretary of Labor.
96. Fletcher, *Silent Sell-Out*.

Figure 4.1 White Men in Philadelphia Construction Craft and Labor Occupations as a Percentage of All White Men in Construction in Philadelphia

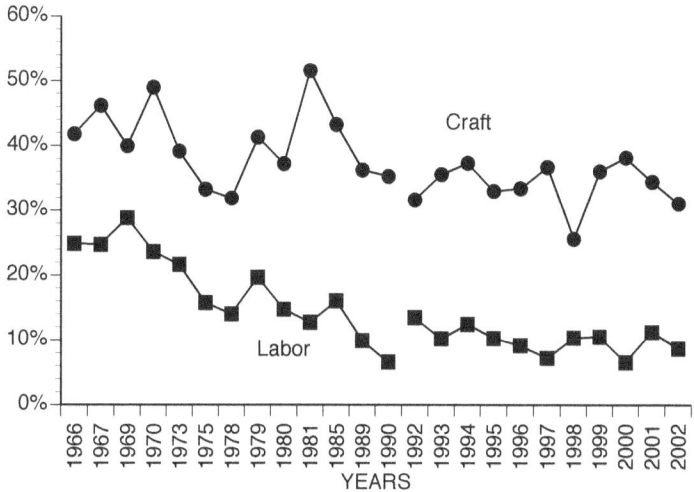

Sources: 1966–90, all men, U.S. Equal Employment Opportunity Commission, "2018 Job Patterns"; 1992–2002, white men, proprietary data tapes obtained by special license from the U.S. Equal Employment Opportunity Commission, Washington, DC.

Blacks have had a far different employment experience than whites in construction. Figure 4.2 shows clearly that until the late 1960s, when the affirmative action programs began, a relatively lower-paying labor position was all that a Black man or woman could expect. Black men carried the bricks and gave them to white men who laid the bricks, regardless of whether the Black man was a skilled bricklayer or not. This was the almost universal racial caste that existed in the construction industry. This situation changed dramatically on the national scene, once the Philadelphia Plans began across the country.

THE COST OF RACIAL EQUALITY

Figure 4.2 Blacks in Construction Craft and Construction Labor Occupations as a Percentage of All Blacks in Construction in the US

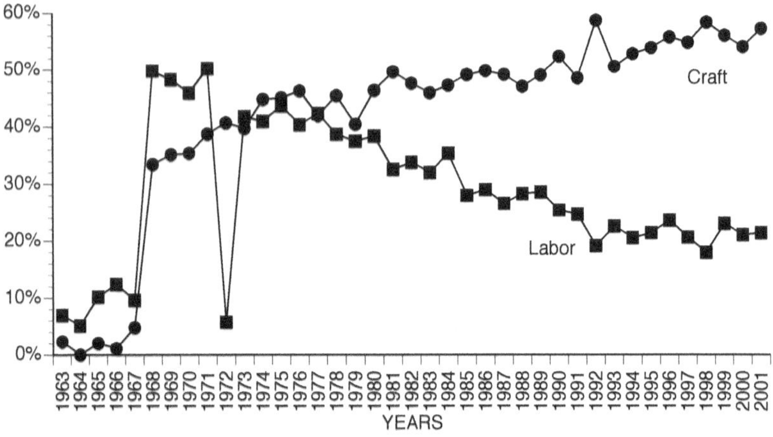

Source: Current Population Survey Datasets, 1962–2001. Washington, DC (machine-readable data files)/conducted by the Bureau of the Census for the Bureau of Labor Statistics. Washington, DC: Bureau of the Census (producer and distributor), 1962–2001. Santa Monica: Unicon Research Corporation (producer and distributor of CPS Utilities), 2001.

Suddenly the employment outlooks for Blacks began to reflect those of whites, as the percentages of Blacks in the higher-paying crafts rose sharply, and the percentages of Blacks in lower-paying labor positions began to decrease just as sharply in the late 1970s. Figure 4.3 clearly shows that this change was dramatic and measurable. Any claims by conservative economists that the civil rights movement did not impact the occupational or employment outcomes for Blacks simply are incorrect.[97] The evidence here is clear.

A Black male Philadelphian working on a construction project for a government building came to work and suddenly received a promotion to a job equivalent to his skill. In figure 4.3, in the late 1960s and early 1970s, 80 percent of Black men in construction in Philadelphia worked as laborers, and only 15–20 percent worked in the higher-paying crafts. The fight to get Blacks into the trades in Philadelphia was long and hard, but after twenty years of affirmative action policy, the percentage of Blacks in crafts and those working as laborers was about equal.

97. Sowell, *Civil Rights*, 49.

Figure 4.3 Black Men in Philadelphia Construction Craft and Labor Occupations as a Percentage of All Black Men in Construction in Philadelphia

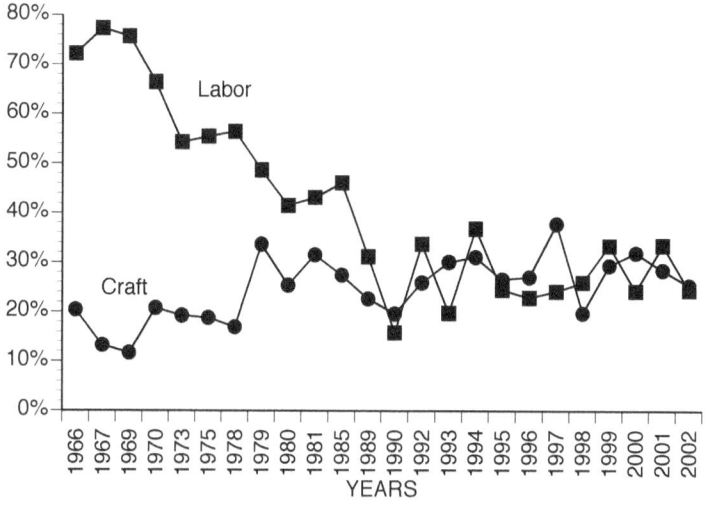

Sources: 1966–90, U.S. Equal Employment Opportunity Commission, "2018 Job Patterns"; 1992–2002, proprietary data tapes obtained by special license from the U.S. Equal Employment Opportunity Commission, Washington, DC.

The Philadelphia Plan worked well, at least by the measure of Black workers moving from labor into craft occupations in construction. The plan nearly created parity between the ratio of Black craft workers to Black laborers and white craft workers to white laborers. In 2001, between 50 and 60 percent of Blacks were in crafts, near the same percentage as whites. About 25 percent of Blacks were in labor in 2001, compared with about 12 percent for whites. In thirty years, strong affirmative action policy broke the back of racism in construction and this victory has continued. In 2018, 64 percent of whites worked in the construction trades in Philadelphia as compared to all construction jobs, while 69 percent of Blacks worked in the construction trades in Philadelphia as compared to all construction jobs, success by any measure.[98]

98. U.S. Equal Employment Opportunity Commission, "2018 Job Patterns," row 8269.

CLAIMS AND COUNTERCLAIMS ABOUT COSTS AND THE LAW

Many could understand Arthur Fletcher's frustration at the change from the fixed and escalating percentages of Black workers moving from labor positions to craft positions in an industry that had practiced blatant racial discrimination. Nevertheless, the Philadelphia Plan was successful. Statements by the Thernstroms, that affirmative action ceased to be effective after 1976, or by Herrnstein and Murray, that large costs to Black labor are from inefficiency, have not been statistically demonstrated.[99] In fact, the data show the opposite.

Evaluating the Philadelphia Plan has provided much information. Black affirmative action can be effective and efficient. The racial imbalances in construction were from racial discrimination and not from labor market skill deficiencies, since Blacks were moved into higher-level occupations so quickly in figure 4.2 there was almost no time to train them; they must already have been fully capable in these jobs. Blacks were promoted from within because all the major business sectors (durable and nondurable goods, transportation, wholesale, and retail trade) were also increasing the percentages of Blacks in the crafts.

Black affirmative action tended to advance only Blacks with merit and skill. In addition, Black affirmative action law did nothing to dismantle decades and centuries of white affirmative action. In this sense, Black affirmative action in the law has a low cost to whites. Breaking the back of racism in the construction trades proved much easier and cheaper than changing individual white cultural attitudes and perceived political costs in the legal systems, which supported the legitimacy of many white construction trades.

The cost of racial equality in the law is primarily cultural because in the history of America, and even today, the law has operated as an extension of white cultural-political power and for white economic gain. From John Adams's dilemma in 1777, about his hatred of slavery versus his desire to avoid disruption of his peace, to the most recent Supreme Court struggles in *Students for Fair Admissions v. Harvard* (2023), the expectations of whites to maintain the status quo of white advantage usually win out.

As the nation quickly becomes majority minority, culturally biased courts may prove to be the obstacle that blocks the will of the new majority to institute substantive racial equality. Justice Ginsburg's dissent in *Fisher II*, that only an ostrich could regard neutrality to race as color blindness, must carry the day if America is to survive. The courts must lead the way in

---

99. Herrnstein and Murray, *Bell Curve*, 487; Thernstrom and Thernstrom, *America in Black and White*, 450.

integrating their own ranks and then lead the nation toward the race consciousness that alone can create true racial equality. In 1968, MLK Jr. said, "America is still struggling with irresolution and contradictions. It has been sincere and even ardent in welcoming some change. But too quickly apathy and disinterest rise to the surface when the next logical steps are to be taken. Laws are passed in a crisis mood . . . but no substantial fervor survives the formal signing of legislation. The recording of the law itself is treated as the reality of the reform."[100] King's claim is as true now as in 1968.

100. King, *Where Do We Go from Here*, 5.

Chapter Five

How Much Affirmative Action Costs America

A LITTLE KNOWLEDGE IS A DANGEROUS THING

Most white Americans—and a sizable minority of Black Americans—think that affirmative action discriminates against whites and is a program of questionable value. What the ramification would be if they are incorrect, however, is worth consideration. If, for example, affirmative action only blocks white racial discrimination against highly qualified Black and minority workers, and whether the programs should continue and/or even be expanded, are questions worthy of attention in spite of the Supreme Court's decision in *Students for Fair Admissions* about affirmative action in higher education.

Imagine a business called B&W Manufacturing, the director of which claimed to be forced by government mandates to replace well-trained, highly efficient white workers with poorly trained, low-skilled Black workers. Suppose, further, that after hiring the Black workers, B&W Manufacturing had an outside consulting firm check their output versus their costs. If B&W Manufacturing found they had higher output at lower cost, we would seriously doubt the claim of B&W Manufacturing that the Black workers were less qualified.

Most people assume lower-quality Black workers dilute the higher quality of the mostly white workforce. The evidence, however, does not support this assumption. Rather, this research shows the reverse seems to be true. Black workers tend to outproduce and outperform white workers. As such, the Black workers are the cream of the workforce and should rise to the top. Only racial discrimination seems to keep them employed below their superior performance levels.

Nobel Laureate and conservative economist James Heckman enunciated this input-output measurement principle when he said part of a "firm's total cost function . . . may be direct loss in output or increase in costs unrelated to employee tastes, that result from a [racially] mixed work force."[1] Failure to anticipate or know the costs of most goods and services, even in a best-case scenario, will generally lead to overspending. A lack of knowledge of costs, or an inaccurate estimate of costs for a business, household, or government, in a worst-case scenario, may lead to bankruptcy or insolvency.

Already, large income, wealth, and health gaps between whites and peoples of color are apparent, and the nation is poised to become mostly peoples of color in less than twenty-five years. With the majority of the peoples-of-color cohort already born, the nation cannot afford to scrap one of the most effective and efficient racial antidiscrimination programs.[2] Few people, or even experts, know how to evaluate affirmative action programs for effectiveness or efficiency.

President Bill Clinton's catchy line "mend it but don't end it," in his July 19, 1995, speech on affirmative action, barely one month after the Supreme Court's decision in *Adarand*, is an example of a skillful politician playing to the popular idea that affirmative action was broken.[3] Few knew that the supporting documents for President Clinton's study of affirmative action contained almost no information on the costs of the programs. Clinton's special report mostly concerned whether affirmative action programs were effective in increasing minority hiring. The evidence showed that they were.[4]

The two Leiter brothers, authors of one of the best textbooks on affirmative action, essentially abandon trying to determine if affirmative action is costly or merit based, claiming "the latest economic review has concluded that 'the theoretical literature from labor economics generates ambiguous results on whether or not affirmative action programs result in efficiency gains or losses.'"[5] The Leiters, who are not economists, cite Holzer

1. Heckman and Wolpin, "Does the Contract Compliance Program Work?," 549.

2. On May 17, 2012, the US Census Bureau reported that 50.4 percent of the nation's population younger than age one were minorities as of July 1, 2011 (United States Census Bureau, "Most Children Younger Than Age 1").

3. *New York Times*, "Excerpts from Clinton Talk," final sentence. In *Adarand v. Peña*, the Supreme Court decided that the federal government must meet the same standards (strict scrutiny, narrowly tailed, compelling governmental interest) for racial programs as do states and municipalities.

4. Stephanopoulos and Edley, *Affirmative Action Review*.

5. Leiter and Leiter, *Affirmative Action*, 85.

and Neumark's article titled "Assessing Affirmative Action" as evidence of ambiguous results for affirmative action efficiency. Holzer and Neumark's eighty-six-page article, however, was a historical summary of theoretical and empirical studies of affirmative action in education, employment, minority business ownership, and government contracting. Setting aside the nearly impossible task of one conclusion for all the theoretical and empirical studies of affirmative action in education, employment, minority business ownership, and government contracting, a close reading of Holzer and Neumark's summary of empirical studies with data on the issue of efficiency and cost reveals that "significant labor market discrimination against minorities and women persists, as do other forms of disadvantage for minorities in the attainment of human capital" and "evidence of weaker performance in the labor market among [minorities] is much less frequently observed or is less credible."[6] Perhaps these were the best conclusions Holzer and Neumark could make, given their mix of areas, goals, and outcomes. Holzer and Neumark's own empirical studies, as opposed to their summarizing of the studies of other researchers, in table 5.1 below, show that Black workers are as qualified or more qualified than their white counterparts.

The courts have generally stayed away from any type of empirical assumptions about the efficiency of affirmative action and have assumed, whether analyzing affirmative action in education, employment, or contracting, that minority students, workers, or contractors are qualified. There have been exceptions to this broad general rule. Students for Fair Admissions (SFFA) in their petition for a writ of certiorari before the US Supreme Court asserted that the "disadvantaged applicants" were less qualified than "the most academically qualified students." If SFFA are correct, we should be able to measure the lower performance of these less qualified applicants after they leave college and enter the labor market.[7] Justice Powell's plurality claim in *Bakke* "that there existed a pool of at least minimally qualified minority applicants to fill the 16 special admissions seats, white applicants could compete only for 84 seats in the entering class, rather than the 100 open to minority applicants" not only misstates the facts, since no minority applicants were admitted as regular applicants, but assumes that minority applicants were only minimally qualified, an assumption not applied to white applicants.[8]

Justice Stanley Mosk, writing for the majority when the *Bakke* case was before the California Supreme Court, better captured the spirit of what

---

6. Holzer and Neumark, "Assessing Affirmative Action," 558.
7. *Students for Fair Admissions v. Harvard*.
8. *Regents v. Bakke*, 289.

efficiency means when he wrote, "While minority applicants may have lower grade point averages and test scores than others, we are aware of no rule of law which requires the University to afford determinative weight in admissions to these quantitative factors. In practice, colleges and universities generally consider matters other than strict numerical ranking in admission decisions.... The University is entitled to consider, as it does with respect to applicants in the special program, that low grades and test scores may not accurately reflect the abilities of some disadvantaged students; and it may reasonably conclude that although their academic scores are lower, their potential for success in the school and the profession is equal to or greater than that of an applicant with higher grades who has not been similarly handicapped."[9]

Chief Justice Rehnquist, joined by Justices Scalia, Kennedy, and Thomas, writing in dissent in *Grutter* in 2003, claimed "the Law School's disparate admissions practices with respect to these minority groups demonstrate that its alleged goal of 'critical mass' is simply a sham. Petitioner may use these statistics to expose this sham, which is the basis for the Law School's admission of less qualified underrepresented minorities in preference to her. Surely strict scrutiny cannot permit these sorts of disparities without at least some explanation."[10] Braswell et al. give other examples of Justices Rehnquist, O'Connor, Scalia, and Kennedy in various cases[11] predicting grievous harm from the stigma of affirmative action preferences, stereotypes and the assumptions of lower-performing affirmative action hires, and the associated costs from "the assumption that the person is less qualified, an assumption that carries over into the post-selection environment."[12] These claims by the justices of lower-performing affirmative action hires, with the associated stigma, did not materialize and were not supported by empirical evidence.

Legal scholarship on affirmative action and cost has tended to be composed of two basic types: 1) those who do not have direct access to the statistical and empirical methods used in econometric analysis and are thus forced to rely on comments in the popular media, which tend to be more social commentary than social science;[13] and 2) legal scholars who are also social scientists who can shed light on the intersection of law and

---

9. *Bakke v. Regents*, 54.

10. *Grutter v. Bollinger*, 382–83.

11. *Metro Broadcasting v. FCC*, 603–4; *Steelworkers v. Weber*, 254–55; *City of Richmond v. Croson*, 493.

12. Braswell et al., "Affirmative Action," 411–12.

13. Mellott, "Diversity Rationale"; Braswell et al., "Affirmative Action."

economics.[14] Table 5.1 examines the work of legal scholars in the latter group. The evidence to support the claims of less qualified minorities in the *Grutter* dissent are strangely missing in the empirical studies in table 5.1.

Effectiveness measures whether a program does what it is supposed to do, which in this case means reducing racial discrimination or inequality. Efficiency measures whether a program performs with reasonable costs, financial or otherwise. Without knowing the costs of affirmative action, determining whether the programs reduce racial inequality at the expense of discriminating against whites is difficult indeed.

With most whites opposing affirmative action, and the Supreme Court's decisions on affirmative action frequently in doubt, the nation could be locked into perpetual racial inequality with a white minority at the top, supported by a non-white proletariat. Such a situation could strategically damage the equality gains of three-quarters of a century and threaten the political stability of the nation. I make this claim based on the concept of strategic equality developed in chapter 3. Strategic equality is the level of equality the nation must have in order to avoid large-scale social disruption and threats to our democratic order.

Failure to know the costs of affirmative action not only renders it impossible to evaluate properly the foremost antidiscrimination program for effectiveness or efficiency. Failure to know costs also suggests that decisions to end such programs could result in increased racial discrimination against Black workers and students. Failure to know costs could also cause the elevation of underperforming whites over better-performing Blacks, creating racial alienation and repression of minority groups who will soon have a voting majority. That is, the foundations of our social and political systems, fairness, merit, democracy, and equality could be seriously challenged if we guess wrong on the costs of affirmative action. And up until now, we do seem to be guessing. Accurate cost information is vital.

While few laypeople frame their views as economic cost issues, their opinions about affirmative action, antidiscrimination, and government help to Blacks are cost statements. Views on affirmative action in employment or education are cost statements, because if Black students or workers are less meritorious than whites, they are less efficient. Declines in efficiency must have a cost in the long run. In the short run, less efficient Black workers can be carried by their superior-performing white colleagues, but as soon as a competitor firm enters the market with more efficient workers, the firm using the less efficient affirmative action workers is at a disadvantage.

14. Ayres, "Fair Driving"; Ayres and Cramton, "Deficit Reduction Through Diversity"; Hiller and Ferris, "Separating Myth from Reality"; Ayres and Vars, "When Does Private Discrimination."

WHITE POPULAR WISDOM VERSUS BLACK POPULAR WISDOM

White opposition to affirmative action, claims of reverse discrimination (Blacks gaining at the expense of whites), and belief that hiring by race is the antithesis of hiring by merit have been termed "white popular wisdom" by Charles Murray, a white conservative writer popular in the 1980s. Murray advised Blacks to listen to white popular wisdom, with the implication that the economy actually functioned in ways imagined by white popular wisdom.[15] Few people on the street think about program or policy costs the way economists do. But when someone says that unqualified Blacks are taking away jobs or university slots from qualified, or more qualified whites, they are making a statement about cost. Whether those thoughts or statements are true is what we want to answer in this chapter.

In 1995, Richard Morin found that 48 percent of whites, who scored the lowest on knowledge about racial facts in America, think that reverse discrimination against whites is a more serious problem than discrimination against minorities.[16] The whites in Morin's *Washington Post* survey, those who know the least about race in America, believe that affirmative action is costly because affirmative action discriminates against whites. The General Social Survey confirms Morin's findings. In 1994, GSS respondents were asked, "What do you think the chances are these days that a White person won't get admitted to a college or university program while an equally or less qualified Black person gets admitted instead? Would you say: very likely, somewhat likely, or not likely."[17] Nearly 80 percent of whites said it is very likely or somewhat likely that an equally or less qualified Black person will get admitted to college over a white person. Fewer than 25 percent of Blacks agreed with this. Rather, over 75 percent of Blacks responded it is unlikely that an equally or less qualified Black person will get admitted to college over a white person.

That same year, 1994, the GSS asked respondents, "What do you think the chances are these days that a White person won't get a job or promotion while an equally or less qualified Black person gets one instead? Is this very likely, somewhat likely, or not very likely to happen these days?" Sixty-eight percent of whites said very likely or somewhat likely. Only 31 percent of whites said not very likely. Twenty-five percent of Blacks said very likely or somewhat likely. Seventy-four percent of Blacks said it was not very likely

---

15. Murray, *Losing Ground*, 146.
16. Morin, "Distorted Image of Minorities."
17. T. Smith et al., "General Social Surveys, 1972–2016," variable colaff.

that a white person won't get a job or promotion while an equally or less qualified Black person gets one instead. Whites believe affirmative action is costly, Blacks clearly do not.

Not much has changed in over twenty years. In 2016, white respondents in the GSS have not changed their views by even a percentage point about an equally or a less qualified Black person obtaining a job or promotion over a white person. Blacks, on the other hand, have changed a great deal. In 2016, 47 percent of Blacks believed an equally or less qualified Black person will obtain a job or promotion over a white person. A majority of Blacks, 52 percent, still find this to be not very likely.[18] As a consequence, this is probably why, in 2016, only 12 percent of whites in the GSS supported preferences in hiring for Blacks because of past discrimination.[19] Seventy-five percent of whites believed that Blacks should work their way up, as, they believe, did white European ethnics and European Jews.[20] A majority of whites have consistently agreed, for nearly half a century, that the government is not obligated to help Blacks because they have suffered systematic racial discrimination.[21]

"White popular wisdom" has been nurtured by the academy. First, many social scientists, with Paul Sniderman among the most prominent, have tended to concentrate on white Americans' beliefs about affirmative action, rather than evaluating the beliefs of white Americans against the more objective costs of affirmative action. For whites, much of American politics, and even some in the judiciary, white perceptions are the realities of what affirmative action is and does. Sniderman's work has tended to show that whites believe they oppose programs that assist non-white groups because favoritism extended on the basis of race violates the American creed of fairness, democracy, equality, and merit.[22]

Second, the late Nobel Laureate economist Gary Becker generated the idea that racial discrimination was inherently uncompetitive or, at the very least, involved costs to those who discriminated against Blacks.[23] This led many of Becker's followers to conclude that affirmative action was expensive because it discriminated against better-performing and more qualified white workers.[24] Also, if anti-Black discrimination was economically

18. T. Smith et al., "General Social Surveys, 1972–2016," variable discaff.
19. T. Smith et al., "General Social Surveys, 1972–2016," variable affrmact.
20. T. Smith et al., "General Social Surveys, 1972–2016," variable wrkwayup.
21. T. Smith et al., "General Social Surveys, 1972–2016," variable helpblk.
22. Sniderman and Piazza, *Scar of Race*, 5.
23. Becker, *Economics of Discrimination*.
24. Arrow, "What Has Economics to Say," 95; Epstein, *Forbidden Grounds*, 9, 41–42;

HOW MUCH AFFIRMATIVE ACTION COSTS AMERICA

expensive, so the claim went, the competitive process alone should drive discrimination out of the marketplace.

Black popular wisdom is almost the antithesis of white popular wisdom. While everyone would be better off without racial discrimination, Black popular wisdom holds that Blacks rather than whites bear most of the costs of discrimination.[25] In the 2018 GSS, respondents were asked, "On the average (Negroes/Blacks/African-Americans) have worse jobs, income, and housing than White people. Do you think these differences are mainly due to discrimination?" The responses were polar opposites based on race. Nearly two-thirds (57.90 percent) of whites said inequality was not due to discrimination; 69.29 percent of Blacks said racial inequality was due to discrimination.[26]

Support or opposition to affirmative action is largely dependent on the framing of the language used. Loaded words, such as "preferences" or "quotas," generate negative responses from respondents because the words sound inherently unfair. Every two years, since 1994, the GSS has asked respondents, "Some people say that because of past discrimination, Blacks should be given preference in hiring and promotion. Others say that such preference in hiring and promotion of Blacks is wrong because it discriminates against Whites. What about your opinion—are you for or against preferential hiring and promotion of Blacks?"[27] The year 1996 was the first year Black support and strong support dropped below 50 percent. This drop in Black support for affirmative action happened right after President Bill Clinton's "Mend It, Don't End It" campaign to assuage white opposition to affirmative action.[28] In 2018, 47 percent of Blacks supported or strongly supported the preferential hiring and promotion of Blacks. That same year, white support or strong support for preferential hiring and promotion of Blacks was 19.51 percent.[29]

Fuchs, *Women's Quest*, 54; Heckman, "Detecting Discrimination," 111; O'Neill, "Discrimination in Income Differences," 13; Sowell, "Free Market vs. Discrimination."

25. Dickens and Dickens, *Black Manager*, 49; Feagin, *Racist America*, 135; Feagin and Sikes, *Living with Racism*, ch. 4; Jencks, *Rethinking Social Policy*, 26; Mays and Nicholson, "Genius of the Negro Church"; Scott and Shaw, "Black and White Performance"; Tomaskovic-Devey, *Gender and Racial Inequality*, 99; R. Williams and Kenison, "Way We Were?"; Mason, "Race, Culture, and Skill"; Bridges and Villemez, "Overeducated Minority Workers."

26. T. Smith et al., "General Social Surveys, 1972–2018," mnemonics racdif1, race, racecensus.

27. T. Smith et al., "General Social Surveys, 1972–2018," mnemonics race, affrmact.

28. Stephanopoulos and Edley, *Affirmative Action Review*.

29. T. Smith et al., "General Social Surveys, 1972–2018," mnemonics race, affrmact.

THE COST OF RACIAL EQUALITY

The MCSUI study asks a more balanced question. "Some people feel that because of past disadvantages there are some groups (Blacks) in society that should receive special job training and educational assistance. Others say that it is unfair to give these groups (Blacks) special job training and educational assistance. What about you?" Over 86 percent of Blacks support such training and over 60 percent of whites support such training.[30] The GSS results show that Blacks generally believe they have to work much harder and be more qualified to have the same jobs as white workers, and they view the labor market and higher education market as fundamentally discriminatory.

In spite of many claims to the contrary and after sixty years of racial equality programs, little information is available about how much affirmative action and antidiscrimination programs cost in terms of corporate markets, finances, or productivity. Without a clear knowledge of the financial, market, and efficiency costs for affirmative action and antidiscrimination programs, little may be said about the relative skill of Black and white workers, the relationship between hiring on the basis of merit versus hiring by race, whether the concept of reverse discrimination is viable, or the degree to which labor and education markets are dominated by racial discrimination.

Failure to know the costs of affirmative action inhibits the determination of whether the program is meritorious or discriminatory. The nation could assume that white majority views in opposition to affirmative action are correct and unwittingly terminate the only racial program that works to eliminate white bias in the work place or in higher education. If left unchecked, however, white popular wisdom could trap the future non-white voting majority in a cycle of racial oppression and inequality. Once this minority becomes a numerical and voting majority, they may retaliate with the same indifference toward whites as whites showed to them.

To avoid the conditions that might lead to race war, permanent racial inequality, and the threatening of our democracy, the financial, market, productivity, and comprehensive costs for affirmative action need clarification. Only this information will reveal whether white or Black popular wisdom is correct and encourage the cultivation of appropriate solutions. Most of the evidence supports Black popular wisdom. Affirmative action operates as a net gain, not a cost, because the market views affirmative action as a plus, there is no financial cost, and Black workers are the most productive (in table 5.2 below).

30. MCSUI was conducted in 1994. The differences in outcome between the GSS and MCSUI, however, are not dependent on year. Even in 1996, the GSS results are similar.

WHY COST MEASURES MERIT

Cost measures merit because the output of most firms is a function of labor and capital inputs, in what is known as a production function (output = labor + capital).[31] If two companies have the same amount of capital (buildings, trucks, machines, inventory, products, money, computers, etc.) and the same labor (number of workers, skill, experience, training, education, motivation, etc.) they should have the same output, all other things being equal. Suppose, however, that one company has a workforce that is 50 percent Black while another company has a workforce that has no Blacks. Most major studies of the efficiency and effectiveness of affirmative action in the workforce are based on the assumption that labor inputs will affect outputs.

Invoking the hypothetical B&W Manufacturing company again, in which the firm was forced to hire Black workers because of a government mandate, suppose the firm complained that the Black workers were inferior. If the number of workers did not change, however, and all the machines and operations remained the same, and B&W Manufacturing produced more widgets at even lower cost, the claim of B&W Manufacturing that the Black workers were inferior would be seriously questioned. This situation would be a case in which the cost to produce the product, or the output level, measures the skill of the workers.

To claim that Black workers and students lack merit and are not the equivalent of white workers and students is to claim a cost to Black labor. The majority of whites make this claim when they say that a less qualified Black person likely will get a job, promotion, or admission to a university ahead of a more qualified white person. This point cannot be stressed too strongly. Without the smoking gun of cost for Black labor, which has gone missing in over sixty years of research, claims by whites that less qualified Blacks take jobs, promotions, and university seats from more qualified whites borders on ludicrous.

In the short run, again, costs can be hidden by transferring work from less skilled Black workers to higher-skilled white labor. The short run ends, however, as soon as competitors enter into the marketplace who do not have to transfer work or have the burden of carrying supposedly less skilled workers on the payroll. There is only so much transferring and reassigning of work that can be done while the business remains competitive.[32]

---

31. Coleman, "Merit, Cost," 122n32; Pearce, *MIT Dictionary*, 348.
32. Coleman, "Merit, Cost," 100n2.

THE COST OF RACIAL EQUALITY

THE COST STUDIES

Almost every major study of affirmative action costs has concluded that our hypothetical B&W Manufacturing has lost not a penny in hiring Black workers. If fact, B&W Manufacturing has gained.

In total, fewer than a dozen cost studies of affirmative action in table 5.1 have verifiable data. Many people are surprised the list is so short. Table 5.1 does not include writers who comment about the cost of affirmative action, but rather persons, some scholars, and other businesspeople, who tried, in some systematic way, to measure the cost of affirmative action.

Table 5.1 divides the cost studies of affirmative action into four groups: market studies, productivity studies, financial studies, and other reports without verifiable data. Table 5.1 is compelling because so many different techniques were used in ascertaining the cost of affirmative action and yet the conclusions are similar, with no significant cost involved.

Table 5.1
Summary of Major Studies of Affirmative Action Costs

	Study	Data, Sample, Years	Study Design	Results
		A. Market Costs for Affirmative Action		
1.	Hiller and Ferris (1993)	28 publicly traded firms receiving exemplary voluntary efforts (EVE) awards for affirmative action hiring, 1986–91	Residual rate of return for firms after notified publicly they received an EVE award	Firms receiving an EVE award had a significantly higher rate of return for two days after an EVE award. The market likes affirmative action.
2.	Ayres and Cramton (1996)	12 minority and nonminority firms bidding for radio frequencies with the federal government, 1993	Price per megahertz in bidding with minority contracts who had a 40 percent bidding handicap compared to price per megahertz in national bidding with no minority handicaps	Government received higher bids when minority contractors were included because it increased competition and drove the prices higher.
3.	Coleman (1999)	164 publicly traded firms in Chicago, 1975–81	Market to book value of the firm compared to non-white employment	No relationship of increasing percentages of non-white employees and market to book values of the firm
		B. Productivity Costs for Affirmative Action		

156

Table 5.1

Summary of Major Studies of Affirmative Action Costs

	Study	Data, Sample, Years	Study Design	Results
4.	Leonard (1984)	Compared industry (two digit) with percent non-white and female in the industrial sector between 1966 and 1977 for over 500 industries	Matched for hours worked per industry percent non-white male, percent female, percent blue collar, and actual sector inventory from the Bureau of Labor Statistics	"The finding here is that neither affirmative action nor Title VII litigation has had a significant impact on productivity" (170).
5.	Bridges and Villemez (1986)	Institute for Social Research Quality of Employment Survey with over 800 respondents, 1972	People were asked about the relationship between the amount of education they needed to do their jobs effectively and the amount of education they had.	Blacks were more overqualified for their jobs by education than were whites.
6.	Conrad (1995)	263 three-digit census industrial codes, 1984–88	Conrad regressed changes in output per worker hour in three-digit SIC code manufacturing sectors onto the change in Black employment levels for the years 1984–88.	"I estimate the total costs at just under $2 billion a year" (46).
7.	Black and Lynch (2001)	Census Bureau national employers survey with over 600 firms, 1994	Regressed race and other variables onto sales per employee	"In manufacturing, everything else held constant, we find that there seems to be little evidence of lower productivity associated with hiring a larger proportion of women or minorities" (444).
8.	Holzer and Neumark (1999)	2,130 business firms in the Multi-City Study of Urban Inequality, 1992–94	Employers asked to rank employees on scale of 1–100, with 50 being average, compared to other employees in same job	"Black females hired under affirmative action obtain higher . . . ratings than white males. . . . white females and Black males also . . . their performance is not lower than that of white males" (561).

Table 5.1
Summary of Major Studies of Affirmative Action Costs

	Study	Data, Sample, Years	Study Design	Results
9.	Holzer and Neumark (2000)	Over 2,000 businesses in the Multi-City Study of Urban Inequality, 1992–94	Relationship of affirmative action in recruiting and hiring to education, competitive performance rating, and hours of training for hires	Generally, affirmative action has no impact on the educational level, competitive performance rating, or training hours of workers.
	Coleman (1999)	164 publicly traded firms in Chicago, 1975–81	Regressed race and other variables onto sales per employee	Minority employees significantly more productive than whites
	C. Financial Costs for Affirmative Action			
10.	Griffin (1992)	Equal Employment Opportunity Commission file combined with Standard and Poors Compustat data and census industry wage data for 555 publicly traded firms, 1980	Compares the cost (return on capital) of affirmative action and non–affirmative action firms against the wages paid to race/gender groups (controls for property, plant and equipment, and net sales plus the changes in the firms inventories from the past to the current year)	Finds that affirmative action firms are paying higher costs than non–affirmative action firms. However, Griffin does not use race/gender wage data by occupation, neither does he use affirmative action and non–affirmative action firms with the same output and sales characteristics.
	Coleman (1999)	164 publicly traded firms in Chicago, 1975–81	Compared percentage of non-white workers to four different financial measures	No relationship of increasing percentages of non-white employees and firm financial performance
	D. Other Cited Reports Without Verifiable Data			
11.	Business Roundtable Study by Arthur Anderson, cited in Leonard (1984)	40 large companies, 1977		Companies spent $217 million in 1977 or $78 per employee or one-tenth of 1 percent of sales.

Table 5.1

Summary of Major Studies of Affirmative Action Costs

	Study	Data, Sample, Years	Study Design	Results
12.	Equal Employment Advisory Council, cited in Leonard (1984)	21 *Fortune* 500 companies, 1981		"The Equal Employment Advisory Council imputed a cost [for affirmative action] of $1.5 billion" (168).
13.	Congressional Research Service, cited in Leonard (1984)	Two companies, 1976		"The Congressional Research Service guessed that $1.6 billion would pay for the cost of affirmative action for all nonconstruction contractors in 1976, based on a sample of two" (168).
14.	Covenant Investment Management, cited in Federal Glass Ceiling Commission (1995)	Standard and Poors 500, 1994	Stock market performance for top and bottom 20 percent of firms in minority and women hiring	Top 20 percent of firms in minority and women hiring averaged an 18.3 annual return compared to 7.9 for bottom 20 percent.

Sources: Ayres and Cramton, "Deficit Reduction Through Diversity"; S. Black and Lynch, "How to Compete"; Bridges and Villemez, "Overeducated Minority Workers"; Coleman, "Merit, Cost"; Conrad, "Economic Cost of Affirmative Action"; Federal Glass Ceiling Commission, *Good for Business*; Griffin, "Impact of Affirmative Action"; Hiller and Ferris, "Separating Myth from Reality"; Holzer and Neumark, "Are Affirmative Action Hires Less Qualified?"; Holzer and Neumark, "What Does Affirmative Action Do?"; Leonard, "Antidiscrimination or Reverse Discrimination."

Leonard divided the country by state and then by industry group within the state. Using aggregate racial employment information from EEOC publications in 1966 and 1977, he compared the output of each industry with the percentage of non-white workers in that state and industrial sector. Leonard concluded, "There is no significant evidence here to support the contention that this increase in (non-White) employment . . . has had marked efficiency costs."[33]

Leonard performed another valuable service by cataloging many older industry studies that have since been lost. One such financial study in table 5.1 is the 1977 Arthur Anderson findings, which indicate that forty large

33. Leonard, "Antidiscrimination or Reverse Discrimination," 101.

firms were spending a total of $217 million for affirmative action costs. These costs amounted to about .1 percent (one-tenth of 1 percent) of sales for the firms and did not involve productivity losses. This base line of .1 percent came to be taken as something of a floor. Firms spending anything around .1 percent of sales were assumed to be paying only minor administrative costs with no losses from Black labor.

Only one serious empirical study by Peter Griffin finds large costs associated with affirmative action.[34] Griffin found no relationship between Black employment, the financial performance of a firm, and whether the firm was a government contractor. This conclusion is important in indicating that the average cost of affirmative action is zero. Griffin did not stop there; he was looking for the worst-case possibilities, so he calculated the difference between the worst-case (lower confidence interval) costs for contractors and non-contractors. He found that the average government contractor had worst-case wage costs of $26 million more than the average non-contractor. Twenty-six million dollars sounds like an extraordinarily large amount of money, but since Griffin studied only large firms with workforces of more than 15,000, $26 million was only 6.5 percent of the average industry wage costs per firm.

Griffin made a number of assumptions that impact his findings. First, he used only 550 large firms, probably the *Fortune* 500, plus a few. The EEOC files contain nearly 200,000 firms per year, 25,000 of which have matching financial data. Griffin did not explain why he chose only the firms he did. Also, Griffin assumed that contractors and non-contractors have the same characteristics for size, sales, wages, property, plant, and equipment and inventory. To assume as Griffin did that contractors and non-contractor firms have the same production function is a mistaken approach. In fact, government contractors differ in many ways from non-contractor firms.

We have no way of knowing which firms Griffin used because his data, like the data in this chapter, comes from proprietary government files. If Griffin's findings were applied to the *Fortune* 500 in 1980, the $26 million extra that government contractors spent in average wages would amount to only .7 percent (seven-tenths of 1 percent) of their average sales of $3.3 billion per firm. Griffin's findings are almost exactly the same as the .4 percent of sales that will be calculated in this chapter. The findings of this chapter and Griffin are not far from the floor of .1 percent paid only for administrative costs cited in the 1977 Arthur Anderson study in table 5.1. And the numbers grow even closer.

---

34. Griffin, "Impact of Affirmative Action."

DOING THE MATH

Table 5.2 is the regression analysis for the financial, market, and productivity measures of cost. Return on capital is the percentage earned on the monetary value of all the business owns. Return on equity is percentage earned from common stock investment or net worth. Return on assets is similar to return on capital, minus debt. Tobin's Q is a market volatility measure (market value versus replacement value). The profit margin is profits as a percentage of sales. Sales per employee is a measure of productivity.

Readers should see that the regression coefficients for Black employment for all of the financial measures are statistically zero for models 1–4 in table 5.2. Affirmative action for Blacks costs business nothing. The regression coefficients in models 5–6 in table 5.2 measure the market and productivity performance of Black workers. Models 5–6 in table 5.2 are statistically significant, and they are also positive, that is, Black employment adds something to the market performance and productivity of firms.

Table 5.3 is essentially a summary table of the variables in table 5.2. The mean value of the denominator (value of capital in table 5.3, model 1= $977 million) is multiplied by the mean rate of return in table 5.3, model 1 (.043). The product of that calculation is multiplied by the lower confidence interval (two times the standard error, or two standard errors subtracted from the regression coefficient for Black workers in table 5.2, model 1 (.043*977,000,000)*((.0129)-(.078*2)). This product gives the lower confidence interval, which is called the worst-case cost here, for the mean percentage of Black workers at the average firm, $6,011,774 million.

Table 5.2

Financial, Market, and Productivity Performance on Black Labor, 1990–2002 (standard errors in parenthesis)

	Model 1	Model 2	Model 3	Model 4	Model 5	Model 6
	Return on Capital	Return on Equity	Return on Assets	Profit Margin	Tobin's Q	Sales per Employee
Percent Black Workers	.0129 (.078)	-.0042 (.113)	.0086 (.030)	-.035 (.052)	.9768* (.6097)	.057*** (.020)
Capitalization Intensity[1]	-.00001 (.0000008)	-.00001 (.00001)	-.000003 (.000003)	-.000004 (.000006)	-.0002 (.00007)	.0003**** (.000009)
Total Employment	-.0000005 (.0000003)	.0000002 (.0000004)	-.0000001 (.0000001)	-.0000001 (.0000002)	-.00001**** (.000008)	-.0000007**** (.00000008)
Total Sales[2]	.000001 (.000001)	.000002 (.000001)	.0000009 (.0000004)	.000001** (.0000007)	.00006**** (.000008)	.000008**** (.0000003)

161

Table 5.2

Financial, Market, and Productivity Performance on Black Labor, 1990–2002
(standard errors in parenthesis)

Total Assets[3]	-.0000001 (.0000003)	-.0000005 (.0000004)	-.0000001 (.0000001)	-.00000008 (.0000001)	-.000004 (.000002)	-.0000003**** (.00000007)
Unionization	.0005 (.0006)	-.0002 (.0009)	.0004* (.0002)	.0005 (.0004)	-.0107** (.0051)	-.0011**** (.0001)
Beta	.033**** (.003)	.036**** (.005)	.011**** (.001)	.008**** (.002)	.2283**** (.0288)	-.0005 (.0009)
Percent Blue Collar	.050*** (.019)	.107**** (.030)	.038**** (.008)	.061**** (.014)	.3297** (.1651)	-.0303**** (.0056)
Constant	-.005 (.013)	-.033 (.019)	-.022**** (.005)	-.041**** (.008)	2.23**** (.1022)	.1932**** (.0035)
Firm Controls	Yes	Yes	Yes	Yes	Yes	Yes
N	14,688	19,249	18,496	19,260	19,233	19,308
Groups[4]	5,247	6,492	6,173	6,477	6,534	6,518
F (df)	12.09 (8)	8.13 (8)	12.62 (8)	4.52 (8)	19.27 (8)	250.76 (8)

*p=10%; **p=5%; ***p=1%; ****p=<.1%, two-tailed test. 1. The deflated value of property, plant, and equipment divided by total labor. Used chain-type quantity indexes for depreciation of fixed assets and consumer durable goods (U.S. Bureau of Economic Analysis, "Table 1.4"). 2. Sales were deflated with chain-type price indices for gross output by industry (U.S. Bureau of Economic Analysis). 3. Assets do not need to be deflated by year because assets are adjusted for liabilities and stockholders equity. 4. Number of firms. Source: Proprietary database created from EEOC confidential files, Standard and Poor's COMPUSTAT, University of Chicago Center for Research in Security Prices and Barry T. Hirsh unionization database.

To find what this worst-case cost is as a percentage of firm sales, the dollar value at the lower confidence interval ($6,011,774) is divided by the mean value of sales for the firms in table 5.3, model 1 ($1,475,700,000), which equals .4 percent (four-tenths of 1 percent). Total sales for manufacturing, wholesale, and retail trade for 2006 was $12.7 trillion. Multiplying $12.7 trillion by .4 percent returns a product of $51 billion. Annual worst-case affirmative action costs for the entire country equal $51 billion. If $51 billion sounds like a lot of money, consider that Wall Street firms pay out about that much each year in bonuses, not salary.[35]

35. On Oct. 25, 2008, ABC News reported the combined bonuses for the top seven Wall Street firms were $20 billion, down about 30 percent from the usual $33.2 billion paid in 2007. Of course, this figure covers only the big seven firms (Lehman Brothers, Citigroup, JPMorganChase, Bank of America, Merrill Lynch, Goldman Sachs, and Morgan Stanley) (ABC News, "Despite Turmoil"). Yearly bonuses for all Wall Street firms would certainly exceed the worst-case costs for affirmative action.

Table 5.3
The Cost of Black Employment, 1990–2002

	Financial Performance				Market Performance	Productivity
	Model 1	Model 2	Model 3	Model 4	Model 5	Model 6
	Return on Capital	Return on Equity	Return on Assets	Profit Margin	Market to Book Value	Sales per Employee
Average Return	4.3%	3.0%	.6%	-1%	2.91 ratio	$198,556
Average Number of Employees[1]	5,333	6,162	6,158	6,184	6,065	6,116
Black Employment	8.9%	8.8%	8.8%	8.8%	8.8%	8.8%
Value of Denominator[2]	$977,000,000	$707,000,000	$2,777,530,000	$1,831,381,000	Not applicable	$1,740,065,000
Total Sales for Each Firm per Year	$1,475,700,000	$1,837,000,000	$1,825,764,000	$1,831,381,000	$1,814,588,000	$1,740,065,000
Worst-Case Loss/Gain per Firm[3]	-$6,011,774	-$4,882,542	-$856,590	Not applicable[6]	2.70	+$4,836
Average Loss/Gain per Firm[4]	+$541,941	-$89,082	+$143,320	Not applicable[6]	2.91	+$16,217
Best-Case Loss/Gain per Firm[5]	+$7,95,657	+$4,704,378	+$1,143,231	Not applicable[6]	5.08	+$27,597
Worst-Case Loss for Total Black Employment as Percentage of Sales for the Firm	.3% (three-tenths of 1 percent)	.02% (two one hundredths of 1 percent)	.003% (three one thousandths of 1 percent)	Not applicable[6]	Not applicable	Worst case is a net gain of $2,603,137 in sales for the entire complement of Black workers.
Number of Observations	14,688	19,249	18,496	19,260	19,233	19,308
Number of Firms	5,247	6,492	6,173	6,477	6,534	6,518

Table 5.3
The Cost of Black Employment, 1990–2002

	Financial Performance				Market Performance	Productivity
	Model 1	Model 2	Model 3	Model 4	Model 5	Model 6
	Return on Capital	Return on Equity	Return on Assets	Profit Margin	Market to Book Value	Sales per Employee

1. From EEOC; COMPUSTAT employment figures are generally higher. 2. The denominator is capital, equity, assets, or sales for the respective column. 3. This is the calculated value at the lower 95 percent confidence interval for a two-tailed test for the total complement of Black employment. 4. This is the calculated value at the regression coefficient for the total complement of Black employment. 5. This is the calculated value at the upper 95 percent confidence interval for a two-tailed test for the total complement of Black employment. 6. Since the average firm did not earn a profit, there is no profit margin. Source: Author's calculations from proprietary database created from EEOC confidential files, Standard and Poor's COMPUSTAT, University of Chicago Center for Research in Security Prices and Barry T. Hirsh unionization database.

Tables 5.2 and 5.3, however, list four financial (models 1–4), a market (model 5), and a productivity measure (model 6) of firm performance. Look at table 5.3, model 6, sales per employee. Sales per employee is a common method used to measure the productivity of the workforce.[36] Notice that even in a worst case, the average firm makes money from its Black workers. Worst case, each firm gains $4,836 in sales per employee for having Black workers, and on average they gain $16,217 in sales per employee. If we multiply the $16,217 increase in sales per worker by the average number of Black workers at these firms (538) the entire complement of Black workers at the firm is associated with a $8.7 million gain, worth about 5 percent of firm sales. A best-case scenario yields a near $15 million gain for the entire complement of Black workers worth about 8 percent of firm sales.

GOVERNMENT CONTRACTS: THE COSTS OF COMPLIANCE

Tables 5.2 and 5.3 use total Black employment as the measure of affirmative action. Because most whites believe that Black employment is synonymous with affirmative action, most scholars (see citations in table 5.1) think this way is the best for measuring affirmative action. Black employment is not the only way to measure affirmative action, however. Most of the early studies of the impact of affirmative action on employment compared race and gender employment for government contractors versus non-contractors as the measure of affirmative action.[37]

36. Coleman, "Merit, Cost"; Huselid, "Impact of Human Resource Management."

37. Ashenfelter and Heckman, "Measuring the Effects"; Burman, "Economics of Discrimination"; Coleman, "Contesting the Magic"; Goldstein and Smith, "Estimated

Chapters 3 and 4 reviewed the history of President Lyndon Johnson's September 28, 1965, Executive Order 11246, which provided for nondiscrimination in employment by government contractors and subcontractors. Section 202(1) provided that "the contractor will take affirmative action to ensure that applicants are employed, and that employees are treated during employment, without regard to their race, creed, color, or national origin."

Executive Order 11246 only applies to federal government contractors with contracts valued at over $50,000 and Executive Order 11246 specifically excludes "preferences," "set-asides," "proportional representation," "quotas," "equal results," or the hiring of unqualified or less qualified persons. Thus, government contractors should pay more for hiring Black or non-white workers, if expectations were rational. White public opinion has driven and controlled the affirmative action debate, and it is to that opinion, right or wrong, that researchers must answer, particularly if they want to be published in the mainstream press.

Table 5.4
Government Contractor Financial, Market, and Productivity Performance on Black Labor, 1990–2002 (standard errors in parenthesis)

	Return on Capital	Return on Equity	Return on Assets	Profit Margin	Tobin's Q	Sales per Employee
Percent Black Workers	-.0035 (.1242)	-.054 (.167)	.0143 (.0446)	-.0041* (.0684)	1.515* (.927)	.1234**** (.0304)
Capitalization Intensity[1]	-.00001 (.00001)	-.00001 (.00002)	-.000003 (.000005)	-.000007 (.000008)	-.0008**** (.0001)	.0002**** (.00001)
Total Employment	-.0000002 (.0000003)	.0000003 (.0000005)	-.00000009 (.0000001)	-.0000001 (.0000002)	-.00001**** (.000003)	-.0000005**** (.00000009)
Total Sales[2]	.000004*** (.000001)	.000003** (.000001)	.000002**** (.0000005)	.000001*** (.0000006)	.00005**** (.000008)	.000008**** (.0000004)
Total Assets[3]	-.000003** (.000001)	-.0000008 (.0000005)	-.000001*** (.0000005)	-.0000001 (.0000002)	-.000003 (.000003)	-.0000001* (.0000001)
Unionization	.0005 (.0008)	-.0002 (.001)	.0001 (.0002)	.0003 (.0004)	-.01527*** (.0062)	-.0010**** (.0002)
Beta	.0337**** (.0050)	.037**** (.007)	.0118**** (.0018)	.0086*** (.0028)	.2703**** (.0393)	-.0010 (.0012)
Percent Blue Collar	.0837*** (.0354)	.150*** (.050)	.0564**** (.0134)	.0852**** (.0210)	.1243 (.2846)	-.0660**** (.0095)

Impact"; Heckman and Wolpin, "Does the Contract Compliance Program Work?"; Holzer and Neumark, "Assessing Affirmative Action"; Holzer and Neumark, "What Does Affirmative Action Do?"; Leonard, "Antidiscrimination or Reverse Discrimination"; Leonard, "Employment and Occupational Advance"; J. Smith and Welch, "Affirmative Action."

Constant	-.0095 (.0201)	-.032 (.026)	-.0203*** (.0074)	-.0342*** (.0110)	2.42**** (.1491)	.2028**** (.0050)
Firm Controls	Yes	Yes	Yes	Yes	Yes	Yes
N	7,939	11,018	10,312	11,048	10,975	11,035
Groups[4]	3,061	3,947	3,659	3,954	3,961	3,964
F (df)	7.23 (8)	5.24 (8)	8.98 (8)	4.04 (8)	19.57 (8)	156.19 (8)

*p=10%; **p=5%; ***p=1%; ****p=<.1%, two-tailed test. 1. The deflated value of property, plant and equipment divided by total labor. Used chain-type quantity indexes for depreciation of fixed assets and consumer durable goods (U.S. Bureau of Economic Analysis, "Table 1.4"). 2. Sales were deflated with chain-type price indices for gross output by industry (U.S. Bureau of Economic Analysis). 3. Assets do not need to be deflated by year because assets are adjusted for liabilities and stockholders equity. 4. Number of firms. Source: Proprietary database created from EEOC confidential files, Standard and Poor's COMPUSTAT, University of Chicago Center for Research in Security Prices and Barry T. Hirsh unionization database.

Table 5.4 contains the financial, market, and productivity costs for Black employment for 1990–2002 for government contractors only. Similar to table 5.2 for Black employment overall, table 5.4 for government contractors shows that the cost to government contractors for Black employment is zero. The regression coefficient for the percentage of Black workers for the return on capital, return on equity, return on assets, profit margin, and Tobin's Q are statistically zero at normal levels in table 5.4. Again, as in table 5.2, Black workers outperform whites in productivity (sales per employee). The coefficient for sales per employee in table 5.4 is statistically significant and positive. The more Black workers a government contractor has, the higher sales are for each worker.

Table 5.5
The Cost of Black Employment for Government Contractors, 1990–2002

	Model 1	Model 2	Model 3	Model 4	Model 5	Model 6
	Return on Capital	Return on Equity	Return on Assets	Profit Margin	Market to Book Value	Sales per Employee
Average Return	5.3%	4.6%	1.3%	.7%	2.56 ratio	$205,384
Average Number of Employees[1]	5,250	6,774	6,778	6,752	6,717	6,681
Black Employment	8.2%	8.3%	8.2%	8.3%	8.2%	8.2%
Value of Denominator[2]	$1,203,862,000	$931,364,400	$3,520,120,000	$2,296,784,000	Not applicable	Not applicable

HOW MUCH AFFIRMATIVE ACTION COSTS AMERICA

Total Sales for Each Firm per Year	$1,796,575,000	$2,317,596,000	$2,338,415,000	$2,296,784,000	$2,297,868,000	$2,162,644,000
Worst-Case Loss/Gain per Firm[3]	-$19,567,169	-$15,134,360	-$4,389,950	Not applicable	2.26	+$26,996
Average Loss/Gain per Firm[4]	-$223,316	-$2,313,509	+$654,390	Not applicable	2.56	+39,944
Best-Case Loss/Gain per Firm[5]	+$15,625,575	+$11,995,973	+$4,736,321	Not applicable	5.59	+$59,625
Worst-Case Loss for Total Black Employment as Percentage of Sales for the Firm	.8% (eight-tenths of 1 percent)	.5% (seven-tenths of 1 percent)	.1% (one-tenth of 1 percent)	Not applicable	Not applicable	Worst case is a net gain of $14,789,889 in sales per employee.
Number of Observations	7,939	11,018	10,312	11,048	10,975	11,035
Number of Firms	3,061	3,947	3,659	3,954	3,961	3,964

1. From EEOC; COMPUSTAT employment figures are generally higher. 2. The denominator is capital, equity, assets, or sales for the respective column. 3. This is the calculated value at the lower 95 percent confidence interval for a two-tailed test for the total complement of Black employment. 4. This is the calculated value at the regression coefficient for the total complement of Black employment. 5. This is the calculated value at the upper 95 percent confidence interval for a two-tailed test for the total complement of Black employment. 6. Government contractors with contracts of $50,000 or more are required by law to comply with Executive Order 11246, which, until 2000, required that they have "goals and timetables to ... correct ... deficiencies ... [in the] full utilization of minorities and women." After 2000, government contractors must have "placement goals" (41 CFR 60-2.10 [2000]). Source: Author's calculations from proprietary database created from EEOC confidential files, Standard and Poor's COMPUSTAT, University of Chicago Center for Research in Security Prices and Barry T. Hirsh unionization database.

The cost results for table 5.5 are calculated using the information from table 5.4 in the same way we calculated table 5.3. The same results occur as in table 5.3. Worst-case costs for Black employment for the return on capital are $19.5 million per firm, that is, I am 95 percent certain firms pay no more than this. Average costs are only $226,349. On average the market views Black employment positively, and even worst-case costs are only 11 percent of the market to book price (2.56-2.26=.3, .3/2.56=.11) in model 5 of table 5.5.

Table 5.6

Non-Contractor Financial, Market, and Productivity Performance on Black Labor, 1990–2002 (standard errors in parenthesis)

	Return on Capital	Return on Equity	Return on Assets	Profit Margin[5]	Tobin's Q	Sales per Employee
Percent Black Workers	.073 (.1097)	.051 (.175)	.0193 (.0453)	-.0202 (.0883)	.8517 (.8638)	.0224 (.0305)
Capitalization Intensity[1]	-.000006 (.00001)	-.00001 (.00001)	-.000001 (.000004)	.0000003 (.000009)	.00007 (.00009)	.0003**** (.00001)
Total Employment	.00000003 (.0000008)	.0000007 (.000001)	-.0000001 (.0000003)	.0000003 (.0000006)	-.00001* (.000006)	-.000001**** (.0000002)
Total Sales[2]	-.000004 (.000004)	.0000005 (.000006)	-.0000002 (.000001)	-.000001 (.000003)	.0001**** (.00003)	.000008**** (.000001)
Total Assets[3]	.0000005 (.0000005)	-.0000001 (.0000009)	.00000005 (.0000002)	.0000003 (.0000004)	-.00001** (.000004)	-.0000007**** (.0000001)
Unionization	.0002 (.001)	-.0003 (.0019)	.0006 (.0004)	.0003 (.0009)	-.0047 (.0095)	-.00016**** (.0003)
Beta	.0324**** (.0057)	.0425**** (.0091)	.0114**** (.0023)	.009** (.004)	.2142**** (.0443)	.0013 (.0015)
Percent Blue Collar	.0537** (.0254)	.1259*** (.0432)	.0327** (.0110)	.0491** (.0215)	.6833**** (.2120)	-.0139* (.0074)
Constant	-.0157 (.0202)	-.0655** (.0322)	-.0290*** (.0083)	-.0593**** (.0162)	1.93**** (.1583)	.1888**** (.0056)
Firm Controls	Yes	Yes	Yes	Yes	Yes	Yes
N	6,695	8,160	8,116	8,142	8,188	8,201
Groups[4]	2,822	3,343	3,291	3,316	3,371	3,350
F (df)	5.32 (8)	4.12 (8)	4.92 (8)	1.30 (8)	6.97 (8)	90.58 (8)

*p=10%; **p=5%; ***p=1%; ****p=<.1%, two-tailed test. 1. The deflated value of property, plant, and equipment divided by total labor. Used chain-type quantity indexes for depreciation of fixed assets and consumer durable goods (U.S. Bureau of Economic Analysis, "Table 1.4"). 2. Sales were deflated with chain-type price indices for gross output by industry (U.S. Bureau of Economic Analysis). 3. Assets do not need to be deflated by year because assets are adjusted for liabilities and stockholders equity. 4. Number of firms. 5. This is a weak model. There is a 25 percent chance that all the variables may equal zero; see the F statistic. Source: Proprietary database created from EEOC confidential files, Standard and Poor's COMPUSTAT, University of Chicago Center for Research in Security Prices and Barry T. Hirsh unionization database.

Whatever the origin of these costs are for Black employment, certainly they do not stem from "preferences," "set-asides," "proportional representation," "quotas," "equal results," or the hiring of unqualified or less qualified persons. Just as in table 5.3, table 5.5 shows that worst-case costs for sales per employee are positive. Worst case, firms gain $26,996 in sales per employee. If we multiply this by the 547 average number of Black employees at one of these firms, that number equals nearly $15 million in sales associated with Black labor for a government contractor firm. This number is 6 percent of the total sales for a government contractor. A lot of money is positively associated with Black labor.

Regarding firms that are not contractors, table 5.6 contains the regression data. The results for table 5.6 show that for non-contractors no statistical relationship exists between Black employment and any of the financial, market, or productivity measures of firm performance. The numbers in table 5.7 are calculated using the information from table 5.6 with the same method of calculation in table 5.3. Compare tables 5.5 and 5.7. Notice that contractors have more employees and greater sales than non-contractors, that is, contractors are larger. Griffin did not take this factor into account when he compared contractors and non-contractors.

Consider the profit margin, the proverbial bottom line that everyone can understand. On average, non-contractors lost money, and contractors made money. Notice another strange phenomenon that has been constant when comparing contractors with non-contractors: non-contractor firms have more Black workers than do contractors because non-contractors hire more Black female workers and pay lower wages than do contractors.

Who pays more for Black labor, and how much affirmative action costs, if affirmative action costs are the difference paid for Black labor by contractors and non-contractors, are the next questions to consider. The return on capital for contractors in table 5.5 indicates that worst-case costs are $19 million, or .8 percent of sales. Worst-case costs for non-contractors in table 5.7 is only $3 million, or .2 percent of sales. The difference between .2 percent and .8 percent is .6 percent. On average, government contractors pay .6 percent (six-tenths of 1 percent) of sales for the privilege of working as a government contractor. This rate is almost exactly the same as the .7 percent of sales calculated for Griffin's findings.

Table 5.7
The Cost of Black Employment for Non-Contractors, 1990–2002

	Model 1	Model 2	Model 3	Model 4	Model 5	Model 6
	Return on Capital	Return on Equity	Return on Assets	Profit Margin	Market to Book Value	Sales per Employee
Average Return	3%	.9%	-.1%	-3.5%	2.39 ratio	$189,401
Average Number of Employees[1]	5,372	5,282	5,314	5,360	5,135	5,295
Black Employment	9.7%	9.5%	9.5%	9.6%	9.5%	9.5%

Table 5.7

The Cost of Black Employment for Non-Contractors, 1990–2002

Value of Denominator[2]	$699,504,500	$401,364,800	$1,813,680,000	$1,182,939,000	Not applicable	Not applicable
Total Sales for Each Firm per Year	$1,078,377,000	$1,172,685,000	$1,156,988,000	$1,182,939,000	$1,149,887,000	$1,154,262,000
Worst-Case Loss/Gain per Firm[3]	-$3,072,223	-$1,080,072	Not available	Not available[6]	1.54	-$8,414
Average Loss/Gain per Firm[4]	+$2,636,457	+$427496	Not available	Not available	2.39	+$4,883
Best-Case Loss/Gain per Firm[5]	+$6,214,705	+$1,548,779	Not available	Not available	4.93	+$18,180
Worst-Case Loss for Total Black Employment as Percentage of Sales for the Firm	.2% (two-tenths of 1 percent)	.09% (nine hundredths of 1 percent)	Not available	Not available	Not applicable	Not applicable
Number of Observations	6,695	8,160	8,116	8,142	8,188	8,201
Number of Firms	2,822	3,343	3,291	3,316	3,371	3,350

1. From EEOC; COMPUSTAT employment figures are generally higher. 2. The denominator is capital, equity, assets, or sales for the respective column. 3. This is the calculated value at the lower 95 percent confidence interval for a two-tailed test for the total complement of Black employment. 4. This is the calculated value at the regression coefficient for the total complement of Black employment. 5. This is the calculated value at the upper 95 percent confidence interval for a two-tailed test for the total complement of Black employment. 6. Since the average firm did not earn a profit or a return, computing the average profit margin or rate of return for Black labor becomes nonsensical. Source: Author's calculations from proprietary database created from EEOC confidential files, Standard and Poor's COMPUSTAT, University of Chicago Center for Research in Security Prices and Barry T. Hirsh unionization database.

The dollar amount is also very close. Griffin found that contractors paid $26 million more in wages than non-contractors. Tables 5.5 and 5.7 find that contractors pay about $16 million more. Subtracting the worst-case return on capital costs in table 5.5 for contractors ($19,567,169) from the same for non-contractors ($3,072,223) in table 5.7 results in $16.4 million, about .002 percent (two-tenths of 1 percent) of the average $1 billion in sales for these firms.

Griffin assumed the higher costs for contractors came from affirmative action's inefficiency. His conclusion cannot be realistic because Black workers for contractors in table 5.5, even in a worst-case situation, are associated with higher productivity. The same is not the case for non-contractors in table 5.7. No wonder the market views a government contract with its affirmative action guidelines and oversight as a plus. A government contract is associated with increased performance for firms in almost every measure (financial, market, and productivity), regardless of the slightly higher costs to administer the programs. From this point forward, affirmative action costing at or around 1 percent of sales should not cause any alarm whatsoever.

Direct costs by the federal government concern the EEOC and OFCCP, the two agencies tasked with most affirmative action monitoring. The entire mission of these two agencies is not strictly racial, of course (OFCCP also sets goals for gender affirmative action). Taking a rough estimate of the yearly racial case load, multiplied by the yearly budget for the EEOC ($139 million) and OFCCP ($67 million) in 2000, reveals that together those two agencies spend $206 million per year on affirmative action enforcement. Using New York as a model for state government direct costs, New York's Human Rights Division spends $10 million each year on antidiscrimination enforcement and monitoring, $1 million of which comes from the EEOC. If all fifty states spent the same as New York, the total would be $450 million, but most spend far less; hence this cost is a worst-case scenario. Thus, total state and federal government spending is less than $1 billion.

AGAINST THE CLOCK: AFFIRMATIVE ACTION COSTS OVER TIME

The reasonable conclusion from the above analysis is that when firms pay even as much as .8 percent of their sales costs for affirmative action, Black employment, or government contractor status, it is not due to the lower productivity of Black workers. In all likelihood, administrative costs have risen.

Figure 5.1 shows the worst-case costs for financial performance (return on capital) for government contractors and non-contractors. Contractors consistently outperformed non-contractors over the entire thirteen-year period from 1990 to 2002. Notice that contractors and non-contractors are influenced by the same events; their financial fortunes generally rise and fall together.

Figure 5.1 Worst-Case Gain or Loss from Return on Capital for Black Employment, 1990–2002

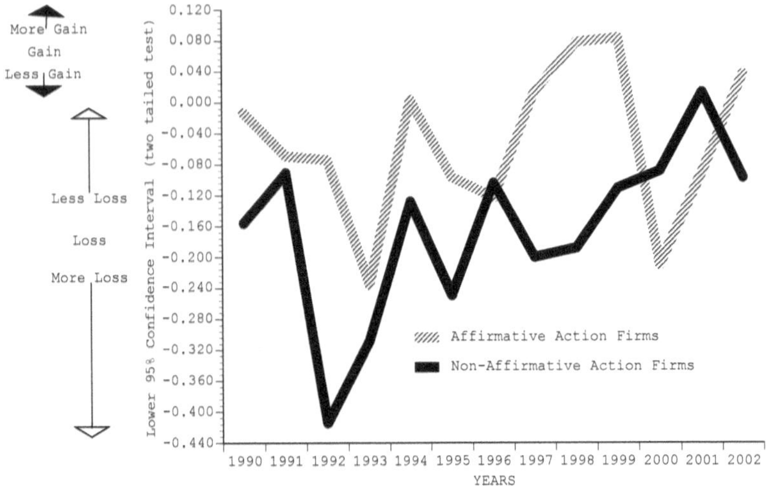

N=14,688. Results from OLS regression. Independent variable=return on capital. Dependent variables include percent of Black employees, total employment, capitalization intensity, total sales, assets, unionization, firm-specific rush, industry, and region. Source: Author's calculations from proprietary database created from EEOC confidential files, Standard and Poor's COMPUSTAT, University of Chicago Center for Research in Security Prices and Barry T. Hirsh unionization database.

Figure 5.2 shows market performance over time for contractors and non-contractors. The same results occur as in figure 5.1. Affirmative action firms outperform non–affirmative action firms and have consistently higher market to book value. Except for a few years, the railroad-track effect is present, as described in chapter 2, and indicates that both groups are subject to the same economic factors.

Figure 5.2 Worst-Case Market to Book Ratio for Black Employment, 1990–2002

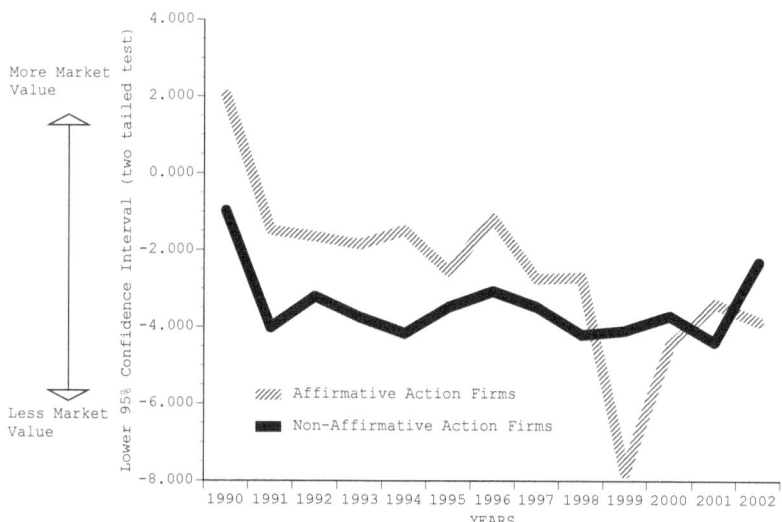

N=19,163. Results from OLS regression. Independent variable=market to book value of the firm. Dependent variables include percent of Black employees, total employment, capitalization intensity, total sales, assets, unionization, firm-specific rush, industry, and region. Source: Author's calculations from proprietary database created from EEOC confidential files, Standard and Poor's COMPUSTAT, University of Chicago Center for Research in Security Prices and Barry T. Hirsh unionization database.

Figure 5.3 measures productivity performance associated with Black employment for contractors and non-contractors from 1990 through 2002. Even though the productivity associated with Black workers for both contractors and non-contractors rises and falls together, the lines never meet. Contractors consistently have higher, not lower, productivity associated with their Black workers than do non-contractors.

Figure 5.3 Worst-Case Sales per Employee for Black Employment, 1990–2002

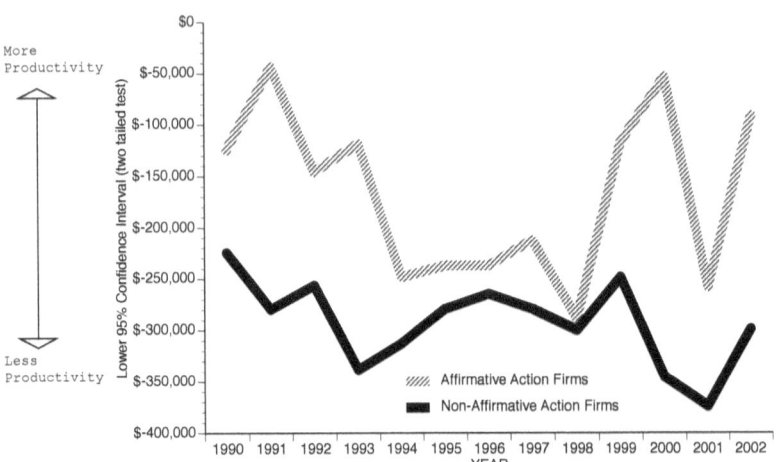

N=19,236. Results from OLS regression. Independent variable=sales per employee. Dependent variables include percent of Black employees, total employment, capitalization intensity, total sales, assets, unionization, firm-specific rush, industry, and region. Source: Author's calculations from proprietary database created from EEOC confidential files, Standard and Poor's COMPUSTAT, University of Chicago Center for Research in Security Prices and Barry T. Hirsh unionization database.

FORCED TO OUTPERFORM

White popular wisdom asserts that affirmative action causes unqualified Blacks, or less qualified Blacks, over better qualified whites, to get jobs, promotions, or admission into universities. Black popular wisdom holds that to have a job nearly equal to a white person, Blacks must be more qualified.

Considering employment rather than education is important for two reasons. First, grades and test scores are notorious for their lack of relationship to on-the-job performance.[38] Second, the education market generally feeds into the labor market, not vice versa, so the place to look for outcomes from education is in the labor market.

Black popular wisdom and white popular wisdom seem to be on a collision course. Perhaps it is possible for both to be correct. Given the nearly polar opposites of the views of Blacks and whites in response to GSS questions about "What do you think the chances are these days that a White person won't get a job or promotion while an equally or less qualified Black

38. Coleman, "African American Popular Wisdom."

person gets one instead?," it is difficult to imagine such a middle ground, however. If whites are correct about less qualified Blacks, a way must be available to measure the lower performance level of Blacks against whites in equal jobs.

When pushed about the impact of discrimination on racial inequality in the 2016 GSS, nearly two-thirds of whites said inequality was not due to discrimination, while nearly two-thirds of Blacks said racial inequality was due to discrimination.[39] Any election with two-thirds of the vote for one candidate would be considered a landslide. A middle ground does not work here. The numbers are equally telling on which popular wisdom wins. Blacks consistently outperform whites.

Most of the evidence points to discrimination as the major factor that encourages Black workers to be so productive and outperform their white counterparts. The higher productivity of Black workers is not caused by firm location, physical or financial size, product market sector, geographic location, capitalization intensity, unionization, percentage of blue collar workers, or market volatility. All of these factors were matched in the calculations. That means the normal explanations do not fit.

Given what much of the literature has had to say about discrimination in labor markets, the higher relative education Black workers have, the longer Black workers remain in their positions, the closer supervision, and the lower promotion rate, Black workers are probably better at their jobs because they are discriminated against. Black popular wisdom shows up in the statistical measures. Blacks work longer and harder than comparable whites do, and they make money for their firms even though Black workers earn less money. White workers are promoted on the basis of their promise; Black workers are promoted only on the basis of their proven performance. Two very different standards.[40]

Tables 5.2 and 5.3 also support these conclusions about the relationship of market performance to affirmative action and Black employment. On average, Black employment is associated with an increase of the market to book ratio. Even the worst case has only a small, 7 percent (.21) decline from 2.91 to 2.7. The market views Black employment positively.

---

39. T. Smith et al., "General Social Surveys, 1972–2016," variable racdif1.

40. Dickens and Dickens, *Black Manager*, 49; Feagin, *Racist America*, 135; Feagin and Sikes, *Living with Racism*, ch. 4; Jencks, *Rethinking Social Policy*, 26; Mays and Nicholson, "Genius of the Negro Church"; Scott and Shaw, "Black and White Performance"; Tomaskovic-Devey, *Gender and Racial Inequality*, 99; R. Williams and Kenison, "Way We Were?"; Mason, "Race, Culture, and Skill"; Bridges and Villemez, "Overeducated Minority Workers."

The 1977 Arthur Anderson Business Roundtable report in table 5.1 found that firms spent .1 percent of sales for affirmative action with no loss of productivity. Griffin's costs for affirmative action were calculated as .7 percent of sales. Table 5.2 worst-case costs for affirmative action (return on capital) are .4 percent of sales for the firms in this study. We know these small costs have no impact on productivity because sales per employee are always positive, even in a worst-case situation.

Table 5.2 confirms almost all information from prior studies of affirmative action. The market evaluates Black employment positively; Black workers seem to understand that they face significant obstacles that whites do not have. Even though Blacks earn significantly less than whites for equivalent jobs, their efforts show that their work is associated with higher firm sales per employee—and greater productivity. There is no indication that firms pay even small administrative costs for affirmative action. Depending on the financial measures used in table 5.2, on average, firms make money from Black employment.

Only in the later years, after the effects of the attacks on affirmative action programs by the Supreme Court in *Adarand v. Peña* (1995) and California's Proposition 209 (1996) began to be felt, did government contractors begin to lose some of their financial performance advantages in financial and market performance. That is, the attacks against affirmative action and attempts to dismantle it increased, rather than decreased, the costs to more efficient government contractors. Affirmative action seems to have experienced more rending than mending in the Clinton years. This is unfortunate because affirmative action was broken only in the minds of whites. Nevertheless, white popular wisdom could have no impact on the productivity performance advantage of the Black workforce. President Johnson's Executive Order 11246 was firmly based on the reality of the efficiency of Black workers and affirmative action policy in employment. President Trump's Executive Order 14173 revoking 11246 and calling DEI dangerous, demeaning, and immoral is based on white popular wisdom, which is not supported by the evidence. No nation can long survive with policies that have no basis in reality.

Black popular wisdom is well grounded in social and economic fact. Only the discrimination lingers.

Chapter Six

The Price of Wage Discrimination, Poverty, and Wealth Inequality

POVERTY, WEALTH, AND WAGES: THE GREAT RECESSION AND COVID-19

Most white people believe that inequality in jobs, income, and housing between Blacks and whites is caused by the personal failure of Blacks themselves. This view may be the reason most whites believe it is not the job of the government to rectify the situation. The overwhelming majority of people, regardless of race, believe that poverty is caused by a lack of effort. The evidence on wage discrimination, poverty, and wealth, however, does not support the idea that poverty is caused by laziness or indolence.[1]

Evidence indicates that racial inequality in wages, disproportionate Black poverty, and wealth inequality are caused by historic and contemporary racial discrimination. If racial inequality in income, wages, and wealth are caused by racial discrimination, and the government does not attempt to eliminate racial discrimination in these areas, the eventual costs to all of us will exceed greatly what we might have paid for affirmative action, if there were indeed any costs to affirmative action at all.

Figure 6.1 shows the increases in poverty for all races from the Great Recession of December 2007 to June 2009. In 2007, before the recession occurred, poverty stood at 12.5 percent for all people. In 2010, after the official recession had passed, poverty for all people had increased to 15.1 percent. However, as late as 2016, poverty levels had not returned to prerecession levels. Overall poverty rates did not return to pre–Great Recession levels of

---

1. T. Smith et al., "General Social Surveys, 1972–2010," variables race, racdif4, whypoor4, helpblk.

around 10.5 percent until 2017–18. Then came the COVID-19 pandemic. Poverty during COVID did tick up from 10.5 percent in 2019 to 11.5 percent in 2020 and remains at COVID levels from the latest figures. Notice also in figure 6.1 the now-familiar railroad-track effect. Black and white poverty rise and fall together, but never meet, indicating they are caused by the same factors, with only racial factors keeping them from meeting.

Figure 6.1 Poverty and Race in the US, 1959–2022

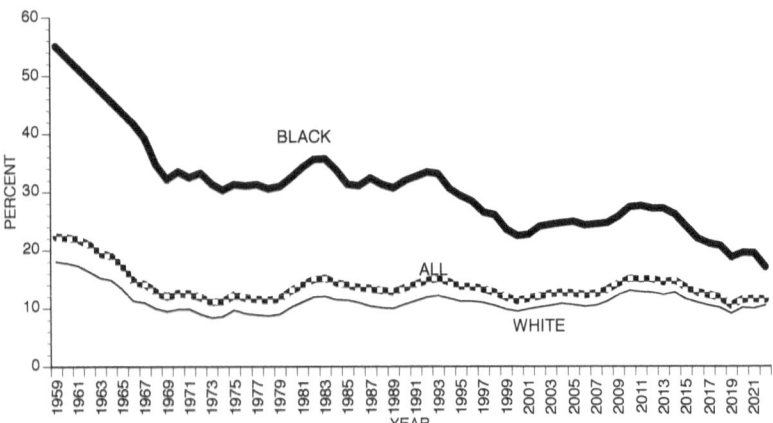

Source: Current Population Survey Datasets, Annual Social and Economic Supplements. For information on confidentiality protection, sampling error, non-sampling error, and definitions, see U.S. Census Bureau, *Current Population Survey*, table 2, "Poverty Status of People by Family Relationship, Race, and Hispanic Origin: 1959 to 2022."

Figure 6.2 makes the ratio for Black to white poverty easier to see. The ratio of Black poverty has fallen from the highs of 3 to 3.5 times (350 percent) that of white poverty in the mid-1960s to about 1.5 times (162 percent) the rate of white poverty in 2022. From 1959 to 2022 the Black poverty ratio has been between 3 times and 1.5 times that of whites. Black and white poverty are at their closest point in US history.

Figure 6.2 Ratio of Black to White Poverty in the US, 1959–2022

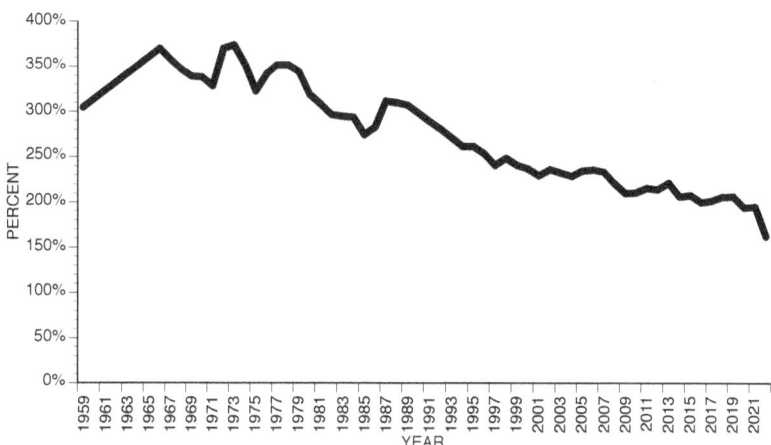

Source: Current Population Survey Datasets, Annual Social and Economic Supplements. For information on confidentiality protection, sampling error, non-sampling error, and definitions, see U.S. Census Bureau, *Current Population Survey*, table 2, "Poverty Status of People by Family Relationship, Race, and Hispanic Origin: 1959 to 2022."

In 2018, almost a quarter (24.5 percent) of the American population, over 79.8 million people, were considered to be poor or near to poverty at 175 percent of the poverty line ($35,000 per year for a family of three).[2] The resistance of the Black to white poverty ratio to change, the high percentage of all Americans who are poor or nearly poor, suggests that, unlike the ideas of most Americans, most higher rates of Black poverty are systemic and not caused by personal failures. The same is true for wealth and wage inequality: the Black to white ratios are constant through many economic cycles and indicate the presence of a racial discrimination factor.

Given what we know of the politico-economic impact of the Great Recession on other nations and the US, we may reasonably assume that racial wealth inequality, disproportionate poverty for Blacks, and wage discrimination based on race will cost all Americans dearly. The COVID-19 pandemic; the Great Recession; the political turmoil in the Middle East called the Arab Spring; the politico-economic crises in Greece, Spain, and the European Union; and the roiling boiling worldwide protests over anti-Black

---

2. For information on confidentiality protection, sampling error, non-sampling error, and definitions, see U.S. Census Bureau, *Current Population Survey: 2019 Supplement*, table 5, "Percent of People by Ratio of Income to Poverty Level: 1970 to 2018."

police abuse since the Black Lives Matter movement demonstrate that economic inequality may impact an entire polis, not just out-groups.[3]

Racial wealth inequality, disproportionate poverty for Blacks and Latinos, and wage discrimination based on race costs all of us because the whole society and culture are diminished when a large number of citizens, such as these minorities, are not productively engaged. This situation was true in 1969, and it seems to be just as true today. In 1966, Thurow estimated that while whites gained $15 billion from employment discrimination in 1960 (approximately $131 billion in 2020 dollars), overall "the total potential output of the country is always less, since productive resources are inefficiently allocated." And that because of these high losses, "eliminating government discrimination has the highest priority since it is the most effective weapon to create and enforce many of the monopoly powers that are behind the different types of discrimination." By "government discrimination" Thurow means lax antidiscrimination enforcement.[4] Locking people out of wealth means they have nothing to invest in their future. People without a future for themselves or their families have little reason to support the system. People outside the system are ripe for dissension and revolt. A large potentially revolutionary mass can destabilize any society.

To avoid the conditions that might lead to race war, permanent racial inequality, and a threat to our democracy, we need to know, at minimum, the relative financial costs for racial wealth inequality, disproportionate poverty for Blacks, and racial wage discrimination. This information will reveal whether affirmative action costs are reasonable in relation to higher priced options such as trying to fix wealth, wage, and poverty discrimination. Most of the evidence shows that not only are gaps in wealth, poverty, and wages caused by racial discrimination, but also the financial price to close these gaps is far greater than worst-case Black affirmative action costs to whites.

MEASURING WAGE DISCRIMINATION COSTS

Historic evidence, surveys, job audits, and the most common statistical modeling can help measure wage discrimination. Advocates who claim massive racial wage discrimination in US labor markets usually create regression models, which match for race, demographics, labor market, and human capital factors. Any wage residual between Black and white workers is evidence of racial discrimination.

3. Carlo and Sadian, "Arab Spring"; Puddington, *Freedom in the World 2012*.
4. Thurow, *Poverty and Discrimination*, 133–34, 138.

THE PRICE OF WAGE DISCRIMINATION

Other economists counter, however, that these racial wage differences need not evince racial discrimination at all. Rather, in all likelihood, some claim, missing skill variables not included in the statistical models must be factored by employers into pay scales.[5]

This dispute probably never will be settled. Nearly all of the evidence, however, supports the claim that statistical models are indeed measuring the impact of racial discrimination in wages and not racial skill differences.

First, aside from racial discrimination, both historic and contemporary, no conceivable reason is evident for Black differences in human capital, demographics, or labor market characteristics unless skin color alone makes people think and act differently. Blacks are the only racial group that still lives primarily in the Southern United States. What could cause demographic difference, other than their historic connection to Southern slavery, is unclear. Chapter 5 showed conclusively that Blacks do not lack skill for their jobs compared to whites.

The Italian immigrants came to the American urban North, a region quite unlike their roots in southern Italy, which was warm and primarily agricultural. Little Italian migration occurred in the American South, which was more closely aligned with their Italian homeland. Historic legacies have consequences. Because of this, statistical models match for region. Why Blacks in the South, with the same education and age, and who work in the same industry, still would earn less than similar whites, other than the legacy of slavery, is a question worth much consideration. This is a historical assumption, but it does not stand alone.

Second, the evidence in figure 3.6 shows that in the late 1970s and early 1980s, Black women almost reached wage parity with white females. If skill variables were missing in the economic models, Black females earned considerably more than white females. This conclusion is unlikely.[6]

Third, MCSUI offers the ability to measure skill directly. The MCSUI employer survey asked supervisors, whose own job performance depends on their ability to evaluate subordinates, to rate an employee. The MCSUI employer survey asked employers: "On a scale of 0–100 where 50 is average and 100 is the best score, how would you rate this employee's performance in this job?" The survey then asked employers: "On a scale of 0–100, how would you rate the typical employee's performance in this job?" The competitive performance rating calculation occurred by subtracting the score on the former question from the score on the latter question.

---

5. See Coleman: "Job Skill"; "Racism in Academia," for a discussion.
6. Coleman, "Strategic Equality," 33.

THE COST OF RACIAL EQUALITY

When Black and white employees are matched for their competitive performance rating, wages for Blacks drop even further behind whites. Discrimination might cause little increase in the wages of Blacks, who have the same skill as whites, but logically, wages should not decline for equally skilled Blacks. The prevalence of wage discrimination suggests that skilled Blacks seem to be punished for their skill.[7]

Fourth, statistical models seem to be correctly capturing wage discrimination because the researchers claiming that the wage gaps are not evidence of discrimination use nearly identical models and claim they can capture skill deficiencies. A few years ago, a group of white researchers were claiming the Armed Forces Qualification Test (a measure of skill) and other variables explained nearly all income differences between white and Black families. The implication was that racial inequality was caused by skill deficiencies in Black families, not from racial discrimination by whites. However, several Black researchers later matched for the age that respondents took the AFQT, and the income gaps reappeared.[8]

Table 6
Wages on Race, Human Capital, Demographics, Labor Market, and Poverty, 2006
(standard errors in parenthesis)

	Model 1	Model 2	Model 3	Model 4	Model 5
	Race	Human Capital	Demographics	Labor Market	Poverty
Black	-10397****	-5793****	-4462****	-3718****	-3261****
	(492)	(465)	(466)	(444)	(445)
Latino	-14061****	558	-556	-1153***	-800**
	(410)	(409)	(410)	(391)	(391)
Age		413****	398****	251****	242****
		(11.1)	(10.9)	(10.5)	(10.5)
Education		5147****	5247****	3751****	3697****
		(52.0)	(50.9)	(56.9)	(57.0)
Sex			18046****	13557****	13475****
			(278)	(306)	(306)
Midwest			-3919****	-4254****	-4148****
			(417)	(394)	(394)
South			-768*	-2201****	-2148****
			(398)	(377)	(377)
West			-1589****	-1872****	-1829****

7. Coleman, "Job Skill."
8. Coleman, "Racism in Academia."

Table 6

Wages on Race, Human Capital, Demographics, Labor Market, and Poverty, 2006 (standard errors in parenthesis)

	Model 1	Model 2	Model 3	Model 4	Model 5
	Race	Human Capital	Demographics	Labor Market	Poverty
			(422)	(400)	(399)
Professional				-9477****	-9481****
				(500)	(499)
Service				-19622****	-19286****
				(542)	(542)
Sales				-14527****	-14339****
				(595)	(594)
Admin Support				-20142****	-20239****
				(520)	(519)
Farming, Fishing, Forestry				707	894
				(1762)	(1761)
Construction				-21887****	-21691****
				(841)	(840)
Install/Maint/Repair				-20640****	-20666****
				(799)	(798)
Production				-23808****	-23676****
				(709)	(708)
Transportation				-23363****	-23222****
				(701)	(701)
Armed Forces				10802	9438
				(9776)	(9766)
Mining				47968****	47482****
				(2065)	(2063)
Construction				28604****	28246****
				(1362)	(1360)
Manufacturing				35779****	35369****
				(1262)	(1261)
Trade				27973****	27568****
				(1252)	(1251)

Table 6

Wages on Race, Human Capital, Demographics, Labor Market, and Poverty, 2006 (standard errors in parenthesis)

	Model 1	Model 2	Model 3	Model 4	Model 5
	Race	Human Capital	Demographics	Labor Market	Poverty
Trans/Comm/Util				35073****	34630****
				(1340)	(1338)
Information				33366****	32970****
				(1468)	(1467)
Financial				36181****	35733****
				(1280)	(1279)
Professional Services				32455****	32183****
				(1255)	(1254)
Education and Health				26054****	25639****
				(1244)	(1243)
Leisure				25133****	24886****
				(1293)	(1292)
Other Service				22999****	22741****
				(1336)	(1335)
Public Admin				32614****	32105****
				(1335)	(1334)
Armed Forces				dropped	dropped
Part Time, Full Year				-20310****	-19882****
				(459)	(459)
Full Time, Part Year				-15988****	-15282****
				(433)	(435)
Part Time, Part Year				-27749****	-26795****
				(542)	(545)
Nonworker				-32271****	-29853****
				(758)	(776)
Poverty					-7981****
					(558)

Table 6

Wages on Race, Human Capital, Demographics, Labor Market, and Poverty, 2006 (standard errors in parenthesis)

	Model 1	Model 2	Model 3	Model 4	Model 5
	Race	Human Capital	Demographics	Labor Market	Poverty
Constant	40006****	-49199****	-57790****	-36519****	-34961****
	(175)	(845)	(895)	(1540)	(1542)
Adjusted R Squared	.0150	.1258	.1642	.2561	.2577
N	93,755	93,755	93,755	93,755	93,755

*p=10%; **p=5%; ***p=1%; ****p=<.1%, two-tailed test. Omitted categories are whites, northeast, managers, agriculture, full time full year. Predicted value of white wages is $40,006.48. Source: Current Population Survey Datasets. Unicon Research Corporation 1640 Fifth Street, Suite 100, Santa Monica, CA 90401 (producer and distributor of CPS Utilities), Washington, DC.

Statistical models appear to be capturing wage discrimination that is all too real. Statistical models that control for race, human capital, demographics, and labor market differences consistently show Black and Latino losses that exceed any gains they may receive from affirmative action.

Table 6.1 is a statistical analysis of wages regressed on racial categories, human capital, demographics, labor market characteristics, and poverty. Whites are the omitted category, which means that the other races, Blacks and Latinos, are compared to the omitted group: whites. Model 1 matches groups only by their race. In table 6, model 1, Black workers receive $10,397 less per year than do white workers. A worker is defined as someone in the workforce, even if temporarily not working. Table 6 computes these figures using the CPS for 2006. Multiplying racial wage discrimination times the Black civilian labor force in 2006 (17,314,000 people) results in a figure of $180 billion, far more than the $51 billion worst-case affirmative action costs found in chapter 5 and very close to Thurow's estimates of $131 billion for gains to whites from discrimination in the 1960s.

More difference exists between white and Black workers than skin color, however. White workers generally bring more human capital to the job. Usually age and education come to mind as measures of skill. Table 6, model 2, controls for race and human capital. If Blacks and whites have the same human capital, Black wages are $5,793 per year less than whites. Multiplying by the same number of Blacks in the labor force above used in model 1 gives us a cost to Blacks for wage discrimination of $100 billion. The cost to Blacks from discrimination is far higher than any costs to whites from affirmative action, even if such affirmative action costs existed, and they probably do not.

Table 6, model 3, matches workers for race, human capital, and demographics. The average Black worker is female; the average white worker is male. Blacks live primarily in the South, with lower wages. When we match these demographics and other factors, the cost to Blacks for wage discrimination is $4,462 per year per worker. That number ($4,462) times the number of Black civilians in the labor force in 2006 (17,314,000 people) results in a figure of $77 billion in losses to Blacks from wage discrimination.

Table 6, model 4, matches workers for race, human capital, demographics, and labor market differences. Blacks and whites have different occupations and work in different industries. In addition, more Black workers are out of work. Matching these variables in table 6, model 4, does not substantially lessen the blow from anti-Black discrimination, which equals $3,718 per worker and totals $64 billion for all Black workers. Blacks lose more from wage discrimination than any worst-case losses to society from affirmative action.

EDUCATION AND THE LAW OF DIMINISHING RETURNS

If racial skill differences form the basis of racial wage differences, more skills should close the gaps, but they do not. Figure 6.3 shows graphically what happens to Blacks who strive for the top; many end up at the bottom. In this regard, not much has changed for Blacks since the 1960s.

Figure 6.3 Black Male Wages as a Percentage of White Male Wages by Years of Education, 1966–2006

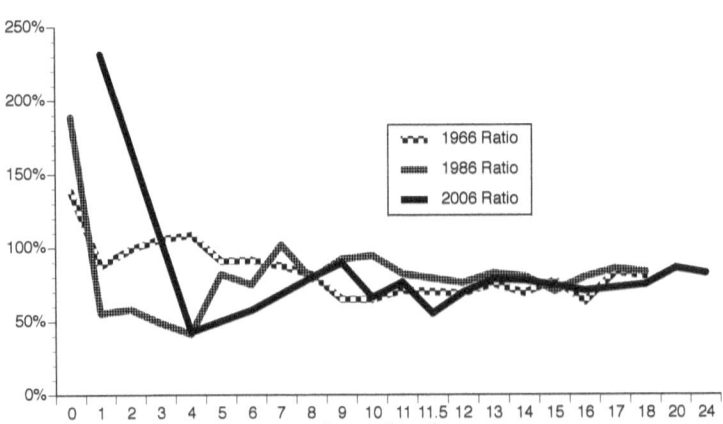

Source: Current Population Survey Datasets, 1962–2006. Conducted by the Bureau of the Census for the Bureau of Labor Statistics. Washington, DC: Bureau of the Census (producer and distributor), 1962–2006. Santa Monica: Unicon Research Corporation (producer and distributor of CPS Utilities), 2006.

Figure 6.3 shows the ratio of Black male wages as a percentage of white male wages by years of education. In 1966, Black men with less than four years of education made as much or more than similar white men. After five years of education, however, a Black man found himself falling further and further behind his white male colleagues. If he managed to graduate from college and go to graduate school, he made only about 80 percent of the income of a white male with the same education as his. These statistics raise the question of why Blacks would continue to try to advance against the law of diminishing returns.

Twenty years later, a Black man's son would face the same problems his father faced. In 1986, only Black men with less than five years of education made as much or more than similarly educated white men. The reason Black men with little education do so well relative to whites is that more Black men with little education work, while fewer white men with little education work.

If a Black man thought his grandson would advance by getting a good education, he was also wrong. By 2006, Black men were in the same position relative to white men as they were in 1966. In figure 6.3, for 2006, after about nine years of education, Black men start falling further and further behind in wages against white men with similar education. With a postgraduate degree such a man almost has hit rock bottom, with his earnings at some of the lowest wages relative to white men, about 75–82 percent. What is so amazing is the resilience of Black workers who continue to outproduce their white colleagues in spite of the odds (see model 6 in table 5.2 and fig. 5.3).

THE PRICE OF POVERTY

Labor market discrimination costs Blacks more than disproportionate poverty, but the price of poverty to Blacks and to society is still very high. In 2008, 39,829,000 people, or 13.2 percent of the population, were below poverty. Of those, 9,882,000 were Black (24.6 percent of the Black population) and 10,987,000 were Latino (23.2 percent of the Latino population). Since half of the poor are Black or Latino, minorities are disproportionately poor, since in 2001 Blacks and Latinos comprise just 27 percent of the population.[9]

How much of racial inequality is due to this disproportionate poverty is the next question to consider. Median family income in 2006 for whites, Blacks, and Latinos, respectively, was $60,400, $31,875, and

9. Current Population Survey Datasets, table 2, "Poverty Status of People by Family Relationship, Race, and Hispanic Origin: 1959 to 2008."

$35,000. Removing the poor from the averages results in family income of $65,600, $43,456, and $45,000 respectively for whites, Blacks, and Latinos. Thus, higher poverty rates cost Black and Latino families about 20 percent ($6,381/$31,875) and 14 percent ($4,800/$35,000), respectively, of their family income compared to whites. Multiplied by the 8.6 million Black families, disproportionate poverty costs Blacks $54.8 billion. Multiplied by the 7.5 million Latino families in 2000, disproportionate poverty costs Latino families $36 billion per year for a total of $91 billion per year for both Blacks and Latinos.[10]

Living outside the labor force has a similar impact. Lower labor force participation rates (LFPRs) cost Black families about 7 percent ($2,312/$31,875) of their family incomes, about $19.8 billion per year. Not participating in the labor force had no impact on Latino family incomes: Latinos gained about 3 percent ($1,212/$35,000), or $9 billion in family income, as opposed to white families because Latinos have higher LFPRs than whites. This figure totals $10.7 billion, if multiplied by the 8.6 million Black families and 7.5 million Latino families in 2000.[11]

Because the poverty threshold is artificially low, many social scientists use the poverty threshold plus 50 percent as a more realistic estimate of who is poor. Taking all those who are within 150 percent of the poverty line, and subtracting them from average family incomes, white, Black, and Latino families earn $70,130, $50,900, and $52,010 respectively. This more realistic poverty level costs Blacks almost 30 percent of their family incomes ([$70,130–$60,400]-[$50,900–$31,875]=$9,295; $9,295/$31,875) and Latinos 20 percent ($7,280/$35,000) of their family income. Multiplied by the 8.6 million Black families and 7.5 million Latino families in 2000, that number reaches approximately $134 billion per year, or approximately $44 billion more than the official poverty thresholds cost Blacks and Latinos. Poverty is an important marker, and counting everyone who was within 150 percent over the poverty line encompassed over 20 percent of the US population in 2018.[12] A family of three with $19,995 or less was poor in 2018. Nearly poor for a family of three in 2018 was a little less than $30,000 per year.[13] Anyone can imagine trying to pay rent, electricity, heating, and

---

10. Current Population Survey Datasets; Fields and Casper, *America's Families*.

11. Current Population Survey Datasets; Fields and Casper, *America's Families*.

12. For information on confidentiality protection, sampling error, non-sampling error, and definitions, see U.S. Census Bureau, *Current Population Survey: 2019 Supplement*, table 5, "Percent of People By Ratio of Income to Poverty Level: 1970 to 2018."

13. For information on confidentiality protection, sampling error, non-sampling error, and definitions, see U.S. Census Bureau, *Current Population Survey: 2019 Supplement*, table 1, "Weighted Average Poverty Thresholds for Families of Specified Size:

air conditioning and buy clothes and food for three people in any American city on less than $30,000 per year would be challenging. Owning a car, having healthcare, cable TV, a cell phone, vacations, a college education, and a host of other items some people take for granted would have to be eliminated if one is poor or even nearly poor.

Be aware that poverty and existing outside the labor market are not mutually exclusive categories. Many of the poor are outside the labor market, and many of those outside the labor market are poor. Also, remember that the figures cited above are only the cost for the disproportionate—that is, higher levels of poverty and lack of labor force participation that Blacks and Latinos have in comparison to whites, not the total cost for poverty and living outside the labor force.

The total cost for poverty is far greater than simply considering the disproportionate poverty of Blacks and Latinos. Per CPS data, in 2006, poor Black families had $45,028 less income than nonpoor Black families. Not joining the labor force cost a family $12,829, and racial discrimination took a $26,847 bite out of a Black family's income. A white poor family bore a cost of $69,453 in income compared to nonpoor white families in 2006. Being poor or living outside the labor force is expensive, no matter what the race.

Rather than measuring from the bottom up (the cost of food times three), most international agencies measure from the middle down: assessing what percentage of the median income the poor make. Reasonably, anyone with less than 60 percent of the median income in their nation is poor. In 2006, the median poor family had an income of only $8,240 compared to the nonpoor median family income of $60,000. To bring all the 28.5 million poor families in America in 2008 up to 60 percent of the median family income would cost $27,760 per poor family for a total of $791 billion. Three-quarters of a trillion dollars is a lot of money, but still it is not high-cost equality.[14]

CHOOSE YOUR PARENTS VERY CAREFULLY

Because most wealth is inherited, wealth inequality measures the effects of not only the current social, political, and economic discrimination, but also the past racial discrimination. Americans seem fascinated with wealth, and no wonder, wealth is extremely rare. In their *New York Times* bestseller

---

1959 to 2018."

14. Current Population Survey Datasets, table 2, "Poverty Status of People by Family Relationship, Race, and Hispanic Origin: 1959 to 2008."

The Millionaire Next Door, Stanley and Danko surveyed households with a net worth of between $1 and $10 million and listed their occupations, businesses, and spending habits. Stanley and Danko said that "this level of wealth can be attained in one generation. It can be attained by many Americans." The list of factors that make a person a millionaire reads like a classic lesson in American rugged individualism: live below your means, be efficient, strive for financial independence before social status, do not rely on parents, have independent adult children, target market opportunities, and choose the right occupation.[15]

While Stanley and Danko do not specifically say that anyone can make it big in America, this is implied. Stanley and Danko try hard to show that the millionaire next door is similar to the average person, but their own information belies this claim. Over half of their millionaires had college paid for by their parents; 95 percent have a bachelor's degree, and the average education is graduate school; a high percentage received an inheritance (we are not told how many); and nearly 20 percent inherited over $100,000.

Stanley and Danko's claims are difficult to imagine. First, even though Stanley and Danko claim they surveyed 11,000 people and conducted focus groups with 500, none of the millionaires is Black, Latino, or Asian. Second, the 11,000 respondents figure is close to the number of respondents in the SIPP database. Third, 58 percent of all whites in the General Social Survey name more than one country of ancestry or do not know their ancestry, yet all of Stanley and Danko's respondents seem to know their ancestry. Fourth, Stanley and Danko claim that 4.5 percent of their respondents are Native American, although less than 1 percent of the US population identifies themselves as of Native American ancestry.

In many surveys, most of those who claim to be Native Americans are European Americans who do not understand that their ancestry is not native to the Americas. If even some of what the authors claim is true, then their respondents come from some of the wealthiest families in the country, even if they are not what most would consider to be the superrich.

The great concentration of wealth in the hands of relatively few in the United States strongly implies that movement in and out of wealth must be extremely limited. Even Stanley and Danko admit that 3.5 percent of the population hold almost half of the wealth. Stanley and Danko provide no evidence of the occupation, education, income, or wealth of the parents of their respondents.

The Internal Revenue Service also seems interested in showing that American society is not based on concentrated, inherited, race-based

---

15. Stanley and Danko, *Millionaire Next Door*, 12.

wealth inequality. In a report on the 400 highest income tax returns, the IRS said, "Less than 25 percent of taxpayers appear more than once in the top 400 returns over the last 9 years." Such information measures only income and says nothing about wealth concentration, which the IRS does not measure in the report.[16]

The SIPP data indicate that in 1988 the top 1 percent owned 20 percent of the net financial assets and over ten times their share of net worth, at 11.6 percent. Since most of the wealth of the average individual is in the equity they have in their personal residence, the overall wealth held by the top 1 percent is understated. The SIPP data show that 43 percent of white wealth and 62.5 percent of Black wealth is in home equity. Considering only net worth, minus owner-occupied housing, yields the top 1 percent owning 48 percent of the wealth in the United States.[17]

The Federal Reserve sponsored SIPP, with nearly 12,000 households in 1987–89, and the data show that having a millionaire next door is rare for most Americans and even rarer for Black Americans. The average (median) white American family has less than $50,000 in net worth, and most of this worth is in home equity. Average (median) white families have less than $7,000 in net financial assets. Such a family could barely survive for six months, even at poverty standards, without a wage or salary. Black families have only $3,700 in median net worth, and zero net financial assets, not counting their house and their car. Whites have nearly twelve times the net worth of Blacks.[18]

The question is how important starting conditions are in terms of income, occupation, education, and parents' SES for the acquisition of wealth. Stanley and Danko fail to mention an almost indispensable ingredient to wealth: choosing the right parents.

The SIPP data show that attaining wealth is highly correlated with the occupation of parents. Respondents with white-collar parents have nearly twice the net worth of respondents with lower-blue-collar parents. Of the *Forbes* 400 richest Americans, 225 (56 percent) inherited what could be considered great wealth.[19]

Of the *Forbes* 400 who did not inherit wealth, nearly all came from elite backgrounds, attended elite schools, or had advantages that up until the 1970s were dispersed on a highly racialized basis almost exclusively to

16. Parisi and Strudler, "Highest Adjusted Gross Incomes," 7.

17. Oliver and Shapiro, *Black Wealth/White Wealth*, 64, 69; Sklar, *Chaos or Community?*, 6.

18. Oliver and Shapiro, *Black Wealth/White Wealth*, tables 4.2 and 4.4.

19. Jonathan Davis, *Forbes Richest People*. Author's analysis of the *Forbes* 400 biographies.

whites. Examples of white advantage include parents in prestigious occupations, loans from wealthy relatives, opportunities in WWII, lucky breaks in sales jobs or access to specialized training, contacts with elites, etc. These types of advantages often are referred to as cultural capital. Perhaps only 3 of the *Forbes* 400 could be considered to have come from poor, but white, backgrounds. Nevertheless, even whites who are poor have nearly the same net financial assets as high-income Blacks. Say Oliver and Shapiro, "Poverty means one thing for Whites and another for Blacks."[20]

Blacks do not have "old money." As late as 1997, not a single Black family or individual inherited wealth sufficient for the *Forbes* 400. The question is why. Blacks have been in America as long as any European American group and much longer than most South, Central, and Eastern European groups. With all the writers who imply that few structural impediments exist to even great wealth, the question still pertains: why more Blacks cannot seem to find more luck.

Oliver and Shapiro offer an answer, and that is racist government policies that have existed since before the end of slavery. These policies distribute opportunities for wealth based on race. These policies are classic examples of white affirmative action, which are rarely discussed. Even though enslaved persons were forbidden by law to have wealth, many enslaved persons were allowed to save money using the same habits of thrift and industry that Stanley and Danko mention. Often, however, enslaved persons used this money to purchase their own freedom and the freedom of loved ones.

The failure to give the freedmen their forty acres and a mule meant that they emerged from slavery with no material assets. While many of the New European groups today are proud of their rise from penniless immigrants, the conditions Blacks faced were far worse. The major differences were that Blacks were much poorer and faced continued racialized violence for nearly a century after the New Europeans arrived. Blacks found themselves trapped in the South with its low wages and lack of a voting franchise where their numbers were the greatest, and in many cases, that situation was the exact opposite for the New Europeans.[21]

Racist practices by the FHA made sure that banks made few if any loans in Black areas, and that loans were targeted for the suburbs, which kept Black buyers out. In fact, the FHA even included model restrictive covenants in its official handbook, to make sure that Blacks were kept out of white neighborhoods. Oliver and Shapiro described the housing boom

20. Oliver and Shapiro, *Black Wealth/White Wealth*, 101.
21. Lieberson, *Piece of the Pie*; Myrdal, *American Dilemma*; Steinberg, *Ethnic Myth*.

in the post-WWII era as the greatest mass wealth opportunity in US history, and it was administered in a most racist fashion. Most recently the examples of discrimination include mortgage lending, which rejects Blacks at rates two to three times more often than whites of similar income, and the discrimination against Black farmers by the US Department of Agriculture, which resulted in an almost $1 billion settlement.

In the year 2000, fewer than .37 percent (three-tenths of 1 percent) of all tax returns had incomes of over $200,000 (constant 1976 dollars). The ratio of high–income tax filers has not grown very much either, compared to the general population, but increased from .05 percent (one twentieth of 1 percent) in 1976. Of the $1.7 trillion in income for those over $200,000, less than half was in wages or salaries. Most income for high-income earners was from the sales of capital assets (property), income from partnerships and small corporations, interest, dividends, and business and professional income.[22]

Since 1962 Blacks have had wages about 59–68 percent of those earned by whites. Dividend income of Blacks, as an indicator of wealth or property ownership, however, varies from single digits in the mid-1970s to about 28 percent that of whites in 2006.[23]

Using Oliver and Shapiro's data on race and wealth inequality, the racial wealth gap in net worth (includes home equity) is $27,075 for each Black household or family. In 2000, Black families numbered 8.6 million. That number times $27,075 equals the $232.8 billion it would cost to equalize racial wealth disparity. Considering only net financial assets (and removing home equity) the wealth gap is reduced to $123 billion ($14,354*8.6 million Black families), again using Oliver and Shapiro's figures.[24]

A 2019 study by Thomas et al. found that rather than the racial wealth gap decreasing, the wealth gap between Blacks and whites is increasing. The idea popularized in the 1980s by sociologist William Julius Wilson that race was declining, not disappearing, as a significant variable in social science is rejected when we analyze race and wealth. We are not in a post-racial period, conclude Thomas et al. In 1989, Blacks had $6,101 of wealth compared to $81,921 of wealth for whites. In 1999, Blacks had $11,918 of wealth compared to $101,515 of wealth for whites. In 2009, Blacks had $5,000 of wealth compared to $92,000 of wealth for whites.[25] These racial wealth gaps are shocking for a nation soon to be made up mostly of people of color. The

22. Balkovic, "High-Income Tax Returns for 2000," table 5.
23. Current Population Survey Datasets.
24. Oliver and Shapiro, *Black Wealth/White Wealth*, 131.
25. Thomas et al., "Race and the Accumulation of Wealth," 29, fig. 1.

recent Supreme Court decision in *Students for Fair Admissions v. Harvard*, which struck down postsecondary affirmative action programs, shows how little a court controlled by white political interests is able to respond to the necessities of strategic equality.

Any computations of average wealth inequality can only understate the wealth gap since the superrich, few of whom are Black, rarely if ever factor into this count. Given the high degree of wealth concentration in the US, with the top 1 percent owning 50 percent of the NFA (net financial assets), the real Black to white wealth gap must be more than double our best computations.

CORPORATE POWER

The differences in size between Black and white control of capital are great. The June 2003 issue of *Black Enterprise* magazine reported that CAMAC, an energy-related firm, was the largest in sales of the "Black Enterprise 100" (the 100 largest Black-controlled firms), with slightly over $1 billion in sales for 2002.[26] Neiman Marcus, the upscale department store chain, was number 500 in the April 2003 list in *Fortune* magazine of the 500 largest US corporations, with $2.9 billion in sales, three times larger than the largest Black-controlled company.

Not much progress has occurred in the last decade, when the June 1990 issue of *Black Enterprise* showed that the late upstart financier Reginald F. Lewis managed a buyout of Beatrice International, a *Fortune* 500 company, which instantly became the largest Black-controlled business.[27] Even with Lewis's firm, which was six times larger than Johnson Publishing Co., the number 2 Black firm in sales, the April 1989 issue of *Fortune* showed that the bottom of the *Fortune* 500 was about twice the size in sales of the top Black firms. If anything, Black firms are falling behind, and the 1997 *Survey of Minority-Owned Business Enterprises* from the Department of Commerce seems to support this finding, since the rate of growth in business receipts between 1992 and 1997 was 32.5 percent for Black firms and 40.2 percent for the nation as a whole.[28] Most of the Black Enterprise 100 are privately held firms, but the results are the same, even worse, compared with publicly held firms. When it comes to corporate control, Blacks control little, and control of large corporations is much of what runs America.

---

26. Dingle, "Reinvention Through Innovation," 96.
27. *Black Enterprise*, "B.E. 100s Overview," 98.
28. U.S. Department of Commerce, *1997 Economic Census*.

THE PRICE OF WAGE DISCRIMINATION

Large corporations control where people live, how much they earn, where workers' kids go to school, the amount of advertising people see, American materialism, urban and regional development, what types of transportation people use, the quality of our natural environment, and the work environment. As evidenced by many of the high-profile racial discrimination law suits, corporations, through their CEOs and managers, also determine much of the racial inequality in America.[29] In 1997, 5.5 million business establishments had employees, and they employed 105 million workers, yet nearly half of all those workers, 50 million, worked for the 16,000 largest businesses with 500 or more workers. That is, half of all employees work for two-tenths of 1 percent of the employers. In that same year, the 458 corporations of the *Fortune* 500 employed over 21 million workers. This data represents a huge amount of large corporate control, with one-quarter of all employees working for fewer than 500 of the 5.5 million employers. Fewer than 1 percent of *Fortune* 500 firms have Black CEOs, and even that is a recent innovation. The August 2003 issue of *Savoy* magazine reported that Richard Parsons (AOL Time Warner), Stanley O'Neal (Merrill Lynch), Kenneth Chenault (American Express), and Franklin Raines (Fannie Mae) all were on the list of the top ten business titans. All headed *Fortune* 500 firms. Strangely, two of these men, O'Neal and Raines, both had to exit because of the subprime mortgage crisis that accrued blame for the Great Recession.[30]

Black control of business capital and receipts is far out of proportion to the Black population of the US. With Blacks comprising over 13 percent of the population in the 2010 census, the *Survey of Minority-Owned Business Enterprises* shows that Black business receipts in 1997 totaled $71 billion. This number is less than .9 percent (nine-tenths of 1 percent) of the total $7,763 billion for white-controlled firms in the US for that same year, and only .3 percent of total business receipts in the US. Asset information on Black firms is not available, but such information probably would show an even-greater disparity, since the largest Black firms generally are in the service area.[31]

Anyone would notice the high number of Black faces among the Power 100 in the July 8, 2002, issue of *Forbes* magazine.[32] This list comprises the greatest income earners among famous people, with the most weight going to "celebrity earnings over the past 12 months." Twenty of the Power 100

---

29. Greenberg, *American Political System*, 128–29.
30. U.S. Small Business Administration, "Private Firms, Establishments."
31. United States Census Bureau, *Statistical Abstract: 2002*, table 718.
32. Badenhausen, "Celebrity 100."

are Black, including Tiger Woods (golf), Oprah Winfrey (talk show host), Michael Jordan (basketball), Shaquille O'Neal (basketball), Kobe Bryant (basketball), and Michael Tyson (boxing), ranking as the top six Blacks of the Power 100.

None of the Blacks in the Power 100 are listed in the July 9, 2001, article titled "The Richest People in the World" issue in *Forbes* magazine.[33] Oprah Winfrey, the first Black women to be listed among the richest people in the world in 1995, was not on the list in 2001. Only Michael Lee-Chin (ranked 488), a Canadian Chinese-Jamaican who owns one of Canada's largest mutual funds as reported by *Forbes*, and Robert Johnson (ranked 312), founder of the Black Entertainment Network (BET), were the two Black people listed in the 2001 *Forbes* 400. *Forbes* states that Johnson, who sold BET to Viacom (number 66 on the 2003 *Fortune* 500 list) for $2.7 billion, is the first African American to have a net worth over $1 billion.

As of 2008 the wealth picture did not change much for Blacks since the late 1990s, if the *Forbes* 400 is any guide. If anything, the situation deteriorated. In 2008, at least $1.3 billion was necessary to make the bottom of the *Forbes* 400 list.

What is discouraging about the *Forbes* 400 list is the number of young and new money faces on the list in some years. Examples in 2008 include Seth Merrin, aged forty-eight, who founded a financial services company; Todd Wagner, aged forty-eight, who started a live internet sports broadcasting firm and sold it to Yahoo; Leonard Blavatnik, aged fifty-one, whom *Forbes* describes as arriving penniless from the former Soviet Union in 1978 and who built an industrial holding company; Aubrey McClendon, aged forty-nine, was cofounder of an energy company; John Arnold, aged thirty-four, made money in oil trading; Google guys Sergey Brin and Larry Page, both aged thirty-five; Pierre Omidyar, aged forty-one, founded eBay; Mark Zuckerberg, aged twenty-four, founded Facebook.

The 2008 *Forbes* listing or the October 31, 2019, *Forbes* listing do not change the analysis from the 1997 listing of the *Forbes* 400. We are interested in long-term trends, not what happened yesterday. Still, nearly all of the *Forbes* 400 have old money inherited from their parents, had elite backgrounds, attended elite schools, or had other advantages highly correlated with white privilege. In 2001, two Blacks were on the *Forbes* 400 list, but neither Michael Lee-Chin or Robert Johnson could keep up with the white wealth pace. In 2019 again there were only two Black people on the *Forbes* 400 list, Oprah Winfrey and Robert Smith. Black super-wealth is such a rare occurrence that the cover of the *Forbes* March 31, 2018, special issue "The

---

33. Dolan and Kroll, "Richest People in World."

World's Richest People" featured a photo of Robert Smith with the caption "The Secret Behind His $4.4 Billion Fortune." *Forbes* listed Robert Smith as "the nation's wealthiest African-American," ranked 163 in 2019. Oprah Winfrey was ranked number 155 in 2008 with $2.7 billion, but ranked only 298 with $2.8 billion in 2019. Even Oprah Winfrey is slipping as she struggles to hold her own among increasingly superrich whites. And for those who are not satisfied unless they have the very latest and up-to-the-minute information, in late 2024, four persons who identify as Black made the *Forbes* 400 list of the richest in the nation: 1) David Steward (sales and finance) with $11.4 billion; 2) Robert Smith (investment), again, with $10.8; 3) Alexander Karp (tech) with $4.1; and 4) Michael Jordan, of basketball fame, with $2.4.[34]

With all the educated Blacks, opportunity, access, and civil rights laws, 3, 4, or even 5 percent of the *Forbes* 400 realistically should be Black, yet we see .0075 percent. The paucity of Blacks among the superrich exemplifies the present and historic racial inequality in American wealth.

WHITES WIN BIG IN THE DISCRIMINATION GAME

Losses to Blacks from wage discrimination, poverty, and wealth disparities do not count lower returns to education for Blacks or the dearth of Blacks among the superrich. Also, these losses do not count the impact of discrimination on lost political power.

Some economists would argue that it is not fair simply to measure the difference in wages between whites and Blacks without considering other factors such as human capital, demographics, occupation, industry, gender, and skill. This calculation, however, indeed is fair. My models include all these variables. Except for discrimination, Blacks should not differ substantially from whites in labor markets, human capital, gender, or skill.

Blacks are the only racial group in the country who live primarily in the poorest region—the South. This fact is not an accident. The location of Blacks is related to their historic connection to American slavery. Asking Blacks to move to other regions assumes they would have the same opportunity structures as whites. Clearly such a move is not the case, however, since controlling for region does not equalize wages. We have compared the worst-case losses to the economy from affirmative action ($51 billion) to Black and Latino losses from poverty and near poverty ($91–134 billion), wage discrimination ($64–180 billion [table 6, models 1–4]), and wealth loss ($123–232 billion). Even if affirmative action were a net gain to Blacks

34. Oluwadara, "Meet Four Black Billionaires."

and Latinos and a net loss to whites (and the evidence does not support this), affirmative action is not sufficient to compensate Blacks or Latinos for poverty, wage, and wealth losses.

Chapter Seven

Trouble Ahead

The Danger of Political Power on the Cheap

AMERICA'S FOUNDING FATHERS UNDERSTOOD that good government requires protection of minority rights from majority perceptions and interests. Any group that had more than half the votes could dominate the entire polis with little concern for the whole. Such a situation could threaten the stability of the state. James Madison (1751–1836), secretary of state under Thomas Jefferson and fourth president of the United States, noted that "complaints are everywhere heard . . . that the public good is disregarded in the conflicts of rival parties, and that measures are too often decided, not according to the rules of justice and the rights of the minority party, but by the superior force of an interested and overbearing majority."[1] By "interested" Madison meant some uniting passion unrelated to the common good. The majority were dangerous because they frequently were those who "are without property" and used their numbers to abuse "those who hold" property.[2] Madison's solution was either a call to national unity unrelated to the majority will or division of the society into smaller parts so that no real majority existed.[3]

British philosopher John Stuart Mill (1806–73) noted that even if the majority is in the right, "it is always probable that dissentients have something worth hearing to say for themselves, and that truth would lose something by their silence."[4] Majorities that have to concern themselves with only their own passions, without regard to a minority who disagrees,

1. A. Hamilton et al., *Federalist Papers*, 72.
2. A. Hamilton et al., *Federalist Papers*, 74.
3. A. Hamilton et al., *Federalist Papers*, 320.
4. Mill, *On Liberty*, 49.

are a dangerous majority, a state of affairs sometimes referred to as majority tyranny.[5] If the majority decide that the minority should not vote, should receive substandard education, and should have to work for lower wages simply because they are Black, few would consider such a government democratic. The American government was in such a state until a little more than fifty years ago; there was no difference between what whites perceived and reality. White perception determined what reality was. To be white politically means to vote on political, social, cultural, and economic issues without any concern that your vote is racialized or may have serious negative impacts on peoples of color.

For the founding fathers, these minority rights that needed protection did not include enslaved Africans or their progeny. James Madison was born into a family who grew rich from the work of enslaved Blacks. Madison recognized the economic importance of slavery in his strong support for a constitution based on Black oppression when he said, "I should conceive this clause [recognizing rights of Southern states in slaves] to be impolitic, if it were one of those things which could be excluded without encountering greater evils. . . . But in this Constitution, 'no person held to service or labor, in one State, under the laws thereof, escaping into another, shall, in consequence of any law or regulation therein, be discharged from such service or labor; but shall be delivered up on claim of the party to whom such service or labor may be due.' This clause was expressly inserted to enable owner[s] of slaves to reclaim them. This is a better security than any that now exists."[6]

Even before the Second Reconstruction, however, the Progressive Era of the early twentieth century produced many thinkers who understood what Martin Luther King Jr. would later say at the June 1965 commencement address at Oberlin College: "We must learn to live together as brothers or perish together as fools."[7] The costs of neglecting civic unity have led to civil war in the past and can do so again. Until the twentieth century, America embraced racial Darwinism and thought of white Americans as the master race.[8] With the former master race declining numerically, and those thought of as subordinate races in the ascendency, the cost of neglecting political equality seems higher now than at any time in American history. Ignoring racial political polarization can delegitimize the system

5. Guinier, *Tyranny of the Majority*, 4.
6. Madison, "Slave Trade and Slaveholders' Rights," para. 2.
7. King, *Where Do We Go from Here*, 171.
8. R. Smith, *Civic Ideals*, 469, 74.

called democracy as the current minority and future plurality, Blacks and Latinos, find no interests worth supporting.[9]

A minority with nothing to lose is a dangerous minority with little incentive to remain part of any government. Conversely, a majority who do not care about the oppression experienced by the minority cannot be a democracy at all. With Black, Latino, and Asian newborns already outnumbering white newborns, ill treatment of these children will not endear them to our system of government. Minority children will become the majority in less than thirty years. If they are ill treated by the majority-white population of today, the majority-minority population of tomorrow is likely to feel justified in treating whites the same way whites treated them.

The first step, the minimal plan, in ending racial polarization and instituting racial equality is to know the difference between the perceived costs and intrinsic costs involved. Intrinsic political costs are those that cause a political group, a political party, to change its most fundamental beliefs or ideology. Perceived political costs are those the party would have to pay in terms of lost votes or party influence with the public. Chapter 1 notes that once an issue becomes a political football, and the parties take sides to attract a voter base, perceived costs can rise exponentially. In the US, intrinsic political costs for racial equality are relatively low, while perceived political costs seem to be very high.

Intrinsic political costs for racial equality are low because most of these measures and policies have already been enshrined into the law and accepted as socially and politically correct. Examples of intrinsic political costs include the right of Blacks to vote, hold public office, live in white neighborhoods, attend integrated schools, and be free of discrimination in wages or salaries or when applying for jobs. Perceived political costs tend to be high because while the laws reflect one reality, the reality in the minds of most white voters is the deciding factor in their political (voting) decisions regardless of any empirical reality or impact.

THE POWER OF THE PLATFORM

Party platforms show polarization over issues with little or no intrinsic cost. Antidiscrimination in many domains is already the law, so asserting this law as right and fair has little to do with fundamental beliefs or ideology. Today, few politicians or political parties would say they favor racial discrimination.

---

9. Guinier and Torres, *Miner's Canary*, 198.

Here the difference between intrinsic and perceived costs becomes clear, however. Since the civil rights movement and the increasing power of the Black vote, the parties have tended to move toward their most loyal voter bases. For the GOP, that movement has meant using the language of white voters who identify themselves by their race and as "conservative," whatever conservative might mean to white voters.

Richard Nixon was the first Republican of the civil rights era to recognize that he must either court Black votes or pursue white voters because they were white. Nixon and his pursuit of the "silent majority" of resentful whites set the GOP on a track that mixes white political and religious conservatism.

In the past, code words for voting white were "states' rights," "law and order," "forced bussing," and "neighborhood schools." Today those words are "family values," "rule of law," "merit," "right to life (abortion)," "school choice," "parental rights," and opposition to "judicial activism." The 2008 GOP party platform does not use the words "race," "racism," "civil rights," "affirmative action," "discrimination," or "African American" anywhere in the platform. The only rights mentioned are human rights, civil liberties, and women's rights. The platform is devoid of issues that impact the lives of most Blacks on a daily basis. The GOP platform uses the words "values" and "abortion" to appeal to the white religious right, which is its core.[10]

The 2008 Democratic Party platform uses almost all the code words Blacks and other minority groups recognize as signals that the party is for and about them. The Democrats use the word "race" in the context of "discrimination," support "affirmative action," and promise to fight for "civil rights." The word "racism" does not appear in either major party platform in 2008, but the Democratic Party platform promises to end racial profiling and "to provide every American an equal chance at employment, housing, health, contracts, and pay."[11]

The 2012 Democratic Party platform differed little from the 2008 platform in terms of code words used to rally the faithful. "Racism" was not mentioned, nor was "affirmative action," words that may offend whites in the coalition. "Race," however, was on prominent display, as were "civil rights," "discrimination," "racial profiling," and "equal opportunity." "Integration" appeared only in the context of immigrants and the disabled, not

---

10. Republican National Committee, "2008 Republican Party Platform."

11. Democratic National Committee, "2008 Democratic Party Platform," s.vv. "A More Perfect Union."

the traditional civil rights and race perspective.[12] These words are fully in line with national law and the Civil Rights Act of 1964.

The 2012 GOP platform differed markedly from 2008. The GOP platform used the words "race," "equal opportunity," "antidiscrimination," "bigotry," and "racism" in the traditional civil rights context. The GOP seems clearly to have been seeking Black votes.

The GOP, however, rejected the concept of affirmative action and talked about "individual merit," rejecting "preferences, quotas, and set-asides."[13] The GOP platform talked about "traditional family values and the sanctity of innocent human life."[14] These words rally the white religious right, who are strongly opposed to pro-choice concepts.

Democrats came out strong in 2016 using words to electrify Black voters: race, racism, racial, systematic racism, environmental racism, civil rights, modern slavery. The 2016 Democratic platform said nothing about affirmative action or reparations but called out the names of civil rights heroes and heroines: Dr. King, Rosa Parks, and John Lewis.

Chapter 3 provided evidence that many whites have difficulty accepting that systematic racism exists, yet the 2016 party platform of the Democratic Party devoted two pages to the problem of systematic racism: "the war on drugs ... disproportionately [impacts] people of color."[15] The Democratic Party pledged to "fight to end institutional and systematic racism in our society."[16] Readers should note that while laws exist against racial discrimination in certain cases, there is no law against ideological racism, the belief that certain racial groups lack human characteristics. The point here is that while policies seriously addressing systematic racism might never have emerged, the 2016 Democratic platform nonetheless purposefully appeals to peoples of color and their white allies.

The 2016 GOP party platform opposes discrimination based on race, sex, religion, etc., and denounces "bigotry, racism, anti-Semitism."[17] "Race"

---

12. Democratic National Committee, "2012 Democratic Party Platform."

13. Republican National Committee, "2012 Republican Party Platform," s.vv. "We the People: A Restoration of Constitutional Government."

14. Republican National Committee, "2012 Republican Party Platform," s.vv. "The Sanctity and Dignity of Human Life."

15. Democratic National Committee, "2016 Democratic Party Platform," s.vv. "Bring Americans Together and Remove Barriers to Opportunities: Reforming Our Criminal Justice System."

16. Democratic National Committee, "2016 Democratic Party Platform," s.vv. "Bring Americans Together and Remove Barriers to Opportunities: Ending Systemic Racism."

17. Republican National Committee, "2016 Republican Party Platform," s.vv. "A

and "racism" appear only once. The GOP platform pledges, however, to "end the government's use of disparate impact theory in enforcing anti-discrimination laws with regard to lending."[18] The word "discrimination" never appears in relation to Blacks or civil rights. Frequent use of the word "values" in conjunction with "family values," "cultural values," and independence is a common theme in the 2016 GOP platform. "Merit and hard work" and the "inalienable right to life" are prominent in the GOP platform. Civil rights apply to businesses, American Indians, and persons with disabilities. Unlike the Democrats, the GOP simply is saying they support most current statutes, but not judicial determinations like disparate impact.

If anything, 2020 showed an even wider divergence between the GOP and Democratic Party platforms than in recent years. For 2020, with a very close election predicted, the GOP kept the exact same platform as in 2016 without changing so much as the year designation or the title page. The Republican National Committee stated the reason for this was the COVID-19 crisis.[19] The Republican Party seemed to believe it had only to appeal to the same base it had in 2016 and support for general antidiscrimination law without any particular appeal to peoples of color. This strategy appeared to pay off. Table 7.3 shows that in 2016, 8 percent of Blacks voted for the Republican presidential candidate, while in 2020, 12 percent of Blacks voted for Donald Trump for president. In table 7.1, Blacks went from less than 1 percent of the GOP coalition in 2016 to over 3 percent in 2020. The data cannot tell us if this increase in Black GOP votes is for the GOP, against the Democratic Party, or both. Still, overall, the GOP lost ground in table 7.1 as their percentage of the popular vote declined from 47.6 percent in 2016 to 46.9 percent in 2020.

Unlike the Republican Party, the Democratic Party was fielding a new candidate in Joseph Biden, former vice president for eight years under President Obama. Biden's campaign was slipping until Biden received the backing of Representative James Clyburn (D, South Carolina), member of the Black caucus and assistant Democratic Party leader in the House of Representatives. Once in the White House, President Biden returned the favor by appointing Clyburn's assistant, Jamie Harrison, as chairman of the Democratic National Committee. Biden did more than just appoint high-ranking Blacks. The Democratic Party platform uses the word "racism" eleven times

---

Rebirth of Constitutional Government: We the People."

18. Republican National Committee, "2016 Republican Party Platform," s.vv. "Restoring the American Dream: Freeing Financial Markets."

19. Republican National Committee, *Republican Platform 2016*, s.vv. "Resolution Regarding the Republican Party Platform."

and supports Black Lives Matter. When the Democratic Party platform says, "We believe Black lives matter, and will establish a national commission to examine the lasting economic effects of slavery, Jim Crow segregation, and racially discriminatory federal policies on income, wealth, educational, health, and employment outcomes; to pursue truth and promote racial healing; and to study reparations,"[20] they are using all the code words that say this is the party for people of color. Democrats oppose the Confederate battle flag and statues of Confederate leaders on public property. "Discrimination" is mentioned eighteen times in the Democratic platform, "Civil Rights" eleven times, "Black Americans" nineteen times, "Latino" twelve times, "Asian American" ten times, and "Native American" eleven times. The 2020 Democratic platform specifically opposes "the voices of racism, misogyny, anti-Semitism, anti-Muslim bigotry, or white supremacy."[21] The Democratic Party platform, 2020 and 2024, takes the grammatically correct but little-used route of capitalizing "Black," because it is the name of the Black racial group that Blacks themselves have chosen, while "white" is not capitalized because it designates only a skin color. The 2016/2020 GOP platform does not include the name of a single racial group.

The 2024 GOP platform uses the word "race" only twice: 1) to "cut federal funding for any school pushing critical race theory,"[22] and 2) to "restore Parental Rights in Education, and enforce our Civil Rights Laws to stop schools from discriminating on the basis of Race."[23] The 2024 GOP platform also mentions "law and order"[24] and "school choice."[25] Without understanding code words, mentioned earlier this chapter, it may be difficult for the uninitiated to decipher exactly what the GOP is talking about. This language is part of the package of classic code words for the rights of whites. This is clear because the 2024 GOP platform never mentions Blacks or African Americans. "Parental rights" are code words meaning the rights of white parents to block ideas they consider to be offensive or erroneous, such as the structural racism upon which critical race theory is based. "School choice" are particularly complex code words in that they are often used by the political right and left. Yet, Orfield and Frankenburg

---

20. Democratic National Committee, "2020 Democratic Party Platform," s.vv. "Achieving Racial Justice and Equity."

21. Democratic National Committee, "2020 Democratic Party Platform," s.v. "Preamble."

22. Republican National Committee, "2024 Republican Party Platform," s.v. "Preamble," point 16.

23. Republican National Committee, "2024 Republican Party Platform," ch. 7.5.

24. Republican National Committee, "2024 Republican Party Platform," chs. 2, 8.

25. Republican National Committee, "2024 Republican Party Platform," ch. 7.2.

make it clear that "forgetting the history of choice policies in our country and ignoring research from other nations showing that unrestricted choice produces unequal, segregated schools that reinforce the underlying stratification of society, policy makers have been swept up in the faith in markets to solve deeply embedded educational and societal problems. This is not research—this is theology."[26] The concept of school choice is bandied about like the phrase "a rising tide lifts all boats," from chapter 3, when the evidence in figure 3.7 shows the concept to be false when applied to race and unemployment. The ability of markets alone to create educational equality is also shown to be false in the next chapter. Code words and magic elixirs are not serious policy.

The 2024 Democratic platform uses the word "race" five times in the traditional Black civil rights context to combat discrimination in heath care, housing, wages, and higher education.[27] Clear messages for the support of all peoples of color.

UNIVERSAL NONSUPPORT FOR THE EEOC

Neither 2024 party platform mentions the nation's top antidiscrimination enforcement agency: the Equal Employment Opportunity Commission (EEOC). However, the 2024 Democratic Party platform does promise to "strengthen enforcement and penalties for safety, wage, and other labor and employment violations."[28] Budgetary support for the EEOC is one method to measure the relationship between campaign promises and a commitment to real change. The 2012 Democratic Party platform mentions the EEOC but tones down support from 2000 or even Obama's campaign support.

The issue of EEOC funding serves to make the point that once an issue becomes involved in a tug-of-war, the perceived costs can rise quite high. The EEOC is a federal agency and operates within the law. By supporting the EEOC, the GOP could challenge the grip of the Democratic Party on Black votes. Support for the EEOC may lose white votes in the GOP, however, and supporting the EEOC too strongly by Democrats might cost white votes in the Democratic Party. Supporting issues perceived to be Black loses white support.[29]

26. Orfield and Frankenburg, *Educational Delusions?*, 258.
27. Democratic National Committee, '24 *Democratic Party Platform*, 18, 25, 51, 55, 61.
28. Democratic National Committee, '24 *Democratic Party Platform*, 9.
29. Bobo and Charles, "Race in the American Mind."

In 2000, the Democratic Party Platform stressed the increases in support that "Clinton-Gore" gave to the EEOC, stating, "Over the last eight years, we have fought hard to end discrimination. We have increased funding for civil rights enforcement—so that the laws on our books are not just pleasant words, but pledges of justice."[30] While it is true that, since the inception of the EEOC, every administration has increased the funding of the agency in real (or current) dollars (fig. 7.1), EEOC funding in constant dollars (that is, dollars corrected for inflation) has been stagnant. Jimmy Carter was the last president who increased the EEOC budget adjusted for inflation. Yes, the EEOC budget has been stagnant since Jimmy Carter, and neither Reagan, George H. W. Bush, Clinton, George W. Bush, Barack Obama, nor Donald Trump did much of anything to change this situation. Since 1980, nearly half a century ago, the top antidiscrimination agency in the nation has not received any budgetary increase, once adjusted for inflation. The agency actually got less funding in 2023 than in 1980, in constant dollars. EEOC staffing has also not kept pace with population growth, even considering technological advances with computers. In 1980, the EEOC had a staff of 3,390, small for the task of monitoring and enforcing antidiscrimination for a nation of 226 million people. But in 2023, the EEOC was staffed at only 2,173 people for a nation with a population of over 330 million.

Figure 7.1 EEOC Budget in Current and Constant Dollars, 1966–2023

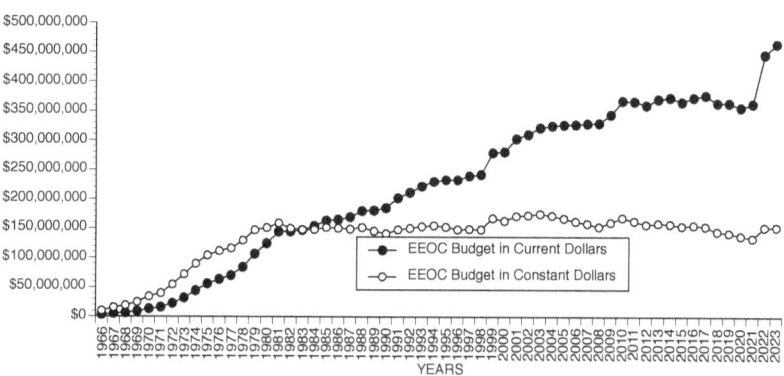

Sources: 1966–79: Bloch, *Antidiscrimination Law and Minority Employment*; 1980–2023: U.S. Equal Employment Opportunity Commission, "EEOC Budget and Staffing History." Author's computations.

30. Democratic National Committee, "2000 Democratic Party Platform," s.vv. "Fighting for Civil Rights and Inclusion."

THE COST OF RACIAL EQUALITY

Worse than that, as a percentage of the gross domestic product (total value of goods and services in the US) EEOC funding has been in steady decline since early in President Reagan's administration (fig. 7.2). This decline continued with Clinton, and not even Obama proposed changing the situation. As America grows, it spends less and less on antidiscrimination enforcement. Indicators suggest, however, that discrimination is not decreasing in healthcare, wages, hiring, or a number of other areas. Adequate funding of the primary federal antidiscrimination enforcement agency is as basic to Black equality, or as politically safe for the Democrats or Republicans, as saying they support statutory law.[31]

Figure 7.2 EEOC Budget as Percentage of GDP, 1966–2023

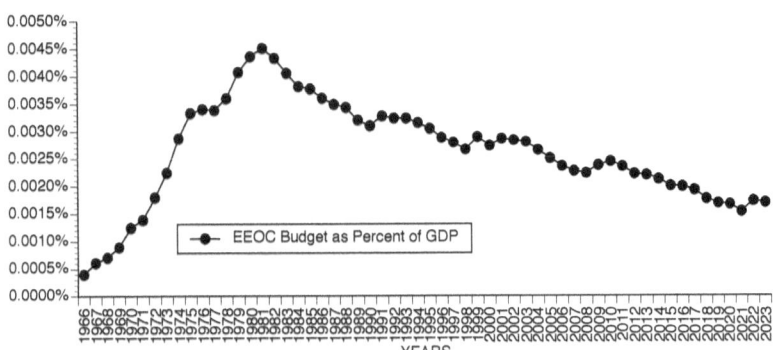

Sources: 1966–79: Bloch, *Antidiscrimination Law and Minority Employment*; 1980–2023: U.S. Equal Employment Opportunity Commission, "EEOC Budget and Staffing History." Author's computations.

Few people are aware that the EEOC unofficially cannot use one of the most powerful tools in the antidiscrimination arsenal: job audits or testing, in which Black and white paired testers apply for jobs and measure the results of which tester gets the job. In 1991, Republican Senator Alan K. Simpson introduced a bill to prohibit the EEOC from using auditors to test firms for discrimination. The prohibition never became legislation, but just the threat was sufficient to warn the EEOC, and the agency has never engaged in testing.[32]

---

31. Bendick, in discussion with author, Dec. 30, 2004. Marc Bendick finds that as many as 20–25 percent of employers are "hard[-]core" discriminators (Bendick and Egan, "Changing Workplace Cultures," 7).

32. See "Civil Rights Amendments of 1991," S. 478, 102nd Congress, 1st session (Feb. 22, 1991), in *Congressional Record* 137 S.2259 (1991).

Much evidence illustrates that job discrimination is not an isolated phenomena but rather is systematic, pervasive, and ubiquitous. Not allowing the agency that is the equivalent of the FBI for employment discrimination to conduct antidiscrimination sting operations can mean only a lack of serious concern with the life-threatening issues that most Blacks face in a major societal sector.

The economic cost of doing a top-quality job audit is less than $1,000. If the EEOC audited every firm subject to EEO-1 reporting requirements (about 250,000 firms) every year, the cost would be $250 million at the most. This amount would not even double the annual budget of the EEOC. Even though the costs for such job audits are relatively modest, both parties perceived the political cost to be quite high and thus the "no-audit" policy stands.[33]

Funding of this critical enforcement agency was a test for the Obama Administration. Obama targeted EEOC enforcement, funding, and staffing during his campaign.[34] Increased funding could have been a sign that the administration was serious about change. Proper funding of the EEOC requires a 400 percent increase in funding, however, just to keep the same relation to the GDP as in 1981. Survey, statistical, and job audit evidence show that employment discrimination is widespread. Proper funding of the EEOC requires that the agency conduct random job audits of every firm covered by Title VII of the 1964 Civil Rights Act at least every two years.[35] Approximately one million firms with twenty or more people currently are operational in the US.[36] A top-quality audit for each firm every two years would cost $500 million per year.

On January 30, 2009, Joe Nocera reported for *The New York Times* that the $18.4 billion in bonuses that Wall Street distributed in 2008, "the sixth-largest haul on record," angered President Obama. Cadillac-quality funding for the EEOC is 6 percent of Wall Street bonuses.

The inability to form the political will to spend $500 million that virtually would eliminate the practice of racialized job discrimination is the difference between intrinsic costs and perceived costs. Job discrimination is already illegal, and society, the GOP, and the Democratic Party condemn it, which suggests that the intrinsic cost is low. Both political party platforms welcome equal opportunity and antidiscrimination. The topic is so hot,

---

33. Bendick, in discussion with author, Dec. 30, 2004. Bendick reports that a "Cadillac" level of audit quality costs anywhere from $500 to $1,000 per audit.

34. Greenspan, "Changes Expected."

35. All firms with fifteen or more employees.

36. United States Census Bureau, *Statistical Abstract: 2009*, table 736, "Establishments, Employees, and Payroll by Employment-Size Class: 1990–2005."

THE COST OF RACIAL EQUALITY

however, that neither party can risk offending white voters and allowing the EEOC to conduct job audits or even to fund the EEOC adequately.

Table 7.1

Presidential Vote by Party and Race, 1948–2024

Year	Candidate	Percent Popular Vote	Electoral College Vote	Winning Margin Percent	Percent White	Percent Black	Percent Latino	Percent Asian	Percent Native	Percent Other
	Democrats									
1948	Truman*	49.6	303	4.5	94.61	5.39				
1952	Stevenson	44.4	89		91.3	8.3				0.4
1956	Stevenson	42	73		93.15	6.26				0.59
1960	Kennedy*	49.7	303	.2	92.6	6.95				0.45
1964	Johnson*	61.1	486	22.6	87.2	12.53				0.27
1968	Humphrey	42.7	191		79.33	19.95				0.71
1972	McGovern	37.5	17		75.27	21.2	1.06	1.41	1.06	
1976	Carter*	50.1	297	2.1	80.33	15.13	2.57	1.66	0.3	
1980	Carter	41	49		70.94	25.65	0.79	2.62	0	
1984	Mondale	40.6	13		70.91	20.56	2.44	5.57	0.52	
1988	Dukakis	45.6	111		66.49	20.14	3.74	8.73	0.89	
1992	Clinton*	43	370	5.6	69.04	21.83	2.54	5.84	0.76	
1996	Clinton*	49.2	379	8.5	69.78	18.03	3.01	7.68	1.5	
2000	Gore	48.4	266	.5	72.02	18.31	1.9	4.84	2.94	
2004	Kerry	48	252		66	20	10	2		
2008	Obama*	53	365	7	62	23	10	2		
2012	Obama*	57.97	332	18	44.77	31.39	18.05			5.79
2016	Clinton	47.6	218	.0008	62.02	17.74	11.95	3.23	.51	3.89
2020	Biden*	51.3	306	2.7	53.2	21.3	16.2	4.7		4.3
2024	Harris	48.2	226		60.5	19.2	11.3	3.35		2.5
	Republicans									
1948	Dewey	45.1	189		96.61	3.39				
1952	Eisenhower*	55.1	442	10.7	98.54	1.46				0
1956	Eisenhower*	57.4	457	15.4	97.62	2.38				0
1960	Nixon	49.5	219		97.35	2.43				0.22
1964	Goldwater	38.5	52		99.72	0				0.28
1968	Nixon*	43.4	301	.7	98.37	0.61				1.02
1972	Nixon*	60.7	520	23.2	96.18	1.76	1.18	0.59	0.29	

210

Table 7.1

Presidential Vote by Party and Race, 1948–2024

1976	Ford	48	240		95.85	0.77	2	0.92	0.46	
1980	Reagan*	50.7	489	9.7	95.54	1.42	1.22	1.62	0.2	
1984	Reagan*	58.8	525	18.2	92.34	1.88	1.63	3.52	0.63	
1988	Bush (father)*	53.4	426	7.8	92.38	1.59	1.59	3.33	1.11	
1992	Bush (father)	37.4	168		89.89	1.81	2.17	3.61	2.53	
1996	Dole	40.7	159		92.38	0.23	2.08	2.77	2.54	
2000	Bush (son)*	47.9	271		89.08	1.53	3.83	3.64	1.92	
2004	Bush (son)*	51	274	3	88	2	7	1		
2008	McCain	46	173		90	1	6	1		
2012	Romney	39.29	206		84.06	1.01	9.6			5.33
2016	Trump*	47.6	289		89.24	.96	4.42	1.61	.24	3.05
2020	Trump	46.9	232		81.6	3.3	8.8	2.6		3.4
2024	Trump*	50.0	312	1.8	80.0	3.0	10.0	2.0		3.0

*indicates winner
Significant third-party candidates: 1968, George Wallace, 13.5 percent; 1980, John Anderson, 6.6 percent; 1992 and 1996, Ross Perot, 18.9 percent and 8.4 percent; 2000 and 2004, Ralph Nader, 2.7 percent and .003 percent.
Sources: 1948–2004: Sapiro and Rosenstone, "American National Election Studies" (Ann Arbor, MI: University of Michigan, Center for Political Studies [producer], 2004; Ann Arbor, MI: Inter-University Consortium for Political and Social Research [distributor], Sept. 25, 2007).
2008: *New York Times*, "Where Candidates Found Support."
2012–16: 2012 Time Series Study (Stanford University and the University of Michigan [producers]); Time Series Cumulative Data File.
2020: Andre et al., "National Exit Polls."
2024: NBC News, "2024 President Results."

RACIAL VOTING AND THE POWER OF PERCEPTION

Voting rights are another example of low intrinsic costs but high perceived costs for Black political rights. Voting rights have low intrinsic costs because voting rights are the law of the land. Both parties support equal rights in voting; few politicians would say Blacks should not have the right to vote. Such remarks would mimic the language of just fifty years ago, when the Mississippi Freedom Democratic Party challenged the regular all-white Democratic Party delegation from Mississippi.

Intrinsic costs are those that would cause a political party to change its most fundamental beliefs or ideology. In terms of support for voting rights, neither party has much to change. The GOP supports the principle of "honest elections and the right to vote" in its 2016 platform.[37] The "Democrats believe we are stronger when we protect citizens' right to vote" in their 2016 platform.[38] Intrinsically, voting rights are not a political issue or even a divisive area.

Perceived costs, however, are those a party would have to pay in terms of lost votes or party influence with their voter base. Perceived costs for voting rights for Blacks seem high. The problem is that as whites age and lose the population race, Black and Latino voters begin to dominate national politics, not because minority voters are a majority, but because white voters still split their votes, to some extent, between the two major parties.

VOTING RIGHTS AND THE PARTIES

Table 7.1 shows that in 2012, over 31 percent of the Democratic Party coalition was Black. Without Black voters, the Democratic Party is not viable. Yet, the 2012 Democratic Party platform begins with support for the voting rights of Americans with disabilities. For the Democratic Party to begin its support for voting rights with groups other than those for whom the 1965 VRA was championed seems incongruous.

The 2012 Democratic Party platform has a large section supporting "civil rights" on the basis of "race, ethnicity, national origin, language, religion, gender, sexual orientation, gender identity, or disability status."[39] Civil rights for women, lesbians, gays, bisexual, and transgender citizens dominates the section on civil rights.

The 2012 Democratic Party platform also has a specific voting rights section comprised of 118 words, which is preceded by a section supporting the rights of women of over 700 words. The platform opposes voter identification laws because they "disproportionately burden young voters, people of color, low-income families, people with disabilities, and the elderly."[40]

The 2012 Democratic Party platform seems designed to appeal to the 44.77 percent of its base who are white in table 7.1, without antagonizing the 31.39 percent who are Black and the 18.05 percent who are Latino. The Democratic Party has to recognize, however, that the Black and Latino

---

37. Republican National Committee, "2016 Republican Party Platform," s.vv. "A Rebirth of Constitutional Government: Honest Elections and the Right to Vote."

38. Democratic National Committee, "2016 Democratic Party Platform," s.v. "Preamble."

39. Democratic National Committee, "2012 Democratic Party Platform," s.vv. "Protecting Rights and Freedoms: Civil Rights."

40. Democratic National Committee, "2012 Democratic Party Platform," s.vv. "Protecting Rights and Freedoms: Voting Rights."

voters believe they have no alternative except to vote Democratic, and that produces the relatively minor position given to Black voting rights as opposed to the rights of women and other nonracial groups.

The Republican 2012 platform opposes popular vote initiatives as a "mortal threat" to our system of government.[41] For a party with a voter base that was over 84 percent white in the 2012 presidential elections, it is understandable that they would oppose any national electoral system based on raw popular vote, which would minimize regionalism and the impact of the South, overwhelmingly GOP.

The GOP also supports "voter integrity," in stating that illegal and fraudulent votes rob citizens of their votes.[42] The Republican Party supports picture identification regulations. With only 1 percent of its voter base comprising Blacks in 2012 and less than 10 percent from Latinos in the same year, the Republican Party may feel it has little to gain and a lot to lose from supporting any issue that favors encouraging votes.

The 2016 GOP platform devotes 444 words to states' rights and individual freedoms, classic rallying cries for the South. Almost as many words, 398, apply to "honest elections" and "the right to vote" by the GOP. The GOP platform demands "legislation to require proof of citizenship when registering to vote and secure photo ID when voting."[43] In 2016, the GOP did not connect the right to vote to civil rights or Black rights.

The Democratic Party used 685 words to "protect voting rights, fix our campaign finance system and restore our democracy" in their 2016 platform. The Democrats claim that the "right to vote is at the heart of our national vision," and that "our democracy suffers when nearly two thirds of our citizens do not or cannot participate, as in the last midterm elections." The Democrats promised to "rectify the Supreme Court decision [see *Shelby County v. Holder* (2013) below] gutting the Voting Rights Act, which is a profound injustice." The 2016 Democratic platform also promises to "stop efforts by Republican governors and legislatures to disenfranchise people of color, low-income people, and young people, and prevent these voters from exercising their right to vote through onerous restrictions."[44]

---

41. Republican National Committee, "2012 Republican Party Platform," s.vv. "We the People: A Restoration of Constitutional Government: The Continuing Importance of Protecting the Electoral College."

42. Republican National Committee, "2012 Republican Party Platform," s.vv. "We the People: A Restoration of Constitutional Government: Voter Integrity to Ensure Honest Elections."

43. Republican National Committee, "2016 Republican Party Platform," s.vv. "A Rebirth of Constitutional Government: Honest Elections and the Right to Vote."

44. Democratic National Committee, "2016 Democratic Party Platform," s.vv.

Voting rights do connect to race in the 2016 GOP platform. The GOP's voter "photo ID," "states' rights," and "individual rights" are traditional code words to vote white. Voting rights are also a racial issue in the 2016 Democratic Party platform. Given that in table 7.1, less than 1 percent of the GOP voter base was Black and less than 5 percent was Latino in 2016, the GOP seems to have little to gain from connecting voting rights with peoples of color. In 2016, almost 18 percent of the Democratic Party coalition was Black and nearly 12 percent was Latino in table 7.1. Fifty-three percent of the Democratic coalition was white in 2020, compared with over 82 percent of the GOP coalition that was white. As with employment, Democratic claims often do not match their actions once in office. The GOP reasonably could make similar promises to attract Black votes.

THE VOTING RIGHTS ACT OF 1965

Chapter 4 listed five twenty-first-century legal issues showing the high perceived cost of the law. Actually, there could be a sixth legal issue that shows the high cost of the law, which was reserved for this chapter because of its political nature: the June 2013 Supreme Court decision in *Shelby County v. Holder* declaring section 4(b) of the 1965 VRA unconstitutional.

The 1965 Voting Rights Act may be one of the most radical pieces of legislation in twentieth-century American history. The VRA of 1965 has had its temporary provisions renewed four times: 1) in 1970 (Nixon Administration, Republican); 2) in 1975 (Carter Administration, Democrat); 3) in 1982 (Reagan Administration, Republican); and 4) in 2006 (Bush [the son] Administration, Republican). Both parties subsequently supported this national legislation, made law during a Democratic administration.

Intrinsic political costs are those that would cause a political party to change its most fundamental beliefs or ideology. Intrinsic political costs for voting equality are low because both parties support the basic principles of the VRA of 1965, which is that "no voting qualifications or prerequisite to voting, or standard, practice, or procedure shall be imposed or applied by any State or political subdivision to deny or abridge the right of any citizen of the United States to vote on account of race or color."[45] These provisions are permanent national law, and apparently no one has proposed changing

---

"Protect Voting Rights, Fix Our Campaign Finance System, and Restore Our Democracy."

45. Voting Rights Act of 1965, Pub. L. No. 89–110, sec. 2, 79 Stat. 437 (1965), codified at 42 U.S.C. § 1973(a), current through Pub. L. No. 113–22 (2013).

them. Even if someone did propose changing these provisions, little support likely would arise in either major political party.

Nevertheless, the perceived political costs are high because the two major national political parties know that, at present, Blacks vote overwhelmingly Democratic. For the Republican Party to support the intricate coverage formulas and federal oversight imposed on the Southern states by the 1965 VRA would be perceived as diminishing white political power. The 1965 VRA not only enfranchised an entire race, but also changed the political landscape.

The 1965 VRA allowed the federal courts to appoint federal examiners whenever the attorney general instituted a proceeding to enforce the Fifteenth Amendment right to vote. The 1965 VRA required states that fell under the enforcement provisions to suspend the use of tests or devices if the court found that such tests or devices were used to deny the right to vote based on race. Further, in the original act, no new voting restrictions could be imposed for a period the court deemed appropriate until it was found that the tests did not deny the right to vote based on race.[46]

The toughest provision of the VRA specified, however, that only in the United States District Court for the District of Columbia could the states contest the attorney general's proceedings to enforce the act. This stipulation took enforcement of the act completely out of the hands of Southern state courts or even Southern federal courts, which were long thought to be sympathetic to the Southern states and nothing more than hybrid state courts.

The provisions of the 1965 VRA applied to any state that on November 1, 1964, maintained any test or device to determine the right to vote (for example, a literacy test or grandfather clause), and in which less than 50 percent of the voting age population was registered to vote or in which less than 50 percent of the voting age population had voted in the presidential election of 1964. Probably the most galling provision of the 1965 VRA for the South was a determination by the attorney general or the director of the census that a state that fell under the provisions of the 1965 VRA was not subject to review in any court.

---

46. Voting Rights Act of 1965, Pub. L. No. 89–110, sec. 3(b), 79 Stat. 437 (1965), codified at 42 U.S.C. § 1973(a),(b).

Table 7.2

Voters and Nonvoters by Race and Year in the South: Percentages

Year	Registered and Voted		Registered, Didn't Vote		Not Registered	
	White	Black	White	Black	White	Black
1952	60.12	15.74	12.99	2.78	26.89	81.48
1956	62.09	16.87	15.35	13.25	22.56	69.88
1960	76.51	32.65	8.72	8.16	14.77	59.18
1964	71.07	53.33	11.52	12.22	17.42	34.44
1968	68.14	67.16	11.36	8.96	20.50	23.88
1972	78.47	79.25	7.65	13.21	13.88	7.55
1976	68.57	59.05	9.89	16.19	21.54	24.76
1980	72.58	69.77	6.99	12.79	20.43	17.44
1984	69.12	64.66	9.22	12.03	21.66	23.31
1988	59.19	52.55	14.36	22.63	26.45	24.82
1992	70.12	60.56	6.30	15.00	23.58	24.44
1996	77.03	63.03	10.27	18.49	12.70	18.49
2000	75.72	69.52	11.23	9.52	13.05	20.95
2004	71.98	60.68	11.21	17.09	7.33	6.84
2008	77.93	79.05	9.39	9.84	12.68	11.11
2012	73.09	76.23	17.24	15.57	9.67	8.20
2016	79.61	78.33	10.85	15.27	9.54	6.40

Sources: 1948–2004: Sapiro and Rosenstone, "American National Election Studies" (Ann Arbor, MI: University of Michigan, Center for Political Studies [producer]. Inter-University Consortium for Political and Social Research [distributor], Sept. 25, 2007); ANES Time Series Cumulative Data File (1948–2012). 2008: ANES 2008 Time Series Study (Ann Arbor, MI: Inter-University Consortium for Political and Social Research [distributor], June 10, 2009). 2012: 2012 Time Series Study (Stanford University and the University of Michigan [producers]) . 2016: Time Series Cumulative Data File.

So powerful was this law that table 7.2 shows that by 1968 no practical difference existed between Blacks and whites who were registered and voted, and by 1972 Blacks voted at a higher rate than whites in the Southern states when controlled for socioeconomic status. As late as 1964, the rate of Black to white voters who were registered and voted in the South was 53 percent for Blacks compared to over 70 percent for whites. In 1952, the ratio of Black to white voters was 15 percent, compared to 60 percent in table 7.2.

A state that fell under the enforcement provisions of the act could apply to be released from the enforcement provisions if "the United States District Court for the District of Columbia . . . has determined that no such test or device has been used during the five years preceding the filing of the action."[47]

Since all the states that came under the enforcement provisions of the 1965 VRA had such tests or devices in 1965, the earliest date for release from the enforcement provisions would have been 1970. In 1970, the five-year provision was extended by legislation to ten years until 1975.[48] In 1975, the ten-year provision was extended to seventeen years from the last time a voting test or device had been used until 1982.[49]

In 1982, the seventeen-year enforcement provisions were extended to nineteen years, 1965 until 1984. Section 4(a), however, was amended to require that before a state could receive a declaratory judgment releasing them from the enforcement provisions of the 1965 VRA from the district court for the District of Columbia, that state would need to satisfy four requirements: 1) no test or device used to prohibit voting for ten years prior to asking for the declaratory judgment, 2) no final judgments from any court of denials or abridgements of the right to vote, 3) no federal observers assigned, 4) no objections by the attorney general of the US. These new provisions extended for twenty-five years until 2006.[50]

In 2000, the Supreme Court considered *Reno v. Bossier Parish School Board II*. Three years earlier the Bossier Parish School Board had asked the attorney general for a "preclearance" in accord with section 5 of the 1965 VRA, to allow their new voting districts (*Reno v. Bossier Parish School Board I*). Even though the Bossier Parish School District was 20 percent Black, and the Black residents were "sufficiently numerous and geographically compact as to constitute a majority in two single-member districts," the school board had not a single majority Black district.[51]

The attorney general denied the preclearance and the school board instituted an action in the district court for the District of Columbia. The district court allowed the plan because the new plan was not worse than the old plan, which also had no Black districts. The attorney general appealed to the Supreme Court that the issue was not simply whether the new plan was worse than the old plan (retrogressive) or whether the intent was to be retrogressive, but whether the plan had a discriminatory purpose.

47. Voting Rights Act of 1965, Pub. L. No. 89–110, sec. 4(a), 79 Stat. 438 (1965), codified at 42 U.S.C. § 1973(b).

48. Voting Rights Act Amendments of 1970, Pub. L. No. 91–285 (1970), codified at 42 U.S.C. § 1973(b).

49. Pub. L. No. 94–73, 89 Stat. 400 (1975).

50. Voting Rights Act Amendments of 1982, Pub. L. No. 97–205, 96 Stat. 131 (1982).

51. *Reno v. Bossier Parish School Board II*, 528 U.S. at 324.

In *Reno v. Bossier Parish School Board I* (1997), the Supreme Court returned the case to the district court and stated that the issue was not simply whether the new plan was not retrogressive, but whether it had a retrogressive intent, which is forbidden by the 1965 VRA. The district court again granted the preclearance and found no evidence of such a discriminatory but non-retrogressive purpose.

In *Reno v. Bossier Parish School Board II* (2000), the Supreme Court rejected the attorney general's claim that section 5 of the VRA prohibits a discriminatory purpose (failure to create Black districts when it was possible to do so) that is not retrogressive (voting districts that decrease the strength of the Black vote). The 5–4 vote by the justices in *Reno v. Bossier Parish School Board II* was along party lines, excepted only by Justice David Souter, who had been appointed by a Republican president, but who nonetheless has consistently supported affirmative action principles in the lineage of Justices William O. Douglass, Thurgood Marshall, and William Brennen.

The Supreme Court ruled again in 2003 in *Georgia v. Ashcroft* that a state could satisfy the requirements of section 5 of the Voting Rights Act of 1965 even when the state diluted supermajority-minority districts (example, a Black district where Blacks vastly outnumber any other racial group), if the state could show that Blacks could form voting coalitions with white voters as an alternative to electing a Black representative. Justice Sandra Day O'Connor wrote:

> In assessing the totality of the circumstances, a court should not focus solely on the comparative ability of a minority group to elect a candidate of its choice. While this factor is an important one in the §5 retrogression inquiry, it cannot be dispositive or exclusive.... There are communities in which minority citizens are able to form coalitions with voters from other racial and ethnic groups, having no need to be a majority within a single district in order to elect candidates of their choice.[52]

The 5–4 vote in *Georgia v. Ashcroft* followed the same party lines as in *Reno v. Bossier Parish School Board II*. The Bush Justice Department and the district court for the District of Columbia both opposed the plan of the state of Georgia. Justice David Souter, in dissent, wrote:

> If the State's evidence fails to convince a factfinder that high racial polarization in voting is unlikely, or that high white crossover voting is likely, or that other political and demographic

---

52. *Georgia v. Ashcroft*, 539 U.S. at 480, 481.

facts point to probable minority effectiveness, a reduction in supermajority districts must be treated as potentially and fatally retrogressive, the burden of persuasion always being on the State.[53]

In 2006, President George W. Bush signed the Fannie Lou Hamer, Rosa Parks, and Coretta Scott King Voting Rights Act Reauthorization and Amendments Act of 2006. This act found that

> the effectiveness of the Voting Rights Act of 1965 has been significantly weakened by the United States Supreme Court decisions in *Reno v. Bossier Parish II* and *Georgia v. Ashcroft*, which have misconstrued Congress' original intent in enacting the Voting Rights Act of 1965 and narrowed the protections afforded by section 5 of such Act.[54]

The VRA amendments of 2006 essentially overruled the preceding Supreme Court decisions by changing section 5 to prohibit discriminatory purpose and stating that the purpose of subsection (b) is to protect the ability of such citizens to elect their preferred candidates of choice. The Fannie Lou Hamer, Rosa Parks, and Coretta Scott King Voting Rights Act Reauthorization and Amendments Act of 2006 would have expired in 2032.[55]

In June 2013, the Supreme Court declared section 4(b) of the 1965 VRA unconstitutional in *Shelby County v. Holder*. Section 4(b) determined which states fell under the enforcement provisions of the VRA of 1965. Section 5 contained the provisions by which states could seek preclearance of proposed changes to voting laws. Even though the 5–4 majority issued no holding on section 5, without a coverage formula that applied to the Southern states, section 5 preclearance requirements are moot.

The majority in *Shelby County v. Holder* found no current reason to target the Southern states, all of whom had voting restrictions in 1964, just because Blacks were denied the vote forty years ago. Chief Justice John Roberts in the majority opinion wrote: "If Congress had started from scratch in 2006, it plainly could not have enacted the present coverage formula. It

---

53. *Georgia v. Ashcroft*, 539 U.S. at 493.

54. Fannie Lou Hamer, Rosa Parks, and Coretta Scott King Voting Rights Act Reauthorization and Amendments Act of 2006, Pub. L. No. 109-246, 120 Stat. 577 (2006), codified at 42 U.S.C. § 1973(b).

55. Fannie Lou Hamer, Rosa Parks, and Coretta Scott King Voting Rights Act Reauthorization and Amendments Act of 2006, Pub. L. No. 109-246, sec. 4, 120 Stat. 577 (2006), codified at 42 U.S.C. § 1973(b). By simply exchanging the name of the act in 42 U.S.C. § 1973(b)(a)(8) from "Voting Rights Act Amendments of 1982," to "Fannie Lou Hamer, Rosa Parks, and Coretta Scott King Voting Rights Act Reauthorization and Amendments Act of 2006," the act was extended to 2032.

would have been irrational for Congress to distinguish between states in such a fundamental way based on forty-year-old data, when today's statistics tell an entirely different story."[56]

In dissenting, Justice Ruth Bader Ginsburg addressed why the South was still worthy of special treatment. "There is no question, moreover, that the covered jurisdictions have a unique history of problems with racial discrimination in voting. . . . Although covered jurisdictions account for less than 25 percent of the country's population, the Katz study revealed that they accounted for 56 percent of successful §2 litigation since 1982."[57]

The point is that while both parties supported equal voting rights, the enfranchisement of the Black vote changed the political landscape in fundamental ways. The Democrats, the party most responsible for the Second Reconstruction, have been the main beneficiaries of the Black vote. Consequently, the GOP either must pander for Black votes or appeal to white voters on a racialized agenda. This political reality affects judicial appointments and the 5-4 splits on the Supreme Court.

President Donald Trump's 2020 claims about voter fraud are an easy target as the reason for the rash of bills making it more difficult for registered voters to actually cast a ballot.[58] COVID-19 required that many states allow greater access to voting by mail, absentee, and early voting than in the past. These efforts were successful and the 2020 presidential election had record voter turnout not seen for nearly a century. In November of 2020, 66.7 percent of the eligible voters cast ballots.[59] The turnout rates were 52.2 percent, 62.8 percent, 58.1 percent, and 60.1 percent in 1948, 1964, 1992, and 2016 respectively. One would have to go back to 1900 (William McKinley, Democrat, versus William Jennings Bryan, Republican) for a higher turnout rate of 73.7 percent.[60] However, the thesis here is that what we see today in attempts to limit particularly the impact of votes by peoples of color is just a continuation of America's historic efforts to enforce the power of whites and maintain white privileges. The declining white population will make those efforts ever more difficult without some sort of limits on legitimate Black and Latino voting power. However, laws designed to limit the increasing power of the vote of people of color risks destroying the legitimacy of the courts and destabilizing the entire political system.

56. *Shelby County v. Holder*, 133 S. Ct., 2630-31.
57. *Shelby County v. Holder*, 570 U.S. 529, 576-78.
58. Brennan Center for Justice, "Voting Laws Roundup."
59. McDonald, "2020 November General Election."
60. McDonald, "National General Election."

On October 2, 2020, the United States Supreme Court agreed to hear the case of *Brnovich v. Democratic National Committee*. The Arizona attorney general appealed after the Ninth Circuit Court of Appeals sitting en banc found that Arizona laws requiring that voters cast ballots only in their own voting precincts, that no one but a family member could be in possession of an early ballot, and it was a felony for a third party to be in possession of an early ballot, violated the VRA of 1965. "Since at least 1970, Arizona has required voters who choose to vote in person on election day to cast their ballots in their assigned precinct and has enforced this system by counting only those ballots cast in the correct precinct."[61] On its face, this law, standing alone, does not seem particularly strange. However, "since 1997, it has been the law in Arizona that 'only the elector may be in possession of that elector's unvoted early ballot' (A.R.S. §16-542[D]). In 2016, Arizona amended A.R.S. §16-1005 by enacting H.B. 2023, which limits who may collect a voter's voted or unvoted early ballot."[62] Essentially, only family members by blood, marriage, or other legal status, mail carriers, or election officials may collect a ballot from another person. Also it is a felony for anyone other than those approved by law to collect ballots. The Arizona Democratic Party (Democratic National Committee, the Democratic Senatorial Campaign Committee) sued the Arizona secretary of state at the time, Republican Michele Reagan, and the Arizona attorney general, also a Republican, Mark Brnovich, claiming these laws violated the 1965 VRA. The federal district court allowed the Arizona Republican Party, and other Republican-interested GOP groups, to join as defendants in the case.

What is strange about the Arizona law is that some counties have what are called "voting centers," which can print ballots for any voter in the county and which limit the voting options on a particular ballot to those applicable to that particular voter's precinct. Some counties, mostly rural and sparsely populated, have voting centers allowing out-of-precinct voting; other counties, mostly urban, do not. The Arizona Democrats produced expert testimony that the laws had a harmful impact on Black, Latino, and Indian voters, that Arizona had a long history of voter suppression of Black, Latino, and Indian voters, and that out-of-precinct voting was "negligible in majority-white precincts, but increases dramatically in precincts where Hispanics and Native Americans make up majorities."[63] The Arizona Democrats "allege that the challenged laws violate §2 of the Voting Rights Act of 1965 (VRA) by adversely and disparately impacting the electoral

61. Democratic Nat'l Comm. v. Reagan, 329 F. Supp. 3d 824, 840 (D. Ariz.).
62. Democratic Nat'l Comm. v. Reagan, 329 F. Supp. 3d 824, 839 (D. Ariz.).
63. Democratic Nat'l Comm. v. Reagan, 329 F. Supp. 3d 824, 835 (D. Ariz.).

opportunities of Hispanic, African American, and Native American Arizonans, who Plaintiffs claim are among their core constituencies."[64]

The federal district court held that the Arizona laws only minimally burdened voters' voting and associated rights and that prohibiting third-party collection of early ballots served important regulatory interests. The United States Court of Appeals for the Ninth Circuit three-judge panel affirmed the judgment of the district court, concluding

> that the district court did not err in holding that H.B. 2023 and the OOP [out-of-precinct] policy did not violate the First and Fourteenth Amendments because they imposed only a minimal burden on voters and were adequately designed to serve Arizona's important regulatory interests. We also conclude that the district court did not err in holding that H.B. 2023 and the OOP policy did not violate §2 of the VRA. Given the minimal burden imposed by these election practices, DNC failed to show that minority voters were deprived of an equal opportunity to participate in the political process and elect candidates of their choice. Finally, we conclude that the district court did not err in holding that H.B. 2023 did not violate the Fifteenth Amendment, because DNC failed to carry its burden of showing that H.B. 2023 was enacted with discriminatory intent. We reject DNC's urging to toss out the district court's findings, reweigh the facts and reach opposite conclusions.[65]

Sidney R. Thomas, the chief judge of the Ninth Circuit, wrote a dissenting opinion stating, "Arizona's policy of wholly discarding—rather than partially counting—votes cast out-of-precinct has a disproportionate effect on racial and ethnic minority groups. It violates §2 of the Voting Rights Act (VRA), and it unconstitutionally burdens the right to vote guaranteed by the First Amendment and incorporated against the states under the Fourteenth Amendment. H.B. 2023, which criminalizes most ballot collection, serves no purpose aside from making voting more difficult, and keeping more African American, Hispanic, and Native American voters from the polls than white voters."[66]

However, when the Ninth Circuit sat en banc (all eleven judges together) the court reversed and made four findings:

> 1) Arizona's policy of wholly discarding, rather than counting or partially counting, ballots that were not cast in voters'

---

64. Democratic Nat'l Comm. v. Reagan, 329 F. Supp. 3d 824, 832 (D. Ariz.).
65. Democratic Nat'l Comm. v. Reagan, 904 F.3d 686, 697 (9th Cir. 2018).
66. Democratic Nat'l Comm. v. Reagan, 904 F.3d 686, 732 (9th Cir. 2018).

assigned precinct, and social and historical conditions in Arizona, constituted impermissible vote denial in violation of §2 of VRA; 2) Arizona statute criminalizing the collection and delivery of another person's ballot, unless the third party was an official engaged in official duties, or was a family member, household member, or caregiver of the voter, constituted impermissible vote denial under "results test" of §2 of VRA; 3) [The] plaintiff established that racial discrimination was motivating factor leading to enactment of Arizona statute as required to allege enactment of statute constituted intentional discrimination in violation of §2 of VRA; and 4) [The] statute would not have been enacted without racial discrimination as a motivating factor, as required for enactment of statute to constitute intentional discrimination in violation of §2 of VRA and Fifteenth Amendment.[67]

Even though the press warned that in *Brnovich* the US Supreme Court gutted most of what remains of the landmark Voting Right Act 1965, more was at stake in the July 2021 *Brnovich* decision by the Supreme Court than just the constitutionality of the Arizona laws.[68] The Democratic Party won Arizona in the 2020 presidential elections for the first time since Bill Clinton in 1996. Before that you would have to go back to Harry Truman's win in 1948 to find the state of Arizona voting for a Democratic candidate. Whites are slowly losing voting power to peoples of color. This is based on the demographic changes in figure 7.3. The Democratic Party won in Arizona in spite of the restrictive laws. Laws designed to stave off the inevitable decline of white voting power can foster disrespect for the laws and the courts that uphold such laws. The recently GOP-packed Supreme Court risks undercutting its own legitimacy by supporting such laws.

In *Brnovich*, with Justice Samuel Alito writing for the 6–3 majority, including Justices Roberts, Thomas, Gorsuch, Kavanaugh, and Barrett, the court held that "Arizona's out-of-precinct policy and HB 2023 do not violate §2 of the VRA, and HB 2023 was not enacted with a racially discriminatory purpose."[69]

The majority found that "the size of the burden imposed by a challenged voting rule is highly relevant. The concepts of 'open[ness]' and 'opportunity' connote the absence of obstacles and burdens that block or seriously hinder voting, and therefore the size of the burden imposed by

67. Democratic Nat'l Comm. v. Hobbs, 948 F.3d 989 (9th Cir.); *Brnovich v. Democratic Nat'l Comm.*

68. Totenberg, "Supreme Court Deals."

69. *Brnovich v. Democratic Nat'l Comm.*, 2350.

a voting rule is important. After all, every voting rule imposes a burden of some sort. Voting takes time and, for almost everyone, some travel, even if only to a nearby mailbox. Casting a vote, whether by following the directions for using a voting machine or completing a paper ballot, requires compliance with certain rules. But because voting necessarily requires some effort and compliance with some rules, the concept of a voting system that is 'equally open' and that furnishes an equal 'opportunity' to cast a ballot must tolerate the 'usual burdens of voting.'"[70]

Next, the majority found that "the racial disparity in burdens allegedly caused by the out-of-precinct policy is small in absolute terms. The district court accepted the plaintiffs' evidence that, of the Arizona counties that reported out-of-precinct ballots in the 2016 general election, a little over 1 percent of Hispanic voters, 1 percent of African American voters, and 1 percent of Native American voters who voted on election day cast an out-of-precinct ballot. For nonminority voters, the rate was around 0.5 percent. A policy that appears to work for 98 percent or more of voters to whom it applies—minority and nonminority alike—is unlikely to render a system unequally open.[71]

Justice Kagan writing in dissent, joined by Justices Breyer and Sotomayor, said the legislative history of the 1965 VRA shows that intent does not matter "if minority citizens are denied a fair opportunity to participate . . . the system should be changed, regardless of what motives were in an official's mind."[72]

Said Kagan, "And whatever the majority might say about the ordinariness of such a rule, Arizona applies it in extra-ordinary fashion: Arizona is *the* national outlier in dealing with out-of-precinct votes, with the next-worst offender nowhere in sight."[73] Kagan showed that Arizona used its out-of-precinct rules to throw out some forty thousand ballots between 2008 and 2016, over 300 percent higher than any other state in the country.

Kagan stated that "elections are often fought and won at the margins—certainly in Arizona. Consider the number of votes separating the two presidential candidates in the [2020] election: 10,457. That is fewer votes than Arizona discarded under the out-of-precinct policy in two of the prior three presidential elections."[74] Challenging the majority's statistics, Kagan demonstrated that "in 2016, Hispanics, African Americans, and

70. Brnovich v. Democratic Nat'l Comm., 2338.
71. Brnovich v. Democratic Nat'l Comm., 2344–45.
72. Brnovich v. Democratic Nat'l Comm., 2357.
73. Brnovich v. Democratic Nat'l Comm., 2366.
74. Brnovich v. Democratic Nat'l Comm., 2367.

Native Americans were about twice as likely—or said another way, 100 percent more likely—to have their ballots discarded than whites."[75] The Arizona voting statute made it a crime to collect or deliver another person's ballot, unless the third party was an official engaged in official duties or was a family member, household member, or caregiver of the voter. On some Indian lands, voters can live up to a two-hour drive from the nearest mailbox. If you lived alone, without a car, your neighbor or even a friend would be prohibited from mailing your ballot. If this is not a violation of a right to vote, nothing is.

The Supreme Court's decision in *Brnovich*, if left unchecked, will destabilize the American democracy. Just as Nat Turner's raid was insignificant compared to the Civil War that followed, the January 6, 2021, attack on the nation's Capitol by Trump supporters will pale in significance to a voting majority made up of peoples of color who wake up one morning realizing American democracy has been stolen from them by the courts and a political system dominated by white supremacy. Any voting rule that impacts races differently and is sufficient to impact state or national election outcomes based on those differing racial impacts is a serious discrepancy and should certainly be a violation of the 1965 VRA. The politically driven decision in *Brnovich* is as grave an error as the Supreme Court decisions in *Dred Scott* and *Plessy*.[76]

WHY ALL BLACK POLITICS IS RADICAL

Black political interests have high intrinsic and perceived political costs for American politics because they are based on substantive equality between the races, which most whites still oppose. Black political interests here imply real interests, not those issues presented as the standard fare for Black voters by the major political parties in their platforms mentioned above: civil rights, antidiscrimination, integration, equal opportunity, voting rights.

Real Black interests tend to challenge white hegemony because they seek substantive equality with whites, not merely incremental improvement in the Black politico-economic position. Many examples are available of these types of substantive Blacks interests. In 1972, Black nationalists dominated the National Black Political Convention in Gary, Indiana, and called for Black self-determination. The Black Manifesto called for reparations from white churches. Even many of Martin Luther King Jr.'s demands would seem radical by the standards of today, such as redistribution of property,

75. *Brnovich v. Democratic Nat'l Comm.*, 2368.
76. *Dred Scott v. Sandford*; *Plessy v. Ferguson*.

wealth and opportunity, guaranteed incomes, and employment. King never voiced unqualified support for the Civil Rights Act of 1964 and criticized the bill because it did not end inequality in income or occupation.[77]

The next topics include the strategic position of the Black vote, the top ten substantive equality interests, and why Black interests demand Black faces. These are the contemporary Black equality proposals.

THE THRILL OF VICTORY AND THE AGONY OF DEFEAT

Whites see substantive equality for Blacks as a threat to their privileges. The Black vote has been a threat to whites since its inception during the Reconstruction era. The Black vote, when it was viable, was often the balance of power immediately after the Civil War. By 1867, over seven hundred thousand Black voters were registered, and that number was larger than the winning margin of every presidential election from 1864 to 1900. Since most Blacks voted for the party of Abraham Lincoln until FDR's second election in 1936, the Democratic Party, which controlled nearly the entire South, was locked out of the White House for over thirty years with the exceptions of Grover Cleveland (a Northern Democrat) in 1884 and 1892. From Lincoln to FDR in 1932, the only Democratic presidents were Cleveland and Woodrow Wilson, also from the North.

As the Black vote was slowly eliminated in the South through various means, the South became a one-party region, almost wholly controlled by Democrats in Congress. The lack of competition in the South gave the Democratic senators in Congress seniority on most of the important committees. It became almost impossible to pass effective civil rights legislation. As Blacks moved North and congregated in Northern cities, however, they became important members of the New Deal Coalition. Table 7.1 illustrates that since 1948, Blacks have been the winning margin in eight of the last nineteen presidential elections (1948, 1960, 1976, 1992, 1996, 2008, 2012, and 2020) and the popular vote margin in over half of the last nineteen elections (1948, 1960, 1976, 1992, 1996, 2000, 2008, 2012, 2016, 2020). That is, few Democratic candidates can win, or even come close to winning, without Black votes, with the only exception as LBJ in 1964, who nonetheless took all of the Black vote.

---

77. Marable, *Race, Reform, and Rebellion*, 121–23; Strickland, "Gary Convention"; Forman, "Black Manifesto"; Coleman, "Affirmative Dilemma," 213–17; King, *Where Do We Go from Here*; King, "*Playboy* Interview."

Table 7.3
Presidential Vote by Race and Gender, 1948–2024

	RACE											
	White		Black		Latino		Asian		Native		Other	
	DEM%	GOP%	DEM%	GOP%	DEM%	GOP%	DEM%	GOP%	DEM%	GOP%	DEM%	GOP%
Year												
1948	53.02	46.98	64.71	35.29								
1952	40.02	59.98	80.39	19.61							100	0
1956	39.24	60.76	64	36							100	0
1960	48.42	51.58	73.81	26.19							66.67	33.33
1964	64.50	35.50	100	0							66.67	33.33
1968	40.93	59.07	96.55	3.45							37.50	62.5
1972	30.28	69.72	86.96	13.04	33.33	66.67	57.14	42.86	66.67	33.33		
1976	45.97	54.03	95.24	4.76	56.67	43.33	64.71	35.29	40	60		
1980	36.52	63.48	93.33	6.67	33.33	66.67	55.56	44.44	0	100		
1984	35.64	64.36	88.72	11.28	51.85	48.15	53.33	46.67	37.50	62.50		
1988	39.06	60.94	91.87	8.13	67.74	32.26	70	30	41.67	58.33		
1992	52.21	47.79	94.51	5.49	62.50	37.50	69.70	30.30	30	70		
1996	51.1	48.9	99.08	.92	66.67	33.33	79.31	20.69	45	55		
2000	47.28	52.72	92.98	7.02	35.48	64.52	59.57	40.43	62.96	37.04		
2004	41.67	58.33	88.14	11.86	59.57	40.43	41.18	58.82	30.77	69.23		
2008	44.24	53.68	99.28	.48	76.34	22.22					73.81	21.43
2012	42.58	54.24	97.26	2.12	71.84	25.92					58.06	36.29
2016	37	58	88	8	65	29	65	29			56	37
2020	41	58	87	12	65	32	61	34			55	41
2024	42	57	86	13	51	46	55	40			41	55
MALES												
1948	54.4	45.6	57.14	42.86								
1952	40.69	59.31	85.19	14.81							100	0
1956	42.69	57.31	62.5	37.5							100	0
1960	51.84	48.16	68.42	31.58							66.67	33.33
1964	63.45	36.55	100	0							0	100
1968	39.71	60.29	100	0							25	75
1972	27.77	72.23	84.62	15.38	14.29	85.71	33.33	66.67	100	0		
1976	46	54	92.68	7.32	58.33	41.67	42.86	57.14	50	50		
1980	33.43	66.57	88.64	11.36	0	100	40	60	0	100		
1984	32.81	67.19	83.33	16.67	41.67	58.33	47.83	52.17	25	75		
1988	37.24	62.76	92.5	7.5	61.54	38.46	60	40	33.33	66.67		
1992	48.32	51.68	92.96	7.04	60	40	88	12	42.86	57.14		
1996	45.69	54.71	97.3	2.7	41.67	58.33	85	15	50	50		
2000	42.82	57.18	87.76	12.24	12.5	87.5	57.14	42.86	30.77	69.23		
2004	38.24	61.76	80	20	54.84	45.16	37.50	62.50	41.67	58.33		
2008	40.23	56.90	100	0	69.61	27.45					70.00	25.00
2012	39.77	55.85	95.63	3.21	72.49	25.27					51.13	42.11
2016	31	63	80	13	62	33					61	32
2020	38	61	79	19	59	36						
2024	38	60	77	21	44	54						
FEMALES												
1948	51.38	48.62	70	30								

THE COST OF RACIAL EQUALITY

Table 7.3
Presidential Vote by Race and Gender, 1948–2024

	RACE											
	White		Black		Latino		Asian		Native		Other	
1952	39.38	60.62	75	25								
1956	36	64	65.38	34.62							100	0
1960	45.29	54.71	78.26	21.74								
1964	65.43	34.57	100	0							100	0
1968	41.85	58.15	94.12	5.88							50	50
1972	32.38	67.62	88.37	11.63	45.45	54.55	75	25	57.14	42.86		
1976	45.95	54.05	96.88	3.12	55.56	44.44	80	20	33.33	66.67		
1980	39.11	60.89	96.72	3.28	37.5	62.5	75	25				
1984	40.58	59.42	91.57	8.43	72.22	27.78	80	20	50	50		
1988	55.48	44.52	95.5	4.5	63.64	36.36	58.54	41.46	0	100		
1992	55.48	44.52	95.5	4.5	63.64	36.36	58.54	41.46	0	100		
1996	56.47	43.53	100	0	86.67	13.33	76.32	23.68	41.67	58.33		
2000	50.81	49.19	96.92	3.08	60	40	61.54	38.46	92.86	7.14		
2004	44.51	55.49	94.12	5.88	68.75	31.25	44.44	55.56	21.43	78.57		
2008	47.22	51.28	98.80	.80	80.23	19.21					77.27	18.18
2012	45.36	52.66	98.48	1.30	71.20	26.58					66.09	29.57
2016	53	43	94	4	68	26					62	32
2020	44	55	90	9	69	30						
2024	46	53	92	7	58	39						

Sources: 1948–2004: Sapiro and Rosenstone, "American National Election Studies" (Ann Arbor, MI: University of Michigan, Center for Political Studies [producer]. Inter-University Consortium for Political and Social Research [distributor], Sept. 25, 2007. 2008: ANES 2008 Time Series Study (Ann Arbor, MI: Inter-University Consortium for Political and Social Research [distributor], June 10, 2009. 2012: 2012 Time Series Study (Stanford University and the University of Michigan [producers]). 2016: CNN, "Exit Polls." 2020: Andre et al., "National Exit Polls."

In 1960, Blacks provided nearly 7 percent of John Kennedy's .2 percent winning margin. In 1964, Blacks cast over 12 percent of the votes for Lyndon Johnson, but Johnson beat Barry Goldwater by over 20 percent. In 1968, Blacks provided nearly 20 percent of the votes for Hubert Humphrey, who lost by .7 percent to Richard Nixon in a three-way race with George Wallace. In 1976, Jimmy Carter won the popular vote by 2 percent over Gerald Ford, with Blacks providing over 15 percent of Carter's votes.

The year 1992 was another one with a third-party candidate (Ross Perot). In that year, Bill Clinton had 5.5 percent more votes than George H. W. Bush, with Blacks contributing over 21 percent of Clinton's votes. Clinton garnered 49.2 percent of the votes to Bob Dole's 40.7 percent in 1996, and Blacks pushed Clinton over the top for a second time with over 18 percent of the Democratic Party's votes. Table 7.3 shows that in 1996 Blacks voted for Bill Clinton at a rate of 99.08 percent, a high number that had not occurred since LBJ's win in 1964, with 100 percent of the Black votes. If a Black person did not vote for Johnson in 1964, no polltaker could find that individual.

Even in 2000, with Al Gore losing the electoral college vote but winning the popular vote by .5 percent over George W. Bush, Gore would have had no chance at all without the 18.31 percent of the Democratic Party votes that came from Blacks. George W. Bush's dilemma in seeking a second term in 2004 was how to garner more white votes without losing any of the

Black votes that he received in 2000. Appointing a Black secretary of state (Colin Powell) and national security advisor (Condoleezza Rice) might have helped, as well as Bush's belated opposition to former Senate Majority Leader Trent Lott for making comments supporting the 1948 segregationist presidential campaign of Senator Strom Thurmond. Bush, however, would have won without a single Black vote. Blacks made up 2 percent of the GOP coalition for Bush in 2004, but Bush won by 3 percent.

Since 1948 the Black vote was not the margin of victory for any GOP presidential candidate, until Trump in 2024. Trump won by 1.8 percent in 2024, with Blacks providing 3 percent of his votes, making Trump's vicious attacks of DEI even harder to understand. Trump's coalition is anything but stable. No wonder the GOP has struggled to cultivate coalitions with Blacks. To say that racial polarization has taken away the balance of power from Blacks is not to say that the Black vote is not strategic. The pattern of election irregularities concentrated in Black communities in Florida and Ohio in both 2000 and 2004 speak to the importance of either maintaining, or eliminating, the Black vote in seeking the White House. Black voters were relatively cool to John Kerry, but Kerry would have lost even if Blacks had given him their normal 90 percent-plus voting for the Democratic Party. Black voters were equally cool to Hillary Clinton in 2016 and gave her only 88 percent of their votes in table 7.3.

Figure 7.3 White (non-Hispanic) Votes as a Percentage of Major Party Coalitions—1948-2024

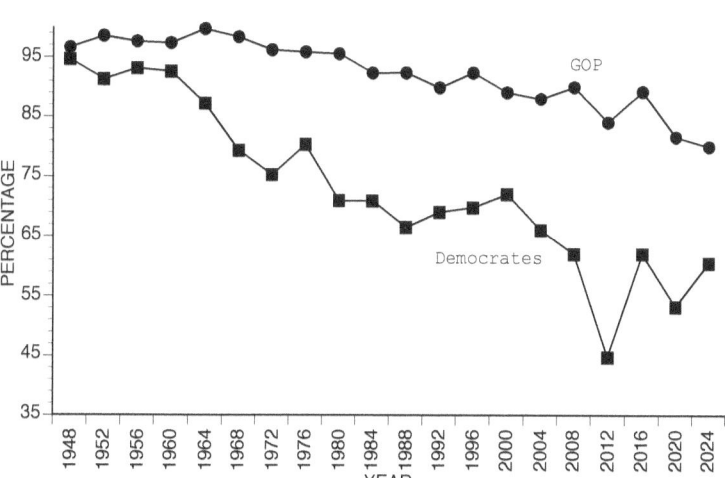

Source: American National Election Studies. "American National Election Studies Cumulative Data File (1948-2016)." 2018. 2020 New York Times, National Exit polls: How Different Groups Voted, conducted by Edison Research for the National Election Pool, https://www.nytimes.com/interactive/2020/11/03/us/elections/exit-polls-president.html?action=click&pgtype=Article&state=default&module=styln-elections-2020&region=TOP_BANNER&context=election_recirc, accessed December 1, 2020. Results for 2024 NBC, "2024 President Results: Trump Wins, National Election Pool, Accessed February 2, 2025, https://www.nbcnews.com/politics/2024-elections/president-results

The problem for Blacks and the Democratic Party is that the passage of the major civil rights legislation in the 1960s garnered nearly all of the Black vote. The GOP had almost nothing in terms of Black voters and little incentive to do anything except appeal to white voters because they were white. Figure 7.3 demonstrates that the percentage of white voters making up the Democratic Party coalition has steadily declined. The perception that Black and white interests are diametrically opposed makes it difficult for the two groups to coexist in one party. Obama garnered 99.28 percent of the Black vote in 2008 and 97.26 percent of the Black vote in 2012 in table 7.3, but he received the lowest percent of white voters in the history of the Democratic Party New Deal Coalition in table 7.1, 62 percent and 44 percent for 2008 and 2012 respectively. Note the difference between tables 7.1 and 7.3, the first of which measures the racial makeup of the major party coalitions, and the second, the presidential vote by race and gender.

The GOP experiences a similar declining white phenomenon to a lesser degree as Latinos take a larger share of the GOP coalition. George W. Bush (the son) received the highest percentage of the Latino vote up to that time in 2000 and 2004 (table 7.1). Romney in 2012 and Trump in 2016 had higher percentages than Bush as a ratio of the GOP coalition. White votes as part of the GOP coalition nonetheless continue to decline. Note in figure 7.3 that whites as a percentage of the major party coalitions are in decline for the GOP and the Democrats at the same time. This phenomenon occurs because the overall white population is in sharp decline. In many ways, the future majority minority is already here.

WHAT REAL BLACK INTERESTS ARE

Table 7.3 illustrates that Barack Obama put together a coalition of Black and white voters in 2008 that no one had seen since Bill Clinton's second election in 1996. In 2012, Obama bested Bill Clinton's two-election average. Other than LBJ, Barack Obama is the top Black vote getter. The percentage of Blacks voting for the Democratic Party has remained high since 1964, when Lyndon Johnson made civil rights the central issue of his presidency. Blacks are so heavily identified with the Democratic Party that anything less than 95 percent of the Black vote seems like a loss for the Democratic Party. Blacks were not impressed with John Kerry in 2000 (92 percent), Hillary Clinton in 2016 (88 percent), or Joe Biden in 2000 (87 percent). Those candidates' percentages of the Black vote seems miniscule compared to LBJ's 100 percent in 1964, Bill Clinton's 99 percent in 1996, and Obama's 99 percent in 2008.

Nevertheless, little in the policies of either major party speaks directly to Black issues. The main Black issue is equality. The voting franchise, Black elected officials, alliances and coalitions, and an informed electorate are all necessary but not sufficient for substantive equality. Real equality is not improvement.[78] Political scientists have difficulty constructing policy lists for Black equality. Most lists focusing on the most important issue facing the nation today dwell in the realm of the possible, rather than what is unlikely to become reality. I am aware of no survey of what issues Black survey respondents believe are most important for full equality. Few survey respondents think in terms of detailed policy initiatives for achieving politico-economic racial equality.

Nevertheless, the evidence that is available shows that while clear differences of opinion are apparent between Black and white respondents regarding the most important issue facing the nation, more similarity exists than difference. The NES cumulative data file codified "the most important national problem." In 1964, 20 percent of respondents thought that racial issues were the most important problem and were third behind social welfare (24 percent), foreign affairs, and defense (37 percent). That same year, 43 percent of Blacks reported race was the most important problem, with social welfare second (33 percent) and foreign affairs and defense a distant third at 9 percent.[79]

In 2000, only 1.03 percent of the nation thought that racial issues ranked number one, compared to 8.79 percent for Blacks in the NES. Joy Wilke of the Gallup organization reported on August 16, 2013, that 16 percent of whites responded that unemployment and jobs were the most important problem, compared to 25 percent for non-whites. No listing appeared for racial issues.

Scholars, policy makers, and civil rights leaders, however, have put forth ideas for policies necessary for substantive equality.

1. Reparations for slavery must be a point of discussion.[80]
2. Integrated and effective schools for Black children[81]
3. A new Constitution devoid of the racist language and old structures[82]

78. King, *Where Do We Go from Here*.
79. See Time Series Cumulative Data File.
80. America, *Wealth of Races*; Robinson, *Debt*; Brooks, *Atonement and Forgiveness*.
81. Ogletree, *All Deliberate Speed*; Orfield, *Must We Bus?*; Orfield, *Schools More Separate*; Orfield, *Reviving the Goal*; Orfield and Eaton, *Dismantling Desegregation*; King, *Where Do We Go from Here*.
82. Bell, *Race, Racism, and American Law*, chs. 1–2; Perea et al., *Race and Races*, 112, #4.

4. Constitutional amendments that recognize societal injustice as well as individual violations of civil rights and statutory change making employment discrimination a general intent violation[83]
5. Full healthcare for all Americans[84]
6. Ending the use of the criminal justice system to destabilize Black families[85]
7. Merit-based population parity goals in employment and education[86]
8. The EEOC must be enlarged and expanded into the employment equivalent of the FBI and empowered to conduct job audits and to prosecute businesses that discriminate.[87]
9. Proportional representation in Congress[88]
10. National urban development to determine industrial plant locations, taxes, and the rehabilitation of existing housing in central cities[89]

Many other issues also would need to be addressed: more effective approaches to substance abuse, child health, Black business development, poverty, and housing. The most important Black issues always are the causes, consequences, and solutions to Black/white politico-economic inequality.

Some of these initiatives have not been tested in the court of public opinion, but those that have show strong white opposition. Over 90 percent of Blacks support reparations for slavery, compared to only 6 percent for whites.[90] Orfield reports that most parents want diversity for their children, with over 90 percent reporting that acceptance of people of different racial and ethnic backgrounds should be taught in school and that a large majority prefers integrated education.[91] When asked whether "the government in Washington should see to it that White and Colored children go to the same schools," fewer than a third of whites say yes.[92] Two-thirds of whites

---

83. King, *Where Do We Go from Here*, 130.

84. Armstrong and Armstrong, *Universal Health Care*; Levy, "How Is Health Insurance Affected?"; Smedley et al., *Unequal Treatment*.

85. Jaynes and Williams, *Common Destiny*, 453–507; J. Miller, *Search and Destroy*.

86. Kerner, *Kerner Report*, 414; King, *Where Do We Go from Here*, 197.

87. Bendick and Egan, "Changing Workplace Cultures."

88. Guinier, *Tyranny of the Majority*, 92.

89. Judd and Swanstrom, *City Politics*, 250, 429; Sugrue, *Origins of the Urban Crisis*, 140–41.

90. Unnever and Gabbidon, *Theory of African American Offending*, 31.

91. Orfield, *Schools More Separate*.

92. Sapiro and Rosenstone, "American National Election Studies," variable

oppose school bussing, the most cost-effective means to achieve equality in schools.[93] Sociologist Joe Feagin writes that white opposition to government intervention to achieve equality is one of the reasons most whites can be classified as racist.[94]

Generally whites support a criminal justice system that oppresses Black men and families.[95] Fifty-seven percent of whites and 66 percent of Blacks oppose quotas in employment. Blacks are about evenly split over the issue of "preferences" in employment, while 82 percent of whites in 2010 oppose "preferences in hiring Blacks."[96]

BLACK FACES FOR BLACK ISSUES

Whether Black voters need Black representatives to support their interests was central in Justice Sandra Day O'Connor's opinion in *Georgia v. Ashcroft* in 2003. At the heart of the debate is the necessity of creating congressional districts with large Black majorities. Carol Swain, a Black political scientist, sees two types of political representation, descriptive and substantive. Descriptive representation is having a representative who looks like the constituent: Black skin, female, and so forth. Substantive representation is having a representative who typifies a person's political and policy interests. Swain implies that Black interests are as varied as white interests on political issues, such as prayer in schools, pollution, abortion, and budget deficits.[97]

Swain finds that Democratic representatives are far more likely to prefigure Black interests than Republican representatives. White Democrats in the North and South, however, regardless of the number of Blacks in their districts, show a high congruence with Black political interests. Swain concludes, "Black representatives are thus not the only source of Black representation in Congress—White Democrats also appear to represent Blacks well."[98]

Swain's conclusions derive from her definition of a Black interest. She measures Black interest by congressional votes of white representatives

VCF0816. The year 2000 was the last year this question was asked.

93. T. Smith et al., "General Social Surveys, 1972–2010," variable busing. The year 1996 was the last year this question was asked.

94. Feagin, *Racist America*, 101.

95. Peffley and Hurwitz, "Persuasion and Resistance"; J. Miller, *Search and Destroy*.

96. T. Smith et al., "General Social Surveys, 1972–2010," variables racquota, affrmact.

97. Swain, *Black Faces, Black Interests*.

98. Swain, *Black Faces, Black Interests*, 19.

for civil rights legislation. The problem with this approach is that much of what is required for substantive Black equality is outside the mainstream of American politics. Few Blacks likely would support the higher levels of poverty, unemployment, wage and job discrimination, and poor-quality education that Blacks face today. The beginnings of chapters 2 and 3 illustrate a basic divide between Blacks and whites about the fundamental causes for Black inequality. Most Blacks think racial inequality has roots in discrimination by whites; most whites do not agree (see ch. 3, "Long-Term Disconnection").

Swain measures only legislation that is likely to pass. In the political world of today, that means white support. Such legislation can be only incremental and moderate in terms of Black equality. Real Black interests radically challenge white hegemony and power and ask for a fundamental change in the structure of race in the US.

Unfortunately for researchers, elected officials vote on few of these more structural proposals for racial equality. One such bill, the Commission to Study Reparation Proposals for African-Americans Act, however, has been introduced each year since 1999 by Rep. John Conyers (D, Michigan). The bill calls for an examination of reparations for slavery, and Representative Sheila Jackson Lee (D, Texas) introduced this bill in the 115th Congress, 1st Session, January 3, 2017.[99]

Most would consider reparations for slavery or any idea designed to achieve substantive economic equality for Blacks as radical, costly, and certainly outside the domain of normal politics. White representatives are not as likely as Blacks to support such measures. Of the thirty-five cosponsors of the bill in the 108th Congress (2003), twenty-five were Black, one was Asian, and the rest were white. All except two were Democrats. No Latino congressional representatives, male or female, supported the bill. Since such a bill likely never will make it out of committee, sponsorship is tantamount to voting in support.[100]

The most important factor in determining sponsorship of the bill was not the party of the representative, as Swain found for her study, but the race of the representative. In fact, assuming the representative comes from the same region, race is the only significant factor in predicting who will sponsor the reparations bill. Sixty-five percent of Black representatives cosponsored the bill, while fewer than 3 percent of white representatives cosponsored the Commission to Study Reparation Proposals for African-Americans Act.

---

99. Commission to Study and Develop Reparation Proposals for African-Americans Act, HR 40 116th Congress, 1st Session, Jan. 3, 2019.

100. The bill was referred to the Judiciary Committee.

Black representatives were nineteen times more likely to support the bill, regardless of party, gender, or the Black population in the district. On issues of substantive racial equality and opposition to white hegemony, Black interests demand Black faces. In the 116th Congress (2019–20), 122 cosponsors were available, up from the 35 cosponsors in 2003.

US Senator Cory Booker, a Black Democrat from New Jersey, became one of the first candidates seeking the nomination of a major political party to make wealth equality a major campaign platform when he championed the American Opportunity Accounts Act, popularly known as "baby bonds."[101] Hamilton and Darity developed the baby bonds concept in which children, not just Black children, at birth, receive financial accounts with increasing amounts for lower-income families.[102] At certain higher income levels, no deposits are given. Each year, deposits become available for advantages, such as college education when the child reaches age eighteen. The political power of people-of-color is increasing.

BLACK, LATINO, AND PEOPLE-OF-COLOR COALITIONS

A thesis of this book is that the future of America is a majority minority consisting mostly of Blacks, Latinos, and other peoples of color. Another contention is that present-day America is comprised of a peoples-of-color political coalition, particularly at the presidential and congressional levels. Not everyone agrees that this numerical majority will represent a voting or political majority. That white elected officials can represent Blacks as well as Black politicians is not the only challenge to Black interests in politics. Rather than assuming a majority minority is in store for the future of America, Vaca asserts that "Blacks and Latinos have a history of competing over jobs and resources."[103] Vaca continues:

> As Latinos and African Americans increasingly live side-by-side in large urban centers as well as suburban clusters, the idealized concept of a "rainbow coalition" would suggest that these two disenfranchised groups are natural political allies. Such a notion presumes a commonality between the two groups that serves as the glue for forming political and economic alliances on a mass level. Contrary to this theoretical approach, however,

---

101. S. 3766, American Opportunity Accounts Act, 115th Congress (2017–18), introduced Dec. 18, 2018. See also Booker, "Booker, Pressley Reintroduce."

102. D. Hamilton and Darity, "Political Economy of Education."

103. Vaca, *Presumed Alliance*, 24.

stands evidence that few formal or even informal coalitions exist among Latinos and African Americans.[104]

To support his claim, Vaca has two primary examples: 1) the Mexican "tsunami" in small Southern towns in Georgia and South Carolina has overwhelmed the local Black populations; and 2) the political fights and contention between Blacks and Latinos in the big-time state and city politics of California. If Vaca's examples were not enough, add in the recent example of the California Proposition 16 to repeal the 1996 Proposition 209, which banned the use of race-based and sex-based affirmative action in state college admissions and California state government contracts. Proposition 16 failed to pass, with 57 percent voting no and only 42.8 percent voting yes. Some journalists have claimed that the Latino vote was critical in the defeat of Proposition 16.[105] Nonetheless, even accepting Vaca's evidence and the possible impact of Latino voters on California Proposition 16, the evidence still supports a future majority minority made up mostly of Blacks, Latinos, and peoples of color in opposition to the majority of white voters. Five reasons for this assumption are: 1) the Hispanic Caucus of the US Congress showed strong support for the Commission to Study and Develop Reparation Proposals in the 116th Congress in 2019; 2) since we have been able to measure, Black and Latino voters have selected different candidates at the national level only three times, and only once did the split between Blacks and Latinos impact a national election; 3) Blacks and Latinos are locked together in the Democratic Party at the local, state, and national level; 4) regardless of which Latino group we are considering, the overall Latino vote is consistently Democratic nationally; and 5) America already has a rainbow coalition of peoples of color standing in opposition to most white voters.

Above we saw that no Latino Congresspeople supported the Commission to Study Reparation Proposals for African-Americans Act in the 108th Congress in 2003. In the 116th Congress, the cosponsorship grew from 35 members in 2003 to 173 members in 2019, and 13 members from the Hispanic Caucus cosponsored the bill. The Hispanic Caucus consists of Latino Congresspeople, voting and nonvoting, from both the House and the Senate and totals 38 members. Support from the Hispanic Caucus for a Black slave reparations bill is important because this issue might divide Blacks and Latinos, since those who stand to gain are only Blacks. Nevertheless, Latino support is growing and strong in Congress.[106] Cecilia Márquez explains that much of the anti-Latino legislation proposed in Southern states

---

104. Vaca, *Presumed Alliance*, front flyleaf.
105. M. Powell, "Liberals Envisioned a Multiracial Coalition."
106. Congress, "H.R. 40."

was blocked by "strong Black/brown coalitions, often led by powerful Black legislative caucuses that fought these anti-immigrant measures."[107]

Whether Blacks and Latinos will form a coalition in the future is a moot point since the voting coalition already exists. Few support the idea that Latinos, or other peoples of color, prefer white candidates to what Besco calls "racialized" candidates. Besco studied racial minorities in Canada and found

> no discrimination among racialized respondents against other ethnocultural minorities, that is, there is no preference for white candidates over candidates of a different racialized background. Second, there are affinity effects for candidates of the same ethnocultural group. Third, there appears to be at least some affinity for candidates of different ethnic minority groups. Finally, the likelihood of affinity is positively correlated with the strength of ethnic affinity; respondents who identify strongly with their ethnocultural group are much more likely to support a racialized candidate, either of their own ethnicity or of a different ethnic minority group, than those who identify only weakly.[108]

McClain and Karnig studied Blacks and Hispanics in forty-nine US cities with populations over 25,000. Similar to Besco, McClain and Karnig found more cooperation than competition between Blacks and Latinos, stating,

> Where [Blacks, Hispanics, or Whites] prosper ... with respect to education, income, employment and nonpoverty, the other groups do significantly better as well.... There is no significant relationship between Black and Hispanic election to mayoral posts or council seats, although there is a mild positive link between the proportionality of their council representation. This evidence indicates neither widespread direct political competition nor prominent mutual support—although it is possible that both exist and simply cancel one another in the aggregate. However[,] there is evidence of political competition between Hispanics and Whites and (particularly) between Blacks and Whites.[109]

Researchers in the area of Black and Latino political coalition at the national presidential level find Black and Latino cooperation because of the consistent voting behavior of the two groups. Hajnal notes that "the contest

107. Márquez, *Making the Latino South*, 171.
108. Besco, "Rainbow Coalitions," 323.
109. McClain and Karnig, "Black and Hispanic," 537.

between Hillary Clinton and Donald Trump pitted the clear majority of Whites on one side against the overwhelming majority of racial and ethnic minorities on the other.... Without a doubt, race is a central factor in the vote today."[110] Besco says, "A rainbow coalition, moreover, typically implies mutual co-operation and support of members, rather than just a coincidental coalition of groups voting for the same party or candidate.... Analysis of the 2008 and 2012 US presidential elections seemed to suggest that such a coalition might be in the offing."[111]

For Haynie, "Obama became the visible embodiment of a version of the aphorism 'demographics are destiny,' which holds that the population transformation would give rise to a powerful African American and Latino-led rainbow coalition that would lead to Democratic Party dominance in presidential elections, enhance Democratic political power in several states, and result in more African American and Latino elected officials at all levels of government. The term 'rainbow coalition' refers to a political alliance of multiple racial, ethnic, religious, and class groups that advocates for political empowerment and policy responsiveness on behalf of those who are disadvantaged or disenfranchised." Thus, Haynie concludes that "when we examine recent demographic data and population change patterns, we find evidence that an African American and Latino-dominated rainbow coalition has indeed emerged on the political landscape."[112]

Most of the aforementioned studies concerned Black and Latino cooperation at the local level. Support of Blacks and Latinos for the Democratic Party at the national level is even stronger than Black and Latino coalitions at the local level. The evidence is clear that coalitions of peoples of color at the national level are far more than just coincidental, and tables 7.1 and 7.3 show Black and Latino coalitions are not a future possibility but already exist at the level for presidential voting. Latinos have broken with Black voters only three times since measurements began: 1) McGovern v. Nixon (1972), 2) Carter v. Reagan (1980), and 3) Gore v. Bush (2000). Even in 2000, only Latinos (men) voted for Bush, instead of Latinas (women) (table 7.3). The Latino/Latina split also happened in 1984, Mondale v. Reagan, but Latinas won, with the majority of the Latino vote going Democratic. The year 2000 is the only year in which the Black/Latino split impacted the election (table 7.1). Table 7.3 shows that Black Democratic Party voting between 1972 and 2000 averages 92.49 percent versus 57.4 percent for Latinos. Compare this statistic to the 41.96 percent average for whites voting for the Democratic

---

110. Hajnal, *Dangerously Divided*, 45.
111. Besco, "Rainbow Coalitions," 305.
112. Haynie, "Containing the Rainbow Coalition," 245.

Party for the same years. Latinos firmly are in the Democratic camp, and any assertion that Latinos would consistently vote with whites would have an uphill battle. Blacks and Latinos do not necessarily march in lockstep, but they do form a powerful coalition at the national level. The future of America is majority minority.

Table 7.4				
Democratic Party Voting on Race Logit Odds Ratios (standard errors in parenthesis)				
	Model 1	Model 2	Model 3	Model 4
	Presidential Vote		Congressional Vote	
Race				
White	Omitted			
Black	30.1****	29.0****	8.07****	2.23****
	(3.03)	(2.93)	(.538)	(.071)
Asian	1.86****	1.73****	1.46***	.483****
	(.265)	(.247)	(.208)	(.143)
Indian	2.50****	2.43****	1.62**	.575***
	(.592)	(.580)	(.333)	(.206)
Latino	3.27****	2.93****	2.44****	1.08****
	(.198)	(.183)	(.150)	(.064)
Demographics				
Gender	.814****	.813****	.981	-.058**
	(.026)	(.026)	(.024)	(.028)
Age	.997***	.995****	.994****	-.002***
	(.0009)	(.0009)	(.0007)	(.0008)
Education	1.05****	1.02*	.921****	-.019**
	(.010)	(.011)	(.006)	(.009)
Family Income	.832****	.840****	.881****	-.164****
	(.013)	(.013)	(.011)	(.014)
Northeast	Omitted			
Midwest	.804****	.785****	.838****	-.235****
	(.038)	(.038)	(.029)	(.041)
South	.589****	.563****	1.04	-.166****
	(.028)	(.027)	(.038)	(.041)

Table 7.4

Democratic Party Voting on Race
Logit Odds Ratios (standard errors in parenthesis)

	Model 1	Model 2	Model 3	Model 4
	Presidential Vote		Congressional Vote	
West	.928	.902**	1.02	-.060
	(.047)	(.046)	(.040)	(.044)
Year				
1968				-.232**
				(.107)
1970				-.089
				(.114)
1972		.627****		-.060
		(.057)		(.099)
1974				.214*
				(.112)
1976		1.28***		-.024
		(.120)		(.104)
1978				.049
				(.107)
1980		.844		-.194*
		(.089)		(.111)
1982				.031
				(.116)
1984		.797**		-.148
		(.075)		(.103)
1986				.034
				(.109)
1988		.945		-.049
		(.092)		(.107)
1990				.231**
				(.115)
1992		1.58****		.011
		(.150)		(.101)
1994				-.528****
				(.110)
1996		1.69****		-.448****

Table 7.4				
Democratic Party Voting on Race Logit Odds Ratios (standard errors in parenthesis)				
	Model 1	Model 2	Model 3	Model 4
	Presidential Vote		Congressional Vote	
1998		(.171)		(.107) -.482****
				(.124)
2000		1.33***		-.267**
		(.135)		(.112)
2004		.979		-.346***
		(.107)		(.118)
2008		1.44****		-.327***
		(.140)		(.107)
2012		1.25***		-.403****
		(.103)		(.092)
2016		1.23**		-.446****
		(.106)		(.095)
Constant	1.62****	1.85****	2.92****	1.04****
	(.145)	(.205)	(.205)	(.112)
X^2	3426.31	3680.54	2409.95	2431.45
df	11	23	11	32
N	18,313	18,313	27,977	27,790

*p=10%; **p=5%; ***p=1%; ****p=<.1%. Whites are the omitted category. Source: Time Series Cumulative Data File.

Voting behavior is influenced by more than just race. Voting behavior is influenced by gender, age, education, income, location, and a host of other issues. Further discussion of how these many factors influence voting behavior requires regression and maximum likelihood analysis. Table 7.4 regresses Democratic Party voting at the presidential level on race, demographics, and year. The year variables are operationalizations for economic, political, or social issues taking place in a given year.[113] Table 7.4, model 1, shows that Blacks are 30 times (3,000 percent) more likely to vote Democratic than are whites, the omitted category. Latinos are 3.27 times (320 percent) more likely to vote Democratic than are whites. The overwhelming support of Blacks for the Democratic Party makes the 320 percent likelihood of Latinos look small, when being 3.27 times more likely to vote

113. Henderson, "Military Spending and Poverty."

Democratic than GOP is quite significant. Model 1 in table 7.4 shows that Asians are almost twice as likely to vote Democratic at the presidential level than are whites. Native Americans are 2.5 times (250 percent) more likely to vote Democratic than are whites in table 7.4, model 1. Women are more likely to vote Democratic than are men, as are younger voters in table 7.4, model 1. More education and lower income are associated with voting Democratic in table 7.4, model 1.

Model 2 in table 7.4 adds year indicator variables. Year indicator variables are rough operationalizations for any politico-economic issues during a particular year. Whatever these issues may be for individual voters, they have almost no impact on a peoples-of-color rainbow coalition. Table 7.4, model 2, illustrates that Blacks, Asians, American Indians, and Latinos are 29, 1.7, 2.4, and 2.93 times, respectively, as likely to vote Democratic than are whites. The demographic variables in table 7.4, model 2, are almost unchanged from model 1.

Models 3 and 4 of table 7.4 address peoples-of-color coalitions at the congressional level. The coalition remains strong at the congressional level in model 3, regardless of the issues involved in model 4. In model 3 of table 7.4 Blacks, Asians, American Indians, and Latinos are 8.07, 1.46, 1.62, and 2.44 times, respectively, as likely to vote Democratic than are whites. Gender has no impact in model 3. Younger age, less education, and less income are associated with voting Democratic at the congressional level. Congressional voting involves local issues particular to the district. Model 4 takes account of these issues. The peoples-of-color coalition is somewhat fractured when local issues come into play. Asians and Native Americans are less likely than whites to vote Democratic at the congressional level when issue operationalization (year) indicators are added in table 7.4, model 4. The important note from table 7.4, model 4, is that the Black and Latino coalition holds up strongly at the congressional issue level, regardless of local issues.

Blacks and Latinos are senior partners in the rainbow coalition, and as such, investigating the Black and Latino coalition further makes sense, as does addressing the issue of Latino nationality, politics, and racial identification as Alamillo, Fletes, and Clemons do. Alamillo is interested in why Latinos voted for Trump in 2016 despite Trump's saying, "When Mexico sends its people, they're not sending their best. They're not sending you. They're not sending you. They're sending people that have lots of problems, and they're bringing those problems with us [sic]. They're bringing drugs. They're bringing crime. They're rapists."[114]

---

114. Alamillo, "Hispanics para Trump," 457.

Answering why Mexicans would vote for a candidate who claims Mexicans are rapists, Alamillo finds:

> Denial of racism serves a measure of a Latino's desire to achieve Whiteness. Taking these findings into account suggests that while Trump's rhetoric may have reduced his support among Latinos at large, his explicit racial appeals may have played a large role in motivating support for him among the subset of Latinos holding disproportionately higher levels of denial of racism. . . . Cubans are much more likely to identify as Republicans and support Republican candidates, while Mexicans, Puerto Ricans, and Central Americans are more likely to be Democrats. To this point, when predicting Republican versus Democratic partisanship among Latinos, research suggests the strongest predictor of identifying as a Republican is being Cuban.[115]

Characterizing Blacks and Latinos as either cooperators or competitors can be difficult to analyze because race, nationality, colorism, and politics are all combined and may have unlikely outcomes. Fletes recognizes these difficulties when she says,

> Going beyond the Black and White binary can be a tricky task that could carry unintended consequences. Latinos and Asian Americans are outpacing the growth of the Black population. This is true even in areas where the Black community arduously fought for and won majority-minority districts. Careful consideration is needed to balance the voting rights of Black and Latino voters, particularly if voting behaviors diverge between the two groups. However, these changing demographics do not necessarily carry negative and unintended consequences for Black Americans; when minority coalitions have formed, Black, Latino, and Asian American voters have been successful in obtaining and enforcing voting rights protections.[116]

Clemons discusses the problem of white racial identity for some Latinos and the implications this racial identity has for a Black-Latino coalition. "Even though there are commonalities between Blacks and Latinos that can be instrumental in uniting them, the diversity within the Latino community poses a special challenge. While some moderate shifts may already be underway, research has demonstrated that Puerto Ricans, Dominicans, and Cubans believe they have more in common with each other than with Mexicans, Salvadorans, and Guatemalans. It has also been shown

115. Alamillo, "Hispanics para Trump," 458–60.
116. Fletes, "Voter Justice," 26–27.

that Puerto Ricans have the greatest affinity toward Blacks in the United States.... Although as a group they are culturally different, many Latinos continue to identify racially as white."[117]

All of the issues and points raised by Alamillo, Fletes, and Clemons are valid and supported by the data in this study: 1) Blacks and Latinos are in a political coalition on many, but not all, levels; 2) white racial identity as a political issue takes on more salience depending on which Latino group is under scrutiny; and 3) the Black and Latino coalition is more related to Latino nationality than Latino racial identity.

Between 2000 and 2018, excluding Spaniards and Basques, 63 percent of Latinos identified as Mexican, 13 percent as Puerto Rican, and nearly 5 percent as Cuban, totaling 81 percent of those calling themselves Hispanic in the GSS.[118] However, only 47 percent of Mexicans and Puerto Ricans respectively self-identify as white. Cubans identify as white 76 percent of the time. Excluding Spaniards and Basques, only a minority of all Latinos identify as white, 49 percent. The lack of a white racial identity does not mean Latinos identify as Black. Overall, only 3.86 percent of all Latinos identify as Black. Mexicans, Puerto Ricans, and Cubans identify as Black at rates of 1 percent, 13 percent, and 8 percent, respectively. Most Latinos identify as other, Hispanic, Latino or by their nationality in the GSS.

Table 7.5				
Democratic Party Voting on Latino Nationality Logit Odds Ratios (standard errors in parenthesis)				
	Model 1	Model 2	Model 3	Model 4
	Presidential Voting		Congressional Voting	
Nationality				
Mexican	Omitted			
Puerto Rican	.958	.951	.544***	.574**
	(.219)	(.221)	(.125)	(.134)
Cuban	.531****	.534****	.417****	.403****
	(.070)	(.072)	(.057)	(.057)
Latino Unknown	1.07	.899	1.38	1.58
	(.395)	(.343)	(.646)	(.762)
Demographics				

117. Clemons, "Beyond the Barriers," 53.
118. T. Smith et al., "General Social Surveys, 1972–2018."

Table 7.5

Democratic Party Voting on Latino Nationality
Logit Odds Ratios (standard errors in parenthesis)

	Model 1	Model 2	Model 3	Model 4
	Presidential Voting		Congressional Voting	
Gender	.882	.902	.879	.901
	(.104)	(.109)	(.110)	(.115)
Age	.993*	.990**	.994	.995
	(.003)	(.003)	(.003)	(.003)
Education	.942	.924**	.896***	.921**
	(.035)	(.035)	(.035)	(.038)
Family Income	.716****	.722****	.749****	.742****
	(.042)	(.043)	(.048)	(.049)
Northeast	Omitted			
Midwest	.518**	.511**	.879	.939
	(.160)	(.161)	(.292)	(.316)
South	.392****	.366****	.443****	.438****
	(.092)	(.088)	(.107)	(.108)
West	.695	.635*	.613*	.625*
	(.170)	(.159)	(.153)	(.159)
Year				
1980			.247	
			(.221)	
1982			.572	
			(.638)	
1984		.656	.380	
		(.340)	(.318)	
1986			1.12	
			(1.10)	
1988		1.22	.650	
		(.622)	(.536)	
1990			.620	
			(.533)	
1992		1.09	.321	
		(.550)	(.259)	

Table 7.5

Democratic Party Voting on Latino Nationality
Logit Odds Ratios (standard errors in parenthesis)

	Model 1	Model 2	Model 3	Model 4
	Presidential Voting		Congressional Voting	
1994			.265	
			(.217)	
1996		2.43*		.272
		(1.30)		(.220)
1998				.860
				(.747)
2000	.853		.216*	
	(.454)		(.179)	
2004	1.03		.293	
	(.547)		(.241)	
2008	2.33*		.520	
	(1.09)		(.404)	
2012	1.78		.311	
	(.810)		(.238)	
2016	2.28*		.281	
	(1.09)		(.219)	
Constant	26.3****	20.1****	34.9****	82.1****
	(9.35)	(11.5)	(13.5)	(68.5)
X^2	112.43	148.51	112.75	143.69
df	10	19	10	25
N	1,515	1,515	1,415	1,415

*p=10%; **p=5%; ***p=1%; ****p=<.1%. Source: Time Series Cumulative Data File.

Regardless of racial identification, table 7.4 showed that Latinos on a whole do not vote at all like whites and are in a strong voting coalition with Blacks at the presidential and congressional levels. Table 7.5 is a similar analysis of Latinos by nationality. Mexicans are the omitted category in table 7.5 and they vote for the Democratic Party at a rate of 75 percent. Model 1 in table 7.5 shows that Puerto Ricans vote for the Democratic Party at 95 percent of the rate of Mexicans, but statistically, there is no difference. Cubans vote the Democratic Party at only 53 percent of the rate of Mexicans. Alamillo's claim that "the strongest predictor of identifying as a Republican is being Cuban" is upheld.[119] But Latinos who do not know their nationality also vote with Mexicans, that is, Democratic. Issues do not much influence how Latinos vote at the presidential level as the results from model 1 hold true in model 2 with the year variables as operationalizations for issues: Mexicans, Puerto Ricans, and Latinos vote Democratic; Cubans do not. At the congressional level in models 3 and 4 the Latino Democratic coalition reforms around Mexicans and Latinos without a known nationality, leaving Cubans strangely allied with Puerto Ricans and the GOP. Models 3 and 4 are similar regardless of political or other issues in the various years. Politics makes strange bedfellows that are not always easily understood with normal criteria. Nevertheless, we have learned that the Black and Latino peoples-of-color rainbow coalition is real at both the presidential and congressional level. The same can be said for the Latino coalition, with a bit more shifting depending on nationality.

NOT A NEW ERA

The morning after Obama's first election, *The New York Times* declared "Racial Barrier Falls in Heavy Turnout."[120] If the election of a Black candidate by white voters is applied to the makeup of congressional districts with Black representatives, the statement most certainly is not true. Black representatives still need Black voters to elect them and exceptions do not make rules. Nationally, the parties are as racially divided as at any time since the re-enfranchisement of the Black vote in 1965. The Trump and Biden elections in tables 7.1 and 7.3 add confirmation of the racial polarization of American politics.

Little intrinsic costs arise as a result of antidiscrimination, affirmative action, voting rights, or EEOC funding. The perception that if something helps Blacks, it hurts whites, however, causes racial polarization in the parties and makes perceived political costs for racial equality high.

The short-term solution is to know the intrinsic and perceived costs. The long-term solutions involve a reversal of factors that caused the problems: lack of political leadership, declines in civil rights activism, end of the post-WWII economic expansion, racial bigotry, and racial block voting.

---

119. Alamillo, "Hispanics para Trump," 458–60.
120. Front-page banner of *New York Times*, Nov. 5, 2008.

Chapter Eight

The Fierce Urgency of Now
K–12 Education

A PANIC FOR EDUCATION

People have linked education, citizenship, and democracy since the days of the American founders and the writers the founders were reading.[1] In modern times, however, the relationship between education and the security of the American way of life probably has more to do with the former Soviet Union than the ideas of the founders.

October 1957 changed America in fundamental ways, and it was not the two-week-old crisis in Little Rock, Arkansas, as nine Black school children attempted to attend class in a formerly all-white high school. Before October 4, 1957, Americans felt they were international and technological leaders. After this date, most Americans felt they were playing catch-up and lagged behind the Soviet Union.

In his celebrated film *Sputnik Mania*, David Hoffman features footage of major network news anchors, Howard K. Smith of ABC, Walter Cronkite of CBS, David Brinkley of NBC, all of whom implied that America was behind in the race for space and science. BBC reporter Llewelyn King said in an interview that "everyone loved American cars, cigarettes, but Sputnik was the first sort of doubt about America." The reason that Sputnik so alarmed America and Americans is important to think about.

Ryan Boyle calls Sputnik "nothing short of a total crisis of confidence in the American way of life."[2] Eisenhower, a Republican, was one of the most popular presidents ever. Eisenhower did not believe Sputnik posed

1. Grant and Hertzberg, "John Locke on Education."
2. Boyle, "Red Moon over the Mall," 373.

a serious threat to the US. Nevertheless, the public alarm over the Soviet Union launch of a satellite gave two Democratic senators, LBJ and JFK, an opportunity to show the public that Eisenhower was a lazy old man who did not understand the times. Ike's approval rating dropped from 79 percent to 57 percent in just a few months.[3]

This crisis of American confidence in its scientific prowess prompted calls for educational reform. Boyle writes, "It was the first time that any significant national attention had been paid to school reform since 1917."[4] Roger Launius claims that Sputnik began the space age and was directly responsible for the founding of NASA.[5]

The Sputnik debacle was more than just the launch of one satellite. Not only did the Soviet Union launch the first artificial satellite, but they also launched the second artificial satellite and the first biological spacecraft on November 3, 1957. Sputnik II carried a stray dog named Laika and was thus termed "muttnik."[6] America tried desperately to respond to the threat from the Soviets. The great fear was that these space objects could be used for spying or, worse, the launch of nuclear missiles.[7]

Ike went on national TV on November 7, 1957, to assure the American public that America was not falling behind. Eisenhower even had a recovered nose cone from an American rocket with him as he spoke in the oval office. What Eisenhower could not say was that he knew from US intelligence sources that Sputnik was not a military threat.

The US televised the launch of its first satellite, Vanguard. Unfortunately, Vanguard blew up on the launch pad on December 6, 1957. The second Vanguard launch reached an altitude of four miles before it too blew up on February 5, 1958.[8]

Sputnik turned perceptions in America of educational slippage into a national crisis. Boyle said, "For every American weakness, there seemed to be a newly discovered Russian strength. For example, the United States was turning out 22,000 engineering graduates a year; the Soviet Union, 66,000 a year." Eisenhower was fearful of turning the race for space into a military escalation. The Sputnik panic was the source of Ike's "foreboding . . . about the Military-Industrial Complex . . . in his 1961 farewell speech."[9]

3. Boyle, "Red Moon over the Mall," 373, 379.
4. Boyle, "Red Moon over the Mall," 379.
5. Launius, "Sputnik."
6. Dickson, *Sputnik*, 141.
7. Boyle, "Red Moon over the Mall," 376.
8. Launius, "Sputnik."
9. Boyle, "Red Moon over the Mall," 379.

People were beginning to compare Sputnik to Pearl Harbor.[10] Ike tried to resist the public pressure to respond more aggressively to the new Russian threat. Eventually, pressure from the young guns in the Democratic Party, LBJ and JFK, forced Eisenhower to act with the Defense Education Act (DEA) of 1958. The DEA took several major actions besides providing $635 billion to fund the act between 1959 and 1962. In constant dollars the 1959 DEA appropriation would equal $5.3 trillion, almost nine times what the local, federal, and state governments combined spent on K–12 schooling in 2012–13.[11]

Title I of the DEA Congress found "that an educational emergency exists and requires action by the federal government." Title II established loans to students in institutions of higher education. Title III provided financial assistance for strengthening science, mathematics, and modern foreign language instruction. Title IV created the National Defense fellowships and "gave preferences to individuals who are interested in becoming college teachers." Title V provided funds for "guidance, counseling, and testing" for high schools to identify students with the ability to attend college. There was even money to expand the use of audiovisual aids in teaching. The DEA seemed to cover everything.

EDUCATION AND THE FOUNDERS

Sputnik caused America to reevaluate the relationship between the American government and education. The Elementary and Secondary School Act of 1965 and the report by the National Commission on Excellence in Education, called *A Nation at Risk*, in 1983, were both education reform movements that emerged in response to the Sputnik crisis.[12] This relationship between democracy and an educated citizenry was not new. Thomas Jefferson frequently noted the relationship between democracy, freedom, and education.

> I know no safe depositary of the ultimate powers of the society but the people themselves; and if we think them not enlightened enough to exercise their control with a wholesome discretion, the remedy is not to take it from them, but to inform their

---

10. Clowse, *Brainpower for the Cold War*, 63.

11. Clowse, *Brainpower for the Cold War*; National Center for Education Statistics, "Table 235.10."

12. Boyle, "Red Moon over the Mall"; Johanningmeier, "Nation at Risk."

discretion by education. This is the true corrective of abuses of constitutional power.[13]

Every government degenerates when trusted to the rulers of the people alone. The people themselves, therefore, are its only safe depositories. And to render even them safe, their minds must be improved to a certain degree.[14]

The most effectual means of preventing [the perversion of power into tyranny are] to illuminate, as far as practicable, the minds of the people at large, and more especially to give them knowledge of those facts which history exhibits, that possessed thereby of the experience of other ages and countries, they may be enabled to know ambition under all its shapes, and prompt to exert their natural powers to defeat its purposes.[15]

The information of the people at large can alone make them . . . safe as they are the sole depositary of our political and religious freedom.[16]

THE COST OF FAILURE

Poor public education threatens the political system, technological supremacy, and military strength because the ordinary citizen cannot evaluate the decisions of their government. Most babies born today are not white. In less than fifty years, most citizens will be Black, Latino, and Asian. The majority of Black and Latino children educated today are not receiving a good, basic education. This should alarm America far more than Sputnik.

Technological backwardness, military weakness, uninformed citizens, lack of political participation, and consumerism were all factors that Sputnik brought to the fore. Control of the nation by dictatorial elites, rather than the common citizen, may happen whenever systems of education break down. Jefferson warned of this phenomenon.

Over two hundred years later, another visionary issued the same somber warning. Martin Luther King Jr. told the nation in his famous "I Have a Dream" speech on August 28, 1963, that he and others had come

---

13. Jefferson, "To William Charles Jarvis," para. 1.
14. Jefferson, *Notes on the State of Virginia*, 14:142.
15. Jefferson, "More General Diffusion of Knowledge," para. 1.
16. Jefferson, "To William Duane," para. 1.

to Washington to "remind America of the fierce urgency of now."[17] King said that now is the time to institute the real promises of democracy. King reminded his readers that "the real cost lies ahead. . . . The discount education given Negroes will in the future have to be purchased at full price if quality education is to be realized." In 1968, King found that Blacks lagged one to three years behind whites and that Black segregated schools received substantially less money than white schools.[18]

EQUALITY OF EDUCATION IS A NECESSITY FOR FREEDOM AND DEMOCRACY

Equality of basic education between children of color and whites needs to occur as soon as possible. At the height of the Sputnik crisis, the Soviet Union used the racial crisis at Little Rock to show the world the true character of America.[19] Racial educational disparity is an emergency that must be rectified. The simplest and cheapest method is simply to move children around spatially to high-quality schools that already exist. Maintenance of a system of racially unequal K–12 education threatens democracy, which depends on an informed and educated citizenry.

Children of color must have a superior education to assist in their overcoming the effects of racial discrimination in the society. The fastest and least expensive method economically is spatial movement. No low-cost political solutions seem viable for involving the movement of white students into Black and Latino schools, although this is fair, since political and social interest follows white children, not Black or Latino children. The burdens of spatial movement should be shared equally, not placed only on the victims of racism and the most vulnerable. Failing to end the poor-quality education given to the soon-to-be people-of-color majority risks destroying the educated citizenry upon which democracy stands.

Poor-quality education is maintained by a system of racially segregated schools that combine poverty, spatial isolation, and social pathology with poor academic performance. Rapid racial integration is the only viable solution before America becomes majority minority in 2060. Many factors hamper the implementation of real racial integration: 1) declines in federal funding and failure to keep pace, 2) quarantining Black school districts, 3) rejection of bussing by whites, 4) white student declines in public schools, 5) the failure of ghetto enrichment, 6) concentrated social pathology in minority

17. King, "I Have a Dream," 217–18.
18. King, *Where Do We Go from Here*, 5–7.
19. Hoffman, *Sputnik Mania*.

schools, 7) the use of exceptional schools as models for the general population, and 8) failure to understand the lessons of *Brown v. Board of Education*.

WHO DROPPED THE BALL?

The financial support for public schools is a three-way agreement among local governments, who use property taxes, state governments, and the federal government. State government pays the most: the latest figures indicate 45.84 percent of all public school funding in 2021.[20] Figure 8 shows funding by source on a per-pupil basis in constant dollars. Figure 8 controls both for inflation and increases in the student population. Note in figure 8 that the costs keep climbing; that is, the cost of education is outpacing the cost of living. Most parents and taxpayers know this.

The states have managed to keep their heads above water and made constant improvements. Few lapses or cuts in state funding have occurred. Only the early 1980s and 1990s experienced cuts from the states for education. Notice in figure 8 that in the late 1970s, the states moved ahead of local governments as the primary source for funding of K–12 education.

Figure 8 Funding per Pupil by Source, 1919–2021, in Constant 1982–84 Dollars

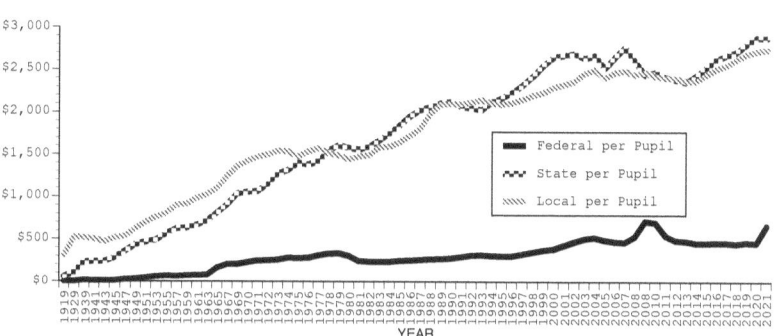

Sources: Snyder and Tan, *Digest of Education Statistics, 2004*, tables 162 and 171. 2005–21: Digest of Education Statistics, table 235.10. Author's computations.

Local funding for public schools balanced for inflation, and student growth becomes clear in figure 8. Municipalities provide 43.60 percent of the funding for public schools, and most of this funding comes from

---

20. Skinner, *Funding for Public Schools*; National Center for Education Statistics, "Table 235.10."

residential and business property taxes.²¹ Municipalities experienced funding difficulties in the 1970s and barely managed to keep funding even with inflation, but local school districts have also generally continued to move forward with the increased number of pupils and increasing costs for education.

The picture for the federal government is quite different in figure 8. The surge in federal support for schools during the "Great Society" years of the 1960s and early 1970s are clear. But the "Reagan Revolution" spelled disaster for K–12 education. Most of the problems began in the Carter years with high inflation and slow economic growth. In 1979–80 the federal government contributed 9.8 percent to school funding but would not reach the same level of funding until 2008–09 at 9.6 percent and 2009–10 at 12.7 percent. The federal government provided only 8.5 percent of school funding in 2014–15. Federal government funding dropped from 10.2 percent in 2012 and 10.5 percent in 2021, the lowest contribution in decades.²² The federal component, although small compared to the states and local governments, is a very important aid to poor and struggling school districts and schools.²³

GHETTO ENRICHMENT

No one is certain how much more funding minority districts need to produce the achievement equivalents of nonminority districts. Large amounts of money have been expended on what has been called "ghetto enrichment," that is, attempts to make minority schools the equal of white schools, while at the same time keeping them separate.²⁴

Orfield reports that after Los Angeles returned to neighborhood schools in 1981, the city received more than $3 billion to equalize minority schools. The school population of the district in 1990 was 625,000 (90 percent Black and Latino in 2000), which means $4,800 per child in extra funds was available if the money was spread equally in the school district, but of course it would be concentrated in poorer schools.

Consider that in 1999–2000 the state of California was spending $7,466 per child, including all federal, state, local, and private funds. The $4,800 in additional money would be more than a 65 percent increase, and more when concentrated on poorer schools. Whether this phenomenal

21. Skinner, *Funding for Public Schools*.
22. Skinner, *Funding for Public Schools*.
23. National Center for Education Statistics, "Table 235.10."
24. Wicker, "Introduction," xviii.

increase in funding in Los Angeles was sufficient to provide equal educational outcomes for those minority students is the next question. Orfield reports that in the mid-1980s the correlation between low math and writing scores and percent minority was nearing -.90, that is, a minority school equals low performance in Los Angeles, in spite of the extra money.[25]

St. Louis had a student population of 43,284 in 1990, and just a decade earlier the federal courts had ordered spending upwards of $1 billion either to improve local schools or increase magnet schools or suburban school transfer programs. If only St. Louis had expended all of the money, that would have amounted to more than $23,000 per student, in a state that spent $7,200 per student in federal, state, local, and private funds in 1999–2000.

What impact this money had is also a topic worthy of consideration. First, 14,000 Black children transferred to St. Louis suburban schools, which indicates how Black families view segregated schools. Most minority students, however, stayed in the city schools and attended either magnet schools or ghetto-enriched neighborhood schools. Measured from their academic starting points, at the high school level, only students transferring to the largely white suburban schools showed significant gains in academic performance. Across all grade levels, the St. Louis magnet schools had the largest academic gains for Black students. The segregated, ghetto-enriched neighborhood schools had no academic gains.[26]

Gary Orfield wrote the court-ordered report that evaluated the effectiveness of the new programs in San Francisco. He found that the only students who made gains were those students transferring to "high-achieving middle-class integrated schools that received no extra money" and those students in low-income schools that hired entirely new staffs, including the principle of being "committed to philosophical principles of integration and intensive reform."[27]

Orfield, who has been a consistent supporter of school integration and bussing, is not the only one to report that financially enriching nearly all-Black, all-poor schools does not produce significant improvement in academic outcomes for the children. The US Department of Education came to the same conclusions in their report.[28]

---

25. National Center for Education Statistics, "Table 42"; National Center for Education Statistics, "Table 157"; Orfield and Eaton, *Dismantling Desegregation*. Author's computations.

26. Orfield and Eaton, *Dismantling Desegregation*, 90.

27. Orfield and Eaton, *Dismantling Desegregation*, 90, 372n29.

28. Puma, *Prospects*, 130.

ELEMENTARY AND SECONDARY SCHOOLS ACT

Chapter 1 of the Elementary and Secondary Schools Act of 1965 (ESEA) provides federal monies to disadvantaged students. In some years Chapter 1 money represents approximately one-half of all program money spent by the US Department of Education. In 2002, $9.2 billion of the $25 billion of the Department of Education was for disadvantaged districts, schools, and students.[29]

In 1993, about 15 percent of first graders nationwide received Chapter 1 money, and about 28 percent of those first graders are Black. The participation rate for Chapter 1 increases as the percentage of students in poverty in a school increase. Chapter 1 participation decreases, however, as the grade increases, so that only about 12 percent of third graders receive Chapter 1 money and about 5 percent of seventh graders in the 1993 cohort. For simplicity, suppose that one-third of the 8.1 million Black schoolchildren, grades 1–12 in fall 2000, receive Chapter 1 funds for disadvantaged children. If those 2.7 million Black schoolchildren received half of the $9.2 billion in ESEA funds, that would be only $1,700 in additional money per student. If all 8.1 million Black schoolchildren received half of the $9.2 billion, each child would have only $550 more in funds. A $900 gap occurs nationally in funding, however, between low-minority and high-minority school districts.[30]

NO CHILD LEFT BEHIND

In January of 2002 President Bush signed the No Child Left Behind Act of 2001, which is an amendment of the ESEA. Title 1 of NCLB promises nothing less than to close the academic performance gap between Black and white students. This endeavor was a bold one. NCLB has five major requirements: 1) states set academic standards in reading, math, and science; 2) states give tests to access whether students reach the standards; 3) the results of the tests give breakdowns by race, ethnicity, language, and income for state, school district, and individual school; 4) states must make "adequate yearly progress" for all students in meeting the standards they set; 5) states must identify schools and districts that are "in need of improvement" and provide corrective action.

---

29. National Center for Education Statistics, "Table 365."

30. National Center for Education Statistics, "Table 40"; National Center for Education Statistics, "Table 42"; Puma, *Prospects*, 135, 153.

The corrective action available appears quite rigorous. A school that fails to make adequate yearly progress for two consecutive years must allow students to transfer to another school in the district that is not in need of improvement. A school that fails to make adequate yearly progress for three consecutive years must provide tutoring for low-income students. A school that fails to make adequate yearly progress for four consecutive years must take corrective action, such as replacing school staff, implementing a new curriculum, decreasing management authority at the school level, appointing an outside expert to advise, etc.

Funding for the act was $13.5 billion for fiscal year 2002 and increased in 2007 by about $2 billion per year to $25 billion for the next five years. Of course, little of the appropriations are new money. The total increase for the ESEA is about $6.7 billion or 15 percent over fiscal year 2001.[31] Even if the entire $6.7 billion went only for the 8.1 million Black children (and it does not), that would be less than $1,000 extra per Black child. If the enormous sums spent on Black students in the St. Louis neighborhood school plan could not produce equal outcomes, the small increases of NCLB were unlikely to make much of a change.[32]

Two provisions of NCLB were particularly exciting: 1) providing detailed statistics on student performance by race and school is a boon to researchers and should stop states from hiding poorly performing schools and racial groups; and 2) allowing parents the choice of leaving poorly performing schools. Most of the choice provisions of NCLB allow the school district the option of instituting them or not. Examples of choice plans include charter and magnet schools, but conceivably inter-district transfer plans also could be used, at the option of the state and school districts.

If a school fails to make adequate yearly progress for two consecutive years, the school district must allow the student to transfer to another higher-performing school in the same district and must provide transportation (unless prohibited by state law). If the school fails to make AYP for three consecutive years, the school must provide "low-income families the opportunity to receive instruction from a supplemental services provider of their choice"—that is, tutoring.[33]

No Child Left Behind sounds like powerful medicine against a failing school. NCLB has no power, however, over a failing unitary school district, from which students cannot transfer, or which makes AYP but still provides a substandard education for students. An example of this outcome

31. Canales et al., *No State Left Behind*.
32. 107 Pub. L. No. 110, title 1, sec. 1002(a), 20 U.S.C. 6302.
33. Canales et al., *No State Left Behind*, 23.

is Wyandanch, New York, called a suburban ghetto, some thirty-five miles east of New York City on Long Island.

BLACK EDUCATION, AMERICAN STYLE: THE CASE OF WYANDANCH, NEW YORK

America has failed to educate Black children, and Wyandanch, New York, exemplifies that deficiency. Wyandanch is an unincorporated hamlet in the township of Babylon, New York. The unitary school district offers no escape for its victims, not even with the provisions of No Child Left Behind. Wyandanch is also the site of the incinerator of the township, where all the white neighborhoods dump their trash. These environmental and educational/racial issues of Wyandanch are emblematic of the problems of Black K–12 education in the nation. In many respects, Wyandanch was the Black Levittown of its day. "Interracial housing" was advertised in the *Amsterdam News*, a well-known Black newspaper in New York City. Carver Park was a housing development built by two Black businesspersons, and homes were sold to middle-class and upwardly mobile Blacks from New York City. Wyandanch quickly became ghettoized, however, by a lack of development in the town, white racism, and the fact that few whites choose to live in Black neighborhoods, which tends to doom any future home equity.[34]

During the Great Migration in the early part of the twentieth century, Wyandanch was a place where Blacks moving up from the South or trying to escape the confines of New York City could buy land and homes on a nonracial basis. Freedmen and -women lived in Wyandanch as late as the end of WWII. This early success, however, led to white flight and allowed Wyandanch to become the target of white discrimination. As late as 1998, reports indicate that Wyandanch was the poorest and Blackest school district in the state of New York.[35]

Blacks have lived in Wyandanch, New York, since the 1920s, during the Black migrations from the South Atlantic states. Most of the Blacks who came to Wyandanch, however, came after WWII and sought to escape the confines of New York City. In the early 1990s, Wyandanch was more than 99 percent Black and had the highest percentage of students receiving free lunches in the state of New York.[36] In 1999, the state of New York reported that Wyandanch was 89 percent Black in the 1996–97 school year. In that year, only Brooklyn District 16 had a higher percentage of Black students,

34. Carr and Kutty, *Segregation*; Koubek, *Wyandanch*.
35. Stashenko, "Neediest Schools."
36. New York State Education Department, *New York, State of Learning* (1993).

89.5 percent. In the 1996–97 school year, Wyandanch ranked sixteenth for the percentage of students receiving free lunches, 87.8 percent.[37]

For years in Wyandanch, earning a diploma that would prepare a student for college was impossible. Wyandanch test scores for nearly every subject lagged years behind white school districts just a few miles away, while Wyandanch spent more money per child.

Wyandanch also is a good example of the impact of NCLB and the pressures on districts to raise their scores if not their performance. Compare Wyandanch and West Babylon, two neighboring school districts, before and after NCLB from the 2001–2 school year to 2006–7. Both school districts were changing.[38]

Wyandanch is becoming less Black and more Latino: .4 percent white, 87.1 percent Black, and 12.3 percent Latino in 2001–2. By 2006–7, Wyandanch was 0 percent white, 75 percent Black, and 24 percent Latino. West Babylon is becoming less white and more Latino: 87.2 percent white, 4.4 percent Black, and 6.3 percent Latino in 2001–2. By 2006–7, West Babylon was 82 percent white, 9 percent Latino, and 5 percent Black. The number of dollars spent per pupil in Wyandanch skyrocketed from $14,000 to nearly $23,000, a 60 percent increase in funding, while West Babylon increased by only 30 percent.

Poverty in Wyandanch dropped from 83 percent to 71 percent of the students receiving free or reduced cost lunches. In West Babylon, 22 percent of the students received free or reduced-cost lunches in 2006–7 compared to 18 percent in 2001–2. Regents diplomas (college-preparatory diplomas in New York) were given to 90 percent of West Babylon students and 89 percent of Wyandanch graduates in 2006–7. It seemed that Wyandanch was closing some big gaps.

Nevertheless, the failure rates for English, Global History, and US History increased substantially in Wyandanch but not in West Babylon. It seems impossible for Wyandanch to equal the Regents diploma rate of West Babylon in just four years and have lower pass rates for exams at the same time. Something is wrong.

The changes in math scores are even more confusing. New York switched to a new math curriculum called Math A and B. Math A is the lower level. In Wyandanch, 75 percent of the students were taking the higher level Math B exams, compared to only 41 percent in West Babylon, and the pass rate in Wyandanch matched that of West Babylon, 72 percent to 74

---

37. New York State Education Department, *New York, State of Learning* (1999).

38. New York State Education Department: "Archive of West Babylon"; "Archive of Wyandanch."

percent. What is unusual is that West Babylon was administering the newer Math A and B curriculum since the 2003–4 school year, and Wyandanch began the tests only in 2006–7. The pass rates were equal, however, and even Wyandanch was ahead in the percentage of students taking Math B.

Surprisingly, Wyandanch caught up to West Babylon in one year. The college-bound students in Wyandanch were only 6 percent of those graduating compared to 91 percent for West Babylon, yet supposedly Wyandanch students were passing the highest-level math test. No one can be sure what these numbers mean, but the combination of suddenly similar Regents diploma outcomes for Wyandanch and West Babylon in such a short time does seem strange with the starkly differing underlying pass rates for exams.

In 2016–17 West Babylon was no longer the exclusive white enclave it once was. West Babylon was only 65 percent white, 7 percent Black, and 22 percent Latino. Wyandanch was 1 percent white, 48 percent Black, and 50 percent Latino.[39] In Wyandanch, 67 percent of students qualified for free lunch compared to 31 percent in West Babylon.

Academic performance in Wyandanch still lagged far behind West Babylon in 2016–17. In Wyandanch only 24 percent of students were in Level 4 English (for those students who exceed standards), compared to 73 percent for West Babylon. In Wyandanch only 5 percent of students were in Level 4 Math (for those students who exceed standards), compared to 33 percent for West Babylon. In Wyandanch only 3 percent of students were in Level 4 Global History (for those students who exceed standards), compared to 45 percent for West Babylon. Students who graduated with a Regents diploma were 5 percent and 73 percent respectively for Wyandanch and West Babylon. The successful-looking exam numbers for Wyandanch turned out to be illusory.

In the 2018–19 school year, West Babylon Senior High School was composed of a student body that was 63 percent white, 8 percent Black, and 23 percent Latino. West Babylon had 46 percent of its students in a category called "economically disadvantaged." Wyandanch High School was 1 percent white, 44 percent Black, and 54 percent Latino.[40] In Wyandanch, 91 percent of the students were considered economically disadvantaged. Again, New York State changed how the state measures student performance and had four proficiency levels: Level 4 Advanced Proficient, Level 3 Proficient, Level 2 Partially Proficient, and Level 1 Not Proficient. In West

---

39. New York State Education Department: *New York, State of Learning* (2018); "West Babylon UFSD."

40. New York State Education Department, "Wyandanch Memorial High School Data."

Babylon, 91 percent of the students were at Level 3 or 4 for English, 70 percent for Algebra I, 68 percent for Geometry, 88 percent for Algebra II, 60 percent for Earth Sciences, and 83 percent for History. In West Babylon in 2018–19, 90 percent of the students graduated in four years. In Wyandanch, 55 percent of the students were at Level 3 or 4 for English, 48 percent for Algebra I, 29 percent for Geometry, 58 percent for Algebra II, 35 percent for Earth Sciences, and 70 percent for History. In Wyandanch in 2018–19, 47 percent of the students graduated in four years. Two school districts that border each other, with two high schools only 3.7 miles and eleven minutes apart, one mostly white, the other mostly Black and Latino, are nonetheless worlds apart. Most of West Babylon's students are proficient. Most of Wyandanch's students are not, and that is Black education American style.

THE DEATH OF THE SCHOOL BUS

White Americans do not oppose bussing or want neighborhood schools. Whites oppose school desegregation and use school bussing as a nonracial code word to keep Black students out of white schools and white students out of Black schools. Matthew Delmont makes it quite clear that "bussing" failed to more fully desegregate public schools because school officials, politicians, courts, and the news media valued the desires of white parents more than the rights of Black students."[41] Delmont calls bussing a fake issue since prior to the 1960s it was white kids who proudly rode the busses while Black kids walked to school.

Yes, school desegregation dressed up as school bussing has been soundly rejected by white parents, and Delmont correctly points out that then Senator Joe Biden was a leader of that rejection.[42] But to transport every single Black child to a middle-class white school, and vice versa, would cost 1/1000 ($500 million) of what is already spent on education and far less than the $13 billion for No Child Left Behind, while possibly giving far better results.

Market competition and school choice models of K–12 education reform are generally averse to bussing, which is nothing more than school choice, for Blacks, on a mass scale. This aversion may have an origin in white opposition. Orfield finds that the desire for neighborhood schools should not be taken as opposition to diversity or integration, and he cites Gallup poll data showing that nearly 89 percent of persons asked described as important or very important that their children be exposed to a more

41. Delmont, *Why Busing Failed*, 2, 3, 210.
42. Delmont, *Why Busing Failed*, 1.

diverse student body if free choice of public or private schools were allowed in their community.[43]

Nevertheless, school integration via bussing does not seem to be popular with most people anymore. School bussing is still unpopular with whites, although opposition is declining at a rapid rate, according to the General Social Survey. Between 1972 and 1982, over 85 percent of white parents were opposed to cross-district bussing. From 1983 to 1987, opposition fell to 78 percent for whites, and to 70 percent between 1988 and 1991. In 1996, the last year the GSS asked this question, 66 percent of whites opposed school bussing. Blacks, on the other hand, usually favor bussing. The highest Black opposition to bussing was in the 1972–82 period, when 46 percent of Blacks opposed bussing. In 1996, 40 percent of Blacks opposed bussing.

White opposition to bussing seems unusual from a financial cost perspective. What has been called "forced bussing" is often the cheapest form of school transportation, since it involves picking up masses of children from one neighborhood and transporting them to a single school. In the 1960s, whites in the South opposed bussing, even though it reduced expenses from two bus systems to one.[44]

Voluntary bussing of individual kids from anywhere in the school district to anywhere else in the school district (for example, magnet schools, which may attract students from anywhere in the school district) is far more expensive. The Kansas City, Missouri, school district is an example of attempts to implement the *Plessy v. Ferguson* (1896) standard of separate but equal. Between the school district and the state, between 1998 and 1999, the state expended over $2 billion on 38,000 school children (that is over $52,000 per child), over 80 percent Black and Latino. Even though this money helped magnet schools and capital improvement programs for local schools, the schools remained 80 percent Black and Latino.[45]

What was gained is the question. When Kansas City could no longer pay for transportation for nonresident students or keep up its magnet school systems, whites fled. Even with the magnet schools, minority student achievement scores remained significantly below the surrounding districts, and the school district remains just as segregated as before the consent decree.

43. Orfield and Eaton, *Dismantling Desegregation*, 6.

44. Orfield, *Must We Bus?*, 140; Orfield and Eaton, *Dismantling Desegregation*, 102–3.

45. Mawdsley, "*Missouri v. Jenkins*."

By nearly every measure, bussing is inexpensive. Few of the estimates of bussing for integration exceed 3–4 percent of transportation costs or 1–2 percent of school district budgets. In 1999–2000 the states spent $13 billion on student transportation, about $500 per pupil. In the dollars of today, the complete integration of the 43 million school children in American via bussing would cost a mere $500 million, or $11 per student in 2000.[46] Even adjusting for inflation in 2019 the cost for bussing is only $770 million.

Compare the $500 million for bussing to the $16 billion for ESEA for fiscal year 2003, or even the $6.7 billion increase in ESEA over 2001. Even doubling or tripling the bussing for integration figure would not approach the cost of NCLB. Even if school integration expended every single transportation dollar, integration is still far cheaper than "separate but trying to make it equal."[47] The St. Louis desegregation plan is a worst-case scenario. The cost was approximately $2,000 per student, including white students attending city magnet schools. The St. Louis plan, however, allowed any Black child to attend any suburban school, which maximizes transportation costs. To save money and help Black school children, then, bussing still is a viable option.

DISAPPEARING WHITE STUDENTS

Declines in white students in public schools increase the racial segregation of Black and Latino children. Many reasons exist for the declines in the ratios of white students, but the most prominent one is the aging white population and subsequent decline in the white birth rate.

Over fifty years after King spoke about the fierce urgency of now for Black education, much the same situation exists today for Black children.[48] Two facts about race and K–12 education are clear: the number of white students in public schools is declining, and Black and Latino students are becoming more and more segregated. Since 1986 white students have declined by 9.2 percent, while Black and Latino students have increased by 1.1 percent and 6.4 percent respectively. Since 1968 the change is even more dramatic: white students have declined by 17 percent, while Black students have increased by 26 percent and Latinos by 245 percent.[49]

46. National Center for Education Statistics, "Table 51"; Orfield, *Must We Bus?*, 130–34. Author's computations: .04*$13 billion, $5.2 million/43.8 million students in 1999–2000. The increase in the student population since 1978 is already included in the transportation figure. The demographic change in the racial makeup of the student body would have little impact.

47. Wells and Crain, *Stepping over the Color Line*, 102.

48. King, "I Have a Dream."

49. National Center for Education Statistics, "Table 40"; National Center for

Even though white students comprise 61 percent of public elementary and secondary school students nationally, for numerous states, most of the students are Black or minority: California, Hawaii, Louisiana, Mississippi, New Mexico, Texas, and Washington, DC. Even in these states in which white students are a minority in the public schools, however, white students attend schools mostly with other white students. In Washington, DC, only 4.3 percent of the public school students are white, 85.9 percent are Black, and 8.3 percent are Latino. With such a small percentage of white students, whites reasonably should be surrounded in their classrooms by Blacks and Latinos. Not so: fewer than half of Black and Latino students attend a school with the typical white student. White students, even in Washington, DC, are concentrated in mostly white schools.[50] This might be called hyper-segregation.

The largest school districts in the US, in which many of the Black population reside, are more minority than white. The New York City schools are over 70 percent Black and Latino, Los Angeles is 83 percent, and Chicago is 86 percent. The school population reasonably should reflect the city population, but that is not so. New York City is only 53 percent Black and Latino, Los Angeles only 57 percent, and Chicago 62 percent.[51]

Where do the white students go? Orfield finds that the white students are not escaping to private schools. Private school enrollment has been dropping since desegregation began. Most white students flee to the suburbs, but low white birth rates and low white immigration to the US mean relatively fewer white students.[52]

Even today, most Black and Latino students attend schools that mostly include other Black and Latino students—that is, in schools that racially are segregated. This segregation is increasing rather than decreasing. By the mid-1980s the percentage of Black students in schools with nearly 100 percent minority students had declined to a low point of about 32 percent from the nearly 65 percent at the end of the 1960s. In 1999, the percentage of Black and Latino students in almost 100 percent segregated schools, however, had gone up again almost to 37 percent nationally. In 1999, over 70 percent of Black and 76 percent of Latino students attended schools that were 50–100 percent Black and Latino, and this stratification occurred in a nation in which they comprised only 26 percent of the students. These numbers were up from 1980, when 62 percent of Black students and 68

Education Statistics, "Table 42"; Orfield, *Schools More Separate*.

50. Orfield, *Schools More Separate*, table 5.
51. United States Census Bureau, *Statistical Abstract: 2002*, tables 35–36.
52. Orfield, *Schools More Separate*, 7.

percent of Latino students were in segregated schools with 50–100 percent minority. Later figures from the National Center for Education Statistics show that 17.1 percent of K–12 students were Black and 20.5 percent were Latino in 2006. The upshot is that 38.5 percent of Black students and 40 percent of Latino students were in schools with 90–100 percent minority students.[53]

The most segregated schools are not in the South. Michigan, Illinois, New York, New Jersey, Maryland, and Pennsylvania hold the top six slots for segregation (Black students in schools that are 90–100 percent minority). The South, while still not desegregated, showed consistent decreases in segregation until the late 1980s. Orfield finds that the increases in racial segregation in elementary and secondary schools are primarily the result of the rulings of the federal courts, which allow school districts to discontinue desegregation plans while they are still segregated.[54]

WHY ALL BLACK IS ALWAYS BAD

The Education Trust reports that in 2000 Blacks and Latinos had fourth-grade reading scores of 193, while white fourth graders had a score of 225. Each ten points is worth a year of reading level, so minorities are three years behind whites in fourth-grade reading. Fourth-grade math deficiencies are just as great, with Blacks three years behind whites by the fourth grade. By the eighth grade, Blacks and Latinos are nearly four years behind whites in science and math. Nearly 70 percent of Black students and 60 percent of Latino students are below the basic math level in eighth grade, compared to only 24 percent for whites. The rates are nearly identical for the fourth grade.[55] As a general rule, minority schools are poorly performing schools. New York educates more Black children (523,000) than just about any other state (only Florida and Texas educate slightly more, at 548,000 and 534,000 respectively).

The differences in academic performance between Wyandanch and West Babylon are emblematic of the state of New York and the nation as a whole. In fall 2000, 20.1 percent of the students in New York were Black, 55.1 percent were white, and 18.4 percent were Latino. For schools in academic trouble (schools under registration review—SURR), however, nearly

53. National Center for Education Statistics, "Table 42"; National Center for Education Statistics, "Table 41"; Orfield, *Schools More Separate*, table 9; Orfield, *Reviving the Goal*, table 4.

54. Orfield, *Schools More Separate*, 11.

55. Education Trust, *Achievement Gap Summary Tables*.

50 percent of the students were Black, 46 percent were Latino, and only 3 percent were white. Nearly all SURR schools in New York had concentrated poverty of over 90 percent.

The relationship between high percentages of Black and Latino students and poverty is well known. In New York State, in high-minority schools, two-thirds of minority children attend schools in which 40–100 percent of the students are poor. In low-minority schools, fewer than 10 percent of the students are poor. In Chicago, the correlation between percent minority and low income in elementary schools is nearly 90 percent, which suggests that if a school is non-white, 90 percent of the time, it is also poor.[56]

Segregation, i.e., having disproportionately high percentages of Black and Latino children, is associated not only with poverty, but also with poor academic performance. In New York, nearly 80 percent of Black and Latino students attend the "Big Five" school districts: New York City, Buffalo, Syracuse, Rochester, Yonkers. As the percentage of Black/Latino children increases, almost every performance indicator decreases.

In New York, school districts with fewer than 20 percent Black and Latino students, the correlation between percent minority (Black and Latino) and scoring between 85 and 100 on the highest Regents math class (Sequential Math III) is +.10. In school districts with more than 80 percent minority, the correlation is -.77, which suggests that a high-minority school district is synonymous with low Regents math scores. As before, this result does not account for the fact that in low-minority districts, 61 percent of students take the Sequential Math III exams, while in high-minority districts, 78 percent of students do not even take the exams.[57]

Even in New York City, which is one unitary school district, minority schools are poorly performing schools. In low-minority schools, 94.4 percent of students are tested for Regents mathematics, and 75.5 percent pass (i.e., score between 55 and 100). In high-minority schools, only 72 percent are tested, and fewer than half pass.[58]

---

56. Orfield and Eaton, *Dismantling Desegregation*, 56; New York State Education Department, *New York, State of Learning* (2018), 123, appendix B.

57. New York State Education Department, *New York, State of Learning* (2021), 135. Author's computations from the report.

58. New York State Education Department, *New York, State of Learning* (2002), 137, table 4.8.

INTEGRATION STILL IMPORTANT

Racial segregation is still associated with poor academic performance. Integrated schools are associated with higher academic performance for Black children. The degree of the academic differences between Blacks and Latinos versus whites nationally almost guarantees that integration is associated with higher performance, unless, inherently, Black and Latino children are deficient, a thesis that chapter 2 showed to be false.

The large socioeconomic gaps between Blacks and whites necessarily imply that mixed-race schools generally also will be integrated economically, which seems to be as important, if not more important, than racial mixing. Chapter 6 delineates how the white and Black poor are unequal. The white poor have far more resources than the Black poor—and sometimes more wealth than the Black middle class. Also, the white poor tend to live near the white middle class.

Nearly every study has shown that integration is beneficial for minority children, in spite of the frequent claims that Black and Latino children can get a high-quality education in segregated schools if financial expenditures are high enough. While the separate but equal idea theoretically may be possible, the lesson of *Brown v. Board of Education* (1954), which argued that "separate educational facilities are inherently unequal," seems to be as true today as in 1954.[59]

EXCEPTIONS DON'T MAKE RULES

Yes, a few schools nationally have either high percentages of minorities or high poverty and are high performing. The Education Trust estimates that 564,000 Black students and 660,000 Latino students attended what they call "high-flying" schools, that is, high-performing and high-poverty/high-minority schools. A high-flying school is one in which students' reading or math performance was in the top third among all schools in the state at the same grade level. A high-poverty-high-minority school is one in which low income students are at least 50 percent of the students in that school, and the school is in the top third for ratio of low-income students. A high-minority school is one in which Black and Latino students are at least 50 percent of the students in that school, and the school is in the top third for ratio of Black and Latino students. The Black and Latino children in these

---

59. *Brown v. Board of Education*, 495.

high-flying schools, however, comprise only about 5 percent of all Black and Latino students in 2000.[60]

In an article titled "A Private School That Thrives on Rules; Minority Students Excel at Brooklyn Site. Is It a Model or an Anomaly?" published in *The New York Times* on September 24, 2003, Jane Gross wrote that "Trey Whitfield, in East New York, is a hybrid institution. . . . It spends a mere $4,000 per pupil, less than half of classroom spending in New York City public schools. . . . Trey Witfield students perform two to three years above grade level on national achievement tests. On the state reading and math exams, they rack up 3s and 4s on the 1-to-4 scorings system, while 2s are the norm in public school."[61]

Gross goes on to explain that the teachers are not unionized and earn far lower pay than city teachers; students are tested for their IQ and parents' attitudes are monitored. Misbehaving children are expelled, as was an eighth grade boy who asked a girl for oral sex. Obviously a tremendous amount of selectivity occurs at the Trey Witfield school in terms of students and their families. While the school draws from working-class families in eastern Brooklyn, these families are highly motivated and spend $3,000 per year in tuition, when the public schools are free. Unfortunately, in education, as in most other areas, exceptions do not make rules.

Why are minority schools generally poorly performing schools? The answers vary. First, minority schools do receive slightly less state and local funding than majority-white schools. New York has the largest funding gap between low- and high-minority enrollment districts, spending $6,335 on high-minority districts and $8,368 on low-minority districts in 1999–2000, with a gap of 32 percent. Wyoming (27 percent gap) followed New York, then Nebraska (25 percent gap), Kansas (24 percent gap), and Texas (20 percent gap).[62]

Nationally, low-minority districts receive $6,684 in state and local funding compared to $5,782 spent on high-minority school districts, with a gap of over 15 percent or $902. Federal, state, and local dollars respectively make up 7 percent, 49 percent, and 43 percent of school district funding nationally. The $27 billion that the federal government spent for public elementary and secondary schools in 1999–2000 could equalize the $15 billion state and local spending deficiency that minority districts face.[63]

---

60. Jerald, *Dispelling the Myth Revisited*; National Center for Education Statistics, "Table 40."

61. Gross, "Private School," paras. 4–6.

62. Orlofsky, *Funding Gap*.

63. Orlofsky, *Funding Gap*; National Center for Education Statistics, "Table 156."

The problem is that districts with large numbers of poor students, as invariably minority districts have, need more than equal funding, but higher funding to counteract the negative impacts of poverty, less educated parents, disruptive home environments, health concerns, etc. Second, minority school districts are unable to attract the best teachers.

SCHOOL CHOICE

School choice has been touted as a big part of the NCLB Act by the conservative think tank the Heritage Foundation. Kafer reports that "research over the past two years has found that charter schools are typically smaller than traditional schools, serve predominantly at-risk populations, and show achievement gains after two years"; however, no information is available by racial group, and "achievement gains" can be anything but the equal educational outcomes promised by NCLB.[64]

The Education Commission of the States' report is less optimistic. Magnet school students tend to perform better than normal public schools, but this performance seems to be a result of taking the best students, spending more money per student, and attracting better-qualified teachers, rather than raising the performance of students from the poorest and Blackest school districts, such as Wyandanch, New York.[65]

Chubb and Moe are probably the best-known exponents of the ability of competition to increase academic outcomes via parental choice.[66] Little information supports the market competition model. Chubb and Moe's regression analysis does show that schools with positive organizational characteristics have higher student achievement. Chubb and Moe do not test how Black student achievement is impacted by schools with good organizational characteristics matched for selection bias (high-performing Black schools may be comprised of higher-performing Black middle-class students), initial student achievement, socioeconomic status of parents, and economic resources of the school. Controlling (matching) these factors is necessary before reasonable conclusions can be made that markets alone have the ability to fix poor Black schools.[67]

Chubb and Moe essentially compared public schools to nonreligious private schools. Comparing public and private schools is problematic, but

---

Author's computations.
64. Kafer, *School Choice*, xiv.
65. Krueger and Ziebarth, *School Choice*.
66. Chubb and Moe, *Politics, Markets, and America's Schools*, 186–87, 89.
67. Chubb and Moe, *Politics, Markets, and America's Schools*, 126–27.

nonreligious private schools are fewer than 8 percent of all private schools and represent a very select group of schools.[68]

The practice of using exceptional schools to make a rule is a continual issue in evaluating any claims that poor Black schools do not need either money or integration to achieve equal educational outcomes. In Carter's book *No Excuses: Lessons from 21 High-Performing, High-Poverty Schools*, almost half of the schools are private, magnet, or charter schools, including the late Marva Collins, a nationally renowned school in Chicago. How unreasonable it seems that these exceptional schools will be the best models to replicate across the nation for the 8.1 million Black school children, perhaps one-third of whom are poor, with little or no additional funding and racial segregation.

BETTER THAN EQUAL EDUCATION

Black school children need better education, not just equal education, to counteract the tremendous socioeconomic disadvantages of growing up as a Black child in America. Eighty percent of Black school children in New York State attend schools in the Big Five (New York, Buffalo, Yonkers, Syracuse, and Rochester), which spend between $10,000 and $14,319 per child. That number is between the 50th and 90th percentile of dollars per student in New York State. At the 99th percentile in 2001, New York State expended $24,903 on each child.

Obviously giving the over 500,000 Black school children in New York State the highest amount of spending per student would cost more money, about $6 billion. To spend at the highest rates in New York State for the 8.1 million Black children in the nation would require $145 billion.[69] These estimates are much higher than the real cost, since New York State has some of the highest living costs in the nation. The costs for high-level education would be recurring, but after time the costs should diminish as Blacks and whites reach equality.

68. F. Fowler, "Shocking Ideological Integrity."
69. New York State Education Department, *New York, State of Learning* (2002). The Big Five spend an average of $11,600 per child. This number represents 80 percent of Black children in New York State. To give Black children the highest spending in the state, about $24,000, would require the spending to double for over 500,000 children. The average spent nationally in high-minority districts is approximately $6,000 per student. New York's 99th percentile is $24,000 per student. The difference of $18,000 is multiplied by 8.1 million.

THE PROMISE OF BROWN

What advantages will accrue with more complete racial integration of schools? Racial integration appears to have huge educational benefits for minority children even today. In their study of desegregation of the St. Louis school system, Wells and Crain found that even though many parents, students, and educators told them the money spent on desegregation could have served better in improving the St. Louis schools, the authors disagree.[70]

If a Black student went to school in the suburbs of St. Louis with whites and endured all the problems associated with that decision (long bus rides, insensitive white teachers, etc.), that student would have a 40 percent chance of going to college. If that same student stayed in the St. Louis city schools, they would have a 6 percent chance of going to college. These statistics take into account all the capital improvements expended on the St. Louis schools.

The reason for such a difference is important to consider. Wells and Crain explain that for Black students, poverty, crime, violence, discrimination, and isolation from the labor market take time away from the learning process, and Black students fail to make the direct link between school and work. In addition, in the suburbs, college-educated parents insist that the schools prepare their students for college. The school administrators know this challenge and make appropriate demands of the suburban students, say Wells and Crain.[71]

Many studies are available about the effects of school desegregation on the achievement of Black school children. One problem with trying to evaluate the studies about what impact integration or segregation has on Black achievement is that many of the studies do not use good methods. For example, some studies compare Black and white students in the same desegregated community. If white students are generally pulling ahead of Blacks in achievement for reasons unrelated to segregation (e.g., income), however, the study may assume that integration does not work.

The best way to evaluate any social program is by randomly assigning subjects to the control group (such as Black students in segregated schools) or the experimental group (Black students placed in integrated schools). The problem is that this type of test is rarely possible in society. Those studies that do use the most rigorous methods show that racial integration is

---

70. Wells and Crain, *Stepping over the Color Line*, 199, 336.
71. Wells and Crain, *Stepping over the Color Line*, 199.

associated with one-third of a year or more in increased academic performance for Black children.[72]

How the increased performance from racial integration compares with the increased performance from the market competition model or the ghetto enrichment model is the next question. At this writing, no good way to answer this question is available. First, little or no evidence exists that ghetto enrichment, the *Plessy v. Ferguson* standard, produces equal outcomes between Black and white schools. This fact should be important to anyone interested in the education of Black school children. Wells and Crain, Orfield, and the US Department of Education come to this conclusion. The conservative Heritage Foundation, Chubb and Moe, and others disagree; they have nothing but exceptional cases to support their claims, however, that market competition or increased spending can make segregation work for Black children.

David Armor, a proponent of magnet schools and voluntary desegregation, and an opponent of mandatory bussing, uses the Pasadena court-ordered desegregation plan as his main exhibit to illustrate that desegregation does not improve Black student achievement compared to whites. Armor uses a figure showing that white reading scores remained almost constant from 1970 to 1973, while Black reading scores rose from 1970 to 1971, then declined sharply from 1971 to 1973.[73]

For Armor and the official report by the Pasadena School District, desegregation "has proven harmful ... inasmuch as desegregation has resulted in substantial losses of White enrollment and significant decreases in levels of district median achievement." Surprisingly, in a 326-page report by the Pasadena School Board, no information comes forth on the changes in the racial makeup of the individual schools.[74]

What Armor does not mention is that at no time did Black and Latino school children attend majority-white schools; that is, the Pasadena schools never were desegregated, even at the height of the desegregation plan. Between 1967 and 1974, the percentage of Black and Latino children in the Pasadena district rose from 18 percent to nearly 70 percent. In 1972–73, just two years after desegregation began, Black and Latino children comprised a majority of the district at 55 percent. Today in the Unified Pasadena School District, only 15 percent of the students are white, and Black academic scores are two years behind those of white students in the district.

---

72. Mahard and Crain, "Research on Minority Achievement."
73. Armor, *Forced Justice*, 78.
74. Kurtz, *Education and Demographic Consequences*, xxxvii.

WHY SEGREGATION IS INHERENTLY UNEQUAL

Why the presence of white students is so important for Black student achievement is an important question. Justice Thomas raised this challenge in his concurrence in *Missouri v. Jenkins* (1995), in which the Supreme Court in a 5–4 decision "struck down a district court degree and held that orders designed to make the district more attractive to Whites living outside it constituted a remedy beyond the scope of the identified harm."[75] Said Thomas in *Missouri v. Jenkins*, "It never ceases to amaze me that the courts are so willing to assume that anything that is predominantly Black must be inferior.... First, the court has read our cases to support the theory that Black students suffer an unspecified psychological harm from segregation that retards their mental and educational development. This approach not only relies upon questionable social science research rather than constitutional principle, but it also rests on an assumption of Black inferiority."[76]

In theory, Black children do not need white students at all. If Black children and their parents have the same resources, funding, socioeconomic advantages, social support, and job opportunities, and are treated exactly as are white citizens, then simply having Black skin should not cause children to underachieve. Ogletree makes this resource argument clear, saying the "challenge [of *Brown*] was not to environment alone; it was also to equal resources. Whether you are in an all-Black or an integrated setting, equal resources and integration of differing ideas are essential to a well-rounded education. Thomas ignores what I believe to be the central goal of *Brown* and its progeny, with little regard for the impact these decisions will have on the African-American children struggling in the under-resourced schools. Furthermore, [Justice Thomas] seems to not recognize the obvious impact of cutbacks on decisions that try to implement the *Brown* mandate. The effect is unconscionable: the resegregation of the very same schools that Marshall and others fought so hard to integrate, upgrade, and bring within acceptable constitutional standards."[77] Thomas also opposed using the enormous powers of the federal government to integrate schools, feeling using these powers violated federalism. For Thomas, the needs of Black school children was secondary.

Justice Clarence Thomas was not the first one to assert the inherent equality of Black school children. However, Thomas makes three errors: 1) he ignores the imbalance of resources between Black and white schools; 2)

---

75. Ogletree, *All Deliberate Speed*, 233.
76. *Missouri v. Jenkins*, 115.
77. Ogletree, *All Deliberate Speed*, 235.

he assumes the separate but equal funding is a political reality; and 3) he does not address the need of Black schools for more than just equal funding to overcome the disadvantages of racial discrimination, which causes poverty, violence, abuse, pathology, and overall inequality.

W. E. B. Du Bois made a similar argument half a century earlier when he claimed that separate schools "are needed just so far as they are necessary for the proper education of the Negro race. The proper education of any people includes sympathetic touch between teacher and pupil; knowledge on the part of the teacher, not simply of the individual taught, but of his surroundings and background, and the history of his class and group; such contact between pupils, and between teacher and pupil, on the basis of perfect social equality, as will increase this sympathy and knowledge; facilities for education in equipment and housing, and the promotion of such extra-curricular activities as will tend to induct the child into life."[78] Thomas argues for de facto segregation to spare whites the intrusions of the federal government. Du Bois argues for voluntary separation to spare Black children the ravages of white hatred and instill Black pride.[79] Regardless of their differing reasons, the impact of segregation and separation on the lives of Black school children is similar.

Du Bois debated with Walter White over this same issue; racial integration versus voluntary Black separation is legendary.[80] Walter F. White led the NAACP as executive secretary from 1929 until his death in 1955. Du Bois was the founding editor of *The Crisis* magazine, the official journal of the NAACP, from 1910 until his resignation in 1934. Randy and Jackson Stakeman, of the Walter White Project, note that the failure of "[Du Bois's] attempts to move the [NAACP] in a new direction, the loss of control over *The Crisis* and his dislike of Walter White all came to a head in one incident. [Du Bois] published an editorial in *The Crisis* saying the gathering together of strength in voluntarily segregated communities (which would later be espoused by Black nationalists and Black power advocates) was a tactic that should be considered. The organization, built on the idea that all walls of segregation should be torn down immediately, reacted with articles in *The Crisis* magazine disagreeing with Du Bois and calling him to task."[81]

The most fierce debates occur when both parties are correct. If inherent Black inferiority is rejected, then Du Bois's first argument seems intuitively correct that "theoretically, the Negro needs neither segregated schools

78. Du Bois, "Does the Negro Need Separate Schools," 328.
79. Delmont, *Why Busing Failed*, 111.
80. Brabri, "W. E. B. Du Bois's Writings."
81. Stakeman and Stakeman, "Departure of W. E. B. Du Bois," para. 4.

nor mixed schools. What he needs is Education. What he must remember is that there is no magic, either in mixed schools or in segregated schools. A mixed school with poor and unsympathetic teachers, with hostile public opinion, and no teaching of truth concerning [B]lack folk, is bad."[82]

The Rev. Francis James Grimké (1850–1937) helped found the NAACP and was a prominent Black leader in civil rights and pastor of Washington, DC's Fifteenth Street Presbyterian Church. Grimké challenged Du Bois in a fierce rebuttal published in *The Crisis* magazine, saying,

> Underlying the idea of race segregation is that of inferiority. It is always a badge of inferiority, and is so intended by those who impose it. It is one way of expressing contempt for the segregated, on the part of those who impose the segregation. In sheer self-respect, therefore, on the part of the segregated, it should be resented. It may be necessary for a time to endure it, but it should never be accepted as a finality. Segregation produces a condition that is not conducive to the best interest of either race. It tends to build up a false or artificial sense of superiority in the one, and is sure to create or engender in the other, feelings of resentment, of hatred, of discontent, out of which no good can come to either, but will continue to be a source of friction, of irritation.[83]

Du Bois was asserting more than just the evils of segregation, however. He posited a second, more profound, empirical claim that "a segregated school with ignorant placeholders, inadequate equipment, poor salaries, and wretched housing, is equally [as] bad [as an integrated school with] . . . poor and unsympathetic teachers, with hostile public opinion, and no teaching of truth concerning Black folk. . . . Other things being equal, the mixed school is the broader, more natural basis for the education of all youth. It gives wider contacts; it inspires greater self-confidence; and suppresses the inferiority complex. But other things seldom are equal, and in that case, Sympathy, Knowledge, and the Truth, outweigh all that the mixed school can offer."[84]

Unfortunately, this important discussion between W. E. B. Du Bois and Walter Frances White, two of the greatest race leaders of that era or any era, about segregated versus integrated schools, devolved into a series of personal attacks. Francis J. Grimké asked, "Why Dr. Du Bois has reopened the question of segregation in *The Crisis* I am at a loss to know. Can it be

82. Du Bois, "Does the Negro Need Separate Schools," 335.
83. Grimké, "Segregation," 173.
84. Du Bois, "Does the Negro Need Separate Schools," 335.

possible that in the remotest part of his brain he is beginning to think, after all, that it is a condition that ought to be accepted...? If so, then his leadership among us is at an end."[85]

For his part, Walter White said almost nothing publicly against Du Bois at the time, except to write in a private letter in February 1934: "So far as I know, the question of freedom of expression in *The Crisis* to Dr. Du Bois has never arisen." Mélissa Brabri records that "Walter White specified that the eviction of Du Bois was more a question ... of finance [the Depression, the worsening income of the organization, and the magazine's circulation], than a question of freedom of expression." Brabri concludes that while "we can still question the validity of [White's] words ... it is true that the magazine was victim of financial problems."[86]

Unfortunately, W. E. B. Du Bois was less circumspect or private and wrote in the April 1934 edition of *The Crisis*, the official journal of the NAACP, the organization of which Walter White was executive secretary, "In the first place, Walter White is white. He has more white companions and friends than colored."[87] Less than three months later, Du Bois resigned.

Du Bois's opinions about Black education will always be important as historical references. Du Bois had no empirical evidence, however, to support his second empirical claim at the time and, as pointed out above in reference to ghetto enrichment, few examples of large-scale segregated but equal Black education have emerged since. Given the racial history of America, it is difficult to debate Du Bois's claim that Black school children suffer at the hands of even well-meaning white teachers and administrators in so-called integrated settings. To claim that Black children do better in segregated settings is an empirical claim, however, that needs empirical evidence.

Why this important discussion about the future of Black children in segregated versus integrated schools was taking place on the pages of *The Crisis*, with little input from the best social science at the time, is uncertain. Du Bois had a PhD in history from Harvard but had broad training in social science and wrote the first case study of a Black community in Philadelphia in 1899.[88] The research necessary to address some of Du Bois's questions was available. The first of the Great Commissions had just been published thirty-six months before Du Bois started his series on segregation in *The Crisis*. Charles Johnson's *The Negro in American Civilization*,

85. Grimké, "Segregation," 173.
86. Brabri, "W. E. B. Du Bois's Writings," 75–76.
87. Brabri, "W. E. B. Du Bois's Writings," 72.
88. Rudwich et al., "W. E. B. Du Bois."

like the other Great Commissions that were to follow over the decades, was a comprehensive study of race in the US that had been commissioned by groups of organizations sympathetic to the plight of Blacks. Designed to be as scientific and empirical as possible, the study had little of the anti-Black or pro-Black racial bias so typical with individual writers on the topic. The National Interracial Conference, chaired by Mary van Kleeck, lent the power of their name to Johnson's study and contributed the foreword to the report.[89] Van Kleeck was a trained social scientist in her own right and a contributor to Du Bois's magazine at the time of the series on segregation in February 1934. Why the information on segregation versus integration in K–12 education from Johnson's study did not make its way into the pages of *The Crisis* probably never will become known.

First, Johnson specifically addressed Du Bois's question by saying that "the effect of the segregated school system upon the attendance and progress of the Negro student has not often been studied."[90] Second, Johnson studied three types of schools in the South: 1) schools segregated by state constitution, 2) schools segregated by custom but not required by law, and 3) schools "which make no legal or extra-legal attempt to segregate the children of different races."[91] Among the factors considered by Johnson in determining quality education was per capita spending per child above the US average. Third, Johnson found that "this [spending] inequality became greater as the counties were more densely populated by Negroes" and that "the crux of the problem of Negro education is in the first group of states here referred to as requiring racial segregation by constitutional enactment."[92] That is, the gravest threat to Black children was poor funding in schools that mandated segregation, not in schools with no such mandates.

Johnson also studied Northern schools. New Jersey maintained segregated as well as integrated grade schools. However, all high schools were integrated. Johnson found:

> With relatively larger numbers enrolled in the grades and smaller numbers in the high schools, Negro students in New Jersey appear to remain in and graduate from high school in larger proportions than whites. Studying separately the mixed and separate schools, it is revealed, that Negro students enter high school in larger proportions from the separate schools. The conclusion is scarcely warranted, however, that this fact constitutes

89. Van Kleeck, "Foreword."
90. C. Johnson, *Negro in American Civilization*, 268.
91. C. Johnson, *Negro in American Civilization*, 259–60.
92. C. Johnson, *Negro in American Civilization*, 236, 260.

an argument in favor of the separate schools. For while Trenton, one of the larger cities, erected a building exclusively for Negroes at a cost of nearly $1,000,000, and secured superior Negro teachers to conduct the school, other cities have fallen into the practice most feared where separate schools exist, of providing grossly inferior accommodations and instructors.[93]

That is, Johnson found that during the age of Jim Crow, with New Jersey providing superior funding and attention to segregated schools containing the children of the Black middle class along with the Black poor, these segregated schools were in fact superior to the white schools in almost every way. However, these exceptional schools did not provide any warrant for segregation because of the very fact they were an anomaly.

In Detroit, Black students coming from the segregated Southern schools lagged further behind than did students coming from other integrated Northern schools. In Minneapolis, Black students transferring into the integrated Minneapolis school system showed the greatest age-related deficits but closed the gap with white students for each year they remained in the integrated Minneapolis schools.[94] Johnson admitted that "the Negroes are by no means in agreement for or against segregation. . . . The intense discussions in Pennsylvania over the Cheyney Normal School, a separate Negro institution, and Philadelphia's separate public schools are indications of this difference in views. Some Negroes view the segregation as an unmitigated evil, dangerous to the status of the Negro in northern sections, while others see many benefits to the race in the form of closer racial solidarity, greater inspiration to Negro youth, and more positions for Negro teachers."[95]

Regardless of the differing views of Black parents, little if anything in the Johnson study supported Du Bois's contention that segregation, even with its inequality, resulted in superior or even equal outcomes for Black children twenty years before *Brown v. Board of Education*.

Lewis and Diamond investigated the evils of tracking in supposedly integrated schools and discussed the pluses and minuses in an ethnographic study of the pseudonymous "Riverview School" in the suburbs of "Metro." Lewis and Diamond describe how tracking gives the false impression of integration as opposed to mere desegregation. Notice that the Lewis and Diamond study specifically addresses Du Bois's hypothesis, however, that Blacks are better off in ghetto-enriched schools and find the evidence in

93. C. Johnson, *Negro in American Civilization*, 268.
94. C. Johnson, *Negro in American Civilization*, 270–71.
95. C. Johnson, *Negro in American Civilization*, 268.

opposition. "The graduation rate for the district's racial subgroups is higher than for their counterparts in the state as a whole. And when those students graduate from Riverview, between 75 and 80 percent attend college."[96]

Both Tyson and Harris also considered the problems caused by tracking for Black students. "Acting white" was a racial slur that Tyson discovered among Black students tracked into lower-performing classes in majority-white schools. In mostly Black schools, high academic performance was not associated with whiteness, and thus no such racial slurs occurred. Tracking creates a self-fulling prophecy that pushes supposedly gifted and mostly white students ahead and holds supposedly slower and mostly Black students back. Tyson went on the claim that while "many youth today are attending racially diverse schools, there is little evidence that they are benefitting from that diversity, because, as the experiences of the student in this book show, their classrooms remain largely segregated."[97]

Tyson's claim that students do not benefit from integration needs to be supported with: 1) evidence that Black students who are tracked in desegregated schools perform no better than Black students in segregated schools; or 2) a comparison of randomly selected Black youth in segregated schools versus those in integrated but tracked school settings. Tyson does not provide such evidence. Mahard and Crain, and Johnson and Nazaryan, do; their views stand somewhat in opposition to Tyson, although Tyson never asserted that children did better in segregated settings, only that most Black students in the segregated tracked classes were deprived of the benefits of the gifted integrated classes in the desegregated but tracked school. Harris is more circumspect and does not make claims about ghetto enrichment versus integration. Harris recognizes, however, that "many studies suggest that school personnel treat Black children differently than they do White and Asian American children, perhaps stemming from their beliefs that Black youth are resisting educational goals."[98] Johnson and Nazaryan, in their book *Children of the Dream: Why School Integration Works*, find that "contrary to popular wisdom, integration has benefited—and continues to benefit—African Americans, whether that benefit is translated into educational attainment, earnings, social stability, or incarceration rates. Whites, meanwhile, lose nothing from opening their classrooms to others. Overall, society benefits from a decrease in the kind of prejudice that, in the past several years, has threatened to tear us apart."[99] The Johnson and Nazary-

---

96. A. Lewis and Diamond, *Despite the Best of Intentions*, xv–xvi.
97. Tyson, *Integration Interrupted*, 160–61. See also 6.
98. A. Harris, *Kids Don't Want to Fail*, 196.
99. R. Johnson and Nazaryan, *Children of the Dream*, 3.

an study is one that illustrates the rarity of randomly controlled student placement so as to isolate the impacts of integration, and their findings are that "the medicine called integration works. When we say 'integration works,' let's be clear: our argument is not predicated on the false notion that poor and minority children can't learn in schools without white and non-poor children. Likewise, any assessment of a school's quality based solely on the racial composition of its students would be woefully incomplete. So what makes integration 'work'? It's in part the resultant impacts of integration on both school resources and school practices."[100]

Certainly almost all controlled studies of school integration show benefits for Black school children, even with tracking, over segregated but ghetto-enriched schools. The problem with ghetto enrichment is that it is not enriched sufficiently. The large, poor, segregated, Black but high-performing school district, with Afrocentric and sympathetic but under-resourced Black teachers and staff, must at this point be considered a work of historic fiction and myth. In a society that is 70 percent white, however, Black children would not be going to mostly Black schools if the society were treating them equally. The reason separation is inherently unequal is that the purpose of the separation is to make Black children, their parents, and their society unequal and to advance the myth of inherent white superiority.

The work of Kenneth Clark and others cited by the court in *Brown* showed that segregation has detrimental psychological effects for Black children. That finding occurred during the age of state-sponsored segregation, however. Recent studies suggest that while preferences of Black children for lighter skin tones still exist, no necessary connection exists between these preferences and self-esteem.[101] Today suggestions are plentiful for why integration works. For example: 1) Black children have more control over their environment in an integrated setting because it responds to them in positive ways, 2) middle-class students provide behavior models, 3) teachers teach differently because of less disruption, 4) more resources, 5) more parental interest in the schools, 6) socioeconomic integration, and 7) integration helps Blacks avoid overestimating the racial hostility in society.[102]

The purpose of school integration is to help break down the social and economic differences between white and Black children, which are substantial. Thirteen percent of whites under eighteen years old live in poverty; this

---

100. R. Johnson and Nazaryan, *Children of the Dream*, 55, 57.

101. Byrd et al., "Modern Doll Study."

102. Mahard and Crain, "Research on Minority Achievement"; Ryan, "Schools, Race, and Money."

number is high, but one-third of Black children live in poverty. To recap, in every study that evaluates Black children randomly assigned to integrated schools at an early age, the academic performance of Black children is markedly superior to those who remain in segregated schools.

The latest findings support the general theme developed by Johnson in 1930, that racial segregation harms Black children.[103] "There is a vast body of research on segregation and desegregation conducted in the more than 65 years since *Brown v. Board of Education*. Ironically, even as desegregation efforts were rolled back, increasing evidence has shown that the Supreme Court and the civil rights movement had been correct in their understanding of the central role of school segregation in perpetuating racial inequality."[104] Orfield shows that the percentage of white school enrollment declined from 79 percent in 1970 to only 47 percent in 2018. At the same time, Black and Latino school enrollment increased from 20 percent in 1970 to 42 percent in 2018.[105] In 2019, the average Black, Latino, and Indian student attended a school that was 63 percent, 58 percent, and 67 percent, respectively, low income, compared to the average white student attending a school that was only 39 percent low income.[106] Poverty is an important inhibitor of quality education because "middle class schools have networks, contacts, and resources that schools of low-income children rarely have."[107] The percentage of Black students in poverty-stricken schools is increasing, not decreasing. In 1976, 62 percent of Black students were in schools that were more than 50 percent non-white. In 2018, the figure was 81 percent. In 1980, 33.2 percent of Black students were in schools that were more than 90–100 percent non-white. In 2018, the figure was 40 percent.

It is important to remember that "segregation does not only harm people of color. Isolation of white students in schools means they also do not reap the benefits from having Black and brown classmates, including growth that comes from having friendships across racial lines, improved cultural competency, greater collaboration, improved critical thinking and problem solving skills. As a country, society is harmed by the racial divides that segregation creates, and diminishes the ability for all students to be successful in a workforce that is increasingly diverse."[108] Cohen lists the many disadvantages of segregated schools, including less experienced teachers,

103. C. Johnson, *Negro in American Civilization*.
104. Orfield and Jarvie, "Black Segregation Matters," 11.
105. Orfield and Jarvie, "Black Segregation Matters," 19, fig. 2.
106. Orfield and Jarvie, "Black Segregation Matters," 27, table 9.
107. Orfield and Jarvie, "Black Segregation Matters," 27.
108. Cohen, *NYC School Segregation Report Card*, 16.

higher teacher turnover, limited curricula, fewer advanced placement and honors courses, lack of advanced math courses (which are required for college-level STEM classes), higher rates of expulsion, and discipline of children of color.[109]

Equality in K–12 education requires racial integration and massive funding increases for Black students, not just equal funding, as the Wyandanch schools demonstrate. Black school children must cope with the entire weight of opposition from white society, white culture, white politics, and economic discrimination, which causes far higher amounts of violence, home-life disruption, single-parent families, poverty, unemployment, and low parental education. Far fewer white children face this opposition. The Wyandanch, New York, school district, almost all Black and Latino, spends $14,724 per student, while neighboring West Babylon, 86 percent white, spends $11,868 per student with far higher scores. In 2017, 53 percent of Black students in Wyandanch received a Regents high school diploma, the ticket to a college future. Only 7 percent of Black students in Wyandanch received a Regents diploma with advanced designation, the highest high school diploma in the state of New York. In 2017, 62 percent of Black students in West Babylon received a Regents diploma and 23 percent received a Regents diploma with advanced designation. Selection factors or no, the words of Chief Justice Earl Warren seem to be as true today as when they were written the better part of a century ago: "Separate educational facilities are inherently unequal."[110]

---

109. Cohen, *NYC School Segregation Report Card*, 17.
110. *Brown v. Board of Education*, 495.

Chapter Nine

High-Cost Equality

Welfare, Social Security, and Reparations

THE PROBLEM WITH REPARATIONS

Almost 70 percent of Americans think the government should not make cash payments to Black Americans who are the descendants of slaves.[1] In June 2014, Ta-Nehisi Coates published an article in the *Atlantic Monthly* titled "The Case for Reparations." Coates outlined the long history of slavery, Jim Crow discrimination, lynching, anti-miscegenation laws, and official discrimination by the Federal Housing Administration, the Social Security Act, the GI Bill, and segregated and substandard schooling for Blacks.

To the list of offences calling for reparations, Coates added the failures of universal civil rights laws (which apply to whites as well as Blacks) to eradicate racial inequality. Regardless of the horrid history of oppression against Blacks, white Americans are unmoved.

After Coates's article, YouGov conducted a survey of American views of the causes for racial inequality generally and the need for reparations specifically. The YouGov survey is important since few of the major public opinion surveys even have questions on reparations.

American views of the causes for racial inequality in the YouGov survey are similar to responses to Richard Morin's article nearly twenty years earlier.[2] Fifty-one percent of whites do not think slavery is related to contemporary racial wealth disparities. Sixty-four percent of whites think that discrimination is either a minor factor or not a factor at all in current racial

---

1. P. Moore, "Overwhelming Opposition to Reparations."
2. P. Moore, "Overwhelming Opposition to Reparations"; Morin, "Distorted Image of Minorities."

wealth disparities. Only 18 percent, 20 percent, and 20 percent of whites respectively think that racial discrimination against Blacks is a current problem in buying a house, getting a loan, or getting a quality education.

Two-thirds of whites do not even think the government should apologize to Blacks for slavery. A full 79 percent of whites do not believe the government should make cash payments to the descendants of slaves, and 67 percent of whites even reject education programs to Black Americans who are the descendants of slaves. In contrast, while a plurality of whites also oppose payments to Japanese Americans interned during WWII, 53 percent of whites think that Germany should have made payments to Jews who survived the Holocaust after WWII. In 2019, Gallup found that 81 percent of non-Hispanic whites oppose reparations to Blacks, and 73 percent of Blacks support reparations.[3]

Black views are diametrically opposed to those of whites on all these issues. Seventy-five percent of Blacks think that slavery is a major or minor factor in contemporary racial wealth disparities. Eighty-seven percent of Blacks think that discrimination is a major or minor factor in current racial wealth disparities.

Nonetheless, Spath makes five main arguments against reparations: 1) slavery was common in antiquity; 2) slavery was not race based; 3) affirmative action and welfare are the equivalent of reparations; 4) most whites today are not responsible for slavery because they immigrated to the US long after slavery was abolished; and 5) reparations are like tort claims for individual wrongs, not social ills.[4] While Kershnar agrees with most whites in the YouGov survey that slavery has not directly harmed current Blacks, he argues that reparations can still be supported from a lost inheritance perspective. Even Kershnar concludes nevertheless that great difficulty exists in assigning liability to any party responsible for slavery.[5]

JIM VERSUS FRANK

Reparations for slavery would be unprecedented in the US. If reparations are necessary to avoid a more costly alternative, then perhaps they are to be reconsidered. Maybe most whites oppose reparations because they have nothing with which to compare them.

---

3. Gallup, "Race Relations."
4. Spath, "What's Wrong with Reparations for Slavery?"
5. Kershnar, "Reparations for Slavery and Justice."

Kershnar finds it difficult to assign liability for slavery because he models reparations as tortious mob action.[6] The tort model of reparations imagines Jim, a white American, as the second-best tennis player in the world behind Frank, a Chinese American. Because Frank is the best, he makes three times the income of Jim. One day, Frank is with his white girlfriend and is beaten and stabbed to death by a racist mob in Brooklyn, New York. Jim now moves into the number one spot vacated by Frank. Consequently, Jim's income triples. Jim directly benefited from the racial injustice done to Frank. Kershnar explains that Jim does not owe two-thirds of his winnings to Frank's descendants even though Jim's increase in income is directly related to the racial injustice Frank suffered.

The Jim versus Frank scenario proposed by Kershnar likely is not persuasive to most Blacks primarily because Kershnar's hypothetical involves only the actions of individuals. Racial oppression against Blacks was more than just individual action. Consider whether most Blacks see the following scenario. Jim, a European American, is the twentieth best tennis player in the world behind nineteen Black American players. Ninety-five percent of all Black men earn their living playing tennis. Please remember this is a hypothetical. Even though Blacks are the best, Jim makes far more income than any of them because European American tennis promoters book only European American players on national TV.

In addition, federal law bans Black players from any stadium that seats more than one hundred people and that has media coverage. State laws mandate that Black players can travel to games only by personal automobile and cannot use the commercial airlines, busses, or trains. Consequently, Black players typically arrive exhausted at games.

Even in the smaller stadiums, Black games are frequently disrupted by violent white mobs. We know that Black players are better than white players because at private exhibitions, in front of wealthy white audiences, Blacks nearly always win. The selection effect of racial discrimination would tend to eliminate Black professional players who were not exceptional just because the costs for entry are so high.

After one hundred years of such attacks and the lynching of over five thousand Black players, the Black tennis league finally collapsed. The Black players sue but certiorari is denied by the all-white Supreme Court. The US Congress refuses to pass legislation to ban the lynching of Blacks at tennis tournaments.

Nevertheless, the Black population continues to rise, and finally, in 2060, Blacks form a political coalition with other oppressed peoples of

---

6. Kershnar, "Reparations for Slavery and Justice," 301.

color. The Coalition of Oppressed Peoples of Color (COPOC) calls for a constitutional convention. COPOC drafts a new Constitution banning any white person from playing tennis for gain.

The nearly universal bans of Black tennis players and the racially motivated attacks for over a century on Black tennis players take the scenario of Jim and Frank out of the realm of personal tortious conduct. The real issue is how do you remedy crimes against humanity when the survival of the nation may be at stake?

THE COST OF POLITICAL INSTABILITY

Most white Americans' views of the causes for racial discrimination, support for reparations for slavery, or even support for social welfare programs for the poor assume that no immediate crises are on the horizon. When a crisis will arise is uncertain, but what is absolutely certain, particularly as applies to racial issues in the United States, is that crises will arise.

The Revolutionary War, the Civil War, Reconstruction, Jim Crow, the Great Migration, the white race riots of the early twentieth century, the Second Reconstruction, the urban revolts of the 1960s, and the Black Lives Matter movement are examples. The emergency programs instituted during those crises (gradual emancipation in the North, Black men entering the military, the Emancipation Proclamation in the South, the Civil War amendments to the US Constitution, the 1866 and 1975 Civil Rights Acts, the street battles between the forces of Jim Crow, SCLC, SNCC, and CORE, the Civil Rights Act of 1964, the Voting Rights Act of 1965, the Fair Housing Act of 1968, the Great Society, the Philadelphia Plan, affirmative action policies, the sudden national agenda for police reform after the horrendous death of George Floyd in late May of 2020) demonstrate that the nation must and does respond to unusual racial events with extraordinary programs and policies.

The political polarization now in place, the decreasing white population and the increasing population of peoples of color, is certain to challenge the business-as-usual theory of reparations as payment for tortious conduct, advocated by some scholars. With the Great Recession and coronavirus just behind us, imagine what would happen if a majority of the nation were comprised of peoples of color, combined with the great inequality in unemployment, housing, and healthcare during the Great Recession and coronavirus. Even with COVID-19, the Department of Health and Human Services' Office for Civil Rights in Action issued guidelines reminding "entities covered by civil rights authorities" that doctors, hospitals, and caregivers are not authorized to decide who receives access to scarce medical resources based on their age, race, disability, or color.[7] The Institute of Medicine report on health inequality discussed in chapter 2 showed that such racially biased decisions have been made in the past.[8] The difference is that once whites no longer have a voting majority, failure even to talk about reparations or substantive racial equality may make a serious politico-economic crisis unavoidable.

This chapter argues that as the population of peoples of color grows and has greater political leverage, costly reparations for slavery may become a plausible political issue unless social welfare programs are redesigned now to help eradicate racial inequality, combined with substantive social equality programs. America's two largest racial groups, Blacks and whites, had consistent social and economic inequality for at least half a century before the welfare state began. This combination of factors usually signals systematic and institutionalized racialization and racism, rather than decreased effort caused by social welfare, as many whites believe.

Most of the evidence supports the charge that the US is suffering from structural racism that extends to and is replicated in welfare and other social service programs. Contrary to the views of most whites, this institutionalized racism most likely is a result of slavery and slavery's aftermath, poverty, and discrimination. Institutionalized racism that cannot be remedied by social welfare eventually may require reparations for the slave system, which was the original cause of the problem. It is far cheaper, economically, to use social welfare to help alleviate unequal economic conditions than pay slave reparations. This cost calculation may change the minds of white voters as we near mid-century.

MIDDLE-CLASS WELFARE VERSUS WELFARE FOR THE POOR

Whites may disdain the idea of reparations for slavery, or using social welfare as a substitute for reparations, but the middle class receive almost three times the welfare the poor receive, and few complain. I need to be clear here, I am not suggesting that social welfare alone is either a financial substitute for reparations or that social welfare programs alone can create substantive equality. With or without reparations, substantive politico-economic equality between races requires a full panoply of antidiscrimination enforcement mechanisms permanently in place as well as the elimination of poverty and

7. HHS Office for Civil Rights in Action, "Civil Rights, HIPAA."
8. Smedley et al., *Unequal Treatment*.

all forms of racial wage, housing, occupation, health, and educational discrimination listed in table 1 of chapter 1.

Table 9.1
Social Welfare Spending in the US

Social Insurance Programs	
Old-Age and Survivors' Insurance (2023)	$1,237,294,000,000
Medicare (2022)	$944,318,000,000
Unemployment Insurance (2022)	$538,935,000,000
Workers Compensation (2020)	$58,925,000,000
Disability Insurance (2023)	$154,815,000,000
Social Insurance Total	$2,934,287,000,000
Means-Tested Transfer Programs	
Aid to Families with Dependent Children/Temporary Assistance to Needy Families (2022)	$13,368,011,856
Medicaid (2022)	$805,732,000,000
Earned Income Tax Credit (2022)	$57,577,000,000
Housing Aid (2020)	$50,552,000,000
Food Stamps/SNAP (2023)	$113,047,090,000
Head Start (2022)	$10,647,159,826
Women, Infants, and Children (2023)	$6,697,800,000
School Food Programs (2023)	$22,586,000,000
Supplemental Security Income (2022)	$55,772,455,000
Means-Tested Transfers Total	$1,135,979,516,682
All Social Welfare	$4,070,266,516,682

Sources: I am indebted to the prior work of Scholz and Levine, "Evolution of Income." Centers for Medicare & Medicaid Services, "NHE Fact Sheet"; Gross Domestic Product; Head Start, "Head Start Program Facts"; IRS, "Earned Income Tax Credit Statistics"; IRS, "SOI Tax Stats," table 4; National Academy of Social Insurance, *Workers' Compensation*; Office of Management and Budget, "Budget," 2022, table 8.5; Social Security Administration, "DI Trust Fund"; Social Security Administration, "OASI Trust Fund"; USDA Food and Nutrition Service, "Program Data Overview"; USDA Food and Nutrition Service, "SNAP Data Tables"; USDA Food and Nutrition Service, *SSI Annual Statistical Report*; USDA Food and Nutrition Service, "WIC Data Tables."

Middle-class welfare is a type of reparation or compensation to whites for having to live in the same nation with Blacks. Middle-class welfare tends to insulate whites from the major disincentives of a system with great inequality. We call middle-class welfare "entitlements," which indicates that whites and the middle class have a right to these government programs. Middle-class welfare seems white, in that whites receive a disproportionate share of entitlement programs. Entitlements are seen as earned, whereas transfers to the poor are seen as not only unearned, but undeserved.

Entitlements are so ingrained in the American psyche that the programs are not even subject to annual debates about funding. Entitlement funding is written into the law and must be paid. For 2016, the cost for mandatory federal programs was $2.7 trillion out of a federal budget of $3.9 trillion. Thus, about 70 percent of the federal budget was for mandatory programs.[9] These programs provide a basic level of equality to many Americans regardless of their race or ability to pay. Table 9.1 lists the major federal- and state-based public social welfare programs in the US. Table 9.1 shows that middle-class welfare, called social insurance, costs almost $3 trillion per year. Welfare for poor people is a third of social insurance, just over $1 trillion per year. AFDC, the welfare that has created the most anger among the middle class, is one of the smallest welfare programs. In table 9.1, AFDC and TANF amount to three-tenths of 1 percent (.003 percent) of all social welfare dollars.

Those with the most money tend to benefit the most from the system of middle-class welfare. For example, social security taxes cap at an income of $118,000. If a person earns a $1,000,000 per year, that individual pays the same social security taxes as someone who earns $118,000 per year. The $1,000,000 earner would draw the same maximum benefit as someone who had a much lower income, even though the higher-income earner presumably has lower benefit needs.[10]

BLACK WELFARE VERSUS WHITE WELFARE

Blacks get disproportionately less welfare than whites even though Blacks have greater needs.[11] Social welfare as we know it today began with the New Deal, and the design specifically was to exclude the two largest occupations of Blacks (agriculture and domestic service). Today, about 28.8 percent of means-tested programs in table 9.1 go to Blacks, at a total of $327 billion. This figure is based on the percentage of families who are Black and who receive TANF in table 9.2 in 2022. The CPS shows Blacks receive almost population parity in income dollars received from social security, about 11 percent. That would indicate that about $136 billion in social insurance

---

9. Office of Management and Budget, "Budget," 2016, tables 3.2 and 8.5.

10. See Research, Statistics & Policy Analysis, archives for OASDI and SSI Program Rates and Limits, 2016.

11. See ch. 2, "The Black Family Did Not Collapse Any More Than the White Family" and "Welfare Reformed to Subsidize the White Poor."

goes to Blacks. Total social insurance and means-tested dollars from table 9.1 that go to Blacks would be $463 billion per year.[12]

Table 9.2

Race and TANF Receipt

Year	Total	Percent White	Percent Black	Percent Latino	Percent Asian
		Families			
2022	1,862,066	25.5	28.8	37.3	2.0
2021	1,846,913	27.0	29.0	35.3	1.9
2020	2,049,744	27.0	28.6	35.8	1.7
2019	2,078,145	26.7	29.0	35.7	1.9
2018	2,277,663	27.2	28.9	37.8	1.9
2017	2,508,441	28.0	28.4	37.4	2.1
2016	2,782,427	27.6	29.1	36.9	1.7
2015	3,114,455	27.5	29.7	36.9	2.0
2014	3,535,534	27.1	30.5	36.8	1.9
2013	3,807,235	27.4	31.1	36.0	1.9
2012	1,753,021	30.1	31.5	31.1	1.9
2011	1,864,160	30.1	32.7	30.3	1.8
2010	1,847,155	31.8	31.9	30.0	1.9
2009	1,726,560	31.2	33.3	28.8	2.1
2008	1,629,345	31.5	34.2	28.0	2.3
2007	1,696,951	32.4	35.5	27.0	1.9
2006	1,802,567	33.4	35.7	26.1	1.8
2005	1,914,036	32.1	37.1	25.5	2.1
2004	1,983,973	32.9	37.6	24.1	1.8
2003	2,027,581	31.8	38	24.8	2
2002	2,060,328	31.6	38.3	24.9	2.2
2001	2,120,474	30.1	39	26	2.1
2000	2,269,131	31.2	38.6	25	2.2
1999	2,648,462	38.3	24.5	30.5	3.6
1998	3,175,646	39	22.2	32.7	3.4

12. These figures are based on the author's calculations from the 2006 CPS, comparing all income received from wages and social security by racial group.

Table 9.2

Race and TANF Receipt

Year	Total	Percent White	Percent Black	Percent Latino	Percent Asian
		Adults			
2022	439,610	27.1	31.3	33.4	2.9
2021	417,256	29.4	31.5		2.9
2020	447,207	29.7	30.8	30.5	2.4
2019	437,341	30.3	31.3	29.8	2.5
2018	492,385	30.5	31.2	31.8	2.9
2017	565,413	32.5	30.2	30.4	2.9
2016	637,472	32.7	31.0	30.5	2.1
2015	744,257	32.7	32.1	29.3	2.5
2014	845,250	32.3	32.9	28.8	2.4
2013	893,735	33.3	33.1	27.7	2.3
2012	1,009,349	34.0	33.5	25.7	2.4
2011	1,104,266	34.5	34.7	24.2	2.4
2010	1,084,828	36.8	33.0	23.7	2.4
2009	973,580	35.4	34.1	24.2	2.3
2008	869,463	35.2	35.0	23.3	2.6
2007	941,040	35.9	36.4	22.6	2.0
2006	996,312	37.9	37.2	19.9	1.7
2005	1,092,018	36.3	38.6	19.8	1.9
2004	1,168,539	36.7	38.9	19.1	1.5
2003	1,248,570	35.1	38.6	20.5	2
2002	1,315,029	34.2	38.9	21.6	2.2
2001	1,408,752	32.2	39	23.6	2.5
2000	1,578,598	32.8	37.9	23.7	2.6
1999	2,068,024	36.4	23.1	32.4	5
1998	2,631,142	37.1	20	35.6	4.6
1997	2,679,716	35.4	21.2	36	4
		Children			
2022	1,422,456	25.0	28.0	38.5	1.7
2021	1,429,657	26.2	28.2	36.8	1.7
2020	1,602,537	26.2	28.0	37.2	1.5
2019	1,640,805	25.7	28.4		
2018	1,785,278	26.4	28.2	39.5	1.7

Table 9.2

Race and TANF Receipt

Year	Total	Percent White	Percent Black	Percent Latino	Percent Asian
2017	1,943,028	27.5	27.8	38.8	1.8
2016	2,144,955	26.8	28.4	38.9	1.6
2015	2,370,198	25.9	29.0	39.3	1.8
2014	2,690,284	25.4	29.7	39.3	1.8
2013	2,913,501	25.5	30.5	38.5	1.8
2012	3,104,899	25.3	30.9	36.6	2.1
2011	3,316,716	25.5	32.2	35.2	2.0
2010	3,280,153	27.1	31.4	34.7	2.0
2009	3,067,764	26.1	33.1	33.5	2.5
2008	2,911,079	26.2	34.1	32.5	2.6
2007	3,005,064	27.6	36.2	30.1	2.3
2006	3,203,631	28.8	36.4	29.2	2.1
2005	3,457,422	27.7	37.5	28.6	2.5
2004	3,611,277	27.8	38.6	27.1	2.1
2003	3,737,200	27	39.1	27.5	2.5
2002	3,835,256	26.8	39.8	27.4	2.7
2001	4,054,964	25.6	40.8	27.8	2.7
2000	4,384,527	26.8	40.1	26.8	2.8
1999	5,318,722	39.5	26	25.8	4.6
1998	6,329,970	40.2	23.4	28.3	4.2
1997	5,737,023	37.8	22.4	27.7	3.1

Source: Office of Family Assistance Resource Library: "Characteristics and Financial Circumstances of TANF Recipients, Fiscal Year [Various]."

The average social security check for Blacks is 84 percent of what whites receive, but Black wages are only about 66 percent those of whites. Social security therefore is both progressive and regressive. Social security is regressive in that it replicates the inequalities in the labor market. The higher a wage, the more an individual receives in OASI upon retirement. OASI is progressive in "that the system returns a greater percentage of pre-retirement earnings to low-wage workers than to high-wage workers."[13]

13. Hendley and Bilimoria, "Minorities and Social Security," 61.

THE SOCIAL INSECURITY SYSTEM

Regardless of whether the social security system is progressive or regressive, the system was designed to replicate social inequality, not to fix it. The history of the Social Security Act demonstrates this. Stories about the national crisis that met Franklin D. Roosevelt as the Great Depression worsened are difficult to read without thinking about the economic emergency the nation faced in 2007–9. What was called the Great Recession began in December 2007. Few people living had ever seen an economic crisis of this magnitude, and the impacts still are apparent, particularly in the housing market. It is even more difficult to imagine that the COVID-19 crisis may surpass the Great Recession in terms of economic damage and turmoil.

Middle-class whites, who had educations and prestigious jobs in the financial sector, couldn't pay the rent. Unemployment systems of the states were overwhelmed. Millions of homeowners were in default, and those not in default were in houses worth hundreds of thousands of dollars less than they owed. Homelessness was rising. Many commentators said the situation was the worst since the Great Depression. Without the intervention from the Federal Reserve and the Treasury, the banking system in the US almost certainly would have collapsed. No one is certain, or wants to find out, what a banking collapse would have done to the national or world economy. In the 1930s, America found out what would happen.

In the first hundred days in office, FDR restructured the federal government. FDR created: FERA (Federal Emergency Relief Administration), CWA (Civil Works Administration), PWA (Public Works Administration), CCC (Civilian Conservation Corps), NYA (National Youth Administration), NRA (National Recovery Administration), NIRA (National Industrial Recovery Act), and WPA (Works Progress Administration).

FDR signed the Social Security Act on August 14, 1935. According to David M. Gordon et al., "It provided old-age pensions, unemployment compensation, aid to dependent children, and several programs of aid to the disabled, as well as a small program of federal money for maternal and infant health. It has since been expanded but not fundamentally changed, and no new major initiatives were undertaken until President Clinton's medical insurance proposal in 1994."[14]

The Social Security Act set up two systems of aid. Old-Age and Survivors' Insurance (OASI) and unemployment insurance (UI) provided basic social support for those in the programs. These programs were for the deserving, and to make use of them seemed a right and not a privilege. Table

---

14. D. Gordon et al., *Segmented Work*, 253.

9.1 illustrates that OASI is the highest-dollar social welfare program in the US at $1.2 trillion.

Aid to Dependent Children, on the other hand, seemed a privilege given by the state to those who are suspect at best and undeserving at worst. Blacks and women were on the bottom of the social security system, just as they were at the bottom of the social ladder.

Most of the other acts that passed—AAA (Agricultural Adjustment Act), NRA, and FERA—were to assist in immediate relief. The SSA was designed to address the longer-term economic issues that people faced as a result of the Great Depression. FDR ordered his team, the Committee on Economic Security (CES) to create a permanent safety net and a "cradle-to-grave" welfare system.[15]

The Depression hit Blacks especially hard, but the New Deal gave signs of hope. FDR appointed Mary McLeod Bethune and others to his Black Brain Trust, and FDR felt that Black voters could no longer remain in the background. Black leaders saw that the New Deal was reordering society, and opportunity existed for Blacks either to move ahead, or as Ralph Bunche said, permanently to be left behind. The system of Jim Crow gave Blacks only the lowest and most menial jobs, but as the Depression worsened, even these jobs were lost to whites.[16]

Title I of the SSA of 1935 gave the states $50 million to provide plans for old-age assistance. Title II set up a Federal Reserve account for old-age benefits. Title III gave the states $49 million "for the purpose of assisting the States in the administration of their unemployment compensation laws." Title IV was "for the purpose of enabling each State to furnish financial assistance, as far as practicable under the conditions in such State, to needy dependent children." Title V was for maternal and child welfare. Title VI was "for the purpose of assisting States, counties, health districts, and other political subdivisions of the States in establishing and maintaining adequate public-health services, including the training of personnel for State and local health work." Title VII created the Social Security Board to "study the most effective methods of providing economic security through social insurance."[17] Titles VIII and IX created payroll taxes to fund the system. Employee payroll taxes started at 1 percent in 1937 and rose to 3 percent

15. Poole, *Segregated Origins of Social Security*, introduction.
16. Horton and Horton, *Hard Road to Freedom*, 249–59.
17. The original Social Security Act of 1935, HR 7260, is easily found on the Social Security Administration website (http://www.ssa.gov/history/35actinx.html). Other useful information is the Congressional Research Service report for Congress (Sidor, "Major Decisions").

after 1948. Employers paid the same tax as workers. Title X gave grants to the states for aid to the blind, and Title XI contained general provisions.

THE INSIGNIFICANCE OF RACE

By now, everyone knows that the social security system seems deliberately to have discriminated against Blacks.[18] Given the scholarly consensus that the Social Security Act was a case of deliberate racial subjugation, an unpleasant surprise at the fifteenth annual conference of the National Academy of Social Insurance in Washington, DC, January 30–31, 2003, was to hear an elderly white-haired man take the microphone and assert that the exclusion of Blacks was not an act of racial discrimination.

Bob Myers, who was a twenty-one-year-old junior actuary with the Committee on Economic Security in 1934, and ninety years of age in 2003, might not have been far off in his personal recollection of events.[19] Excluding the two largest occupations for Black workers (farm labor and domestic work) was merely an added bonus for a racist system caught in the middle of an economic crisis.

Many today have difficulty believing, accepting, and understanding that Black people were so unimportant in the minds of policy makers of the time that they could quite honestly eliminate these largest Black occupations because they were unwieldy and inconvenient, not because they were Black. The incomes of farm workers and domestic servants were considered too difficult to track. That these occupations were the lifeblood of Black people was not a major consideration. Sadly, most of the evidence supports this claim by Bob Myers.

Title IV of the Social Security Act of 1935 created Aid to Dependent Children, and appropriated $24,750,000 to carry out the purpose of providing assistance "to needy dependent children." Title IV section 402(a) requires that ADC be in effect in all political subdivisions of the state. Further, section 402(a)(4) provides that if the state denies a claim for ADC, an opportunity must be present for a fair hearing, on the record.

Title IV section 402(b) states that the three-member Social Security Board, appointed by the president, shall not approve any state ADC plan that

---

18. Katznelson, *When Affirmative Action Was White*; Oliver and Shapiro, *Black Wealth/White Wealth*; Quadagno, *Transformation of Old Age Security*; Quadagno, *Color of Welfare*; Sitkoff, *New Deal for Blacks*.

19. Social Security Administration, "Remembering Robert J. Myers."

imposes as a condition of eligibility for aid to dependent children, a residence requirement which denies aid with respect to any child residing in the State who has resided in the State for one year immediately preceding the application for such aid or who was born within the State within one year immediately preceding the application, if its mother has resided in the State for one year immediately preceding the birth.

In section 406 a child is defined as any

child under the age of sixteen who has been deprived of parental support or care by reason of the death, continued absence from the home, or physical or mental incapacity of a parent, and who is living with his father, mother, grandfather, grandmother, brother, sister, stepfather, stepmother, stepbrother, stepsister, uncle, or aunt, in a place of residence maintained by one or more of such relatives as his or their own home.

States were free to set up their own requirements for receiving ADC, except for requiring that ADC be available in the entire state, that there be little or no residency requirements, and that a hearing be allowed. The purpose of ADC was to assist needy children, and states used the need requirement to impose a host of moral tests on which children were needy.

Quadagno explains that support for the SSA by the Southern delegation was assured "only if local welfare authorities retained control over the distribution of benefits. As a result, most of the initial ADC beneficiaries were White, widowed women with young children." Katz supports this contention that ADC was originally conceived as a small program for widows and their children.[20]

Hostility to unwed mothers, and to Black women, whether widows or not, led to many of the additional state restrictions designed to keep these two classes of women off the welfare rolls.[21] Seasonal restrictions cut ADC mothers off the welfare rolls during cotton-picking season. "Man in the house" rules allowed caseworkers to make unannounced visits to a home and cut any women from the rolls if a man were living with them. Black-white relationships or the birth of an illegitimate child would mean a woman and her children were unsuitable for ADC.

The racial and moral restrictions for ADC began to collapse in the 1960s as courts struck down many of the restrictions. Welfare mothers began to organize and created the National Welfare Rights Organization (NWRO). NWRO staged sit-ins and confrontations at welfare offices. Table

---

20. Quadagno, *Color of Welfare*, 119; Katz, *In the Shadow of the Poorhouse*, 275.
21. L. Gordon, *Pitied but Not Entitled*, 291, 95, 98; Quadagno, *Color of Welfare*, 119.

9.3 shows that from 1960 to 1969, the number of recipients on AFDC more than doubled.[22]

Table 9.3
Historical Trends in AFDC/TANF Enrollments

Fiscal Year	Families*	Recipients	Children
1960	784,572	2,982,093	2,320,962
1961	844,587	3,240,970	2,502,288
1962	933,213	3,642,237	2,816,103
1963	56,762	3,902,991	2,926,715
1964	996,355	4,125,440	3,092,548
1965	1,049,211	4,374,584	3,282,695
1966	1,082,800	4,501,327	3,396,536
1967	1,178,059	4,854,972	3,658,389
1968	1,355,158	5,515,567	4,135,479
1969	1,612,197	6,400,350	4,770,233
1970	1,909,000	7,429,000	5,494,000
1971	2,532,000	9,556,000	6,963,000
1972	2,918,000	10,632,000	7,698,000
1973	3,123,000	11,038,000	7,965,000
1974	3,170,000	10,845,000	7,824,000
1975	3,342,000	11,067,000	7,928,000
1976	3,561,000	11,339,000	8,156,000
1977	3,575,000	11,108,000	7,818,000
1978	3,528,000	10,663,000	7,475,000
1979	3,493,000	10,311,000	7,193,000
1980	3,642,000	10,597,000	7,320,000
1981	3,871,000	11,160,000	7,615,000
1982	3,569,000	10,431,000	6,975,000
1983	3,651,000	10,659,000	7,051,000
1984	3,725,000	10,866,000	7,153,000
1985	3,692,000	10,813,000	7,165,000
1986	3,747,000	10,995,000	7,294,000
1987	3,784,000	11,065,000	7,381,000
1988	3,748,000	10,920,000	7,326,000
1989	3,771,000	10,935,000	7,370,000
1990	3,974,000	11,460,000	7,755,000
1991	4,375,000	12,595,000	8,515,000
1992	4,769,000	13,625,000	9,225,000

22. Katz, *In the Shadow of the Poorhouse*, 275; Quadagno, *Color of Welfare*, 120.

Table 9.3
Historical Trends in AFDC/TANF Enrollments

Fiscal Year	Families*	Recipients	Children
1993	4,981,000	14,144,000	9,539,000
1994	5,046,000	14,226,000	9,590,000
1995	4,869,000	13,619,000	9,275,000
1996	4,553,000	12,649,000	8,673,000
1997	3,740,000	8,879,760	6,141,146
1998	3,050,000	8,347,000	6,320,000
1999	2,578,000	6,924,000	5,109,000
2000	2,303,000	6,143,000	4,479,000
2001	2,192,000	5,717,000	4,195,000
2002	2,187,000	5,609,000	4,119,000
2003	2,180,000	5,490,000	4,063,000
2004	2,153,000	5,342,000	3,969,000
2005	2,061,000	5,028,000	3,756,000
2006	1,908,000	4,591,000	3,457,000
2007	1,698,795	3,960,907	3,049,679
2008	1,632,369	3,791,678	2,921,367
2009	1,726,799	4,041,292	3,084,413
2010	1,847,683	4,370,844	3,288,506
2011	1,864,187	4,417,445	3,315,576
2012	1,753,737	4,106,881	3,105,952
2013	1,640,654	3,782,146	2,885,147
2014	1,520,894	3,504,648	2,681,139
2015	1,332,064	3,083,993	2,348,971

*Families data 1960–69 is number of cases; 1970–2008 is number of families. Sources: Office of Family Assistance, "TANF Caseload Data 1996–2015"; Committee on Ways and Means: 1996 Green Book; 2008 Green Book.

The social security system that FDR created is much the same system we have today. The original eleven titles have been expanded to twenty-one, but all the basic parts still exist. What started out as a segregated social security system became "the closest thing to a race-blind social program the United States has ever known."[23] Other than slight reductions in recipients in the 1980s, in what would eventually become AFDC (table 9.3), welfare rolls continued to climb until the large decreases in 1997 after passage of Bill Clinton's Personal Responsibility and Work Opportunity Reconciliation Act (PRWORA) in 1996.

23. Lieberman, *Shifting the Color Line*, 67.

By 1950, the exclusions for agricultural and domestic workers were gone. The consensus was that it was advantageous to have as many people paying into the system as possible, even Blacks. In 1954, the self-employed were added to the social security system, and in 1956 professionals (physicians and lawyers) were added. In 1965, President Johnson signed Medicare and Medicaid into law. In some ways Medicare and Medicaid can be considered the start of the "Great Society."[24]

Medicare and Medicaid were added to the Social Security Act as Titles XVIII and XIX respectively. Medicare provides protection for the cost of hospital services and follow-up services after a hospital stay. Plus, Medicare covered nursing home and many outpatient services, tests, home health services, and equipment. Medicare provided direct services to citizens who paid into the social security system.[25] Medicaid started as a program to provide medical help to people receiving help from state social service programs. Participation by states was voluntary, and much variation appeared across states in terms of levels of participation and services provided.[26]

THROWING MONEY AT A PROBLEM REALLY HELPS

The large amounts of money spent during the Great Society years created the greatest increases in racial equality the nation has ever seen. Many of the Great Society programs that elevated poor Blacks out of the ghettos of Wyandanch, New York, are now defunct, however, including the Law Enforcement Assistance Administration (LEAA), the Office of Economic Opportunity (OEO), and the Stay-in-School program. The name "Great Society" recalls a time when all seemed possible.

The bounding possibilities of the Great Society were created not only by the moral high ground provided by the civil rights campaigns of SNCC,

---

24. Pub. L. No. 734, 81st Congress, Social Security Act Amendments of 1950 (HR 6000).

25. The easiest way to find out all of the provisions for Medicare is to go to the Social Security Administration website and read Title XVIII. Go to www.ssa.gov, go to the sitemap, look under "L" for laws, select "Compilation of Social Security Laws." Midgley et al., *Handbook of Social Policy*, 225.

26. "Further, a new federal-state medical assistance program established under Title XIX of the Social Security Act replaced the Kerr-Mills law (medical assistance for the aged that was enacted in 1960). The program was to be administered by the states, with federal matching funds. The new Medicaid program was available to all people receiving assistance under the public assistance titles (Title I, Title IV, Title X, and Title XIV) and to people who were able to provide for their own maintenance but whose income and resources were insufficient to meet their medical costs" (Sidor, "Major Decisions"). See also Midgley et al., *Handbook of Social Policy*, 225.

SCLC, and CORE, or by the increasing shame America felt about its embrace of Jim Crow, but also because the US was awash in money from the post-WWII economic boom. Some of the great-grandchildren of the freedmen in Wyandanch got their first paychecks working as community guides with OEO. Social workers streamed through the ghettos to make sure that garbage cans had lids and running water was available, and frequently it was not.

Figure 9.1 Weekly Wages for Manufacturing and Private-Sector Production Non-Supervisory Workers, and All Industries, All Occupations, in Constant 1982–84 Dollars

Source: BLS Data Finder 1.1: Weekly wages for manufacturing and private sector production non-supervisory workers; weekly wages for all industries and all occupations, first quarter.

Figure 9.1 depicts the extraordinary WWII and post-WWII boom starting in 1939. The shift from war production to civil production from 1945 to 1947 was hardly a hiccup. From 1945 until 1975, the US economy seemed invincible. These days were happy ones for white America and, in some sense, Black America too. Blacks were stifled by Jim Crow in the South and terrible repression in the North, but the burgeoning economy fueled Black wages in the North. Some said that Black auto workers in Detroit in the 1950s were the highest-paid Black workers in the world. Perhaps that claim was true.

A video on the Great Society points out many of the benefits that the Great Society created. The Johnson legislative blitzkrieg was amazing. The first major civil rights legislation in nearly a hundred years—the 1964 Civil Rights Bill, the 1965 Voting Rights Act, the 1968 Fair Housing Act, the Economic Opportunities Act of 1964—all were part of Johnson's Great Society.[27]

27. *American Experience*, "LBJ and Great Society."

The Economic Opportunities Act of 1964 created the Jobs Corps, urban and rural community action programs that included adult education, rural anti-poverty programs, employment programs for the long-term unemployed, work experience programs, and more, such as the legal assistance programs that came from OEO, public broadcasting, the National Endowment for the Arts and Humanities, and the list goes on.

The question is why, even with these helpful programs, did poverty and racial inequality survive. The answers are money, pride, and ambition.

Considering the Great Society or the War on Poverty as a failure is difficult. The reductions in poverty were extraordinary. Figure 9.2 shows that Johnson's War on Poverty was the most effective of our time, or perhaps of any time. Black poverty dropped from over 50 percent in 1959 to less than 35 percent by 1970.

Figure 9.2 Black Poverty, 1959–2021

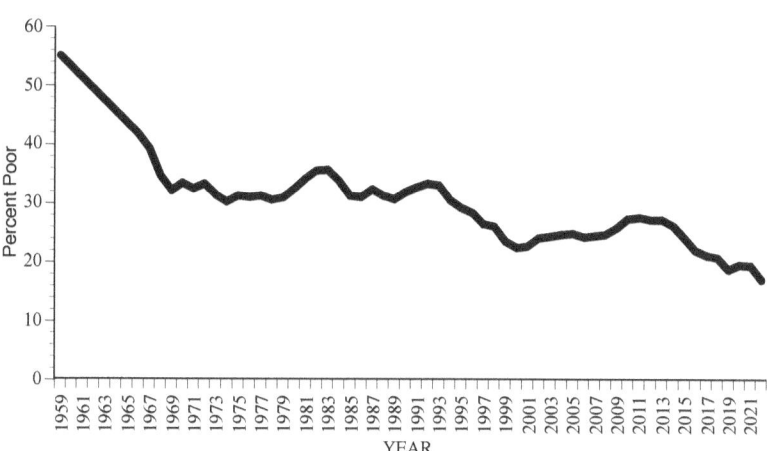

Source: Current Population Survey Datasets, Annual Social and Economic Supplements. For information on confidentiality protection, sampling error, non-sampling error, and definitions, see U.S. Census Bureau, *Current Population Survey*, table 2, "Poverty Status of People by Family Relationship, Race, and Hispanic Origin: 1959 to 2022."

By contrast, Bill Clinton's ending of welfare as we know it has not done nearly so well. From the passage of the Personal Responsibility and Work Opportunity Reconciliation Act (PRWORA) in 1996, the poverty rate for Blacks fell from 28.4 percent to 20.8 percent in 2018, with many ups and downs. The economic crisis of 2007–9 saw rises in the poverty rate for Blacks and whites, however, and these problems are still with us. Erik Eckholm reported for *The New York Times* on September 10, 2009, that the poverty rate in 2008 was the highest in twelve years.[28] Figure 9.2 delineates that for Blacks the poverty rate has gone almost nowhere since 2000 when the rate stood at 22.5 percent and 17.1 percent in 2022. Except for the impact of the Great Recession on whites, whether anyone would notice Black poverty is a question of concern.[29]

The Great Society also saw the most profound reductions in racial wage discrimination. Figure 9.3 measures Black male log wages against white male log wages. For Black men the coefficient is almost always in the minus territory because Black men earn less than white men, even for the same skill. Real progress was occurring, with the Black male log wage coefficient falling rapidly toward zero from 1964 to even the mid-1970s. Then the progress stopped. The obvious reasons for that cessation are the end of the expanding economy and overspending on the Vietnam War, which influenced voters and policy elites to curtail or eliminate equality programs.

Figure 9.3 Black Male Log Wage Coefficient, 1963–2014

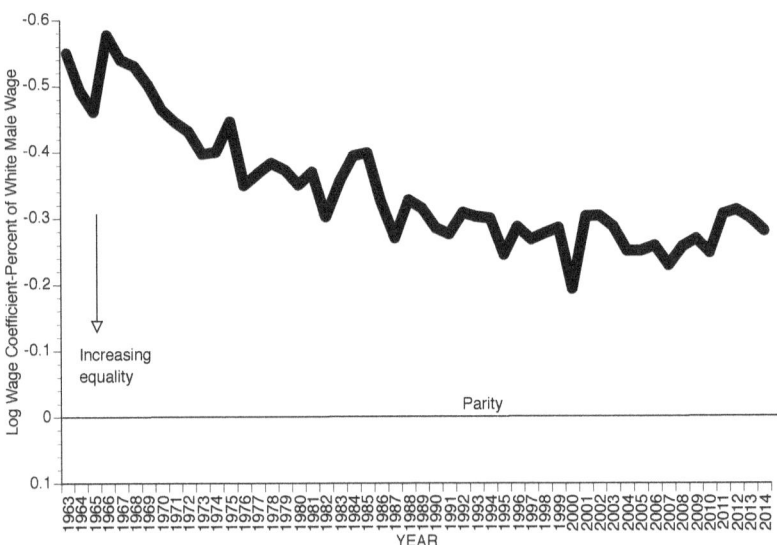

Controls: age, region. Source: Current Population Survey Datasets, 1962–2014. Washington, DC (machine-readable data files)/conducted by the Bureau of the Census for the Bureau of Labor Statistics. Washington, DC: Bureau of the Census (producer and distributor), 1962–2014. Los Angeles: Unicon Research Corporation (producer and distributor of CPS Utilities), 2014.

Black men were not the only ones making progress during the Great Society years. Black women, riding on the policies and programs of the

28. Eckholm, "Last Year's Poverty Rate."
29. DeNavas-Walt et al., *Income, Poverty: 2008*.

Great Society, reached parity with white females in the late 1970s or early 1980s (fig. 9.4). Parity for Black females must be considered against the greater experience and job tenure of Black females compared to white females. Given the greater job tenure and experience of Black females over their white counterparts, only racial discrimination explains why Black females do not earn considerably more than do white females.

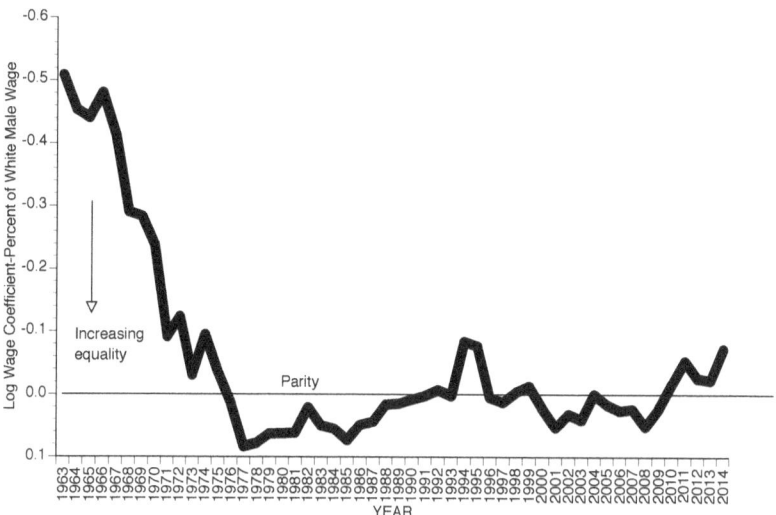

Figure 9.4 Black Female Log Wage Coefficient, 1963–2014

Controls: age, region. Source: Current Population Survey Datasets, 1962–2014. Washington, DC (machine-readable data files)/conducted by the Bureau of the Census for the Bureau of Labor Statistics. Washington, DC: Bureau of the Census (producer and distributor), 1962–2014. Los Angeles: Unicon Research Corporation (producer and distributor of CPS Utilities), 2014.

The expanding economy is not what fueled Black progress during the Great Society. The expanding economy fueled the political environment and consensus, which allowed LBJ to create the programs that fueled Black progress. Since everyone thought they would have more, the argument was that giving Blacks what they want seemed appropriate.[30] The Great Society and the War on Poverty today seem to be Black programs, or mostly so. Only after the urban revolts in the mid-1960s did these programs take on the racial view they now have.[31]

Johnson seemed to care about the poor, and he staked his political career on fighting racism. Johnson's refusal to let go of either the Great Society or the escalating war in Vietnam, however, eventually led to his downfall

30. King, *Where Do We Go from Here*, 6.
31. Davies, *From Opportunity to Entitlement*, ch. 2.

and the end of the Great Society programs. LBJ had no idea how much the Vietnam War would cost. As the war costs grew, he faced cuts to his social programs and the inevitable inflation that came from so much spending on the war and his refusal to raise taxes.[32]

A recent article listed LBJ as the greatest modern president, even above FDR.[33] This author supports that claim if only because LBJ attacked racism directly and not just with the FEPCs, as did FDR. Alvin Tillery and Hanes Walton also rank LBJ as the greatest of the nineteen modern presidents since 1900 in terms of civil rights based on positive editorials in Black newspapers. Tillery and Walton rank Obama as number seven (behind LBJ, Eisenhower, FDR, Truman, Harding, and Teddy Roosevelt) and Clinton as number ten (behind Gerald Ford), in spite of their high rates of Black voting support in table 7.3.[34] Tillery and Walton's analysis matches the economic data in figures 3.5 and 3.6. The greatest income gains for both Black men and women came during the post-WWII boom years of the late 1950s, gaining traction during the LBJ years and continuing until the beginning of the Reagan presidency. The Clinton years saw the greatest declines in incomes for Black men and women relative to whites. The Obama years were stagnant.

But, Johnson's greatest weakness as a president was in deciding not to choose which he wanted, the Great Society or the war in Vietnam. LBJ wanted both, and that was his undoing. Vietnam had little if anything to do with the domestic agenda. LBJ figured that once the soldiers were in the field, it would be impossible for Congress to cut off funds for the war. That assessment was true. At the same time, LBJ figured that he could grow his way out of the costs for the Great Society, that is, economic growth would pay for it. All the while almost no information was available about the cost of the war or the domestic agenda. Both Vietnam and the Great Society began to draw heavily on the budget at the same time—in 1966.[35] From where we sit today it is easy to be critical of LBJ, but looking at figure 9.1 again, imagine that you started your working career in 1939. By the time you were ready to retire, thirty years later in 1969, you would have never seen a decline in your paycheck or what your paycheck could buy. If you worked in manufacturing, the same could be said if you started your career in 1945, as did many GIs. We may never know the full cost of the Great Society. The entire program comprised some 435 individual bills and spread

32. Davies, *From Opportunity to Entitlement*, 106.
33. Taylor, "Ranking Every Modern US President."
34. Tillery and Walton, "Presidential Greatness in the Black Press."
35. Helsing, *Johnson's War*, 9–10.

across dozens of agencies. The Office of Economic Opportunity, one of the most well-known Great Society agencies, was in the Executive Office of the President, and that location made it particularly difficult to track where the money went.[36]

The Senate GOP policy committee put the cost for the Great Society at $54.4 billion in current dollars for the first five years from 1965 to 1970. Another estimate puts the tab at $38.6 billion for a low figure and $65.5 billion for a high figure for the same period. The latest Congressional Research Service report puts the amount spent on the Vietnam War, 1965–75, in current dollars, at $111 billion. By almost any measure LBJ devoted twice as much money to Vietnam as to the Great Society. Yes, the war was twice as long, but even that says something about where national priorities were.[37] The Great Society was more than just money; also prominent was the idea that Blacks were no longer slaves and they, like everyone else, deserved a part of the American dream to be somebody.

STANDING AT THE JORDAN

Martin Luther King Jr.'s plan was to create real, substantive equality. This seemed within reach during the Great Society years. King stated that the Civil Rights Act of 1964 was weak and helped mostly the Black middle class. In 1965, King demanded that Blacks have preferences in jobs, housing, and education, and he estimated that the government would have to spend some $50 billion per year over a ten-year period to achieve "a genuine and dramatic transformation . . . in the conditions of Negro life in America."[38] King's request is over and above the social welfare Blacks receive.

The defense budget during the mid-1960s to the 1970s rarely dipped below $80 billion per year. At that rate, the Great Society was costing about one-tenth of the defense budget or one-fifth of what King was requesting on

36. Shribman, "Lyndon Johnson," 239.

37. Young, *Democrat Spending Plans*; Haveman, "What Antipoverty Policies Cost"; Daggett, "Costs of Major U.S. Wars." Young's report cites Congressional Research Service and Heritage Foundation reports, neither of which have I been able to locate. I was not able to replicate Haveman's exact figures but I came very close. Haveman calculated two scenarios based on the growth in social welfare spending versus the GDP. In scenario A, Haveman subtracted the growth in the GDP (8.9 percent per year) from the actual growth in social welfare spending from 1965 to 1980 (he calculated that to be 12.9 percent per year; I calculated 13.15 percent per year). In scenario B, Haveman subtracted the growth in social welfare spending from 1950 to 1965 (10.7 percent per year) from the growth in social welfare spending from 1965 to 1980. I do not accept Haveman's claim that the Great Society ended in 1980.

38. King, "*Playboy* Interview," 366.

a yearly basis. Even the high figure of $65.5 billion for the Great Society is only 1 percent of the $5.4 trillion in GDP for 1965–70. The priorities seem fairly clear. MLK Jr.'s request for $50 billion per year for ten years totals $500 billion in 1965. King's $500 billion was 1 percent of GDP from 1965 to 1974, ten years. The value of King's request as a percentage of GDP from 2014–23 ($214 trillion), ten years, is $2.1 trillion. The value of King's request based on CPI inflation would equal $4.9 trillion in 2024.[39] In 1990, James Marketti put the price for slave reparations at between $2.1 and $4.7 trillion.[40] The value of Marketti's high figure of $4.7 trillion in 2024 is $11.2 trillion. By comparison, King's $4.9 trillion request looks like an incredible bargain.

With the successes already made in poverty reduction and wage equality for Black men during the Great Society period, and with the funds and commitment that King was requesting, perhaps the nation might have achieved the long-sought-after dream of substantive racial equality. If nothing else, they were very close. The nation spent a large part of those funds on Vietnam. No wonder King and his allies were so intense. They were on the shore of the Jordan, looking at the promised land of racial equality, just on the other side.

WELFARE AS CHEAP HIGH-COST EQUALITY

While social welfare is high cost compared to affirmative action and other programs, welfare is inexpensive as a percent of the total wealth of America. Table 9.1 illustrates that the US government and the states spent over $4 trillion on welfare in the latest figures available. US GDP was $25 trillion in 2022.[41] Social welfare spending is about 16 percent of GDP. However, the government expends only a small portion of that money on the poor. Most welfare in the US is for the nonpoor. Table 9.1 lists the largest public social welfare programs in the US and the amounts of funding. We spend about three times as much on welfare for the middle class as we do on welfare for the poor. Medicare, disability insurance, unemployment insurance, and workers' compensation are examples of middle-class welfare.

Medicare is the health insurance program in the US for people aged sixty-five or older. Certain people younger than age sixty-five can qualify

---

39. Author's calculations using U.S. Bureau of Economic Analysis, table 1.1.5, formerly at https://apps.bea.gov/iTable/iTable.cfm?reqid=19&step=2#reqid=19&step=2&isuri=1&1921=survey; and U.S. Bureau of Labor Statistics, Consumer Price Index for all Urban Consumers, annual, formerly at https://data.bls.gov/pdq/SurveyOutputServlet.

40. Marketti, "Estimated Present Value."

41. See interactive database at Gross Domestic Product.

for Medicare, including those who have disabilities and those who have permanent kidney failure or Lou Gehrig's disease. The program helps with the cost of healthcare but does not cover all medical expenses or the cost of most long-term care.[42]

The Social Security Administration stated, "Social Security Disability Insurance (DI) is financed with Social Security taxes paid by workers, employers, and self-employed persons. To be eligible for a Social Security benefit, the worker must earn sufficient credits based on taxable work to be 'insured' for Social Security purposes."[43]

Unemployment insurance replaces wages lost due to involuntary unemployment or layoffs. Unemployment insurance programs are generally funded by employers who pay taxes on wages paid to employees. "Workers' compensation provides cash and medical benefits to some persons with job-related disabilities or injuries and provides survivor benefits to the dependents of those whose death resulted from a work-related accident or illness."[44]

Social insurance programs are middle-class welfare because persons do not have to be low income to receive them. Social insurance programs are middle class also because social insurance programs are almost never subject to the attacks we see on welfare for the poor. Welfare for the poor includes AFDC/TANF, Medicaid, supplemental security income, food stamps (SNAP), Head Start, housing aid, WIC (a food nutrition program for women, infants, and children), school food programs, and the earned income tax credit.[45]

Little changed in the past thirty years on the relationship between government spending for social insurance and transfers. Also, it matters little how a person looks at the data in terms of percent of GDP, current expenditures, or constant dollars. Middle-class welfare or social insurance is about three times that of poor peoples' welfare or transfers. Figure 9.5 shows social welfare as a percent of GDP from 1933 to 2020. Social welfare as a percent of GDP indicates the importance of social welfare in comparison with the total wealth of the nation, not just what the government chooses to collect. About 8.6 percent of GDP is for middle-class welfare, and about 2.8 percent is for the poor in 2013. Total public social welfare spending in that

   42. Social Security Administration, *Medicare*.
   43. Statement formerly at https://www.ssa.gov (accessed May 20, 2020).
   44. Scholz and Levine, "Evolution of Income," 200.
   45. "Supplemental Security Income (SSI) is a program financed through general revenues. SSI disability benefits are payable to adults or children who are disabled or blind, have limited income and resources, meet the living arrangement requirements, and are otherwise eligible" (formerly at https://www.ssa.gov [accessed May 20, 2020]).

THE COST OF RACIAL EQUALITY

year was about 12 percent of GDP. This number is quite low in comparison with other developed nations.

Figure 9.5 Social Welfare Spending as a Percent of GDP, 1933–2020

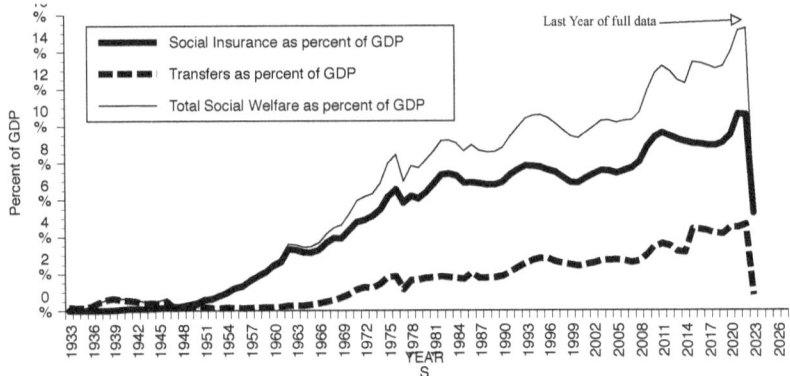

Source: Author's database.

QUALITY LINGERS LONG AFTER THE PRICE IS FORGOTTEN

The higher percentage of GDP that nations spend on social welfare, generally, the better the overall quality of life in the country. And these higher quality of life measures seem to gain far more attention than the prices countries pay for them. Conversely, the poor quality of life measures in the world's richest nation seem to be a constant conversation rather than the low price America pays to protect its people. Compared to other OECD nations, the US spends little for social welfare. Table 9.4 lists social spending by nations for 2019.

Table 9.4	
Social Welfare Spending as a Percent of GDP, 2019	
Country	Percent of GDP
France	30.7
Finland	29.4
Denmark	28.4
Belgium	28.2
Austria	27.7

Table 9.4

Social Welfare Spending as a Percent of GDP, 2019

Country	Percent of GDP
Italy	27.7
Germany	25.6
Norway	25.3
Greece	25.1
Sweden	25.1
Spain	24.6
New Zealand	23.6
Japan	22.8
Portugal	22.3
Luxembourg	21.6
Slovenia	21.5
Poland	21.2
Australia	20.5
OECD Average	20.1
Czechia	19.5
United Kingdom	19.5
Canada	18.8
Iceland	18.7
United States	18.3
Estonia	17.9
Hungary	17.6
Slovak Republic	17.5
Lithuania	17
Latvia	16.5
Netherlands	16.3
Israel	16.1
Switzerland	16.1
Colombia	14.1
Ireland	12.9
Turkey	12.4
Costa Rica	12.3
South Korea	12.3
Chile	11.7
Mexico	7.4

Source: Social Spending.

Note the difference between tables 9.4 and 9.1. Table 9.1 was for federal (with some state) social welfare spending. Table 9.4 is for federal, state, local, and private social spending in various nations.

Table 9.4 shows that the US is near the bottom of the list for public and private social welfare spending. The nations that rank lower than the US are small nations that do not have the per capita wealth of the US. None of the OECD nations in table 9.4 have the overall wealth of the US.[46]

Nations tend to get exactly what we pay for because the more money spent for social welfare, the more social welfare nations receive, measured in equality and health. Many international organizations use income equality and infant mortality as overall measures of social well-being in a nation. Table 9.5 shows countries ranked by their index of income inequality. Again, the US is near the bottom of the list of OECD countries. Nearly all of the industrialized Western nations of Europe spend more for social welfare and have greater income equality.

Table 9.5
Index of Income Inequality, 2019–22
(after taxes and transfers)
Smaller numbers indicate less income inequality.

Country	Gini Coefficient
Slovak Republic	0.217
Slovenia	0.242
Czechia	0.255
Belgium	0.256
Poland	0.261
Denmark	0.268
Finland	0.273
Hungary	0.278
Austria	0.281
Luxembourg	0.284
Norway	0.285
Sweden	0.286
Croatia	0.288
Ireland	0.291
Canada	0.292
Netherlands	0.297

46. Readers should not confuse social welfare spending with the public and private health expenditures discussed in ch. 2. Social welfare spending takes in more than just health spending.

Table 9.5
Index of Income Inequality, 2019–22
(after taxes and transfers)
Smaller numbers indicate less income inequality.

Country	Gini Coefficient
France	0.298
Germany	0.303
Greece	0.312
Portugal	0.313
Romania	0.317
OECD Average	0.317973684
Australia	0.318
New Zealand	0.32
Spain	0.32
Switzerland	0.32
Estonia	0.321
Italy	0.33
Korea	0.333
Israel	0.34
Latvia	0.343
United Kingdom	0.354
Lithuania	0.366
Bulgaria	0.383
United States	0.395
Turkey	0.403
Mexico	0.42
Chile	0.448
Costa Rica	0.472

Source: Income Inequality.

Chapter 2 discussed infant mortality as a measure of social well-being. Black infant mortality in the US is far below white infant mortality. Whether social welfare spending causes greater income equality or lowers infant mortality may be uncertain. Nevertheless, a clear moderate to strong relationship occurs between the greater social welfare spending in table 9.4 and decreased income inequality in table 9.5 ($r=.19$, $n=28$) and lower infant mortality in chapter 2 ($r=.33$, $n=29$).[47] That is, if we know the social welfare

---

47. L. Hamilton, *Modern Data Analysis*, 481, defines the relationship of the coefficient of determination to measures of strength.

spending of the nation, we can predict income inequality and infant mortality, respectively 19 percent and 33 percent of the time, which again, is a moderate to strong relationship.

REPARATIONS VERSUS WELFARE

Reparations are not at all impossible to calculate, and many estimates are available. Larry Neal estimated the present value, in 1983, of the wages, that should have been paid to the slaves. We do not have detailed censuses for all slaves or non-slaves, so Neal uses the US Historical Statistics. Data is available, however, on the prices for slaves. For those who love to figure, please read Neal. His final calculations yield $1.4 trillion, in 1983–84 dollars, that the slaves were worth from 1620 to 1840.[48] James Marketti calculated diverted income and its compounded values from 1790 to 1860. He came up with a figure of $2.1 to $4.7 trillion. David Swinton has a figure of $700 billion for contemporary labor market discrimination based on private assets and wealth. All of the economists used different methods, but all have figures close to or over $1 trillion and up to $5 trillion.[49]

Reparations for slavery alone range from $1.4 trillion to $4.7 trillion. The low figure of $1.4 trillion (in 1983) is equal to the $4.4 trillion (in 2024), about what is spent annually on all social welfare programs in table 9.1. The high figure of $4.7 trillion (in 1990) is equal to $11.2 trillion in 2024, almost three times the annual cost for all social welfare spending for all races in table 9.1. Even the lowest estimates for slave reparations, $1.4 trillion in 1983, which is worth $4.4 trillion today, is almost ten times the $463 billion that Blacks receive for all social welfare programs in table 9.1.

The estimates for reparations from Neal, Marketti, and Swinton were published thirty years ago but were based on 1983 dollars in calendar year 1983.[50] Calculating the value of wage discrimination against contemporary Blacks involves the current value of wage and income discrimination for a given year, converted into constant dollars for all years of labor. The basic model was performed in table 6, model 1. On average, Black workers lose $10,397 per year just for being Black. Model 1 of table 6 assumes that racial differences in human capital, demographics, occupations, gender, and poverty are all caused by racial discrimination. If the 33 million Black workers in 2019 had a forty-year working life, the total value of their losses from

---

48. Neal, "Current Benefits of Slavery."

49. Marketti, "Estimated Present Value"; Swinton, "Racial Inequality."

50. Marketti, "Estimated Present Value"; Neal, "Current Benefits of Slavery"; Swinton, "Racial Inequality."

wage discrimination is approximately $11.7 trillion. These calculations are needlessly arduous. The shorthand is that slave reparations are approximately equal to one year GDP in the US. In 1988, GDP was $4.8 trillion, and Marketti's high figure for slave reparations was $4.7 trillion. Marketti's $4.7 trillion has a value of $12 trillion in 2019 using 1983–84 constant dollars. Adding contemporary wage and income discrimination of $11.7 trillion to slave reparations yields a price of nearly $24 trillion. With a GDP of approximately $24 trillion in 2021, the current value of slave reparations may still be near to one year GDP.

Craemer provides one of the most recent reparations estimates totaling, with interest from 1860 to 2009, approximately $6 trillion based on a twelve-hour work day for persons older than five years of age and $14 trillion based on the total time Blacks were enslaved (twenty-four hours per day) with a relaxed age requirement.

> For the period from 1776 to 1865 since this is the time the United States could have abolished slavery but failed to do so. I present two slavery-reparations scenarios whereby the more conservative estimates the amount of uncompensated work time only, while the more liberal one counts any amount of time the slave was "on the clock." Scenario 1 only counts slaves of working age (five years or older) during daylight working hours (on average roughly 12). Scenario 2 relaxes the age requirement because slave owners were under no legal obligation to observe age limits, and it counts all 24 hours of the day as time to be compensated. Scenario 2 has the advantage of accurately representing the role of downtime and sleep for a slave: it was restoration of energy for further forced labor. It was not spare time in the wage-labor sense with choice of activities and granting it or not was entirely up to the slave owner—no law required it. Granting or denying it was part of the economic calculation of the slave owner and the life expectancy of a slave crucially depended on that utility calculation. . . .
>
> During the Civil War, the slave population dropped, and no reliable census records are available to impute slave population estimates for the years between the 1860 census and 1865. Thus, the resulting figures establish lower boundaries for debt estimates.
>
> From 1860 until 2009, the estimated amount grows each year by the interest rate that is applied (here 3 percent) and the resulting total slavery debt figures for 2009 are $5,931,336,366,538.91 for Scenario 1 and $14,239,934,652,326.70 for Scenario 2. If the number of slave descendants is estimated based on the number

of people who identify as African American or Black in the US Census of 2006–2008 (37,131,771 individuals), per capita reparations would amount to $159,737.50 in Scenario 1 and $383,497.32 in Scenario 2.[51]

What is so interesting about all the authors who undertook the task of actually calculating reparations for slavery is that they used different techniques and time periods but arrived at figures that are relatively close to each other.

THE MIXED-UP MALONES AND WHO SHOULD GET REPARATIONS

The story of the twin Malone brothers, two white firefighters who tried to join the Boston Fire Department in 1975, is memorable. They scored poorly on the entrance examination and were not hired. Then they struck on an idea and claimed to be Black and were hired under a court-ordered affirmative action program that allowed self-identification. All went well for ten years until they sought promotion to lieutenant, and the fire commissioner noticed the twins were listed as Black. They were fired immediately. The "mixed-up Malones" sued. The court used a three-part test to determine their race: 1) visual observation, that is, whether they appeared to be Black; 2) documentary evidence, such as birth certificates and Black ancestry; and 3) their status in the community, that is, did the Malones hold themselves out to be Black. The Malones lost the case.[52]

The story may be amusing to some, but the problem is a serious one. One of the arguments against reparations is that it is impossible to determine who should get them. The answer is simple: the sons and daughters of American slavery. That answer raises another question of exactly who those people are. Conservative talk show host Armstrong Williams raises this question: "One wonders, for example, what percentage of Black blood would entitle a citizen to reparations?"[53]

Economists William A. Darity and A. Kirsten Mullen have made this issue simple.[54]

> The moral-hazard principle alerts us to potential problems in establishing criteria for eligibility for receipt of African-American

51. Craemer, "Estimating Slavery Reparations," 649.
52. Ford, "Administering Identity."
53. A. Williams, "Presumed Victims," 170.
54. Darity and Mullen, *From Here to Equality*, 258–59.

reparations. Reparations would create a premium for being Black in America that previously did not exist. Thus, individuals who had not previously self-identified as Black suddenly will have an incentive to declare their African ancestry. To mitigate this problem, we propose two criterion for eligibility: (i) individuals would have to provide reasonable documentation that they had at least one ancestor who was enslaved in the United State, and (ii) individuals would have to demonstrate that at least 10 years prior to the onset of the reparations programs they self-identified as Black, African American, colored, or Negro on a legal document.[55]

As with the Malones, perhaps a third criteria should be added, that their community considered them as Black, that is, they lived a Black lifestyle. Prior to receiving a payout, anyone wanting to be part of the reparations process would need a Black church, Black friends, Black spouse, Black children, Black neighborhood, or the like, to show they were part of the group of oppressed people, because race is a social construct.

PRECEDENTS FOR REPARATIONS

Reparations are not new. Germany apologized and paid reparations to individual Jews and to the state of Israel. The US has paid reparations of $20,000 per person and apologized to those of Japanese ancestry who were interned during WWII. The Inuit recovered monies from the Canadian government, and Korean women forced into prostitution received reparations from Japan.[56]

Reparations for the enslavement of Africans have been paid in the past. These reparations were not paid to those enslaved, however, but to the slave masters for the loss of their property when slavery was abolished in the British Empire.[57]

REPARATIONS ARE FAIR

The YouGov survey found that most whites do not support the idea of reparations for slavery but the survey did not reveal why whites opposed

---

55. Darity and Frank, "Economics of Reparations."

56. Bell, *Race, Racism, and American Law*, 56; Brooks, *Atonement and Forgiveness*, 107; Robinson, *Debt*, 221; Van Dyke, "Reparations," 73.

57. E. Williams, *Capitalism and Slavery*, 87–89.

reparations for slavery.[58] Spath provides valuable assistance, when he writes from a libertarian perspective, about what is wrong with reparations.[59] Spath's first three objections to reparations concern slavery in antiquity: 1) slavery was common in antiquity; 2) before the Atlantic slave trade, slavery was not race based; and 3) the West should be praised for abolishing slavery. Slavery in antiquity has little if anything to do with the Atlantic slave trade and even less to do with the legality of contemporary inequality. US courts rarely look to ancient Roman law for precedent. Whether the West should receive praise for abolishing slavery depends on the reason the West generally and Britain in particular, the biggest slave transporter and seller of slaves, abolished slavery. Williams argues that ending slavery in the West had little to do with moral compunction and everything to do with the inability of the British system of monopoly to compete with the new industrial order.[60]

Next, Spath attacks the need of Blacks for reparations with four charges: 1) most Blacks are not poor; 2) Blacks do not need government handouts; 3) compared to the rest of the world, African Americans are wealthy; and 4) since Reconstruction, Blacks have succeeded. None of the aforementioned examples of reparations to the Japanese, British landed gentry, European Jews, or Inuit are based on the needs of those injured. Reparations are based on the wrongs committed by governments, unjust enrichments of privileged groups, and losses suffered by those impacted.

Continuing, Spath makes the classic cases for white innocence: 1) most whites were not slave owners; 2) most whites today are the progeny of immigrants; and 3) if the white immigrants made it without special help, so can Blacks. All whites, slave holders or not, benefited from slavery because Black slavery was the foundation of the national economy.[61] All whites today, whether they support racial inequality or not, whether they support white privileges or not, are beneficiaries of white privilege and the compounded discriminations against peoples of color. Black American slavery did not end with the Thirteenth Amendment to the Constitution. The Jim Crow era continued Black oppression for nearly another century, and the Southern, Central, and Eastern European groups who immigrated to the US after the English, Germans, and Dutch, were very conspicuous in their discrimination against Blacks in the North, particularly in trade unions dominated by

---

58. P. Moore, "Overwhelming Opposition to Reparations."
59. Spath, "What's Wrong with Reparations for Slavery?"
60. E. Williams, *Capitalism and Slavery*.
61. Blumrosen and Blumrosen, *Slave Nation*; Goldstone, *Dark Bargain*.

these groups.[62] Northern whites are not innocent. This compounded white privilege is most prevalent in wealth inequality based on race. Comparing Blacks to white immigrants assumes their starting conditions were equal. Most of the evidence indicates that Blacks faced more intense and longer-lasting discrimination than white immigrant groups.[63]

Spath has three final claims: 1) we do not know who is Black, 2) welfare is a substitute for reparations, and 3) reparations are like tort claims and need a living tortfeasor or negligent party. Identifying the descendants of the enslaved Africans would be a challenge, when, for the first time, a premium might exist for self-identification as Black. Different schemes for racial identification exist, but here are four suggested criteria: 1) visual observation, 2) documentary evidence such a birth certificates or other legal document, 3) whether the claimants hold themselves out to be Black in the community, and 4) the Black community considers the claimants members.

Spath asserts that welfare and affirmative action are the equivalent of reparations without any analysis of the economics costs.[64] Table 1 in the introduction and chapter 5 calculated worst-case costs for affirmative action at $51 billion or less. In most cases affirmative action operates as a net gain to American industry, not a subsidy for less qualified Black workers. Chapter 5 also showed that Black workers outperform white workers in productivity. Affirmative action is not a substitute for reparations because affirmative action is not a cost to the nation; rather, affirmative action benefits America more than it benefits Blacks.

Welfare is not a financial substitute for reparations since the cost comparisons are so disparate. Reparations for slavery range in cost from $1.4 to $4.7 trillion. (See the earlier discussion in this chapter for the calculation of total social insurance and means-tested dollars from table 9.1 that go to Blacks as $335 billion per year.) Social insurance, however, is a right for which Blacks and whites pay, not a gift from the government. Blacks receive about $327 billion in means-tested programs, less than a tenth of the lowest estimate for reparations. The cost for means-tested welfare programs is a yearly cost. The figures for reparations are a one-time cost. The reparations figures, however, do not include compounded interest, which would raise the dollar figure for reparations considerably.

Tort models, like criminal law or constitutional law, are poor models for reparations. Brooks makes a good case against the tort model: 1) slavery in the US was not illegal at the time; and 2) international law holds nations

62. Fletcher, *Silent Sell-Out*; Hill: *Black Labor*; "Black Labor."
63. Lieberson, *Piece of the Pie*; Oliver and Shapiro, *Black Wealth/White Wealth*.
64. Spath, "What's Wrong with Reparations for Slavery?," 46.

blameless for the actions of predecessor regimes.[65] Spath nonetheless seems to miss the point. Rather than finding legal means by which reparations need not be paid, suppose the government is controlled by those who were injured by slavery and its aftermath. Suppose the option is to pay reparations, dissolve the state, or face racial or civil war. Under such circumstances, high-cost welfare, with the goal of creating economic equality rather than mere subsistence, or even reparations, may look like an attractive option.

MARTIN LUTHER KING JR. AND COVID-19

In 1965, MLK Jr. was not asking for reparations for slavery or reparations for contemporary discrimination. He wanted only $50 billion per year (in current 1965 dollars), for ten years ($500 billion in current 1965 dollars, $4.9 trillion in constant dollars, balanced for today's prices), to make "a genuine and dramatic transformation . . . in the conditions of Negro life in America."[66] The entire Great Society spent only $65.5 billion in 1965–70 dollars. The $327 billion Blacks receive per year in means-tested welfare programs in table 9.1 does not even equal what King was asking for in 1965, which was over and above the subsistence-level means-tested programs Blacks already received.

From the earliest mention of the Coronavirus Aid, Relief, and Economic Security Act (CARES Act) in the US Senate, on Sunday, March 22, 2020,[67] until the CARES Act became law on March 27, 2020, was only five days. All one hundred senators, Democrats and Republicans, agreed to spend nearly $2 trillion to address the COVID-19 pandemic. The CARES Act is not easy reading but Reed and Schulteis point out that CARES was actually the third act passed in less than a month to address COVID-19. The speed and large funding amounts are evidence that the US government can react very quickly to national crises. Even more funding for COVID-19 may be coming.[68] The amounts already spent for the COVID-19 crisis in the US are beginning to approach what Martin Luther King Jr. was requesting to transform Black life in America. America appears to have the money, lacking only the will.

---

65. Brooks, *Atonement and Forgiveness*, 105.
66. King, "*Playboy* Interview," 366.
67. *Congressional Record* 166, S1897–902.
68. Reed and Schulteis, "President Trump Signs."

Chapter Ten

Penny Wise and Pound Foolish

HOW TO RECOGNIZE AND TREAT CLINICAL DEPRESSION

Robert Burton (1577–1640) coined the term "penny wise and pound foolish" in *Anatomy of Melancholy*.[1] Even though Burton was an Anglican priest, his book was a medical text on how to manage what these days physicians refer to as clinical depression. Burton's book, written under the pseudonym Democritus Junior, is replete with Latin phrases and satiric passages that can be difficult to understand today. Burton suffered from depression, and he wanted to describe some of the strange, illogical actions that depression causes people to do. He includes: "a fond mother, like Aesop's ape, [who] hug[s] her child to death, a wittol wink at his wife's honesty, and too perspicuous in all other affairs; one stumble at a straw, and leap over a block; rob Peter, and pay Paul; scrape unjust sums with one hand, purchase great manors by corruption, fraud and cozenage, and liberally to distribute to the poor with the other, give a remnant to pious uses, &c. Penny wise, pound foolish."[2] Difficult seventeenth-century satire or no, Barton's descriptions of postpartum depression and manic-depressive and bipolar disorders are clear.

The continued strength of anti-Black discrimination has created a strange mix of scrimping or refusing to pay the small costs necessary to fix a racial problem early, and this failure to plan will necessitate larger and inevitable expenditures later to eliminate the expanded problem. A plethora

---

1. Editors of *Encyclopaedia Britannica* et al., "Robert Burton"; Democritus Junior, *Anatomy of Melancholy*.
2. Democritus Junior, *Anatomy of Melancholy*, sec. 378.

of examples of penny-wise and pound-foolish behavior have been well covered in the preceding chapters.

COVID-19 racial discrepancy and cost perspectives have already been discussed in chapters 2 and 9. However, COVID-19 is also a good example of penny-wise and pound-foolish actions in failing to plan. This behavior applies to epidemics as well as racial equality. Although this book is not about any particular presidential administration, past or present, the focus of consideration, rather, tackles the long-term implication of failing to consider the costs of achieving racial equality. COVID-19 began in Wuhan, China, in December 2019, but the problems of COVID-19 in the United States began decades before when the federal government decided that it was better to save money by not following the recommendations of experts to maintain stocks of protective gear and ventilators. The government did save some funds by allowing the supply stocks that all pandemics require to dwindle. The government wasted far more money than it saved, however, when the COVID-19 virus finally arrived. Experts did not know what type of pandemic they would face, but they knew from prior experience that epidemics and pandemics are not new and would inevitably emerge. Epidemics are a normal occurrence, and preparing for them is no different than maintaining a 747 jetliner or an automobile. With proper planning, the maintenance is routine with few surprises. In rare occasions, parts fail prematurely, but even this occurrence is more or less predictable, and routine and regular checks and inspections constantly anticipate and thwart accidents before they can occur.

COVID-19 began battering the US during the first Trump Administration, but the problems predate Trump's presidency by over a century. In 1918, a deadly strain of the influenza virus struck the world. It was called the Spanish flu because it was first recognized in Spain in March 1918, during WWI.[3] The Spanish flu of 1918 has been described as one of the most devastating pandemics in human history with "extreme mortality."[4] The total number of deaths from the Spanish flu may never be known, but estimates are from 25 to 50 million worldwide. In the US alone, 550,000 died from the Spanish flu in 1918. The flu killed ten to twenty per one thousand of those who were infected, or about 1–2 percent. The CDC estimates that for the 2019–20 flu season, 39–56 million persons in the US were infected with the influenza virus and 24,000–62,000 died, which computes as an annual flu

---

3. Editors of *Encyclopaedia Britannica* et al., "Influenza Pandemic of 1918–19," para. 3.

4. Editors of *Encyclopaedia Britannica* et al., "Influenza Pandemic of 1918–19," para. 2.

mortality rate of about one-tenth of 1 percent, .01 percent.[5] Every day the numbers of those infected with the coronavirus change, and those who die. So far, the Johns Hopkins Coronavirus Resource Center reports that in the US COVID-19 kills 6 percent of those infected,[6] which gives COVID-19 a mortality rate six hundred times that of the seasonal flu and three times that of the Spanish flu of 1918.[7] COVID-19 is less contagious than the Spanish flu, but carries a far higher mortality rate.

PLANNING TO FAIL BY FAILING TO PLAN

COVID-19 is new, but pandemics are not. In 2005, the US Department of Health and Human Services issued a report that outlined a plan to anticipate and manage pandemics just like COVID-19. The 2005 *HHS Pandemic Influenza Plan* recommended "distribut[ing] stockpiled ventilators and other medical material needed to treat and care for infected individuals to health departments and federal agencies that provide direct patient care. Equipment and supplies [should be] maintained in the Strategic National Stockpile and state stockpiles sufficient to enhance medical surge capacity."[8] The 2005 HHS pandemic plan also contained recommendations on "infection control" and the "use of personal protective equipment, such as masks, gloves, and gowns; hand hygiene and safe work practices."[9]

On July 11, 2016, Christopher M. Kirchhoff, director for strategic planning at the National Security Council, wrote to Susan Rice, the national security advisor for Barack Obama from 2013 to 2017, about the dangers the Ebola virus presented for PPE procurement and logistics:

> When it came to PPE in the early days, no one had a very good handle on who could produce what at what volumes and where they were in the world, or even what was needed. The Ebola Task Force asked for the assistance of the Department of Commerce and certain contracting mechanisms at DoD to ensure

---

5. CDC, "2019–2020 Flu Seasons."

6. Coronavirus Resource Center, "New COVID-19 Cases Worldwide."

7. National Center for Immunization and Respiratory Diseases, "Coronavirus Disease 2019."

8. U.S. Department of Health and Human Services, *HHS Pandemic Influenza Plan*, 25.

9. U.S. Department of Health and Human Services, *HHS Pandemic Influenza Plan*, F36.

PPE supply chains for US personnel would be adequate for the scale for the response.[10]

The first Trump Administration conducted a drill of a possible pandemic in 2019, called Crimson Contagion, which recommended "guidance to healthcare and public health sector partners regarding strategies to reduce demand, using engineering and administrative controls to reduce the need for personal protective equipment (e.g., N95 face masks, gloves, and respirators)."[11] N95 face masks, gloves, respirators, and PPE are exactly the items that were in critically short supply during the COVID-19 crisis.

The 2005 HHS pandemic plan and the COVID-19 crisis are merely the latest tragedies in a list of failures of executing a plan. The 116th Congress took their seats on January 3, 2019, in the middle of the $5.7 billion border-wall crisis that led to a thirty-three-day government shutdown, the longest in US history. The border wall purportedly would stop the threat of individuals carrying contraband and drugs via desert crossings. The DEA finds that almost all of the drugs that come across the southern border illegally, however, come through legal POEs in POVs and tractor trailers, not illegal desert crossings.[12] A border wall is another example of penny-wise and pound-foolish actions because it does little or nothing to stop the entry of most opioid drugs. These drugs tend either to be legal prescriptions or to come through legal POEs and cost the nation $504 billion per year.[13] Failing to fund the EEOC adequately (fig. 7.2) and prohibiting sting operations to stop employment discrimination is another example of penny-wise and pound-foolish practices. The government saves the price of a $1000 employment audit ($250 million for all firms covered by Title VII), but Blacks lose $180 billion per year (2006) in wage discrimination in table 6. Rather than spend the $500 million in gasoline to racially integrate America's school children immediately, the US would rather spend the $25 billion (2007) for NCLB and achieve neither racial integration nor ghetto enrichment. Just as with COVID-19, this book identifies the many government reports, books, and studies that warn of the dangers of allowing racial equality to lapse and racial discrimination to run unchecked in American society, culture, politics, and economics.

The second Trump Administration seems bent on eliminating DEI programs in the federal government and, if possible, in state, local, and private spheres. This was termed the new anti-structuralism in chapter 3. The

---

10. Kirchhoff, "Memorandum for Ambassador Susan E. Rice," 29.
11. U.S. Department of Health and Human Services, *Crimson Contagion 2019*, 32.
12. DEA Strategic Intelligence Section, *2018 National Drug Threat Assessment*.
13. Council of Economic Advisers, *Underestimated Cost*.

new anti-structuralism is an attempt to use political power to achieve what social science evidence cannot, acceptance of the belief that racial inequality is caused by Black deficiency, an idea thoroughly discredited.

PAY NOW OR PAY MORE LATER, IF YOU CAN PAY AT ALL

Building a border wall to stop the opioid crisis is penny wise and pound fooling because the cost and impact of the wall are insignificant against such a daunting $504 billion problem. Refusing to build the border wall is also penny wise and pound foolish, since the monies saved from the wall are insignificant. The $1.3 billion offered by the Democrats for border security is a mere .002 percent (two-tenths of 1 percent) of the economic cost of the opioid crisis, according to the president's Council of Economic Advisors. In addition, these funds addressed border security, not the problems of employment opportunity, education, poverty, violence, discrimination, and homelessness that drive the opioid crisis. Even with these missteps, the Johns Hopkins Bloomberg School of Public Health suggests that the opioid crisis receives the attention it currently receives only because the opioid crisis affects so many whites.[14]

If America refuses to buy the lowest-cost equality programs now, buying such programs in the future may not produce the desired results, or these programs may not be available. A nation of people on the verge of revolution may not easily be dissuaded with low-cost programs or solutions, such as affirmative action or K–12 school integration. Refusing to pay low costs now is usually an unplanned decision to pay higher costs later on. Paying the small costs now is the best way to avoid larger costs later. Even paying the high costs now is often less expensive than purchasing the programs later, not only because of inflation, but also because the high-cost programs have more impact the sooner they are begun.

In a bit more than twenty years, when America officially becomes majority minority, that is, the American population will comprise mostly peoples of color, none of whom constitute a majority of the nation. When this happens, America will be in an economic, social, political, and cultural position that differs from anything the nation has faced before.

Figure 1 illustrated that while the non-Hispanic white population has rapidly decreased, equality, measured by Black to white family income ratio, has been essentially flat. In only seventy-five years, America has shifted from the historic conditions of post-Reconstruction, through the Jim Crow

---

14. Saloner et al., "Public Health Strategy."

period and the critical conditions of the civil rights movement to the post–civil rights eras of today, and will enter the super-critical conditions of a majority minority to around the year 2045. Yes, soon America will have a largely people-of-color majority supporting a white minority who hold most of the economic power. Such a situation is inherently unstable.

KNOWING THE TYPE AND LEVEL OF COST

Finding out how much racial equality costs is not an easy endeavor, but the effort is necessary to avoid painful wastes, missteps, and possible disasters. Economist Thomas D. Boston has said that today "established scholarship must now compete with social media, much of which is not even based on anecdotes but wishful thinking and extreme ideologies."[15] Chapter 1 considered three levels of economic cost—low, medium, and high—and introduced four types of costs: economic, social, political, and cultural. Avoiding a crisis that threatens our democracy demands at least knowing the levels and types of costs.

Programs with low economic cost arbitrarily were classified as those costing less than $100 billion. The lowest-level equality programs that were effective were school integration, by physically moving students, affirmative action programs in labor, equality under the law including the major civil rights legislation, voting rights, fair housing, and antidiscrimination in employment with strong enforcement from EEOC audits.

Programs with medium economic cost are those between $100 billion and $1 trillion. Some of these include ending labor market wage discrimination; equalizing (not eliminating) Black and white poverty, so that the Black poor do not subsidize the white poor, as they do now; poverty elimination; equalizing the educational outcomes in K–12 education; ending the opioid crisis; and instituting racial wealth equality.

Programs with high economic cost include social welfare and reparations for slavery and contemporary racial discrimination, all of which cost well over $1 trillion and upwards of one year GDP in table 1.

Economic costs are not the only costs involved in racial equality. In fact, political costs are in some sense higher than the economic costs. For example, America already pays social welfare costs over $4 trillion. Some low estimates for slave reparations are not much higher than that. Some of the highest-cost social welfare programs are the most popular: welfare for the middle class (OASI, Medicare, unemployment insurance, workers compensation, disability insurance). More than economic costs are at issue.

15. Coleman, "Reading and Leading."

Political costs divide into intrinsic and perceived political costs to illustrate the difference between the often-changing and shifting nature of racial politics on the one hand and fundamental political ideology on the other. Intrinsic political costs are the difference between a particular policy and the views of the party faithful. Few racial issues carry high intrinsic political costs because few racial issues are naturally divisive. At one time or another, the GOP and Democratic Parties have supported voting rights, racial equality at some level, antidiscrimination, and school integration.

Perceived political costs are another matter, however. Perceived political costs are what a political party would have to pay, say in lost votes and support, for taking a particular stand on an issue. Since the 1965 Voting Rights Act enfranchised the Black vote, gains for Blacks are seen to be losses for whites, even when, like affirmative action or school integration and bussing, evidence demonstrates they are not. Table 1 depicted that all the racial equality programs evaluated here, other than middle-class welfare, carry low intrinsic political costs, but high perceived political costs. Middle-class welfare carries low intrinsic and low perceived political costs. Only racially polarized politics could explain this conclusion.

Social and cultural costs classify as group and individual costs respectively. Social costs are how much a racial group needs to change to match a social science reality. Please do not confuse the sociological concept of costs necessary to change a group's deficiency and the economic term of art that was explained in chapter 1. Cultural costs are the changes individual members of a group need to make to improve their conditions.

Table 1 illustrates that all equality programs, regardless of whether their economic cost is low, medium, or high, carry low social group costs. This conclusion may seem strange, but most of the racial equality programs, though not supported politically, are already the law of the land or accepted as right and proper. Voting rights, diversity in business, antidiscrimination are the law or accepted as improving our social conditions. No single group that supports increases in poverty comes to mind. A few white nationalists may support K–12 school segregation or housing discrimination, but few other groups would, at least not openly. America does not yet have socialized medicine, yet almost all countries that do have socialized medicine in chapter 2 have higher quality of life measures than the US and less inequality in table 9.5. Few dispute this claim. The good news is that, in principle, not much separates us.

Cultural costs, individual costs, are another matter altogether. Quite unlike social and group standards, which are widely accepted, the individual behavior of most whites, at least, departs widely from these social norms. Table 1 illustrated that racial equality programs at all economic levels, low, medium, and high, carry high white cultural costs. This finding is counter to the typical white paradigm, which views individual Black behavior as problematic and even pathological.

Looking for this pathological Black behavior in chapter 2 produced little results. The time and effort to change white stereotypical ideas about Blacks will be costly culturally. These mistaken white ideas will soon run headlong into a majority-minority population, who are in sharp disagreement. The January 6, 2021, riot by mostly white Trump supporters as they stormed the US Capitol with their conspiracy theories is one recent example of this phenomena of wildly divergent white belief systems running headlong into a social reality. However, America has a long history of such white race riots.

LOW-COST EQUALITY

Chapters 2–5 considered programs that carry low economic cost price tags. Black deficiency, white culture, equality under the law, and affirmative action are some of the programs included in this section. Low economic costs do not mean low cultural, social, or political costs, however.

Chapter 2 found that many American programs for Blacks arise from the faulty assumption that racial inequality has a cause in some biological, social, or cultural deficiency on the part of Blacks. Evidence in support of such contentions has always been scarce. Because Black deficiency has little, if any, impact on racial inequality, Black deficiency has low cultural costs. Whatever Black deficiency does exist, a theme that has been with America for centuries, it is almost wholly perpetrated by white racism. For the most part, Blacks manage white oppression with skill, determination, tenacity, and a strong spiritual base that often neutralizes the effect of racism in almost all domains of Black life.

The *Washington Post* survey and the GSS showed that most whites think Blacks prefer welfare to self-help, that racial inequality stems from a lack of motivation and willpower by Blacks, that whites pulled themselves up without government help, and that Blacks need to do the same. After nearly a century of legal slavery at the hands of the United States government, and another century of legal Jim Crow oppression that ended only fifty years ago, the supposition that America owes Blacks nothing is untenable. Chapter 2 also showed how science, not anecdotes, is used to combat these types of erroneous ideas. Science employs observation, recordkeeping, and controlled analysis of the empirical world that is falsifiable by others. Falsification means more than simply to discredit an idea. In the minds of many, the FBI discredited Martin Luther King Jr. The FBI did not demonstrate that King was wrong in his claims about racial inequality. To prove a theory or idea empirically false is to present evidence that the idea cannot be true, not merely that the idea is politically, culturally, or socially unpopular or disfavored.

The evidence against Black deficiency as a cause for racial inequality is strong. As of yet, no one has been able to break the chain of historic causation from the slave past. At no time in American history have Blacks achieved substantive economic, political, and social equality with whites, such that henceforth Blacks and whites could be evaluated equally. Good science says that nothing can be the cause of what came before its existence. Cause must precede effect is a basic rule of good theory testing. Figure 2.1 demonstrates that racial income inequality has been constant and fixed since 1880, over half a century before welfare even existed. Welfare does not create racial inequality between Blacks and whites. The CPS shows a clear hierarchy of races based on income arranged in perfect order with whites on top, followed by Asians, Latinos, and Blacks. This racial income hierarchy is so consistent that every economic survey supports it, including the GSS, CPS, and MCSUI.

Job and housing audits also show that discrimination against Blacks is not the exception, but the rule. Historical analysis of Africa before colonialization has failed to support the concept of inherent Black biological deficiency. All commissioned studies of racial inequality in the US, termed the Great Commissions, have found that white racism, not Black deficiency, is the culprit behind racial inequality. Blacks vote, save, and achieve educations at higher levels than whites, once starting conditions are controlled.

The railroad-track effect in figure 2.2 is the gap in life expectancy that has been constant between Blacks and whites since earliest measurements, which would have included the freedmen. Racial inequality in the US is a phenomenon that survives location, era, behavior, and political change. Table 2.1 and figure 2.5 examined whether female headship was a behavioral issue in Black culture. Table 2.1 evinced that female headship, which is highly correlated with poverty, was not dependent on the behavioral characteristics of Black women. In comparison with white females, neither age, income, education, region, employment status, marital status, nor time significantly affect Black female headship. Figure 2.6 shows that for the better part of a century, Black female heads are 50–100 percent more likely to be poor as white female heads. Clearly Black female headship is a structural component of the American system, based on the inability of Black females to marry anyone but Black men, who are in short supply.

The so-called Black slave mentality is part of white mythology. Blacks detest welfare, which may explain why in figure 2.3 only 2 percent of Blacks received government help while fully 26 percent of Blacks were poor. Figure 2.3 shows the railroad-track effect again, with Black and white welfare receipt rising and falling in unison and showing that receipt of welfare (AFDC/TANF) by Blacks is influenced by the same forces that impact whites.

Statistically, table 2.2 illustrated that while Blacks receive government aid at levels higher than whites, however, once assets, social and financial networks, and resources are matched with whites, Blacks receive no more government aid than do whites. This outcome could be a point of pride, but in reality, Black self-reliance is a boon for whites. Table 2.3 shows that before President Clinton's welfare reform, Blacks received slightly more government aid than their comparative rate of poverty. After welfare reform, even though Blacks are 2.4 times more likely than whites to be poor, they are no more likely than whites to receive welfare. Poor Black people subsidize the white poor by taking far less welfare than their needs demand to meet the needs of the middle class and the white poor. Black deficiency has low cultural costs because Black deficiency does not exist and the historical evidence is that Black deficiency never existed.

Unlike the low cultural cost of Black deficiency, white cultural deficiency in chapter 3 carries high cultural costs because it veers so strongly against the best social science evidence, and erroneous white ideas are entrenched. In the past, white perceptions were considered reality simply because whites controlled almost every economic, political, social, and cultural outlet. This situation no longer is true.

Figures 3.1 to 3.3 demonstrated the distinction between absolute, relative, and strategic improvement in the lives of Black people. Absolute improvement is the difference between now and the beginnings of Black lives in the Americas, the difference between now and slavery, now and Jim Crow. Absolute improvement seems to be more important to whites than Blacks. The fact that Blacks were far better than during the antebellum period may have meaning to whites. Such perceptions may have grave consequences if whites believe such comparisons are meaningful to Blacks.

Relative improvement is the difference between Black and white lives now, in keeping up with the Joneses. Relative improvement is how most people judge their lives. How much do I earn in comparison to my peers? Absolute and relative improvements are not totally without meaning. Figures 3.1 and 3.2 compared Black and white and Latino and white ratios for four-year college degrees. The familiar railroad-track effect is present: seventy-five years of stagnation. Blacks and Latinos lag behind whites by some 25–50 percent and the gaps are not closing. Any ideas that whites may have that the conditions of the life of the average Black or Latino relative to theirs are improving are false.

Strategic improvement is the comparison between where we are now and some important goal or target. At this time, only one target is paramount: substantive racial equality at or before America is composed more of peoples of color than whites, on or about the year 2040. Similar to figure 1, figure 3.3 showed the strategic gap between the safest equality route and the Black to white ratio for baccalaureate completion is actually growing wider over time. Strategically, the US is falling behind in racial equality, not moving ahead. One reason for this strategic malaise is white spatial isolation. Figure 3.4 showed that, in their neighborhoods, whites are the least diversified racial group. White neighborhoods have a higher ratio of whites than exist in the general population. Whites live in a type of fantasy world made up of themselves. They receive little outside information from other racial groups and thus often are out of touch. Table 3.1 shows little progress in the high rate of residential segregation in America.

Another significant obstacle for whites is that their erroneous ideas go far back. Most whites have never believed that racial inequality stems from racial discrimination; the majority of whites still oppose large-scale government programs to eradicate racial inequality and continue to insist that conditions for non-whites are improving relative to theirs. Figures 3.5 and 3.6 put these white ideas into a real politico-economic context. Black male and female wages have not risen relative to whites for almost half a century, with non-white men earning about 70 percent of a white male wage since 1999, and non-white women stuck at about 85 percent of a white female wage since the mid-1980s.

Whites do not believe racial profiling of Blacks on the roads of the nation is a problem, in spite of the fact that the overwhelming majority of Blacks believe racial profiling is a problem, and the statistics support Black views as opposed to whites. White support for the death penalty in chapter 3 actually increases if they think that innocent Blacks are facing execution. Even though Blacks are twice as likely to be without health coverage as whites, whites still believe Blacks have equal or better access to healthcare as they do. The least-informed whites think they are more often the victims of racial discrimination than are Blacks.

Some may believe that as presented the evidence is far too critical and condescending of white views. Against these realities, the only appropriate response is that the days of coddling whites in their ignorance should have been over long before now. Rather, the hope for America is to confront whites with the social science evidence showing them they are incorrect in many of their assumptions. Blacks receive little or no coddling from the long list of so-called experts, both Black and white, who support Black deficiency theories and are constantly challenging Blacks to do better, rather than attacking white anti-Black discrimination, the real cause of racial inequality. These experts, from Thomas Sowell, the Thernstroms, Herrnstein and Murray, J. Philippe Rushton, Lawrence Mead, and David Reich, at best use faulty data and at worst engage in pseudoscience. To the list of academic experts, include the list of public intellectuals with little or no training in social science, such as Bill Cosby, Ben Carson, Dinesh D'Souza, Shelby Steele, and John McWhorter. The list seems endless. These misinformed experts and public figures lead the white public astray by adding fuel to white ignorance and making it more difficult to combat. Most people are familiar with these wild claims: affirmative action does not work, affirmative action does not work anymore, affirmative action worked only in the South, affirmative action does not help the poor, affirmative action does not help Blacks, and the civil rights movement did not help.

Figures 3.5 and 3.6 show the civil rights movement was a glorious economic and spiritual success. The greatest advances in Black male income vis-à-vis white male income came in the years 1963–72, the civil rights years. Figure 3.6 shows that the same was true for Black women. Tables 3.2—3.4 show that affirmative action is a complex social program that does indeed benefit Black men, works outside the South, and is still effective long after the civil rights years. The so-called experts have been incorrect, but the highest costs for white cultural belief systems lie ahead of us. The lead social indicators, those measures of the society that tell us what the future has in store, do not have good news. One assumption is that affirmative action helps the poor, but because affirmative action is merit based, it mostly helps those with skills and abilities. Affirmative action is no more an antipoverty program than is the capital gains tax.

When considering tomorrow, we look to the youth and their K–12 education. When we want a moral compass, we look to the church. Unfortunately, these two institutions are some of the most racially segregated major institutions in American society. Since 1988, school segregation has been increasing rather than decreasing. Churches remain segregated to the point of religious apartheid. White churches, neighborhoods, and schools have built a wall to insulate themselves from peoples of color. It will be difficult and expensive even to reach whites to educate them out of their racial ignorance.

Because laws are the basis of most economic systems, all economic costs are included in the costs of the law. However, isolating the most important costs just for the law is important. The cost of the law in chapter

4 highlighted the cultural cost for individuals and the perceived political costs for the institution of the courts.

Three examples illustrate why the courts carry high perceived political costs: 1) The refusal of the US Senate in 2016 to vote on Barack Obama's Supreme Court replacement for Antonin Scalia, with a moderate Democrat, almost a year before the end of Obama's presidency, shows a new level of political hardball involving not only a Black president but the racial polarization between the Democrats and the GOP. 2) The affirmative action case *Fisher v. University of Texas* in 2016 (*Fisher II*) was the right decision for an inappropriate reason. The Supreme Court held correctly that the affirmative action plan of the university was constitutional. The reasoning of the court was that diversity in this case was a compelling government interest and that the plan was narrowly tailored to meet that interest. The court, rather, should have decided that the affirmative action was constitutional because the state had engaged in disparate treatment of Blacks for most of its history. 3) The 2014 Michigan affirmative action case showed the Supreme Court allowing the state of Michigan to pass a law disallowing race-based affirmative action, which is permissible under the US Constitution, but allowing alumni, athletic, regional, class-and-grade-based affirmative action.

Chapter 4 also included the Supreme Court decision in *Students for Fair Admissions v. Harvard* (2023) that diversity did not pass the strict scrutiny standard and that it was the job of the courts to measure how higher educational institutions evaluate the benefits of education. One day this decision will be regarded as illogical as *Dred Scott* (1857), which found that Blacks had no rights whites had to respect, and *Plessy v. Ferguson* (1896), which declared segregation was fully legal as long as it was equal, which was impossible. Having courts overwhelmingly staffed by white elites, regardless of party, makes it difficult for Blacks and their allies to use the courts to foster the large-scale changes that are needed for racial equality, not merely in creating or maintaining diversity.

The erroneous idea that race neutrality is even possible, after centuries of purposeful and determined efforts by the courts to ensure that whites have the best and most of everything, is why the cultural cost of the law is so high. Affirmative action may be defined generically to be the operation of governments, institutions, and business to advance the interests of particular racial groups. In this sense most affirmative action applies to whites, not Blacks. The US Constitution set the stage by creating a political system with Blacks as slaves and a Constitution that was difficult to change. Supreme Court rulings provided much of the basis for this white affirmative action by making the Civil War amendments to the US Constitution of little use to Blacks. *Strauder v. West Virginia* (1879) provided states with a model for Jim

Crow laws. The *Civil Rights Cases* (1883) invalidated the Civil Rights Act of 1875, which attacked individual acts of discrimination against Blacks. *Plessy v. Ferguson* (1896) created a nightmare of racism and racial violence that lasted for the better part of a century. Early twentieth-century historians gave the nation the idea that they and their system were just, even in the face of massive racial discrimination and oppression.

Examples of white affirmative action include the economic and political demands of cotton production, the anti-miscegenation laws necessary to be certain that a caste based on Black racial phenotypes was easily identifiable, and inflated educational criteria and spurious qualification demands for employment not based on the actual ability to do the job. All these practices favor whites. The federal government did its best to help whites move ahead of peoples of color. The Federal Housing Administration kept Blacks and Jews out of the financial system that created equity for white-owned homes. Administration of the GI Bill by states discriminated against Black veterans. The Social Security Act of 1935 excluded farm workers and domestics, the two largest occupations of Black workers. Nepotism in business seems to ensure that nineteenth-century white affirmative action will continue into the foreseeable future.

In contrast to white affirmative action, Black affirmative action is mainly a twentieth-century phenomenon. Also, in contrast to white affirmative action, which is generally anti-merit and dominated by nepotism in business, Black affirmative action tends to be super-meritorious. No more illustrative example of this statement is the notorious but highly successful Philadelphia Plan.

Historically, the Philadelphia construction industry was dominated by white men working in the higher-paying construction crafts versus the low-paying labor occupations (fig. 4.1). After concerted efforts by civil rights groups, both the Johnson and Nixon Administrations created hiring plans for construction firms with government contracts that set goals and timetables to increase Black hiring, not only in construction generally but also in the skilled trades. Figure 4.2 showed that the strong Black affirmative action had an immediate and positive effect on Blacks working in skilled crafts. In 1967, fewer than 5 percent of Blacks worked in the high-paying construction crafts in Philadelphia. One year later, the percentage of Blacks working in the high-paying construction crafts in Philadelphia was 33 percent. This percentage continued to rise through the next three decades. Figure 4.3 illustrates a one-to-one ratio between Blacks in construction labor and crafts, a situation different from the 70 percent of Blacks in labor and 20 percent in craft occupations in 1966. Claims by conservative commentators that affirmative action was not effective, or that it had no impact, simply are false and unsupported by the data. When applied correctly, the law can have an important effect in creating equality.

The clash between white popular wisdom and Black popular wisdom has existed since slavery. Whites long have asserted that efforts to promote Blacks violate standards of merit and dilute the quality of the workforce. For decades whites have believed that reverse discrimination is a serious problem. In chapter 5 we found that 80 percent of whites believe a less qualified Black person will be admitted to college instead of a white person. Fewer than 25 percent of Blacks agree and indeed are polar opposites. These findings have held nearly constantly for a quarter of a century, from 1994 to 2016. Elite academicians have not helped in reducing the clash because they have tended to address white attitudes without the economic and statistical data to determine whether white attitudes have a basis in reality. Whites believe assistance to Blacks violates the American creed of merit, equality, and pulling oneself up by one's bootstraps. Conservative economists postulated that racial discrimination was inefficient. This concept led many to think that Black affirmative action was expensive, even without data to support those contentions.

The clash between white and Black views is intense; both cannot be right. While Blacks and whites differ, the fourteen studies on the cost of affirmative action in table 5.1 surprisingly are consistent; affirmative action costs very little, probably involving only administrative costs, rather than operational costs from lower-quality workers.

Six tables, 5.2—5.7, show that, on average, affirmative action is costless financially but makes money for firms with the superior productivity of Black workers. Three different groups of firms were evaluated: 1) firms overall, 2) government contractor firms, and 3) non-contractor firms. The three groups of firms have two tables each with two-cost measures: 1) average cost and 2) worst-case cost, for a total of six tables. These tables are the first time financial, market, and productivity performance have been compared in one study.

Table 5.2 showed no financial costs to affirmative action; the market views affirmative action positively, and worker productivity is positively associated with affirmative action; that is, the more Black workers a manager has, the more productive the work force. This evidence is powerfully in support of Black popular wisdom. Worst-case financial costs for firms overall in table 5.3 are very small, but big productivity gains come from Black labor.

Tables 5.4 and 5.5 measure the financial, market, and productivity of affirmative action for government contractor firms. In table 5.4 the financial coefficients are negative, but statistically zero—that is, on average, affirmative action costs government contractors nothing at all. Markets like affirmative action and, again, strong productivity gains from Black labor. Tables 5.6 and 5.7 are average costs and worst-case cost for firms without a government contract. On average no significant cost arises for Black labor for non-contractors, neither are there productivity gains or losses for Black labor. This outcome is good: no difference is apparent between Black and white workers for firms without a government contract. Worst-case cost for non-contractor firms for Black productivity is only $16.4 million per firm, only .002 percent (two-tenths of 1 percent) of the $1 billion in sales for these firms.

Chapter 5 points out that from 1990 to 2002 in figures 5.2—5.4 affirmative action firms consistently outperformed non–affirmative action firms financially, in the market and in productivity. Chapter 5 concluded that racial discrimination causes the consistent Black productivity advantage by keeping Blacks in jobs far below their skill level, while promoting whites beyond their skill and ability. Black popular wisdom is firmly grounded in the evidence. The same cannot be said for white popular wisdom.

Low-cost equality programs, such as affirmative action in employment, antidiscrimination enforcement, funding for the EEOC, K–12 school integration, correcting the little Black deficiency that exists, correcting white popular wisdom, and equality under the law are not penny wise and pound foolish. These programs work and produce results. They are not full equality programs, however, and never were meant to create across-the-board racial equality. Pay a little and receive little, but a little is certainly better than nothing. To obtain more, pay more. Those who do not want to pay a lot for equality, whoever these people are, naturally should embrace all of the low-cost programs.

MEDIUM-COST EQUALITY

Chapters 6–8 concerned medium-cost racial equality, ranging in economic price from over $100 billion to almost $1 trillion. Poverty, wages, wealth, politics, the opioid crisis, and K–12 education spending were all programs in this middle range. Sometimes the reason a program is in the middle range is not because of its economic cost but rather its social, cultural, or political cost.

Chapter 6 compared losses incurred by Blacks and Latinos from disproportionate poverty, wage discrimination, and wealth losses with possible gains from affirmative action. Claims that affirmative action creates lower performance by giving Blacks more while they do less is not supported by the evidence. Chapter 5 indicated that Black workers consistently return positive productivity to their employers. Figure 6.3 showed Black men receive far lower returns on education than white men. Rather than lowering performance, Blacks do more while they receive less. Essentially, a Black man gains no financial advantage over his white colleagues in closing the wage discrimination gap by going to college, graduate, or professional school.

Those who claim that ending antidiscrimination enforcement and instead concentrating on anti-poverty is a better plan for achieving equality seem to assume that, in terms of race, poverty is a more serious problem than labor market discrimination. This claim may or may not be true and depends on how the measurement occurs. The tab for basic wage discrimination against Blacks based on race alone ($180 billion) is twice as high as what Blacks and Latinos lose from the disproportionate poverty they suffer ($91 billion). Even when controlling for human capital, demographic, and labor market factors, Blacks still lose more from wage discrimination ($64 billion) than from disproportionate poverty ($54.8 billion).

Blacks do not respond or behave differently than do whites to adverse economic conditions. Blacks are not disproportionately poor because they are lazy; in fact, quite the opposite is true. Figure 6.1 demonstrates the familiar railroad-track effect for poverty and race. Black and white rates for poverty rise and fall in unison, a phenomenon that indicates they are influenced by the same events. A racial factor separates Black and white poverty, but that factor is not behavior. Figure 6.2 showed that during the Great Recession, the ratio of Black to white poverty decreased, a statistic that indicates that Blacks are more self-sufficient than are whites during economic distress. Further, in 2022, some 17 percent of Blacks were poor in figure 6.2; however, in figure 2.3 only about 1 percent of Blacks actually receive what is commonly thought as welfare, means-tested transfers. Blacks are extremely self-reliant.

The wealth picture has not changed much for Blacks since the late 1990s, if the *Forbes* 400 members are a guide. If anything, the situation has deteriorated. In 1997, nearly all of the *Forbes* 400 had old money inherited from wealthy parents, had elite backgrounds, attended elite schools, or had other advantages highly correlated with white privilege. In 1997, no Blacks were on the *Forbes* 400 list of the richest Americans. In 2001, two Blacks were on the *Forbes* 400 list. In 2024, still only three Blacks were on the *Forbes* list for a measly .0075 percent. With all the educated Blacks, opportunity, access, and civil rights laws, 3 percent, 4 percent, even 5 percent of the *Forbes* 400 should be Black. Their absence on this list speaks volumes about the significance of present and historic racial inequality in the wealth of America.

Using the data of Oliver and Shapiro, chapter 6 computations showed that Blacks lose $232 billion in wealth if we include home equity for the 8.6 million Black families in the year 2000.[16] If home equity is not a factor, Blacks are behind whites by only $123 billion in wealth. Remember these figures do not include the superrich and capital ownership. With the CPS data on dividend income as a proxy for capital ownership, in 2006, Blacks had only 28 percent the dividend income of whites. The Black to white wealth gap may be many times our best computations.

Politics rarely has a direct economic effect on racial equality, even though politics influences all economics. Political costs in chapter 7 appear as intrinsic costs and perceived costs. Intrinsic costs are those that would cause a political party to change their ideas, platform, ideology, or fundamental beliefs. Little evidence exists that serious intrinsic political costs affect racial equality in the US. This statement may seem implausible in table 7.1, which shows the obvious racial polarization in the two major parties. Essentially, the GOP is an almost-all-white party. In 2016, nearly 90 percent of the GOP coalition was white compared with only 70 percent of the population. Over the last three-quarters of century, the white percentage of the GOP has oscillated between over 99 percent (1964) to 80 percent in 2024.

The Democratic Party holds the lion's share of all the other racial groups and a minority of white voters in 2024. In table 7.3 only 42 percent of whites voted for the Democratic candidate in 2024, compared to 57 percent of whites who voted for the GOP. This result is unlikely to change anytime soon (fig. 7.3), as both parties are losing white voters because of the decline in the white population. Whites have one of the highest average ages of all the racial groups and the lowest birth rate. Latinos are on the opposite end of the spectrum. Look at table 7.3 again. Since Black voters were enfranchised by the 1965 Voting Rights Act, whites and Blacks have never voted for the same party or candidate, except for Bill Clinton in 1992 and 1996. Bill Clinton likely would not have been elected if not for the candidacy of Ross Perot during 1992 and 1996. Perot pulled away 18.9 percent and 8.4 percent respectively of mostly white voters first from Bush (the father) and then from Robert Dole. American politics is highly racially polarized.

Politics has low intrinsic costs because, even though racially polarized, both the Republican Party and the Democratic Party differ little, if at all, in their core beliefs and racial ideologies. An examination of the party platforms shows that both major parties are in sync about racial equality in voting, antidiscrimination in wages and employment, civil rights, open housing, and integrated schools. More is involved in the political cost of

16. Oliver and Shapiro, *Black Wealth/White Wealth*.

racial equality than intrinsic costs. Political costs also include perceived costs, which are the losses or costs in votes, support, or influence a party would incur if they decided to support a program that has become a political football, such as in the case of affirmative action or in significant decreases in the capital gains tax.

Since FDR's second election in 1936, Blacks mostly have voted against the GOP in a presidential contest. After the passage of the major civil rights legislation in the mid-1960s, Blacks have voted so heavily for the Democratic Party as to leave little for the GOP in terms of Black votes. The two most likely avenues for the GOP to gain votes would be either to support Black causes to a greater degree than the Democratic Party or to appeal to whites. Still, other than the lip service of the party platforms, neither party seems prepared to address substantive racial equality initiatives. Funding for the EEOC, the leading antidiscrimination agency in the nation, is an example of difference between intrinsic and perceived political costs. Since the EEOC's creation in 1966 to the beginning of the Reagan years, funding for the EEOC increased in constant and current dollars (fig. 7.1), regardless of the political party in the White House. Beginning with Ronald Reagan in 1980, however, the EEOC has suffered from a paucity of vital resources; even as the number of discrimination claims continues to rise, funding has been flat in dollars controlled for inflation (constant dollars).

What is so strange about the politics of affirmative action is that this research shows little, if any, economic costs to affirmative action and big productivity gains. The GOP party platform does not support affirmative action; the Democratic platform has supported affirmative action from time to time, but neither party funds the EEOC. The only way to explain this situation is that the intrinsic cost of affirmative action is zero, but the perceived political costs are high.

Chapter 8 delineates that Black and Latino children face a threefold threat: 1) on average they receive lower funding for their educations than do white children; 2) Black and Latino children need more than just equal funding to overcome the effects of poverty, poor nutrition, health issues, disruptions in the home, less educated parents, violence, crime, and social and cultural isolation; and 3) racial segregation allows minority schools to be isolated and receive less political attention and resources from the society at large.

Majority Black and Latino schools are poorly performing schools but not because Black and Latino children are inherently poorer performing than are white students. Historically, since *Brown v. Board of Education* in 1954, racial segregation was the culprit, and racial integration, by almost any means, was the cure to unequal educational outcomes for the school children of the nation. In recent decades many scholars have arisen to challenge those historic claims and fixes to educational inequality. The findings of this study are that the historic causes and cures were true when written and still true today.

Academic studies and newspapers regularly report on high-performing schools in high-poverty areas. Some use the existence of high-performing-high-poverty schools to attempt to demonstrate that racial integration is not necessary for educational equality or that ghetto enrichment, expending large sums of money to improve segregated schools (the *Plessy v. Ferguson* standard), is sufficient for educational equality. Investigation of most of these reports shows they are not exceptions to the broad general rule that segregation is inherently unequal because the purpose of the segregation is to ensure inequality. High-performing-high-poverty schools almost always comprise select groups of students, parents, teachers, and techniques for assuring anything but a random sample of the students from the poverty-stricken region of the school. The ability to eliminate disruptive students, something far more difficult in public schools, is one such technique.

Lay readers may assume social scientists have the ability to demonstrate easily that racial integration is positively associated with benefits to Black and Latino school children, and this assumption is true. As ratios of white students increase, ratios of poverty decrease and test scores go up. Few deny this association. The difficulty arises in demonstrating that racial inequality in education is caused by racial separation, and this harmful impact demands remedies that are opposed by white parents, such as transporting Black children into superiorly performing white school districts or transporting white children into poorly performing schools.

Natural and physical science experiments are powerful because they are simple. Natural and physical science experiments have a control group that does not receive or contain the treatment or substance and an experimental group that receives or contains the treatment or substance. Social science experiments always are difficult because human beings, the subject of the experiment, are inherently far more complicated and difficult to control than natural or physical objects. Many scholars who oppose school bussing and support ghetto enrichment rely on poorly designed studies. Comparing Black and white students from the same segregated school district or community assumes no socioeconomic differences between Black and white students in a poor district. This circumstance is rarely the case, as illustrated in chapter 6, in which even the white poor tend to have more wealth than the Black middle class. The proper way to design a study about the impact of integration is randomly to assign Black students to the control group (those who remain in the high-minority districts) and the experimental groups (those who go to school in a low-minority district). Few such studies exist, but those that do show big gains for integrated education.

While the states and local governments have generally kept up with increased enrollments and increased costs (fig. 8), the federal government at times has dropped the ball and failed to keep pace. Figure 8 demonstrated that in the early 1980s the Reagan Administration and in 2010 the Obama Administration provided less funding than in past years. The problem of unequal education for Black and Latino children is not a Democrat versus Republican problem.

Mary Morris was born in slavery in Virginia in 1854 and died in 1945 while living in Wyandanch, New York, with her daughter and granddaughter, in what would become the poorest and most densely populated Black school district in the state. Her progeny would have to wait five generations, until the birth of Mary's great-great-grandchild, for the first child to be born untouched by poverty. Her wait was an almost interminable wait for the effects of slavery to diminish substantially. Mary Morris was the author's maternal great-grandmother. A fierce urgency to ending K–12 educational inequality in funding and in racial segregation should take the place of such multigenerational waiting, particularly as the Black and Latino populations grow.

Some medium-cost equality programs cost little or nothing economically, including K–12 school integration, intrinsic political costs, equal voting, antidiscrimination in employment. Other medium-cost equality programs do rise above the low-cost level, such as poverty equalization, poverty elimination, wealth equality, wage equality, K–12 equality, and ending the opioid crisis. Some of these programs approach $1 trillion. Medium-cost equality programs are not for the faint of heart, but they produce tangible results and attack some of the most dogged racial problems the nation has faced. Far from penny wise and pound foolish, medium-cost programs can be a middle ground, a meeting place for those who want low or no cost and those who want only high-cost efforts. These medium-cost programs are where America should be for serious future work and without further ado to neutralize the lasting effects of slavery and discrimination in the next century.

HIGH-COST EQUALITY

High-cost equality has only one chapter because even though the economic costs start at over $1 trillion and can reach as high as one year of the nation's GDP, relatively few such programs exist. Cost alone is not what makes high-level equality programs expensive. Much depends on political support for the programs, and the amount of political support a program receives is dependent on for whom and what the program serves.

Chapter 9 argues that because Blacks and whites have had consistent social and economic inequality for fifty years before the Social Security Act passed in 1935, welfare is an unlikely source for the cause of racial inequality. The causes of long-term social and economic inequality usually stem from the structural and systemic foundations of a nation from its inception. Rather than seeing welfare as the cause of racial inequality, perhaps a more realistic view is to understand that the welfare system in the US tends to replicate, rather than repair, the economic inequalities that already existed in the system.

Entering into mid-century, with large economic and social inequality firmly in place, with whites no longer having a voting majority, could change the existence of the nation as we know it. Welfare programs that seek to equalize socioeconomic conditions, rather than just maintaining the poor at survival levels, are in the interests of whites. As the population of people of color grows, reparations for slavery may become a viable issue. Cory Booker, a Black Democratic US senator from New Jersey, made history when he became the first US candidate seeking the presidential nomination from a major party to embrace reparations as a major issue. It is far cheaper to stave off claims for reparations by creating real, substantive equality now.

Numerous pieces of evidence support the contention that it is penny wise and pound foolish even to attempt to carry large-scale racial inequality much further with a far poorer people-of-color majority supporting a much better-off white minority. The middle class receives three times the welfare the poor receive, and few complain. Middle-class welfare has become a right, not a privilege. The state systematically has denied support for Blacks, starting with the exclusion of agricultural and domestic service from SSA benefits during the Great Depression, to the failure of social security to compensate fully for the inequality in the labor market. Allowing social welfare benefits to be administered locally left Southern Black women particularly at the mercy of the Jim Crow South.

The Southern states and other states multiplied restrictions on unwed mothers and the poor: seasonal restrictions during cotton picking; the "man in the house" rules, which allowed unannounced visits to cut off women who were caught with adult males in the home; and anyone in an interracial relationship.

Without doubt, the Great Society years and the money provided to attack racial inequality produced real advances for Blacks and declines in racial discrimination. The advances in wages for all workers, regardless of race, during the post-WWII boom years from 1945 to the mid-1970s provided the greatest wage advances in American history (fig. 9.1).

Black poverty plummeted sharply from nearly 55 percent of Blacks being poor in 1959 to fewer than 30 percent of Blacks being poor by 1975 (fig. 9.2). Only in the 1990s did rates for Black poverty experience anything approaching such a decline. Unlike the poverty declines in the Great Society, however, the 1990s declines were short lived, and poverty began a steady rise, beginning in 2000, and is present today. The long-term impact of the COVID-19 crisis on poverty rates is yet undetermined.

Black poverty was not all that was on the decline during the Great Society. Black wages, for both men and women, were playing a tremendous game of catch-up. Wages for Black males rose from only 40 percent of the wages of a white man to almost 80 percent. Black women reached parity with white females in the late 1970s and early 1980s (figs. 9.3 and 9.4). The assertion of this chapter, supported by such evidence, is that the post-WWII boom did not so much push Black progress but rather quelled white resentment toward Blacks because of the economic prosperity whites were enjoying.

With all of this progress and prosperity, the United States has never spent more than 5 percent of its GDP on welfare for the poor (transfers as a percent of GDP [fig. 9.5]). Even with welfare for the poor and welfare for the middle class combined, the US ranks below average on social welfare spending among the industrialized Western nations. Poland spends more as a percent of GDP than does the US (table 9.4).

Income inequality, racial and otherwise, is closely related to social welfare spending (table 9.5), with the US near the bottom of income equality among the industrialized Western nations. Greece, with all its economic woes, has more income equality than the US.

The time to spend money and resources on equality is now. When peoples of color amass the political power to vote on reparations, the game may be over; few options will remain for whites.

Comparing the cost of racial equality in 1968 with what racial equality would cost today is not easy. If nothing else, the successes of the Great Society years demonstrate that racial equality was more than just a dream; it was possible to achieve, at least for a while.

Substantive racial equality would not have been easy to achieve in the 1960s, and it is not easy to achieve now, but the price is calculable. The price always has been high. In the mid-1960s, the price tag requested by MLK Jr. was about $500 billion, to be disseminated over a decade. The US spent $65.5 billion on the entirety of Great Society programs. America has never invested the level of financial resources MLK Jr. was requesting or what was needed to achieve substantive racial equality, even though the US had the money.

Today Blacks receive about $327 billion in means-tested transfers every year. To make a real difference in racial equality, over and above means-tested programs, King requested a bit more than ten times the monies spent on the Great Society. MLK Jr.'s $500 billion, adjusted for inflation using the CPI, equals over $4.9 trillion in 2024. The most current high estimates for slave reparations are rounded to $12 trillion, with another $12 trillion of reparations for contemporary wage discrimination, for approximately one year GDP for the US. Blacks likely would take far less than that. If America ever wanted to make a deal, at a bargain, on racial equality, the time to make that deal is now.

WHAT COMES NEXT

Americans, rich and poor, Black and white, from Wall Street to Main Street and the Beltway seem to be more interested in racial fantasy than racial equality. A rising tide repeatedly has been shown to have little if anything to do with racial equality (fig. 3.7), yet many cling to this belief as if it had magical powers. Mythology about Blacks, poverty, affirmative action, wealth, discrimination, and reverse discrimination are as strong today as they were thirty years ago. Retaining this mythological approach does not bode well for a nation that will be mostly minority in less than half a century.

Students and colleagues ask if more can be done other than to complain and what is the way forward to fix the problem of race and inequality in America. Most such questions seem disingenuous because, so far, America has soundly rejected the easiest, lowest-cost programs to institute racial equality. If we reject what is easy, then doing something even more difficult and costly, like poverty elimination, is unlikely. The idea that the nation can fail to engage in low-cost equality because we are more interested in high-cost programs is ludicrous. If America is unwilling to pay the political and cultural cost for low-level racial programs, the country also likely will be unable to tackle larger issues.

THE DISCOUNT RACIAL EQUALITY OPTION

Six discount racial equality programs should be purchased immediately. These programs have a proven record of accomplishment for success. The economic and intrinsic political cost of these programs is low. They do not have the ability to remake the entire racial landscape, but generally they produce more than the low cost paid in support from Blacks and whites, changed lives, and hope for the future. Even though these six programs, policies, or strategies have low economic cost, they have a lot of bang for the buck.

First: Full support should be available for affirmative action programs in higher education and voluntary employer-sponsored programs based on disparate impact and treatment, not diversity. Blacks, particularly Black men, and Latinos are underrepresented in the labor market and the higher education market. The railroad-track effect between Black and white male unemployment (fig. 3.7) indicates that the racial discrimination gap in unemployment must be closed. The most fiscally conservative political parties should be the strongest supporters of low-cost programs in employment and education, since the cost data presented in chapter 5 shows that these programs are cheap at worst, costless on average, and may make money.

Second: Funding for the EEOC, the top national antidiscrimination enforcement agency, should see increases of a minimum of fourfold and maybe tenfold (figs. 7.1 and 7.2). Even tenfold would result in a cost of only $4.5 billion dollars. For Lester Thurow, ending lax antidiscrimination enforcement was "the highest priority since [antidiscrimination enforcement] is the most effective weapon to create and enforce many of the monopoly powers that are behind the different types of discrimination."[17] The EEOC should perform a high-quality audit of every firm covered by the 1964 CRA every year or several times per year. Chapter 7 details the funding for such endeavors: the current $450 million (budget of the EEOC), plus the audits ($250 million for a once-per-year audit), or better yet, $500 million (for a twice-per-year audit), and double the EEOC budget, is only $1.4 billion.

Since all the evidence shows that job discrimination is pervasive, why not eradicate it in just a few years and do audits four times per year? Effective antidiscrimination enforcement needs to occur, at a zero-tolerance level for racial discrimination, and not simply for improved conditions. This cost is not only low economically but also has a low intrinsic political cost since racial discrimination in employment is already illegal.

The law of diminishing returns in figure 6.3 must be unacceptable in America. Blacks should receive the same returns to education as whites. Progress made against wage discrimination involving Black men and women stopped in the Reagan/Bush years (figs. 3.5 and 3.6). This progress must return. The EEOC needs enforcement tools not only to attack discrimination in hiring but also on the job. The staff, auditors, and investigation tools easily could cost the remainder of the $4.5 billion budget proposed for the

17. Thurow, *Poverty and Discrimination*, 138.

EEOC. Employers must know that around every corner an EEOC investigator is waiting, and the penalties for wage or hiring discrimination are not worth the cost. As in the US military, the numbers of Black workers or students below population parity in any major sector should be a serious problem for the nation.

Third: K–12 equality must be a national priority because, like the church, K–12 education is a leading social indicator. If you want to know what is going to happen to the nation tomorrow, look at K–12 education today. The cost for K–12 equality is over $650 billion. But K–12 integration is less than $1 billion, a super-bargain with big payoffs. Chapter 8 illustrated that the vast majority of whites do not want segregated schools, even though a significant minority of whites still do. A big gap exists between what whites say they want, however, and what they are willing to do for the education of Black school children. The NES demonstrates that most whites never have agreed that it was the job of the federal government to ensure that Black and white children go to school together. If the federal government cannot ensure an equal education, not based on race, then who else could and would step up to this task is unclear.

In the chapter 8 section "The Death of the School Bus," two-thirds of whites oppose school bussing for integration. Orfield has shown repeatedly, however, that a super-majority of Black and Latino school children attend poor-quality, segregated schools. This situation cannot continue. School bussing costs less than $1 billion, even today. Gasoline for moving children is the only economic cost of integration. The cost of *Brown* is not economic; the perceived political cost is high because the political fear of white parents dominates national and local politics. This book does not concern the political limits given the white electorate, however. School bussing for integration must continue if America is to have any chance whatsoever of avoiding a racial crisis of "the coming race war" in fifty years.[18]

Fourth: Poverty equalization. If we cannot or are unwilling to pay the $791 billion to bring all Americans within 60 percent of the median-family income, then low-cost poverty equalization, where Blacks and whites suffer the same levels of poverty, is fairly cheap economically: $90 billion to bring Black poverty down to the level of white poverty (ch. 6). Table 9.1 illustrated, however, that we already spend almost $1.1 trillion on means-tested transfer programs. The problems are not economic; the perception that poverty is Black makes the perceived political cost of even low-level poverty equalization high.

---

18. Delgado, *Coming Race War*; Rowan, *Coming Race War in America*.

Fifth: The bully pulpit. At one time President Obama, the first Black president, winner of a Nobel Peace Prize, had the world at his feet. In terms of racial inequality in wages (figs. 3.5 and 3.6), however, Obama did not use that time well. Perhaps Presidents Trump and Biden never had the world at their feet, but the point is that as the leader of the most powerful and richest nation in the world, any American president must use the power of his office to teach the public that racial polarization and inequality are greater threats to the United States and the world than global warming, terrorism, and pandemics combined. President Biden stressed the need to act strongly and swiftly on his three top priorities, one of which was racial equality.

If the Democratic Party does not teach the public that racial equality is within our reach, and that the cost is reasonable, when we consider alternatives, the GOP should attempt an end run around the Democratic Party and exchange Black voters for the 2 percent of their party who are extremely conservative and the 10 percent who are conservative. This scenario is not impossible. Bush came close in 2004 (table 7.3) with his campaign on family values, which captured nearly 12 percent of Black voters, the highest Black support for the GOP since Nixon's Black capitalism. Blacks made up 2 percent of the GOP coalition in 2004 (table 7.1). And while President Trump managed less than half as many Black voters in 2016 in table 7.1, in 2020, Trump actually surpassed Bush in Black support. Nevertheless, it is difficult to imagine, at this time, a GOP candidate who could electrify the Black electorate. A Colin Powell type comes to mind but the late Colin Powell admitted that while "the elements were present for a credible run for the Republican nomination and the presidency," he did not have "a complete political philosophy to take to the American people. . . . I could speak with passion on my belief in America and its promise. I had strong views on foreign policy. I could be persuasive, I thought, on the issue of the need to return to traditional values. I could make a contribution to restoring racial harmony. But I did not have strong, passionate views on the economy, education, health reform, or the dozens of other domestic issues that I had never dealt with during my years as a soldier. . . . I would be campaigning on the basis of popularity rather than a full political agenda."[19] Without a racial policy focus, Powell overestimated his abilities at restoring racial harmony. But given other presidencies before and after, perhaps Powell set the standard for the presidency much too high.

Sea changes in politics are not easy, but nothing inherent in the histories of either the GOP or Democratic Party makes this change impossible. At different times both parties have been the champions of Blacks. The

---

19. C. Powell, *My American Journey*, 599–600.

Republican Party must recognize and teach that racial equality is what is best for America. Statesmanship and stature are required, not simply trying to get Blacks to vote for the GOP. Trump's current control of the Republican Party seems to limit their ability to address racial issues seriously. However, one remembers LBJ, a Southern Democrat, who had opposed all civil rights legislation but came forward and confronted his former mentors, the entire Southern delegation, with his presidency on the line, to embrace civil rights and fundamentally alter race and voter alignment in the United States.[20] If neither party provides this leadership, the increasing Latino population may force the major parties to compete for non-white votes.

Sixth: Independent advantage. The late Ron Walters stressed the need for "independent leverage."[21] Blacks must make the GOP and the Democratic Party compete for their votes. The current state of affairs with Blacks as slaves to the Democratic Party helps almost no one. Many people say that Blacks have nowhere to go, but conservatives in the GOP also have nowhere to go. The Black electorate can regain its status as kingmaker, if they somehow could start to swing or move between the parties. The current GOP ideology makes this unattractive, but in the political arena, swinging or moving from party to party en masse is what tends to break the logjam of polarization. Strangely, this independent leverage scenario is exactly what took place in the 2024 presidential election in tables 7.1 and 7.3. Blacks provided the margin of victory for Trump, contributing 3 of the votes for his coalition, while he won by only 1.8 percent. The test is whether Blacks can now punish Trump for his relentless attacks on the traditional Black civil rights agenda and shift just as quickly back to the Democratic Party. If these swings by the Black electorate take place, Blacks will have very successfully demonstrated Walter's concept of independent leverage and the power of the Black vote. Also tested will be whether the Democratic Party has learned that the Black agenda is not only about party platforms and symbols but also about real policy, political, economic, and legislative action. At the same time, both parties must teach the white electorate that racial equality, and surrendering the illicit gains of whiteness, is in their strategic interest. Failure to teach and learn this lesson threatens the nation and democracy.

Civil rights groups, churches, and others must hold leaders responsible and not be mere cheerleaders for the Democratic Party. MLK Jr. never endorsed a political candidate. Policy and accountability are more important than party label. Blacks need political clubs and groups that address and listen to real issues and force leaders to be accountable.

20. Leuchtenburg, "Old Cowhand from Dixie."
21. Walters, *Black Presidential Politics in America.*

DEFAULTING TO FULL PRICE

Little evidence exists that America is willing to pay the perceived political and cultural price it takes to institute the low economic cost solutions. The preceding chapters are replete with examples of America's rejection of low-cost solutions, but some of the most recent are: 1) opposition by a majority of State Boards of Education, GOP-led legislatures, and governors, to the Department of Education's "Proposed Priorities" to institute racially and culturally diverse stories about the impact of racism and oppression in America's founding, into K–12 classrooms (the 1619 Project);[22] 2) the Supreme Court's 2021 decision in *Brnovich v. Democratic National Committee* gutting the power of the 1965 VRA to protect the votes of peoples of color; and 3) the Supreme Court's 2023 decision in *Students for Fair Admissions v. Harvard* striking down diversity-based affirmation action in high education. This situation is unfortunate because the high-cost equality programs will have to be purchased at full price, with few discounts, in a crisis.

MLK Jr. asked for $50 billion per year in 1965 for ten years ($500 billion total) to make a substantial impact of the lives of Negro Americans. When King made that request, it equaled about 1 percent of GDP. The value of King's request as a percentage of GDP from 2014 to 2023 ($214 trillion), ten years, is $2.1 trillion, within the range of low-level reparations. It would have been better to have given King what he was requesting in 1968. By many measures racial equality could have been achieved in the 1970s. Wage discrimination was dropping very quickly in the Great Society years (figs. 9.3 and 9.4). The greatest declines in poverty (fig. 9.2) also took place in the Great Society years. With sufficient funds committed, substantive racial equality surely could have been possible before the 1980s.

Today Blacks receive about $327 billion in means-tested transfers every year. Welfare (AFDC/TANF) for Blacks, about $327 billion per year (tables 9.1 and 9.2), is far less than the combined $180 billion in wage discrimination, $134 billion for the disproportionately poor or nearly poor, and $232 billion in wealth discrimination Blacks lose every single year. Welfare is not a substitute for equality.

Only one reason comes to mind as to why the two major political parties do not opt for the low-cost programs: paying low cost is an unattractive option if people believe they can pay no cost. The no-cost option is an illusion, however. The irrational belief that depriving 30 percent of the population, who will soon be the majority, of acceptable and fair schooling, jobs,

---

22. Ryder, "Proposed Priorities."

healthcare, welfare, training, political control, housing, and wealth, and end up with democracy is beyond penny wise and pound foolish: it is madness.

If America ever wanted to avoid the high-cost equality programs, the time to do it is now. Dr. King spoke of "the fierce urgency of now,"[23] which given the consistent refusal of the white electorate to support low-cost affirmative action, school integration, and political equality, the crises of the next fifty to one hundred years seem unavoidable.

The problem is the perceived political costs and cultural costs to whites. Most of the costs for cultural and perceived political changes were high (table 1). White cultural belief systems, the false ideas that a rising tide can create racial equality at no cost, that market competition is more effective in promoting equality than antidiscrimination laws, that Blacks should work their way up, as did the mythical European groups, are so pervasive in white culture that reeducation seems almost impossible, short of a crisis. The rising visibility of white nationalist groups connected with Trumpism is particularly disturbing as is the refusal of the majority of Republicans to accept Trump's lost 2020 election.

In absolute terms, great improvements in the quality of life for both whites and Blacks have taken place since the antebellum and Jim Crow eras. In other areas the relative position of Blacks has changed dramatically in comparison to whites. High school graduation, college attendance, the end of mob violence, de jure segregation and voting rights are but a few examples. The most important measurement of racial equality, however, is strategic equality (figs. 1 and 3.3). In the next fifty years, as America becomes mostly people of color and majority minority, the racial inequality caused by white discrimination in wages, wealth, educational quality, housing, healthcare, elections, occupations, employment, postsecondary and graduate education must dissolve, not merely improve.

Strategically speaking, Black alienation and white racism are increasing. The differing views of Blacks and whites on police abuse, even after the death of George Floyd in May 2020, are evidence of this divide. In a few decades, the low-cost programs will no longer be viable options. We will have a mostly minority electorate supporting a mostly white and aging population who control most of the wealth and capital. This situation should be avoided, even if the cost is high.

Only one identified racial group gave the majority of their support to Trump's second term in table 7.3, whites. Every other racial group opposed him, Blacks, Latinos, and Asians. This is consistent with white acceptance of racial deficiency as the cause for racial inequality, in spite of

23. King, "I Have a Dream," 217–18.

the overwhelming social science evidence against this idea. Little wonder that Trump seeks to reward his followers with rabid opposition to DEI. Nevertheless, such opposition to DEI is doomed to failure because of figure 7.3, diminishing white political power due to demographic decline. The only way to reverse such a decline is through extralegal or unconstitutional means, which signal a serious threat to American democracy. While Trump has shown little hesitancy at using either, the support for Trump by most whites is the more serious issue.

THE NEED FOR ATONEMENT

Chapter 3 mentioned the introduction to the 1988 edition of the Kerner Report, in which Tom Wicker said, "If the cause of the trouble was the society that white racism had created, obviously racism would also be the major obstacle to the great commitment of money and effort that same society was asked to make in order to attack the trouble—a vicious circle indeed."[24] Most white Americans seem to be thoroughly convinced that today's minorities can be subjected to the tyranny of the majority; that white majorities can pass laws and create policies to insure that historic and contemporary non-meritorious white privileges are protected; and that when Black, Latino, Asian and other peoples of color become the majority, these ill-gotten white privileges will be respected, enshrined, and treated as vested rights. Such a scenario seems difficult to imagine. A more likely outcome is that whatsoever the white electorate has sown, that shall it also reap.

If knowing the economic, political, cultural, and social cost for racial equality does not compel us to action, if a mob attacking the US Capitol with the symbols of white supremacy on full display does not raise a national alarm, imagining what would compel us to action is difficult. America would face a spiritual problem that no amount of knowledge could fix. Only an atonement for the past, present, and future of America could save us from ourselves. Over the past few decades, legal scholars from different areas of the law have begun to envisage a process for social reconciliation based on the Christian atonement.[25] As concerns social disruption, these legal scholars have shown little interest in contract relations, tortious conduct, constitutional law, retribution, or deterrence for criminal behavior, or even political solutions. Rather, they use words like wrongdoing, guilt, repentance, apology, restitution, forgiveness, penance, and reconciliation,

---

24. Wicker, "Introduction to the 1988 Edition," xii.

25. Blevins, "Restorative Justice"; Brooks, *Atonement and Forgiveness*; Coleman, "Legal and Natural Atonement Theory"; Garvey, "Punishment as Atonement."

where social groups who have been estranged from each other by genocide, crimes against humanity, enslavement, or war can begin to heal. These legal scholars also seem to sense that without this atoning the future is bleak, no matter how much we praise ourselves or pass procedurally equal laws. A future scientific analysis of what this atonement might look like will provide a guidepost.

Bibliography

1619 Project, The. https://www.nytimes.com/interactive/2019/08/14/magazine/1619-america-slavery.html.

2012 Time Series Study. https://electionstudies.org/data-center/2012-time-series-study/.

ABC News. "Despite Turmoil, Wall Street Bonuses Survive." ABC News, Oct. 25, 2008. https://abcnews.go.com/Business/IndustryInfo/story?id=6105795&page=1.

Abernathy, David B. *The Dynamics of Global Dominance: European Overseas Empires 1415–1980*. New Haven, CT: Yale University Press, 2000.

Adarand Constructors, Inc. v. Peña, 515 U.S. 200 (1995).

Ahuja, Anjana. "Study the Face Below: Now, Why Shouldn't Research Scientists Do That?" *Times*, Oct. 31, 2005. https://www.thetimes.com/article/study-the-face-below-now-why-shouldnt-research-scientists-do-that-6ffl89tnckk.

Alamillo, Rudy. "Hispanics para Trump? Denial of Racism and Hispanic Support for Trump." *Du Bois Review* 16 (2019) 457–87.

Alland, Alexander, Jr. *Race in Mind: Race, IQ, and Other Racisms*. New York: Palgrave Macmillan, 2002.

America, Richard F., ed. *The Wealth of Races: The Present Value of Benefits from Past Injustices*. Contributions in Afro-American and African Studies: Contemporary Black Poets. Westport, CT: Greenwood, 1990.

American Experience. "LBJ and the Great Society." PBS LearningMedia, 2010. Adapted from *American Experience*, "LBJ." https://florida.pbslearningmedia.org/resource/pres10.socst.ush.now.greatsociety/lbj-and-the-great-society/.

America Votes 2006. https://www.cnn.com/ELECTION/2006/pages/results/states/MI/I/01/epolls.0.html.

Anderson, Carol. *White Rage: The Unspoken Truth of Our Racial Divide*. New York: Bloomsbury, 2016.

Andre, Michael, et al. "National Exit Polls: How Different Groups Voted." *New York Times*, Nov. 3, 2020. https://www.nytimes.com/interactive/2020/11/03/us/elections/exit-polls-president.html?action=click&pgtype=Article&state=default&module=styln-elections-2020&region=TOP_BANNER&context=election_recirc.

ANES 2008 Time Series Study (ICPSR 25383). V3. https://doi.org/10.3886/ICPSR25383.v3.

ANES Time Series Cumulative Data File (1948–2012) (ICPSR 8475). V15. https://doi.org/10.3886/ICPSR08475.v15.

BIBLIOGRAPHY

Ards, Shelia D., and Samuel L. Myers Jr. "The Color of Money." *American Behavioral Scientist* 45 (2001) 223–39.

Arizona Republican Party v. Democratic Nat'l Comm., 141 S. Ct. 221, 207 L. Ed. 2d 1165 (2020).

Armor, David J. *Forced Justice: School Desegregation and the Law.* New York: Oxford University Press, 1995.

Armstrong, Pat, and Hugh Armstrong. *Universal Health Care: What the United States Can Learn from the Canadian Experience.* New York: New, 1998.

Arrow, Kenneth J. "What Has Economics to Say About Racial Discrimination." *Journal of Economic Perspectives* 12 (1998) 91–100.

Ashenfelter, Orley, and James Heckman. "Measuring the Effects of an Antidiscrimination Program." In *Evaluating the Labor-Market Effects of Social Programs*, edited by Orley Ashenfelter and James Blum, 46–84. Industrial Relations Section. Princeton, NJ: Princeton University Press, 1976.

Atkinson, Anthony B. *Inequality: What Can Be Done?* Cambridge, MA: Harvard University Press, 2015.

Avivi, Hadar, et al. "Adaptive Correspondence Experiments." *American Economic Association Papers and Proceedings* 111 (2021) 43–48.

Ayres, Ian. "Fair Driving: Gender and Race Discrimination in Retail Car Negotiations." *Harvard Law Review* 104 (1991) 817–72.

Ayres, Ian, and Fredrick E. Vars. "When Does Private Discrimination Justify Public Affirmative Action?" *Columbia Law Review* 98 (1998) 1577–641.

Ayres, Ian, and Peter Cramton. "Deficit Reduction Through Diversity: How Affirmative Action at the F.C.C. Increased Auction Competition." *Stanford Law Review* 48 (1996) 761–815.

Badenhausen, Kurt. "The Celebrity 100." *Forbes* (July 8, 2002) 98–104.

Badie, Rick. "Cosby's Rant Got People Talking." *Atlanta Journal-Constitution*, May 25, 2004.

Bakke v. Regents of University of California, 18 Cal.3d 34 (1976).

Balkovic, Brain. "High-Income Tax Returns for 2000." Internal Revenue Service, 2003. https://www.irs.gov/pub/irs-soi/00hiinco.pdf.

Banfield, Edward C. *The Unheavenly City Revisited.* Boston: Little, Brown, 1974.

Barinaga, Marcia. "African Eve Backers Beat a Retreat." *Science* (1992) 686–87.

Barker, Lucius J., and Mack H. Jones. *African Americans and the American Political System.* 3rd. ed. Englewood Cliffs, NJ: Prentice Hall, 1994.

Barnett, Jessica C., and Edward R. Berchick. "Current Population Reports, P60-260, Health Insurance Coverage in the United States: 2016." Washington, DC: US Government, 2017.

Barrera, Mario. *Race and Class in the Southwest: A Theory of Racial Inequality.* Notre Dame, IN: University of Notre Dame Press, 1979.

Beard, Charles A. *An Economic Interpretation of the Constitution of the United States.* New York: Free, 1986.

Becker, Gary S. *The Economics of Discrimination.* 2nd ed. Chicago: University of Chicago Press, 1971.

Bell, Derrick A., Jr. *Race, Racism, and American Law.* 6th ed. New York: Aspen, 2008.

Belz, Herman. *Equality Transformed: A Quarter-Century of Affirmative Action.* Brunswick, NJ: Transaction, 1991.

Bendick, Marc, Jr., and Mary Lou Egan. "Changing Workplace Cultures to Reduce Employment Discrimination." Paper presented at the Conference on Low-Wage Workers in the New Economy, Washington, DC, May 25, 2000. http://www.bendickegan.com/pdf/Changing_Workplace_Cultures.pdf.

Bennett, Lerone, Jr. *Forced into Glory: Abraham Lincoln's White Dream.* Chicago: Johnson, 2000.

Bergmann, Barbara R. *In Defense of Affirmative Action.* New York: Basic, 1996.

Berlin, Ira. "The Structure of the Free Negro Caste in the Antebellum United States." In *Free Blacks in a Slave Society*, edited by Paul Finkelman, 1–22. Articles on American Slavery 17. New York: Garland, 1989.

Bertrand, Marianne, and Sendhil Mullainathan. "Are Emily and Brendan More Employable Than Lakisha and Jamal? A Field Experiment on Labor Market Discrimination." *American Economic Review* 94 (2004) 991–1014.

Besco, Randy. "Rainbow Coalitions or Inter-Minority Conflict? Racial Affinity and Diverse Minority Voters." *Canadian Journal of Political Science* 48 (2015) 305–28.

Biden, Joseph R. "Executive Order on the Establishment of the Presidential Commission on the Supreme Court of the United States." White House, Apr. 9, 2021. https://bidenwhitehouse.archives.gov/briefing-room/presidential-actions/2021/04/09/executive-order-on-the-establishment-of-the-presidential-commission-on-the-supreme-court-of-the-united-states/.

Black, Edwin. *War Against the Weak: Eugenics and America's Campaign to Create a Master Race.* New York: Four Walls Eight Windows, 2003.

Black, Sandra E., and Lisa M. Lynch. "How to Compete: The Impact of Workplace Practices and Information Technology on Productivity." *Review of Economics and Statistics* 83 (2001) 434–45.

Black Enterprise. "B.E. 100s Overview: Facing the Moment of Truth." *Black Enterprise* 20 (1990) 97–132.

Blevins, Michael F. "Restorative Justice, Slavery, and the American Soul: A Policy-Oriented, Intercultural Human Rights Approach to the Question of Reparations." *Thurgood Marshall Law Review* 31 (2006) 253–322.

Bloch, Farrell. *Antidiscrimination Law and Minority Employment: Recruitment Practices and Regulatory Constraints.* Chicago: University of Chicago Press, 1994.

BLS Data Finder 1.1. https://data.bls.gov/dataQuery/search.

Blumrosen, Alfred W., and Ruth G. Blumrosen. *Slave Nation: How Slavery United the Colonies and Sparked the American Revolution.* Naperville, IL: Sourcebooks, 2005.

Bobo, Lawrence D., and Camille Z. Charles. "Race in the American Mind: From the Moynihan Report to the Obama Candidacy." *Annals of the American Academy of Political and Social Science* 621 (2009) 243–59.

Bonilla-Silva, Eduardo, and Tyrone A. Forman. "'I Am Not a Racist, But . . .': Mapping White College Students' Racial Ideology in the USA." *Discourse and Society* 11 (2000) 50–85.

Booker, Cory. "Booker, Pressley Reintroduce 'Baby Bonds' Legislation to Combat Wealth Inequality." Cory Booker, July 26, 2019. https://www.booker.senate.gov/news/press/booker-pressley-reintroduce-and-ldquobaby-bonds-and-rdquo-legislation-to-combat-wealth-inequality.

Boyle, Ryan. "A Red Moon over the Mall: The Sputnik Panic and Domestic America." *Journal of American Culture* 31 (2008) 373–82.

Brabri, Mélissa. "W. E. B. Du Bois's Writings for the Crisis, 1910–1934, from Integration to Voluntary Segregation?" *Literature* (2013) 1–110.

Branch, Taylor. *At Canaan's Edge: America in the King Years, 1965–68*. New York: Simon and Schuster, 2006.

———. *Parting the Waters: America in the King Years, 1954–63*. New York: Simon and Schuster, 1988.

———. *Pillar of Fire: America in the King Years, 1963–65*. New York: Simon and Schuster, 1998.

Braswell, Michael K., et al. "Affirmative Action: An Assessment of Its Continuing Role in Employment Discrimination Policy." *Albany Law Review* 57 (1993) 365–440.

Brennan Center for Justice. "Voting Laws Roundup: February 2021." Brennan Center for Justice, Feb. 8, 2021. https://www.brennancenter.org/our-work/research-reports/voting-laws-roundup-february-2021.

Bridges, William P., and Wayne J. Villemez. "Overeducated Minority Workers: Does E.E.O.C. Coverage Make a Difference?" In *Affirmative Action: Theory, Analysis, and Prospects*, edited by Michael W. Combs and John Gruhl, 72–90. Jefferson, NC: McFarland & Co., 1986.

Brnovich v. Democratic National Committee, 141 S. Ct. 222, 207 L. Ed. 2d 1165 (2020).

Brooks, Roy L. *Atonement and Forgiveness: A New Model for Black Reparations*. Berkeley: University of California Press, 2004.

Brown v. Board of Education of Topeka, 347 U.S. 483 (1954).

Brown, Walter T. *In the Beginning: Compelling Evidence for Creation and the Flood*. 8th ed. Phoenix: Center for Scientific Creation, 2008.

Bruchey, Stuart. *Cotton and the Growth of the American Economy: 1790–1860*. New York: Harcourt, Brace, 1967.

Buettner, Dan. "The Secrets of Long Life." *National Geographic* 208 (2005) 2–27.

Burman, George. "The Economics of Discrimination: The Impact of Public Policy." PhD diss., University of Chicago, 1973.

Bushnell, Horace. *The Census and Slavery*. Hartford, CT: Hunt, 1860.

———. *God in Christ: Three Discourses Delivered at New Haven, Cambridge, and Andover, with a Preliminary Dissertation on Language*. Hartford, CT: Brown and Parsons, 1849.

Byrd, Diane, et al. "A Modern Doll Study: Self Concept." *Race, Gender and Class* 24 (2017) 186–202.

California Depart of Education. *Ethnic Studies Model Curriculum*. Sacramento: California Department of Education, 2022. https://www.cde.ca.gov/ci/cr/cf/esmc.asp.

Campbell, James T. Review of *The Funding of Scientific Racism*, by William H. Tucker. *Journal of Blacks in Higher Education* 38 (2003) 126–30. https://doi.org/10.2307/3134230.

Canales, Josie, et al. *No State Left Behind: The Challenges and Opportunities of ESEA 2001*. ERIC, Mar. 2002. ED468096. https://eric.ed.gov/?id=ED468096.

Carlo, John, and Gil M. Sadian. "The Arab Spring—One Year Later." *Censei Report* 2 (Feb. 13–19, 2012) 24–33.

Carr, James H., and Nandinee K. Kutty, eds. *Segregation: The Rising Costs for America*. New York: Routledge, 2008.

Carroll, Joseph Cephas. *Slave Insurrections in the United States, 1800–1865*. Mineola, NY: Dover, 2004.

BIBLIOGRAPHY

Carson, Ben. *One Nation: What We Can All Do to Save America's Future*. New York: Random House, 2014.
CDC. "Estimated Flu Disease Burden 2019–2020 Flu Seasons." CDC, Nov. 15, 2024. https://archive.cdc.gov/#/details?url=https://www.cdc.gov/flu-burden/php/datavis/2019-2020.html.
Centers for Medicare & Medicaid Services. "NHE Fact Sheet." CMS, last updated June 24, 2025. https://www.cms.gov/data-research/statistics-trends-and-reports/national-health-expenditure-data/nhe-fact-sheet.
Chronicle of Higher Education. "The Almanac 2011." *Chronicle of Higher Education*, Aug. 26, 2011. https://www.chronicle.com/article/the-almanac-2011/.
———. "Diversity in Academe: Social Class on American Campus." Special issue, *Chronicle of Higher Education* 3 (2010).
Chubb, John E., and Terry M. Moe. *Politics, Markets, and America's Schools*. Washington, DC: Brookings Institution, 1990.
City of Richmond v. J. A. Croson Co., 488 U.S. 469 (1989).
Civil Rights Act, 18 Stat. 335 (1875).
Civil Rights Act of 1957, Pub. L. No. 85-315 (1957).
Civil Rights Act of 1960, 52 U.S.C. § 10101 (1960).
Civil Rights Act of 1964, 42 U.S.C. § 2000 (1964).
Civil Rights Cases, 109 U.S. 3 (1883).
Clemons, Michael L. "Beyond the Barriers: Toward a Durable African American-Latino Political Coalition." *Journal of Latino/Latin American Studies* 5 (2013) 40–56.
Clowse, Barbara Barksdale. *Brainpower for the Cold War: The Sputnik Crisis and National Defense Education Act of 1958*. Westport, CT: Greenwood, 1981.
CNN. "Exit Polls." CNN, last updated Nov. 23, 2016. https://www.cnn.com/election/2016/results/exit-polls.
———. "Nobel Winner in 'Racist' Claim Row." Lipstick Alley, Oct. 18, 2017. https://www.lipstickalley.com/threads/nobel-prize-winner-blacks-less-intelligent.104135/.
Coalition to Defend Affirmative Action, Integration and Immigrant Rights and Fight for Equality by Any Means Necessary (BAMN), et al., v. Regents of the University of Michigan, 701 F.3d 466 (2012).
Coates, Ta-Nehisi. "The Case for Reparations." *Atlantic* (2014) 54–71.
Cohen, Danielle. *NYC School Segregation Report Card: Still Last, Action Needed Now!* Civil Rights Project, UCLA, June 2021. https://escholarship.org/uc/item/5fx616qn.
Coleman, Major G. "The Affirmative Dilemma: The Politics and Reality of Individualistic Remedies for Collective Discrimination." PhD diss., University of Chicago, 1993.
———. "African American Popular Wisdom Versus the Qualification Question: Is Affirmative Action Merit-Based?" *Western Journal of Black Studies* 27 (2003) 35–44.
———. "At a Loss for Words: Measuring Racial Inequality in America." *Review of Black Political Economy* 43 (2016) 177–92.
———. "Contesting the Magic of the Marketplace: Black Employment and Business Concentration in the Urban Context." *Urban Studies* 39 (2002) 1793–818.
———. "Job Skill and Black Male Wage Discrimination." *Social Science Quarterly* 84 (2003) 892–906.
———. "Legal and Natural Atonement Theory." SJD diss., Emory University, 2024.

———. "Merit, Cost, and the Affirmative Action Policy Debate." *Review of Black Political Economy* 27 (1999) 99–127.

———. "Racial Discrimination in the Workplace: Does Market Structure Make a Difference?" *Industrial Relations* 43 (2004) 660–89.

———. "Racism in Academia: The White Superiority Supposition in the 'Unbiased' Search for Knowledge." *European Journal of Political Economy* 21 (2005) 762–74.

———. "Reading and Leading: Interviews with *RBPE* Editors About the Past and the Future of the *Review*." *Review of Black Political Economy* 47 (2020) 125–33. https://doi.org/10.1177/0034644620926515.

———. "Strategic Equality and the Failure of Affirmative Action Law." *International Journal of Discrimination and the Law* 12 (2012) 27–51. https://doi.org/10.1177/1358229112453890.

Coleman, Major G., et al. "Are Claims of Discrimination Valid? The Moral Hazard Effect." Working paper, Pennsylvania State University, 2002.

Committee on Ways and Means, U.S. House of Representatives. *1996 Green Book*. ASPE, Nov. 4, 1996. https://aspe.hhs.gov/1996-green-book.

———. *2008 Green Book*. Washington, DC: U.S. Government, 2008.

Congress. "H.R. 40—Commission to Study and Develop Reparation Proposals for African-Americans Act." Congress, Jan. 3, 2019; last updated June 19, 2019. Sponsored by Rep. Sheila Jackson Lee, D-TX. https://www.congress.gov/bill/116th-congress/house-bill/40.

Conrad, Cecilia A. "The Economic Cost of Affirmative Action." In *Economic Perspectives on Affirmative Action*, edited by Margaret C. Simms, 33–53. Washington, DC: Joint Center for Political and Economic Studies, 1995.

Contractors Association of Eastern Pennsylvania v. Secretary of Labor, 404 U.S. 854 (1971).

Coons, John E., et al. *Private Wealth and Public Education*. Cambridge, MA: Belknap, 1970.

Coronavirus Aid, Relief, and Economic Security Act, Pub. L. No. 116-36, 134 Stat 281 (2020).

Coronavirus Resource Center. "New COVID-19 Cases Worldwide." Coronavirus Resource Center, last updated Mar. 16, 2023. https://coronavirus.jhu.edu/data/new-cases.

Cose, Ellis. *The Rage of a Privileged Class: Why Are Middle-Class Blacks Angry? Why Should America Care?* New York: Harper Perennial, 1994.

Council of Economic Advisers. *The Underestimated Cost of the Opioid Crisis*. Trump White House, Nov. 2017. https://trumpwhitehouse.archives.gov/sites/whitehouse.gov/files/images/The%20Underestimated%20Cost%20of%20the%20Opioid%20Crisis.pdf.

Craemer, Thomas. "Estimating Slavery Reparations: Present Value Comparisons of Historical Multigenerational Reparations Policies." *Social Science Quarterly* 96 (2015) 639–55.

Crime in the United States 2005. https://ucr.fbi.gov/crime-in-the-u.s/2005.

Crowder, Kyle D., and Stewart E. Tolnay. "A New Marriage Squeeze for Black Women: The Role of Racial Intermarriage by Black Men." *Journal of Marriage and the Family* 62 (2000) 792–807.

Current Population Survey Datasets. Last updated Oct. 18, 2024. https://www.census.gov/programs-surveys/cps/data/datasets.html.

Current World Population. https://www.worldometers.info/world-population/.
Daggett, Stephen. "Costs of Major U.S. Wars." Congressional Research Service, 2008. https://congressionalresearch.com/RS22926/document.php?study=Costs+of+Major+U.S.+Wars.
Darity, William A., Jr., and A. Kirsten Mullen. *From Here to Equality: Reparations for Black Americans in the Twenty-First Century.* Chapel Hill: University of North Carolina Press, 2020.
Darity, William A., Jr., and Dania Frank. "The Economics of Reparations." *American Economic Review* 93 (2003) 326–29.
Darity, William A., Jr., and Samuel L. Myers Jr. *Persistent Disparity: Race and Economic Inequality in the United States Since 1945.* Cheltenham: Edward Elgar, 1998.
Davies, Gareth. *From Opportunity to Entitlement: The Transformation and Decline of Great Society Liberalism.* Lawrence: University Press of Kansas, 1996.
Davis, James A., et al. "General Social Surveys, 1972–2004 [Cumulative File]." ICPSR, Sept. 2, 2005. https://doi.org/10.3886/ICPSR04295.v1.
———. "General Social Surveys, 1972–2008 [Cumulative File]." ICPSR, Oct. 16, 2009. https://doi.org/10.3886/ICPSR25962.v2.
Davis, Jonathan T., ed. *Forbes Richest People: The Forbes Annual Profile of the World's Wealthiest Men and Women.* New York: Wiley and Sons, 1997.
DEA Strategic Intelligence Section. *2018 National Drug Threat Assessment.* United States Drug Enforcement Administration, Oct. 2018. DEA-DCT-DIR-032-18. https://www.dea.gov/sites/default/files/2018-11/DIR-032-18%202018%20NDTA%20final%20low%20resolution.pdf.
Delgado, Richard. *The Coming Race War: And Other Apocalyptic Tales of America After Affirmative Action and Welfare.* New York: New York University Press, 1996.
Delmont, Matthew F. *Why Busing Failed: Race, Media, and the National Resistance to School Desegregation.* Oakland: University of California Press, 2016.
Demarest, Jack, and Rita Allen. "Body Image: Gender, Ethnic and Age Differences." *Journal of Social Psychology* 33 (2000) 465–72.
Democratic National Committee. "2000 Democratic Party Platform." American Presidency Project, Aug. 14, 2000. https://www.presidency.ucsb.edu/documents/2000-democratic-party-platform.
———. "2008 Democratic Party Platform." American Presidency Project, Aug. 25, 2008. https://www.presidency.ucsb.edu/documents/2008-democratic-party-platform.
———. "2012 Democratic Party Platform." American Presidency Project, Sept. 3, 2012. https://www.presidency.ucsb.edu/documents/2012-democratic-party-platform.
———. "2016 Democratic Party Platform." American Presidency Project, July 21, 2016. https://www.presidency.ucsb.edu/documents/2016-democratic-party-platform.
———. "2020 Democratic Party Platform." American Presidency Project, Aug. 17, 2020. https://www.presidency.ucsb.edu/documents/2020-democratic-party-platform.
———. '*24 Democratic Party Platform.* Democrats, n.d. https://democrats.org/wp-content/uploads/2024/08/FINAL-MASTER-PLATFORM.pdf.
Democratic Nat'l Comm. v. Hobbs, 948 F.3d 989 (9th Cir. 2020).
Democratic Nat'l Comm. v. Reagan, 904 F.3d 686 (9th Cir. 2018).

Democritus Junior [Robert Burton]. *The Anatomy of Melancholy*. Project Gutenberg, 2004. Edited by KTH. Ebook 1080. https://www.gutenberg.org/files/10800/10800-h/10800-h.htm.

DeNavas-Walt, Carmen, et al. *Income, Poverty and Health Insurance Coverage in the United States: 2008*. United States Census Bureau, Sept. 2009. Report P60-236 (RV). https://www.census.gov/library/publications/2009/demo/p60-236.html.

———. *Income, Poverty and Health Insurance Coverage in the United States: 2012*. United States Census Bureau, Sept. 2013. Report P60-245. https://www.census.gov/library/publications/2013/demo/p60-245.html.

Department of Commerce, Bureau of the Census. *Occupations*. Edited by William C. Hunt. Vol. 4 of *Population: 1920; Fourteenth Census of the United States Taken in the Year 1920*. Washington, DC: U.S. Government, 1923. https://www.census.gov/library/publications/1923/dec/vol-04-occupations.html.

Department of Education. "Required Instruction Planning and Reporting." *Florida Administrative Code & Florida Administrative Register*, last updated July 2, 2024. https://www.flrules.org/gateway/ruleno.asp?id=6A-1.094124.

Digest of Education Statistics. https://nces.ed.gov/programs/digest/.

Dingle, Derek T. "B.E. 100s, 31st Annual Report on Black Business: Reinvention Through Innovation." *Black Enterprise* 33 (2003) 94–103.

Dolan, Kerry A., and Luisa Kroll. "The Richest People in the World." *Forbes* (July 9, 2001) 110–24.

D'Souza, Dinesh. *The End of Racism: Principles for a Multiracial Society*. New York: Free, 1995.

Durose, Matthew R., et al. *Contacts Between Police and the Public, 2005*. Bureau of Justice Statistics, Special Report, Apr. 2007. NCJ 215243. https://bjs.ojp.gov/content/pub/pdf/cpp05.pdf.

Dickens, Floyd, Jr., and Jacqueline B. Dickens. *The Black Manager: Making It in the Corporate World*. New York: American Management Association, 1982.

Dickey, Jack. "The Revolution on America's Campuses." *Time*, May 31, 2016. https://time.com/4347099/college-campus-protests/.

Dickson, Paul. *Sputnik: The Shock of the Century*. New York: Berkley, 2003.

Donaldson, Gary A. *The First Modern Campaign: Kennedy, Nixon, and the Election of 1960*. Lanham, MD: Rowman & Littlefield, 2007.

Dred Scott v. Sandford, 60 U.S. 393 (1857).

Drinnon, Richard. *Facing West: The Metaphysics of Indian-Hating and Empire-Building*. New York: Meridian, 1980.

Du Bois, W. E. B. "Does the Negro Need Separate Schools?" *Journal of Negro Education* 4 (1935) 328–35.

———. *The Souls of Black Folk*. Norton Critical ed. New York: Norton, 1999.

———. *The Suppression of the African Slave-Trade*. Baton Rouge: Louisiana State University Press, 1969.

Eckholm, Erik. "Last Year's Poverty Rate Was Highest in 12 Years." *New York Times*, Sept. 10, 2009. https://www.nytimes.com/2009/09/11/us/11poverty.html.

Editors of *Encyclopaedia Britannica*, et al. "Influenza Pandemic of 1918–19." *Britannica*, July 20, 1998; last updated July 11, 2025. https://www.britannica.com/event/influenza-pandemic-of-1918-1919.

———. "Robert Burton." *Britannica*, July 20, 1998; last updated Feb. 4, 2020. https://www.britannica.com/biography/Robert-Burton.

Education Trust, Inc. *Achievement Gap Summary Tables*. Education Trust, Winter 2002–3. https://edtrust.org/wp-content/uploads/2013/10/sstables.pdf.

Entine, Jon. *Taboo: Why Black Athletes Dominate Sports and Why We're Afraid to Talk About It*. New York: Public Affairs, 2000.

Epstein, Richard A. *Forbidden Grounds: The Case Against Employment Discrimination Laws*. Cambridge, MA: Harvard University Press, 1992.

Evrie, John H. Van. *White Supremacy and Negro Subordination*. Vol. 3 of *Anti-Black Thought, 1863–1925*. Edited by John David Smith. New York: Garland, 1993.

Feagin, Joe R. *Racist America: Roots, Current Realities, and Future Reparations*. 2nd ed. New York: Routledge, 2010.

Feagin, Joe R., and Melvin P. Sikes. *Living with Racism: The Black Middle Class Experience*. Boston: Beacon, 1994.

Federal Glass Ceiling Commission. *Good for Business: Making Full Use of the Nation's Human Capital; The Environmental Scan*. GovInfo, Mar. 1995. https://www.govinfo.gov/app/details/GOVPUB-Y3-PURL-LPS3994.

Fields, Jason, and Lynne M. Casper. *America's Families and Living Arrangements: March 2000*. United States Census Bureau, June 2001. P20-537. https://www.census.gov/library/publications/2001/demo/p20-537.html.

Fireside, Harvey. *Separate and Unequal: Homer Plessy and the Supreme Court Decision That Legalized Racism*. New York: Carroll and Graf, 2004.

Fisher v. University of Texas, 570 U.S. 297 (2013). [*Fisher I*.]

Fisher v. University of Texas, 136 S. Ct. 2198 (2016). [*Fisher II*.]

Fletcher, Arthur. *The Silent Sell-Out: Government Betrayal of Blacks to the Craft Unions*. New York: Third, 1974.

Fletes, Christina. "Voter Justice: Why Latinos Must Be a Key Part of the New Coverage Formula for the Voting Rights Act." *Harvard Kennedy School Journal of Hispanic Policy* 29 (2017) 23–35.

Fogel, Robert William, and Stanley L. Engerman. *Time on the Cross: The Economics of American Negro Slavery*. New York: Norton, 1989.

Foner, Eric. *The Fiery Trial: Abraham Lincoln and American Slavery*. New York: Norton, 2010.

———. *Reconstruction: America's Unfinished Revolution, 1863–1877*. New York: Harper and Row, 1988.

Forbes. "The Forbes 400." *Forbes* (Oct. 6, 2008) 44–280.

Forbes. "The Forbes 400: The Richest People in America; The List." *Forbes* (Oct. 31, 2019) 118–84.

Ford, Christopher A. "Administering Identity: The Determination of 'Race' in Race-Conscious Law." *California Law Review* 82 (1994) 1231–85.

Forman, James. "The Black Manifesto." In *Black Manifesto: Religion, Racism, and Reparations*, edited by Robert S. Lecky and H. Elliott Wright, 114–26. New York: Sheed and Ward, 1969.

Fowler, David H. *Northern Attitudes Towards Interracial Marriage: Legislation and Public Opinion in the Middle Atlantic and the States of the Old Northwest, 1780–1930*. New York: Garland, 1987.

Fowler, Frances C. "The Shocking Ideological Integrity of Chubb and Moe." *Journal of Education* 173 (1991) 119–29.

Fraser, Gary E. *Diet, Life Expectancy, and Chronic Disease: Studies of Seventh-day Adventists and Other Vegetarians*. New York: Oxford University Press, 2003.

Fraser, Gary E., et al. "Association Among Health Habits, Risk Factors, and All-Cause Mortality in a Black California Population." *Epidemiology* 8 (1997) 168–74.

Fuchs, Victor R. *Women's Quest for Economic Equality.* Cambridge, MA: Harvard University Press, 1988.

Gallup. "Race Relations." Gallup, 2019. https://news.gallup.com/poll/1687/race-relations.aspx.

Gallup, George. *The Gallup Poll: Public Opinion, 1935–1971.* 3 vols. New York: Random House, 1972.

Gallup, George, Jr. *The Most Segregated Hour: Religion and Values.* Princeton, NJ: Gallup, 2002.

———. *The Most Segregated Hour, Part 2: Religion and Values.* Princeton, NJ: Gallup, 2002.

Garg, Shikha, et al. "Hospitalization Rates and Characteristics of Patients Hospitalized with Laboratory-Confirmed Coronavirus Disease 2019—Covid-Net, 14 States, March 1–30, 2020." *Morbidity and Mortality Weekly Report* 17 (2020) 458–64. https://doi.org/10.15585/mmwr.mm6915e3.

Garvey, Stephen P. "Punishment as Atonement." *UCLA Law Review* 46 (1999) 1801–58.

Georgia v. Ashcroft, 539 U.S. 461 (2003), 123 S. Ct. 2498.

Gish, Duane T. *Evolution: The Fossils Still Say No!* El Cajon, CA: Institute for Creation Research, 1995.

———. *Have You Been Brainwashed?* Seattle: Life Messengers, 1974.

Gittleman, Maury, and Edward N. Wolff. "Racial Differences in Patterns of Wealth Accumulation." *Journal of Human Resources* 39 (2004) 193–227.

Goldstein, Morris, and Robert S. Smith. "The Estimated Impact of the Anti-Discrimination Program Aimed at Federal Contractors." *Industrial and Labor Relations Review* 29 (1976) 523–43.

Goldstone, Lawrence. *Dark Bargain: Slavery, Profits, and the Struggle for the Constitution.* New York: Walker & Co., 2005.

Gordon, David M., et al. *Segmented Work, Divided Workers: The Historical Transformation of Labor in the United States.* Cambridge: Cambridge University Press, 1982.

Gordon, Linda. *Pitied but Not Entitled: Single Mothers and the History of Welfare 1890–1935.* New York: Free, 1994.

Gore, Rick. "Neandertals: The Dawn of Humans." *National Geographic* 189 (1996) 2–35.

Gould, Stephen Jay. "Mismeasure by Any Measure." In *The Bell Curve Debate: History, Documents, Opinions*, edited by Russell Jacoby and Naomi Glauberman, 3–14. New York: Random House, 1995.

Graham, Hugh Davis. *The Civil Rights Era: Origins and Development of National Policy.* New York: Oxford University Press, 1990.

———. "Civil Rights Policy in the Carter Presidency." In *The Carter Presidency: Policy Choices in the Post-New Deal Era*, edited by Gary M. Fink and Hugh Davis Graham, 202–23. Lawrence: University of Kansas Press, 1998.

Grant, Ruth W., and Benjamin R. Hertzberg. "John Locke on Education." In *A Companion to Locke*, edited by Matthew Stuart, 447–65. Blackwell Companions to Philosophy. West Sussex: Blackwell, 2015.

Greenberg, Edward S. *The American Political System: A Radical Approach.* 5th ed. Glenview, IL: Scott, Foresman and Co., 1989.

Greenberg, Edward S., and Benjamin I. Page. *The Struggle for Democracy*. New York: Harper Collins, 1993.

Greenspan, Jesse. "Changes Expected at EEOC, but Nothing Too Radical." Law 360, Nov. 7, 2008. https://www.law360.com/articles/76059.

Grier, William H., and Price M. Cobbs. *Black Rage*. 2nd ed. New York: Basic, 1992.

Griffin, Peter. "The Impact of Affirmative Action on Labor Demand: A Test of Some Implications of the Lechatelier Principal." *Review of Economics and Statistics* 74 (1992) 251–60.

Griggs v. Duke Power Co., 401 U.S. 424 (1971).

Grimké, Frances J. "Segregation." *Crisis* 41 (1934) 173–74.

Gross, Jane. "A Private School That Thrives on Rules; Minority Students Excel at Brooklyn Site. Is It a Model or an Anomaly?" *New York Times*, Sept. 24, 2003. https://www.nytimes.com/2003/09/24/nyregion/private-school-that-thrives-rules-minority-students-excel-brooklyn-site-it-model.html.

Gross Domestic Product. https://www.bea.gov/data/gdp/gross-domestic-product.

Grutter v. Bollinger, 539 U.S. 306 (2003).

Guinier, Lani. *The Tyranny of the Majority: Fundamental Fairness in Representative Democracy*. New York: Free, 1994.

Guinier, Lani, and Gerald Torres. *The Miner's Canary: Enlisting Race, Resisting Power, Transforming Democracy*. Cambridge, MA: Harvard University Press, 2002.

Hacker, Andrew. *Two Nations: Black and White, Separate, Hostile, Unequal*. Rev. ed. New York: Ballantine, 1995.

Hajnal, Zoltan L. *Dangerously Divided: How Race and Class Shape Winning and Losing in American Politics*. Cambridge: Cambridge University Press, 2020.

Hamilton, Alexander, et al. *The Federalist Papers*. Edited by Clinton Rossiter. New York: Signet, 2003.

Hamilton, Darrick, and William A. Darity. "The Political Economy of Education, Financial Literacy, and the Racial Wealth Gap." *Federal Reserve Bank of St. Louis Review* 99 (2017) 59–76.

Hamilton, Lawrence C. *Modern Data Analysis: A First Course in Applied Statistics*. Pacific Grove, CA: Brooks/Cole, 1990.

Haney-López, Ian. "Intentional Blindness." *New York University Law Review* 87 (2012) 1779–877.

Harris, Angel L. *Kids Don't Want to Fail: Oppositional Culture and the Black-White Achievement Gap*. Cambridge, MA: Harvard University Press, 2011.

Harris, Cheryl I., and Kimberly West-Faulcon. "Reading Ricci: Whitening Discrimination, Racing Test Fairness." *UCLA Law Review* 58 (2010) 73–165.

Harris, David A. *Driving While Black: Racial Profiling on Our Nation's Highways*. New York: American Civil Liberties Union, 1999.

Hashimzade, Nigar, et al. "Social Cost." *Oxford Dictionary of Economics*, 2017. https://www.oxfordreference.com/display/10.1093/acref/9780198759430.001.0001/acref-9780198759430-e-2895?rskey=Rb65Is&result=2.

Harris, Paul. *Black Rage Confronts the Law*. New York: New York University Press, 1997.

Hart, H. L. A. *The Concept of Law*. 3rd ed. Oxford: Oxford University Press, 2012.

Haveman, Robert H. "What Antipoverty Policies Cost the Nonpoor." *Challenge* (1986) 37–42.

Haynie, Kerry L. "Containing the Rainbow Coalition: Political Consequences of Mass Racialized Incarceration." *Du Bois Review* 16 (2019) 245–51.

Head Start. "Head Start Program Facts: Fiscal Year 2022." Head Start, last updated Feb. 27, 2025. https://headstart.gov/program-data/article/head-start-program-facts-fiscal-year-2022.

Health, United States—Datafinder. https://www.cdc.gov/nchs/hus/data-finder.htm.

Heaton, Tim B., and Cardell K. Jacobson. "Intergroup Marriage: An Examination of Opportunity Structures." *Sociological Inquiry* 70 (2000) 30–41.

Heckman, James. "Detecting Discrimination." *Journal of Economic Perspectives* 12 (1998) 101–16.

Heckman, James J., and Kenneth I. Wolpin. "Does the Contract Compliance Program Work? An Analysis of Chicago Data." *Industrial and Labor Relations Review* 29 (1976) 544–64.

Helsing, Jeffrey W. *Johnson's War, Johnson's Great Society: The Guns and Butter Trap.* Westport, CT: Praeger, 2000.

Henderson, Errol Anthony. "Military Spending and Poverty." *Journal of Politics* 60 (1998) 503–20.

Hendley, Alexa A., and Natasha F. Bilimoria. "Minorities and Social Security: An Analysis of Racial and Ethnic Differences in the Current Program." *Social Security Bulletin* 62 (1999) 59–64. https://www.ssa.gov/policy/docs/ssb/v62n2/v62n2p59.pdf.

Herring, Cedric, and Sharon M. Collins. "Retreat from Equal Opportunity? The Case of Affirmative Action." In *The Bubbling Cauldron: Race, Ethnicity, and the Urban Crisis*, edited by Michael Peter Smith and Joe R. Feagin, 163–81. Minneapolis: University of Minnesota Press, 1995.

Herrnstein, Richard J., and Charles Murray. *The Bell Curve: Intelligence and Class Structure in American Life.* New York: Free, 1994.

HHS Office for Civil Rights in Action. "Bulletin: Civil Rights, HIPAA, and the Coronavirus Disease 2019 (COVID-19)." American Association on Health & Disability, Mar. 28, 2020. https://www.aahd.us/wp-content/uploads/2020/04/ocr-bulletin-3-28-20.pdf.

Hill, Herbert. "Black Labor and Affirmative Action: An Historical Perspective." In *The Question of Discrimination: Racial Inequality in the U.S. Labor Market*, edited by Steven Shulman and William Darity Jr., 190–267. Middletown, CT: Wesleyan University Press, 1989.

———. *Black Labor and the American Legal System: Race, Work and the Law.* Madison: University of Wisconsin Press, 1985.

Hiller, Janine S., and Stephen P. Ferris. "Separating Myth from Reality: An Economic Analysis of Voluntary Affirmative Action Programs." *Memphis State University Law Review* 23 (1993) 773–803.

Hine, William C. "Black Politicians in Reconstruction Charleston, South Carolina: A Collective Study." *Journal of Southern History* 49 (1983) 555–84.

Hoffer, Peter Charles. *Cry Liberty: The Great Stono River Slave Rebellion of 1739.* New Narratives in American History. Oxford: Oxford University Press, 2012.

Hoffman, David, dir. *Sputnik Mania.* Santa Cruz, CA: Varied, 2008.

Holzer, Harry J., and David Neumark. "Are Affirmative Action Hires Less Qualified? Evidence from Employer-Employee Data on New Hires." *Journal of Labor Economics* 17 (1999) 534–69.

———. "Assessing Affirmative Action." *Journal of Economic Literature* 38 (2000) 483–568. https://doi.org/10.1257/jel.38.3.483.

———. "What Does Affirmative Action Do?" *Industrial and Labor Relations Review* 53 (2000) 240–71.
Hopwood v. Texas, 78 F.3d 932 (5th Cir. 1996).
Horsman, Reginald. *Race and Manifest Destiny: The Origins of American Racial Anglo-Saxonism*. Cambridge, MA: Harvard University Press, 1981.
Horton, James Oliver, and Lois E. Horton. *Hard Road to Freedom: The Story of African America*. New Brunswick: Rutgers University Press, 2001.
Huselid, Mark A. "The Impact of Human Resource Management Practices on Turnover, Productivity, and Corporate Financial Performance." *Academy of Management Journal* 38 (1995) 635–72.
Income Inequality. https://www.oecd.org/en/data/indicators/income-inequality.html.
International Database: World Population Estimates and Projections. https://www.census.gov/programs-surveys/international-programs/about/idb.html.
IRS. "Earned Income Tax Credit Statistics." IRS, last updated Dec. 5, 2024. https://www.irs.gov/credits-deductions/individuals/earned-income-tax-credit/earned-income-tax-credit-statistics.
———. "SOI Tax Stats—Individual Income Tax Returns." IRS, last updated Mar. 26, 2025. https://www.irs.gov/statistics/soi-tax-stats-individual-income-tax-returns.
Jacobs, David, and Robert M. O'Brien. "The Determinants of Deadly Force: A Structural Analysis of Police Violence." *American Journal of Sociology* 103 (1998) 837–62.
Jacoby, Russell, and Naomi Glauberman, eds. *The Bell Curve Debate: History, Documents, Opinions*. New York: Times, 1995.
Jaynes, Gerald David, and Robin M. Williams Jr., eds. *A Common Destiny: Blacks and American Society*. Washington, DC: National Academy Press, 1989.
Jefferson, Thomas. "A Bill for the More General Diffusion of Knowledge, 18 June 1779." Founders Online, 1779. From *1777—18 June 1779*, edited by Julian P. Boyd, 526–35, vol. 2 of *The Papers of Thomas Jefferson* (Princeton, NJ: Princeton University Press, 1950). http://founders.archives.gov/documents/Jefferson/01-02-02-0132-0004-0079.
———. "From Thomas Jefferson to William Charles Jarvis, 28 September 1820." Founders Online, 1820. From *Retirement Series, 1 June 1820 to 28 February 1821*, edited by J. Jefferson Looney et al., 287–89, vol. 16 of *The Papers of Thomas Jefferson* (Princeton, NJ: Princeton University Press, 2019). https://founders.archives.gov/documents/Jefferson/03-16-02-0234.
———. *Notes on the State of Virginia*. TB3052. New York: Harper Torchbooks, 1964.
———. "Thomas Jefferson to William Duane, 16 September 1810." Founders Online, 1810. From *Retirement Series, 12 August 1810 to 17 June 1811*, edited by J. Jefferson Looney, 86–89, vol. 3 of *The Papers of Thomas Jefferson* (Princeton, NJ: Princeton University Press, 2006). http://founders.archives.gov/documents/Jefferson/03-03-02-0052.
Jencks, Christopher. *Rethinking Social Policy: Race Poverty and the Underclass*. Cambridge, MA: Harvard University Press, 1992.
Jerald, Craig D. *Dispelling the Myth Revisited: Preliminary Findings from a Nationwide Analysis of "High-Flying" Schools*. ERIC, 2001. ED462485. https://eric.ed.gov/?id=ED462485.
Johanningmeier, Erwin V. "'A Nation at Risk' and 'Sputnik,' Compared and Reconsidered." *American Educational History Journal* 2 (2010) 347–65.
Johnson, Charles S. *The Negro in American Civilization*. New York: Holt, 1930.

Johnson, Janet Buttolph, and Richard A. Joslyn. *Political Science Research Methods*. 2nd ed. Washington, DC: Congressional Quarterly, 1991.

Johnson, Rucker C., and Alexander Nazaryan. *Children of the Dream: Why School Integration Works*. New York: Basic, 2019.

Jones, JoLissa. "Merrick Garland and the Stalemate Senate: Does the Senate Owe a Vote?" *Thurgood Marshall Law Review (Online)* 3 (2018) 3–22.

Jones, Phillip B. *Southern Baptist Congregations Today*. Southern Baptist Historical Library & Archives, Feb. 2001. http://media2.sbhla.org.s3.amazonaws.com/collections/hmb_namb_reports/hmb-namb-report_154.pdf.

Judd, Dennis R., and Todd Swanstrom. *City Politics: Private Power and Public Policy*. 2nd ed. New York: Longman, 1998.

Kafer, Krista. *School Choice 2003: How States Are Providing Greater Opportunity in Education*. Washington, DC: Heritage Foundation, 2003.

Katz, Michael B. *In the Shadow of the Poorhouse: A Social History of Welfare in America*. New York: Basic, 1986.

Katznelson, Ira. *When Affirmative Action Was White*. New York: Norton, 2005.

Keil, Thomas, and Gennaro F. Vito. "Race and the Death Penalty in Kentucky Murder Trails: 1976–1991." *American Journal of Criminal Justice* 20 (1995) 17–36.

Kennedy, John F. "Remarks in Heber Springs, Arkansas, at the Dedication of the Geers Ferry Dam." American Presidency Project, Oct. 3, 1963. https://www.presidency.ucsb.edu/documents/remarks-heber-springs-arkansas-the-dedication-greers-ferry-dam.

Kerner, Otto. *The Kerner Report: The 1968 Report of the National Advisory Commission on Civil Disorders, with New Introductions by Fred R. Harris and Tom Wicker*. New York: Pantheon, 1988.

Kershnar, Stephen. "Reparations for Slavery and Justice." *University of Memphis Law Review* 33 (2003) 277–306.

Kinder, Donald R., and Lynn M. Sanders. *Divided by Color: Racial Politics and Democratic Values*. Chicago: University of Chicago Press, 1996.

Kindy, Kimberly, et al. "A Year of Reckoning: Police Fatally Shoot Nearly 1,000." *Washington Post*, Dec. 26, 2015. https://www.washingtonpost.com/sf/investigative/2015/12/26/a-year-of-reckoning-police-fatally-shoot-nearly-1000/.

King, Martin Luther, Jr. "I Have a Dream." In *A Testament of Hope: The Essential Writings and Speeches of Martin Luther King, Jr.*, edited by James M. Washington, 217–20. San Francisco: HarperCollins, 1986.

———. "Letter from Birmingham Jail—April 16, 1963." In *African American Religious History: Documentary Witness*, edited by Milton C. Sernett, 519–34. 2nd ed. C. Eric Lincoln Series on the Black Experience. Durham: Duke University Press, 1999.

———. "Nonviolence and Racial Justice." In *The Civil Rights Movement*, edited by Paul A. Winters, 58–61. San Diego: Greenhaven, 2000.

———. "*Playboy* Interview: Martin Luther King, Jr." In *A Testament of Hope: The Essential Writings and Speeches of Martin Luther King, Jr.*, edited by James M. Washington, 340–77. San Francisco: HarperCollins, 1986.

———. "A Testament of Hope." In *A Testament of Hope: The Essential Writings and Speeches of Martin Luther King, Jr.*, edited by James M. Washington, 313–28. New York: Harper Collins, 1986.

———. *Where Do We Go from Here: Chaos or Community?* Boston: Beacon, 1968.

Kirchhoff, Christopher M. "Memorandum for Ambassador Susan E. Rice: NSC Lessons Learned Study on Ebola." *New York Times*, July 11, 2016. https://int.nyt.com/data/documenthelper/6823-national-security-counci-ebola/o5bd797500ea55be0724/optimized/full.pdf.

Kirschenman, Joleen, and Kathryn M. Neckerman. "We'd Love to Hire Them, But . . . : The Meaning of Race for Employers." In *The Urban Underclass*, edited by Christopher Jencks and Paul E. Peterson, 203–34. Washington, DC: Brookings Institution, 1991.

Koslow, Philip, ed. *African American Desk Reference*. New York: Wiley and Sons, 1999.

Koubek, Richard F. *Wyandanch: A Political Profile of a Black Suburb*. New York: City University of New York, Queens College, Institute for Community Studies, 1971.

Kramer, Gerald H. "Political Science as Science." In *Political Science: The Science of Politics*, edited by Herbert F. Weisberg, 11–23. New York: Agathon, 1986.

Krasner, Stephen D. "State Power and the Structure of International Trade." *World Politics* 28 (1976) 317–47.

Krueger, C., and T. Ziebarth. *School Choice*. No Child Left Behind Policy Brief GP-02-08W. Denver: Education Commission of the States, 2004.

Kruger, Justin, and David Dunning. "Unskilled and Unaware of It: How Difficulties in Recognizing One's Own Incompetence Lead to Inflated Self-Assessments." *Journal of Personality and Social Psychology* 77 (1999) 1121–34.

Kuklinski, James H., et al. "Racial Prejudice and Attitudes Toward Affirmative Action." *American Journal of Political Science* 41 (1997) 402–19.

Kurtz, Harold. *The Education and Demographic Consequences of Four Years of School Desegregation in the Pasadena Unified School District*. Pasadena: Pasadena Unified School District, 1975.

Launius, Roger D. "Sputnik and the Origins of the Space Age." NASA, Feb. 2, 2005. https://history.nasa.gov/sputnik/sputorig.html.

Leiter, Samuel, and William M. Leiter. *Affirmative Action in Antidiscrimination Law and Policy: An Overview and Synthesis*. Albany: State University of New York Press, 2002.

Leonard, Jonathan S. "Antidiscrimination or Reverse Discrimination: The Impact of Changing Demographics, Title VII, and Affirmative Action on Productivity." *Journal of Human Resources* 19 (1984) 145–74.

———. "Employment and Occupational Advance Under Affirmative Action." *Review of Economics and Statistics* 66 (1984) 377–85.

Leslie, Charles. "Scientific Racism: Reflections on Peer Review, Science and Ideology." *Social Science and Medicine* 31 (1990) 891–912.

Leuchtenburg, William E. "The Old Cowhand from Dixie." *Atlantic Monthly* (Dec. 1992) 92–100.

Levy, Helen. "How Is Health Insurance Affected by the Economy? Public and Private Coverage Among Low-Skilled Adults in the 1990s." In *Working and Poor: How Economic and Policy Changes Are Affecting Low-Wage Workers*, edited by Rebecca M. Blank et al., 396–425. National Poverty Center Series on Poverty and Public Policy. New York: Russell Sage Foundation, 2008.

Lewis, Amanda E., and John B. Diamond. *Despite the Best of Intentions: How Racial Inequality Thrives in Good Schools*. Transgressing Boundaries: Studies in Black Politics and Black Communities. Oxford: Oxford University Press, 2015.

Lewis, David L. *King: A Biography*. Urbana: University of Illinois Press, 1978.

Lieberman, Robert C. *Shifting the Color Line: Race and the American Welfare State.* Cambridge, MA: Harvard University Press, 1998.

Lieberson, Stanley. *A Piece of the Pie: Blacks and White Immigrants Since 1880.* Berkeley: University of California Press, 1980.

Lillie-Blanton, Marsha, et al. "Site of Medical Care: Do Racial and Ethnic Differences Persist?" *Yale Journal of Health Policy Law and Ethics* 1 (2001) 15–32.

Litwack, Leon F. *North of Slavery: The Negro in the Free States, 1790–1860.* Chicago: University of Chicago Press, 1961.

Logan, John R., and Brian J. Stults. *The Persistence of Segregation in the Metropolis: New Findings from the 2010 Census.* Brown, Mar. 24, 2011. US2010 Project. https://s4.ad.brown.edu/Projects/Diversity/data/report/report2.pdf.

López, Ian F. Haney. *White by Law: The Legal Construction of Race.* New York: New York University Press, 1996.

Louisiana Department of Health. "Coronavirus (Covid-19)." Louisiana Department of Health, 2020. http://ldh.la.gov/coronavirus/. Link discontinued.

Lubenow, Marvin L. *Bones of Contention: A Creationist Assessment of Human Fossils.* Grand Rapids: Baker, 2004.

Lynd, Staughton. *Class Conflict, Slavery, and the United States Constitution.* Indianapolis: Bobbs-Merrill, 1962.

MacDonald, John M. "Analytic Methods for Examining Race and Ethnic Disparity in the Juvenile Courts." *Journal of Criminal Justice* 29 (2001) 507–19.

Madison, James. "Slave Trade and Slaveholders' Rights, [17 June] 1788." Founders Online, June 17, 1788. From *7 March 1788—1 March 1789*, edited by Robert A. Rutland and Charles F. Hobson, 150–51, vol. 11 of *The Papers of James Madison* (Charlottesville: University Press of Virginia, 1977). https://founders.archives.gov/documents/Madison/01-11-02-0091.

Mahard, Rita E., and Robert L. Crain. "Research on Minority Achievement in Desegregated Schools." In *The Consequences of School Desegregation*, edited by Christine H. Rossell and Willis D. Hawley, 103–25. Philadelphia: Temple University Press, 1983.

Marable, Manning. *Race, Reform, and Rebellion.* Jackson: University of Mississippi Press, 1991.

Marketti, James. "Estimated Present Value of Income Diverted During Slavery." In *The Wealth of Races: The Present Value of Benefits from Pat Injustices*, edited by Richard F. America, 107–23. New York: Greenwood, 1990.

Márquez, Cecilia. *Making the Latino South: A History of Racial Formation.* Latinx Histories. Chapel Hill: University of North Carolina Press, 2023.

Mason, Patrick L. "Race, Culture, and Skill: Interracial Wage Differences Among African Americans, Latinos, and Whites." *Review of Black Political Economy* 25 (1997) 5–39.

Mawdsley, Ralph D. "*Missouri v. Jenkins*: Remaking an Urban School District." *Education and Urban Society* 33 (2000) 36–43.

Mays, Benjamin E., and Joseph W. Nicholson. "The Genius of the Negro Church." In *African American Religious History: A Documentary Witness*, edited by Milton C. Sernett, 423–34. 2nd ed. C. Eric Lincoln Series on the Black Experience. Durham: Duke University Press, 1999.

McClain, Paula D., and Albert K. Karnig. "Black and Hispanic Socioeconomic and Political Competition." *American Political Science Review* 84 (1990) 535–45.

McClain, Paula D., and Steven C. Tauber. *American Government in Black and White.* Boulder: Paradigm, 2010.

McDonald, Michael P. "2020 November General Election Turnout Rates." US Elections Project, last updated Dec. 7, 2020. https://www.electproject.org/2020g.

———. "National General Election VEP Turnout Rates, 1789–Present." US Elections Project, n.d. http://www.electproject.org/national-1789-present.

McIntosh, Peggy. *White Privilege and Male Privilege: A Personal Account of Coming to See Correspondences Through Work in Women's Studies.* Wellesley, MA: Wellesley College Center for Research on Women, 1988.

McWhorter, John. *Losing the Race: Self-Sabotage in Black America.* New York: Perennial, 2001.

Mead, Lawrence M. *Beyond Entitlement: The Social Obligations of Citizenship.* New York: Free, 1986.

Meier, August, and Elliott Rudwick. *CORE: A Study in the Civil Rights Movement, 1942–1968.* Urbana: University of Illinois Press, 1975.

Mellott, Jared M. "The Diversity Rationale for Affirmative Action in Employment After Grutter: The Case for Containment." *William and Mary Law Review* (Dec. 2006) 1091–158.

Metro Broadcasting v. FCC, 497 U.S. 547 (1990).

Meyerson, Adam, et al. *Alternatives to Racial Preferences.* Washington, DC: Heritage Foundation, 1998.

Midgley, James, et al., eds. *The Handbook of Social Policy.* Thousand Oaks, CA: SAGE, 2000.

Miles, Robert. *Racism.* Edited by Peter Hamilton. Key Ideas. London: Routledge, 1989.

Mill, John Stuart. *"On Liberty" and Other Writings.* Edited by Stefan Collini. Cambridge Texts in the History of Political Thought. Cambridge: Cambridge University Press, 1989.

Miller, Claire Cain, and Josh Katz. "What Researchers Discovered When They Sent 80,000 Fake Résumés to US Jobs." *New York Times*, Apr. 8, 2024. https://www.nytimes.com/2024/04/08/upshot/employment-discrimination-fake-resumes.html.

Miller, Jerome G. *Search and Destroy: African-American Males in the Criminal Justice System.* 2nd ed. Cambridge: Cambridge University Press, 2011.

Millis, Harry A., and Emily Clark Brown. *From the Wagner Act to Taft-Hartley: A Study of National Labor Policy and Labor Relations.* Chicago: University of Chicago Press, 1950.

Missouri v. Jenkins, 515 U.S. 70 (1995).

Moore, Barrington, Jr. *Social Origins of Dictatorship and Democracy: Lord and Peasant in the Making of the Modern World.* Boston: Beacon, 1966.

Moore, Peter. "Overwhelming Opposition to Reparations for Slavery and Jim Crow." YouGov, June 2, 2014. https://today.yougov.com/politics/articles/9522-reparations.

Morin, Richard. "A Distorted Image of Minorities; Poll Suggests That What Whites Think They See May Affect Beliefs." *Washington Post*, Oct. 8, 1995. https://www.washingtonpost.com/archive/politics/1995/10/08/a-distorted-image-of-minorities/9fcea96f-763d-440b-ad8d-33fee53e5d39/.

———. "Misperceptions Cloud Whites' View of Blacks." *Washington Post*, July 11, 2001. https://www.washingtonpost.com/archive/politics/2001/07/11/misperceptions-cloud-whites-view-of-blacks/6c151d9b-7f2c-409e-b5cc-e6d6376ff582/.

Morone, James A. "Still the American Dilemma: Race and Inequality." Presentation at 16th Annual Meeting of the Association for Health Services Research, Chicago, June 1999.

Morris, John D., and Frank J. Sherwin. *The Fossil Record: Unearthing Nature's History of Life*. Dallas: Institute for Creation Research, 2010.

Moynihan, Daniel. "The Negro Family: The Case for National Action." In *The Moynihan Report and the Politics of Controversy*, edited by Lee Rainwater and William L. Yancey, 39–124. Cambridge, MA: MIT Press, 1965.

Müller, Ingo. *Hitler's Justice: The Courts of the Third Reich*. Translated by Deborah Lucas Schneider. Cambridge, MA: Harvard University Press, 1991.

Murphy, Frederick G., et al. "The Mortality Profile of Black Seventh-day Adventists Residing in Metropolitan Atlanta: A Pilot Study." *American Journal of Public Health* 80 (1990) 984–86.

Murray, Charles. *Losing Ground: American Social Policy, 1950–1980*. New York: Basic, 1984.

Muse, Benjamin. *The American Negro Revolution: From Nonviolence to Black Power, 1963–1967*. Bloomington: Indiana University Press, 1968.

Myrdal, Gunnar. *An American Dilemma: The Negro Problem and Modern Democracy*. New York: Harper & Brothers, 1944.

National Academy of Social Insurance. *Workers' Compensation: Benefits, Costs, and Coverage*. NASI, Nov. 2022. https://www.nasi.org/wp-content/uploads/2022/11/2022-Workers-Compensation-Report-2020-Data.pdf.

National Archives. "National Labor Relations Act (1935)." National Archives, n.d. https://www.archives.gov/milestone-documents/national-labor-relations-act.

National Center for Education Statistics. "Table 40—Enrollment in Public Elementary and Secondary Schools, by Grade: Fall 1986 to Fall 2000." National Center for Education Statistics, Feb. 2002. https://nces.ed.gov/programs/digest/d02/tables/PDF/table40.pdf.

———. "Table 41—Percentage Distribution of Enrollment in Public Elementary and Secondary Schools, by Race/Ethnicity." National Center for Education Statistics, Oct. 2008. http://www.nces.ed.gov/programs/digest/d08/tables/dt08_041.asp.

———. "Table 42—Percentage Distribution of Enrollment in Public Elementary and Secondary Schools, by Race/Ethnicity and State: Fall 1986 and Fall 2000." National Center for Education Statistics, Feb. 2002. https://nces.ed.gov/programs/digest/d02/dt042.asp.

———. "Table 51—Public School Pupils Transported at Public Expense and Current Expenditures for Transportation: 1929–30 to 1999–2000." National Center for Education Statistics, Sept. 2002. https://nces.ed.gov/programs/digest/d02/tables/PDF/table51.pdf.

———. "Table 156—Revenues for Public Elementary and Secondary Schools, by Source of Funds: 1919–20 to 1999–2000." National Center for Education Statistics, May 2002. https://nces.ed.gov/programs/digest/d02/dt156.asp.

———. "Table 157—Revenues for Public Elementary and Secondary Schools, by Source and State: 1999–2000." National Center for Education Statistics, Apr. 2002. https://nces.ed.gov/programs/digest/d02/tables/PDF/table157.pdf.

———. "Table 235.10—Revenues for Public Elementary and Secondary Schools, by Source of Funds: Selected Years, 1919–20 Through 2014–15." National Center for Education Statistics, Aug. 2020. https://nces.ed.gov/programs/digest/d20/tables/dt20_235.10.asp.

———. "Table 365—Federal On-Budget Funds for Education, by Level or Other Educational Purpose, by Agency and Program: Fiscal Years 1965–2002." National Center for Education Statistics, June 2003. https://nces.ed.gov/programs/digest/d02/dt365.asp.

National Center for Health Statistics. *Health, United States, 2006 with Chartbook on Trends in the Health of Americans*. Hyattsville, MD: US Government, 2006.

———. *Health, United States, 2014 with Chartbook on Trends in the Health of Americans*. Hyattsville, MD: US Government, 2014.

National Center for Immunization and Respiratory Diseases (U.S.), Division of Viral Diseases. "Coronavirus Disease 2019 (COVID-19) in the U.S." CDC, Mar. 12, 2020. https://stacks.cdc.gov/view/cdc/85827.

NBC News. "2024 President Results: Trump Wins." NBC News, Nov. 5, 2024. https://www.nbcnews.com/politics/2024-elections/president-results.

NCC Staff. "Looking Back at the *Brown v. Board* Decision." National Constitution Center, Nov. 23, 2015. https://constitutioncenter.org/blog/looking-back-at-the-decision-that-ended-segregation.

Neal, Larry. "A Calculation and Comparison of the Current Benefits of Slavery and an Analysis of Who Benefits." In *The Wealth of Races: The Present Value of Benefits from Past Injustices*, edited by Richard F. America, 91–105. New York: Greenwood, 1990.

News Leaders Association. "Table A—Minority Employment in Daily Newspapers." News Leaders Association, n.d. https://members.newsleaders.org/content.asp?contentid=129.

New York State Education Department. "Archive of West Babylon UFSD Reports." NYSED, n.d. https://data.nysed.gov/archive.php?instid=800000037851.

———. "Archive of Wyandanch UFSD Reports." NYSED, 2018. https://data.nysed.gov/archive.php?instid=800000037741.

———. *New York, the State of Learning: Statistical Profiles of Public School Districts*. Albany: University of the State of New York, State Education Department, 1993.

———. *New York, the State of Learning: Statistical Profiles of Public School Districts*. Albany: University of the State of New York, State Education Department, 1999. https://www.p12.nysed.gov/irs/chapter655/1999/home.html.

———. *New York, the State of Learning: A Report to the Governor and the Legislature on the Educational Status of the State's Schools; Statewide Profile of the Educational System*. Albany: University of the State of New York, State Education Department, 2002. https://www.p12.nysed.gov/irs/chapter655/2002/home.html.

———. *New York, the State of Learning: A Report to the Governor and the Legislature on the Educational Status of the State's Schools; Statewide Profile of the Educational System*. Albany: University of the State of New York, State Education Department, 2018.

———. *New York, the State of Learning: A Report to the Governor and the Legislature on the Educational Status of the State's Schools; Statewide Profile of the Educational System*. Albany: University of the State of New York, State Education Department, 2021.

———. "West Babylon UFSD—School Report Card Data [2016–17]." NYSED, 2018. https://data.nysed.gov/reportcard.php?year=2017&instid=800000037851.

———. "Wyandanch Memorial High School Data." NYSED, n.d. https://data.nysed.gov/profile.php?instid=800000037743.

———. "Wyandanch UFSD—School Report Card Data [2016–17]." NYSED, 2018. https://data.nysed.gov/reportcard.php?year=2017&instid=800000037741.

New York Times. "Excerpts from Clinton Talk on Affirmative Action." *New York Times*, July 20, 1995. https://www.nytimes.com/1995/07/20/us/excerpts-from-clinton-talk-on-affirmative-action.html.

———. "Race, Genetics and a Controversy." *New York Times*, Apr. 2, 2018. https://www.nytimes.com/2018/04/02/opinion/genes-race.html.

———. "Where Candidates Found Support." *New York Times*, Nov. 5, 2008.

North, Douglass C. *The Economic Growth of the United States, 1790–1860*. New York: Norton, 1966.

Nozick, Robert. *Anarchy, State, and Utopia*. New York: Basic, 1974.

Obama, Barack. "President Obama's 100th Day Press Briefing." *New York Times*, Apr. 29, 2009. https://www.nytimes.com/2009/04/29/us/politics/29text-obama.html.

OECD Data Explorer. https://data-explorer.oecd.org.

Office of Family Assistance. "TANF Caseload Data 1996–2015." Office of Family Assistance, May 9, 2018. https://acf.gov/ofa/data/tanf-caseload-data-1996-2015.

Office of Family Assistance Resource Library. https://acf.gov/ofa/resource-library?f%5B0%5D=type%3Aeasychart.

Office of Immigration Statistics. *2017 Yearbook of Immigration Statistics*. Office of Homeland Security Statistics, July 2019. https://ohss.dhs.gov/sites/default/files/2023-12/yearbook_immigration_statistics_2017_0.pdf.

Office of Management and Budget. "Budget of the United States Government." GovInfo, n.d. https://www.govinfo.gov/app/collection/budget.

Ogletree, Charles J., Jr. *All Deliberate Speed: Reflections on the First Half Century of Brown v. Board of Education*. New York: Norton, 2004.

Oliver, Melvin L., and Thomas M. Shapiro. *Black Wealth/White Wealth: A New Perspective on Racial Inequality*. New York: Routledge, 1997.

Oluwadara, Stephen. "Meet the Four Black Billionaires on the Forbes List of 400 Richest Americans." *Urban Geekz*, Oct. 2, 2024. https://urbangeekz.com/2024/10/black-american-billionaires-forbes-400-list-2024/.

O'Neill, June. "Discrimination in Income Differences." In *Race and Gender in the American Economy: Views from Across the Spectrum*, edited by Susan F. Feiner, 13–17. Englewood Cliffs, NJ: Prentice-Hall, 1994.

Orfield, Gary. *Must We Bus? Segregated Schools and National Policy*. Washington, DC: Brookings Institution, 1978.

———. *Reviving the Goal of an Integrated Society: A 21st Century Challenge*. Los Angeles: Civil Rights Project/Proyecto Derechos Civiles at UCLA, 2009.

———. *Schools More Separate: Consequences of a Decade of Resegregation*. Cambridge, MA: Harvard University Press, 2001.

Orfield, Gary, and Carole Ashkinaze. *The Closing Door: Conservative Policy and Black Opportunity*. Chicago: University of Chicago Press, 1991.

Orfield, Gary, and Danielle Jarvie. "Black Segregation Matters: School Resegregation and Black Educational Opportunity." Civil Rights Project, UCLA, Dec. 17, 2020. https://www.civilrightsproject.ucla.edu/research/k-12-education/integration-

and-diversity/black-segregation-matters-school-resegregation-and-black-educational-opportunity/BLACK-SEGREGATION-MATTERS-final-121820.pdf.

Orfield, Gary, and Erica Frankenberg. *Educational Delusions? Why Choice Can Deepen Inequality and How to Make Schools Fair*. Berkeley: University of California Press, 2013.

Orfield, Gary, and Susan E. Eaton. *Dismantling Desegregation: The Quiet Reversal of Brown v. Board of Education*. New York: New, 1996.

Orlofsky, Greg F. *The Funding Gap: Low-Income and Minority Students Receive Fewer Dollars*. Edited by Jeanne Brennan. ED 468 550. Washington, DC: Education Trust, 2002. https://files.eric.ed.gov/fulltext/ED468550.pdf.

Parisi, Michael, and Michael Strudler. "The 400 Individual Income Tax Returns Reporting the Highest Adjusted Gross Incomes Each Year, 1992–2000." Utah Government Digital Library, 2003. https://digitallibrary.utah.gov/#!/s?a=c&q=*&type=16&criteria=lb_document_id%3D106754&b=0.

Paternoster, Raymond. "Prosecutorial Discretion and Capital Sentencing in North and South Carolina." In *The Death Penalty in America: Current Research*, edited by Robert M. Bohm, 39–52. Acj'S/Anderson Monograph 2. Cincinnati: Anderson, 1991.

Pearce, David W., ed. *The MIT Dictionary of Modern Economics*. 4th ed. Cambridge, MA: MIT Press, 1992.

Peffley, Mark, and Jon Hurwitz. *Justice in America: The Separate Realities of Blacks and Whites*. Cambridge Studies in Public Opinion and Political Psychology. Cambridge: Cambridge University Press, 2010.

———. "Persuasion and Resistance: Race and the Death Penalty in America." *American Journal of Political Science* 51 (2007) 996–1012.

Perea, Juan F., et al. *Race and Races: Cases and Resources for a Diverse America*. 2nd ed. St. Paul, MN: Thomson West, 2007.

Perez, Marisol, and Thomas E. Joiner Jr. "Body Image Dissatisfaction and Disordered Eating in Black and White Women." *International Journal of Eating Disorders* 33 (2003) 342–50.

Perry, Pamela. *Shades of White: White Kids and Racial Identities in High School*. Durham: Duke University Press, 2002.

Pew Research Center. *U.S. Religious Landscape Survey: Religious Beliefs and Practices*. Pew Research Center, June 1, 2008. https://www.pewresearch.org/religion/2008/06/01/u-s-religious-landscape-survey-religious-beliefs-and-practices/.

Phillips, Wendell, ed. *The Constitution: A Pro-Slavery Compact, or, Extracts from the Madison Papers, etc*. 3rd ed. New York: American Anti-Slavery Society, 1856.

Piketty, Thomas. *The Economics of Inequality*. Cambridge, MA: Harvard University Press, 2015.

Plessy v. Ferguson, 163 U.S. 537 (1896).

Poole, Mary. *The Segregated Origins of Social Security: African Americans and the Welfare State*. Chapel Hill: University of North Carolina Press, 2006.

Posner, Richard A. "A Political Court." *Harvard Law Review* 119 (2005) 31–102.

Poussaint, Alvin. *Why Blacks Kill Blacks*. New York: Emerson Hall, 1972.

Powell, Colin. *My American Journey*. New York: Ballantine, 1995.

BIBLIOGRAPHY

Powell, Michael. "Liberals Envisioned a Multiracial Coalition. Voters of Color Had Other Ideas." *New York Times*, Jan. 3, 2021. https://www.nytimes.com/2020/11/16/us/liberals-race.html.

Price, S. L. "Whatever Happened to the White Athlete." *Sports Illustrated* (Dec. 8, 1997) 31–55. https://vault.si.com/vault/1997/12/08/what-ever-happened-to-the-white-athlete-unsure-of-his-place-in-a-sports-world-dominated-by-blacks-who-are-hungrier-harder-working-and-perhaps-physiologically-superior-the-young-white-male-is-dropping-out-of-the-athletic-mainstr.

Puddington, Arch. *Freedom in the World 2012: The Arab Uprisings and Their Global Repercussions; Selected Data from Freedom House's Annual Survey of Political Rights and Civil Liberties*. Freedom House, 2012. http://www.freedomhouse.org/sites/default/files/inline_images/FIW%202012%20Booklet--Final.pdf.

Puma, Michael. *Prospects: The Congressionally Mandated Study of Educational Growth and Opportunity; Findings from the 1992 Catholic School Supplement*. ERIC, 1993. ED402657. https://files.eric.ed.gov/fulltext/ED402657.pdf.

Quadagno, Jill. *The Color of Welfare: How Racism Undermined the War on Poverty*. New York: Oxford University Press, 1994.

———. *The Transformation of Old Age Security*. Chicago: University of Chicago Press, 1988.

Ransom, Reverdy C. "The Race Problem in a Christian State, 1906." In *African American Religious History: A Documentary Witness*, edited by Milton C. Sernett, 337–46. 2nd ed. C. Eric Lincoln Series on the Black Experience. Durham: Duke University Press, 1999.

Rawls, John. *A Theory of Justice*. Rev. ed. Cambridge, MA: Belknap, 1999.

Rector, Robert. "Welfare Reform." In *Issues '96: The Candidate's Briefing Book*, edited by Stuart M. Butler and Kim R. Holmes, 197–226. Washington, DC: Heritage Foundation, 1996.

Reed, Katie P., and Monica P. Schulteis. "President Trump Signs into Law the Coronavirus Aid, Relief, and Economic Security (Cares) Act." *National Law Review*, Mar. 29, 2020. https://www.natlawreview.com/article/president-trump-signs-law-coronavirus-aid-relief-and-economic-security-cares-act.

Regents of University of California v. Bakke, 438 U.S. 265 (1978).

Regions in the World by Population. https://www.worldometers.info/world-population/population-by-region/.

Reich, David. *Who We Are and How We Got Here: Ancient DNA and the New Science of the Human Past*. New York: Pantheon, 2018.

Reno v. Bossier Parish School Board I, 520 U.S. 471 (1997), 117 S. Ct .1491.

Reno v. Bossier Parish School Board II, 528 U.S. 320 (2000), 120 S. Ct. 866.

Republican National Committee. "2008 Republican Party Platform." American Presidency Project, Sept. 1, 2008. https://www.presidency.ucsb.edu/documents/2008-republican-party-platform.

———. "2012 Republican Party Platform." American Presidency Project, Aug. 27, 2012. https://www.presidency.ucsb.edu/documents/2012-republican-party-platform.

———. "2016 Republican Party Platform." American Presidency Project, July 18, 2016. https://www.presidency.ucsb.edu/documents/2016-republican-party-platform.

———. "2024 Republican Party Platform." American Presidency Project, July 8, 2024. https://www.presidency.ucsb.edu/documents/2024-republican-party-platform.

———. *Republican Platform 2016*. American Presidency Project, 2020. https://www.presidency.ucsb.edu/sites/default/files/books/presidential-documents-archive-collections/national-political-party-platforms/136059.pdf.

Research, Statistics & Policy Analysis. https://www.ssa.gov/policy/research.html.

Richardson, Heather Cox. *The Death of Reconstruction: Race, Labor, and Politics in the Post–Civil War North, 1865–1901*. Cambridge, MA: Harvard University Press, 2001.

Riley, Jason L. *Please Stop Helping Us: How Liberals Make It Harder for Blacks to Succeed*. New York: Encounter, 2014.

Roberts, Paul Craig, and Lawrence M. Stratton. *The New Color Line: How Quotas and Privilege Destroy Democracy*. Washington, DC: Regnery, 1995.

Robinson, Randall. *The Debt: What America Owes to Blacks*. New York: Plume, 2000.

Rosenberg, Gerald N. *The Hollow Hope: Can Courts Bring About Social Change?* Chicago: University of Chicago Press, 1991.

Rowan, Carl T. *The Coming Race War in America: A Wake-up Call*. Boston: Little, Brown, 1996.

Ruchames, Louis. *Race, Jobs and Politics: The Story of FEPC*. New York: Columbia University Press, 1953.

Rudwich, Elliot, et al. "W. E. B. Du Bois." *Britannica*, July 20, 1998; last updated June 21, 2025. https://www.britannica.com/biography/W-E-B-Du-Bois.

Rushton, J. Philippe. *Race, Evolution, and Behavior: A Life History Perspective*. 2nd special abridged ed. Port Huron, MI: Charles Darwin Research Institute, 2000.

Rushton, J. Philippe, and Anthony F. Bogaert. "Population Differences in Susceptibility to Aids: An Evolutionary Analysis." *Social Science and Medicine* 28 (1989) 1211–20.

Ryan, James E. "Schools, Race, and Money." *Yale Law Journal* 109 (1999) 249–316.

Ryder, Ruth. "Proposed Priorities—American History and Civics Education." *Federal Register* 86 (Apr. 19, 2021) 20348–51. Docket ID ED–2021–OESE–0033. FR Doc. 2021–08068. https://www.govinfo.gov/content/pkg/FR-2021-04-19/pdf/2021-08068.pdf.

Saloner, Brendan, et al. "A Public Health Strategy for the Opioid Crisis." *Public Health Reports* 133 (2018) 24S–34S.

Sapiro, Virginia, and Steven J. Rosenstone. "American National Election Studies Cumulative Data File, 1948–2002." Inter-University Consortium for Political and Social Research, May 2002. https://august.csscr.washington.edu/~data/archive/data8/publicdata/data/anescdf4800/anescdf4800.cod.pdf.

Satel, Sally, and Jonathan Klick. "The Institute of Medicine Report: Too Quick to Diagnose Bias." *Perspectives in Biology and Medicine* 48 (2005) S15–S25.

Scholz, John Karl, and Kara Levine. "The Evolution of Income Support Policy in Recent Decades." In *Understanding Poverty*, edited by Sheldon H. Danziger and Robert H. Haveman, 193–228. New York: Russell Sage Foundation, 2001.

Schuette v. Coalition to Defend Affirmative Action, 572 U.S. 291 (2014).

Schumacher, Alvin J., et al. "Roger B. Taney: 5th Chief Justice of the United States." *Britannica*, July 20, 1998; last updated Mar. 13, 2025. https://www.britannica.com/biography/Roger-B-Taney.

Schwartz, Sarah. "Map: Where Critical Race Theory Is Under Attack." *Education Week*, June 11, 2021. https://www.edweek.org/policy-politics/map-where-critical-race-theory-is-under-attack/2021/06.

Science News. "African Eve Gets Lost in the 'Trees.'" *Science News* 141 (Feb. 22, 1992) 123.
Score, Donald, and Sidra Score, dirs. *Martin's Lament: Religion and Race in America*. Washington, DC: Films for the Humanities, 1995.
Scott, Richard R., and Marvin E. Shaw. "Black and White Performance in Graduate School and Policy Implications of the Use of Graduate Record Examination Scores in Admissions." *Journal of Negro Education* 54 (1985) 14–23.
Screen Actors Guild. "2007 & 2008 Casting Data Reports." Screen Actors Guild, 2008. http://www.sagaftra.org/files/sag/documents/2007-2008_CastingDataReports.pdf. Link discontinued.
Sernett, Milton C., ed. *African American Religious History: A Documentary Witness*. 2nd ed. C. Eric Lincoln Series on the Black Experience. Durham: Duke University Press, 1999.
Shapiro, Thomas M. *Toxic Inequality: How America's Wealth Gap Destroys Mobility, Deepens the Racial Divide, and Threatens Our Future*. New York: Basic, 2017.
Shattuck, Rachel M., and Rose M. Kreider. "Social and Economic Characteristics of Currently Unmarried Women with a Recent Birth: 2011, American Community Survey Reports." United States Census Bureau, May 2013. ACS-21. https://www2.census.gov/library/publications/2013/acs/acs-21.pdf.
Shelby County v. Holder, 133 S. Ct., 186 L.Ed.2d 651, 570 U.S. 529 (2013).
Shribman, David M. "Lyndon Johnson: Means and Ends, and What His Presidency Means in the End." In *The Great Society and the High Tide of Liberalism*, edited by Sidney M. Milkis and Jerome M. Mileur, 233–50. Amherst: University of Massachusetts Press, 2005.
Sidor, Gary. "Major Decisions in the House and Senate on Social Security: 1935–2006." Congressional Research Service, last updated Oct. 25, 2007. Originally written by Geoffrey Kollmann and Carmen Solomon-Fears. https://congressionalresearch.com/RL30920/document.php?study=Major+Decisions+in+the+House+and+Senate+on+Social+Security+1935-2000.
Silverstein, Jake. "Why We Published the 1619 Project." *New York Times Magazine*, Dec. 20, 2019. https://www.nytimes.com/interactive/2019/12/20/magazine/1619-intro.html.
Sitkoff, Harvard. *A New Deal for Blacks: The Emergence of Civil Rights as a National Issue*. New York: Oxford University Press, 1978.
Skinner, Rebecca R. *Funding for Public Elementary and Secondary Schools*. Washington, DC: Congressional Research Service, 2023.
Sklar, Holly. *Chaos or Community? Seeking Solutions, Not Scapegoats for Bad Economics*. Boston: South End, 1995.
Skrentny, John David. *The Ironies of Affirmative Action*. Chicago: University of Chicago Press, 1996.
Sleeper, Jim. *Liberal Racism*. New York: Viking, 1997.
Smedley, Brain D., et al., eds. *Unequal Treatment: Confronting Racial and Ethnic Disparities in Health Care*. Washington, DC: National Academy Press, 2003.
Smith, James P., and Finis Welch. "Affirmative Action and Labor Markets." *Journal of Labor Economics* 2 (1984) 269–301.
Smith, Rogers M. *Civic Ideals: Conflicting Visions of Citizenship in US History*. New Haven, CT: Yale University Press, 1997.
Smith, Stacy L., et al. "Race/Ethnicity in 600 Popular Films: Examining On Screen [sic] Portrayals and Behind the Camera Diversity." Cornell, n.d. https://moodle.

cornellcollege.edu/pluginfile.php/117533/mod_resource/content/1/Race_Ethnicity%20in%20600%20Popular%20Films.pdf.
Smith, Tom W., et al. "General Social Surveys, 1972–2010: Cumulative Codebook." Sage, Mar. 2011. https://study.sagepub.com/sites/default/files/gss_cummulative_codebook.pdf.
———. "General Social Surveys, 1972–2012: Cumulative Codebook." Sage, Mar. 2013. https://study.sagepub.com/sites/default/files/gss_codebook.pdf.
———. "General Social Surveys, 1972–2016: Cumulative Codebook." Sage, Sept. 2017. https://study.sagepub.com/system/files/gss_codebook.pdf.
———. "General Social Surveys, 1972–2018: Cumulative Codebook." NORC, Dec. 2019. https://gss.norc.org/content/dam/gss/get-documentation/pdf/codebook/GSS_Codebook_intro.pdf.
Sniderman, Paul M., and Thomas Piazza. *The Scar of Race.* Cambridge, MA: Harvard University Press, 1993.
Snowden, Frank M., Jr. *Before Color Prejudice: The Ancient View of Blacks.* Cambridge, MA: Harvard University Press, 1983.
———. *Blacks in Antiquity: Ethiopians in the Greco-Roman Experience.* Cambridge, MA: Belknap, 1970.
Snyder, Thomas D. and Alexandra G. Tan. *Digest of Education Statistics, 2004.* National Center for Education Statistics, Oct. 2005. NCES 2006005. https://nces.ed.gov/use-work/resource-library/report/compendium/digest-education-statistics-2004.
Social Security Administration. "DI Trust Fund, a Social Security Fund." SSA, last updated 2024. https://www.ssa.gov/OACT/STATS/table4a2.html.
———. *Medicare.* SSA, Sept. 2009. Publication 05-10043. https://www.ssa.gov/pubs/EN-05-10043.pdf.
———. "OASI Trust Fund, a Social Security Fund." SSA, last updated 2024. https://www.ssa.gov/OACT/STATS/table4a1.html.
———. "Remembering Robert J. Myers." *Social Security Bulletin* 70 (2010). https://www.ssa.gov/policy/docs/ssb/v70n2/v70n2p83.html.
———. *SSI Annual Statistical Report, 2023.* SSA, Oct. 2024. https://www.ssa.gov/policy/docs/statcomps/ssi_asr/index.html.
Social Spending. https://www.oecd.org/en/data/indicators/social-spending.html.
Sowell, Thomas. *Civil Rights: Rhetoric or Reality?* New York: Quill, 1984.
———. *Ethnic America: A History.* New York: Basic, 1981.
———. "Free Market vs. Discrimination." *Forbes* (July 6, 1992) 69.
Spath, Stefan. "What's Wrong with Reparations for Slavery?" *Ideas on Liberty* 52 (2002) 44–47.
Stakeman, Randy, and Jackson Stakeman. "The Departure of W. E. B. Du Bois in 1934." Walter White Project, May 30, 2012. https://scalar.usc.edu/nehvectors/stakeman/the-departure-of-dubois-in-1934.
Stanley, Thomas J., and William D. Danko. *The Millionaire Next Door: The Surprising Secrets of America's Wealthy.* New York: MJF, 1996.
Stashenko, Joel. "Neediest Schools Would Get More Aid." *Syracuse Post Standard*, Mar. 11, 1998.
Stephanopoulos, George, and Christopher Edley Jr. *Affirmative Action Review.* Clinton White House, July 19, 1995. https://clintonwhitehouse4.archives.gov/WH/EOP/OP/html/aa/aa-lett.html.
Steele, Shelby. *The Content of Our Character: A New Vision of Race in America.* New York: St. Martin's, 1990.

Steelworkers v. Weber, 443 U.S. 193 (1979).
Steinberg, Stephen. *The Ethnic Myth: Race, Ethnicity and Class in America*. Boston: Beacon, 1981.
Stiglitz, Joseph E. *The Price of Inequality: How Today's Divided Society Endangers Our Future*. New York: Norton, 2012.
Stout, Cathryn, and Gabrielle LaMarr LeMee. "Efforts to Restrict Teaching About Racism and Bias Have Multiplied across the US." Chalkbeat, July 22, 2021. https://www.chalkbeat.org/22525983/map-critical-race-theory-legislation-teaching-racism.
Straight, Ronald L. "Survey of Consumer Finances: Asset Accumulation Difference by Race." *Review of Black Political Economy* 29 (2001) 67–81.
Strauder v. West Virginia, 100 U.S. 303 (1879).
Strickland, Bill. "The Gary Convention and the Crisis of American Politics." *Black World* 21 (1972) 18–26.
Strigel-Moore, Ruth H., et al. "Eating Disorders in White and Black Women." *American Journal of Psychiatry* 160 (2003) 1326–31.
Students for Fair Admissions v. Harvard, 600 U.S. 181 (2023).
Sugrue, Thomas J. *The Origins of the Urban Crisis: Race and Inequality in Postwar Detroit*. Princeton, NJ: Princeton University Press, 1996.
Swain, Carol M. *Black Faces, Black Interests: The Representation of African Americans in Congress*. Cambridge, MA: Harvard University Press, 1993.
Sweatt v. Painter, 339 U.S. 629 (1950).
Swinton, David H. "Racial Inequality and Reparations." In *The Wealth of Races: The Present Value of Benefits from Past Inequalities*, edited by Richard F. America, 153–62. New York: Greenwood, 1990.
Taylor, Ben. "Ranking Every Modern US President from Worst to First." Inside Gov, Apr. 24, 2015. http://us-presidents.insidegov.com/stories/3995/ranking-modern-us-presidents#13-lyndon-b-johnson. Link discontinued.
Templeton, Alan R., and S. Blair Hedges. "Human Origins and Analysis of Mitochondrial DNA Sequences." *Science* (1992) 737–39.
Thernstrom, Stephan, and Abigail Thernstrom. *America in Black and White: One Nation, Indivisible: Race in Modern America*. New York: Simon and Schuster, 1997.
Thomas, Melvin, et al. "Race and the Accumulation of Wealth: Racial Differences in Net Worth over the Life Course, 1989–2009." *Social Problems* 67 (2019) 22–39.
Thurow, Lester C. *Poverty and Discrimination*. Washington, DC: Brookings Institution, 1969.
Tierney, John, et al. "The Search for Adam and Eve." *Newsweek* (Jan. 11, 1988) 46–52.
Tillery, Alvin B., Jr., and Hanes Walton Jr. "Presidential Greatness in the Black Press: Ranking the Modern Presidents on Civil Rights Policy and Race Relations, 1900–2016." *Politics, Groups, and Identities* 7 (2017) 71–88. https://doi.org/10.1080/21565503.2017.1318760.
Tillman, Zoe. "Obama Nominates Merrick Garland for Supreme Court." *National Law Journal*, Mar. 16, 2016. https://www.propertycasualty360.com/2016/03/16/obama-nominates-merrick-garland-for-supreme-court/?slreturn=20241106120244.
Time Series Cumulative Data File. https://electionstudies.org/data-center/anes-time-series-cumulative-data-file/.

Tocqueville, Alexis de. *Democracy in America*. Translated by George Lawrence. Edited by J. P. Mayer. Anchor Library of Politics. 13th ed. Garden City, NY: Doubleday, 1969.

Tomaskovic-Devey, Donald. *Gender and Racial Inequality at Work: The Sources and Consequences of Job Segregation*. Ithaca: Cornell University Press, 1993.

Totenberg, Nina. "The Supreme Court Deals a New Blow to Voting Rights, Upholding Arizona Restrictions." Houston Public Media, July 1, 2021. https://www.houstonpublicmedia.org/articles/news/politics/2021/07/01/402059/the-supreme-court-deals-a-new-blow-to-voting-rights-upholding-arizona-restrictions/.

Tufte, Edward R. *Data Analysis for Politics and Policy*. Englewood Cliffs, NJ: Prentice-Hall, 1974.

Turner, Frederick Jackson. *The Frontier in American History*. New York: Holt, Rinehart and Winston, 1967.

Turner, Henry McNeal. "Emigration to Africa." In *African American Religious History: Documentary Witness*, edited by Milton C. Sernett, 289–96. 2nd ed. C. Eric Lincoln Series on the Black Experience. Durham: Duke University Press, 1999.

Turner, Margery Austin, et al. *Opportunities Denied, Opportunities Diminished: Racial Discrimination in Hiring*. Washington, DC: Urban Institute, 1991.

Tyson, Karolyn. *Integration Interrupted: Tracking, Black Students, & Acting White After Brown*. Oxford: Oxford University Press, 2011.

United States Census Bureau. "1960 Census: Population, Subject Reports, Occupational Characteristics: Data on Age, Race, Education, Work Experience, Income, etc., for the Workers in Each Occupation." PC(2)-7A. United States Census Bureau, 1963. https://www.census.gov/library/publications/1963/dec/population-pc-2-7a.html.

———. "2022 Annual Social and Economic Supplements." United States Census Bureau, last updated Dec. 6, 2022. https://www.census.gov/data/datasets/2022/demo/cps/cps-asec-2022.html.

———. "Housing Patterns Tables." United States Census Bureau, last updated Oct. 8, 2021. https://www.census.gov/data/tables/time-series/demo/housing-patterns/housing-patterns-tables.html.

———. "America's Families and Living Arrangements: 2013." United States Census Bureau, 2013. https://www.census.gov/data/tables/2013/demo/families/cps-2013.html.

———. "Most Children Younger Than Age 1 Are Minorities, Census Bureau Reports." *Newsroom*, May 17, 2012. https://www.census.gov/newsroom/releases/archives/population/cb12-90.html.

———. "Section 2. Births, Deaths, Marriages, and Divorces." United States Census Bureau, Dec. 30, 2007. From *Statistical Abstract of the United States: 2008* (127th ed.). https://www.census.gov/library/publications/2007/compendia/statab/127ed/births-deaths-marriages-divorces.html.

———. "Section 2. Births, Deaths, Marriages, and Divorces." United States Census Bureau, Aug. 2011. From *Statistical Abstract of the United States: 2012* (131st ed.). https://www.census.gov/library/publications/2011/compendia/statab/131ed/births-deaths-marriages-divorces.html.

———. *Statistical Abstract of the United States: 2001*. United States Census Bureau, Mar. 2002. 121st ed. https://www.census.gov/library/publications/2002/compendia/statab/121ed.html.

———. *Statistical Abstract of the United States: 2002*. United States Census Bureau, Dec. 2002. 122nd ed. https://www.census.gov/library/publications/2002/compendia/statab/122ed.html.

———. *Statistical Abstract of the United States: 2009*. United States Census Bureau, Dec. 2008. 128th ed. https://www.census.gov/library/publications/2008/compendia/statab/128ed.html.

United States Census Bureau. *See also* United States Department of Commerce, Bureau of the Census; U.S. Census Bureau; U.S. Department of Commerce, Bureau of the Census.

United States Department of Commerce, Bureau of the Census. *The Labor Force: Occupation, Industry, Employment and Income*. Edited by Leon E. Truesdell. Vol. 3 of *Population: Sixteenth Census of the United States: 1940*. Washington, DC: U.S. Government, 1943. https://www.test.census.gov/library/publications/1943/dec/population-vol-3.html.

United States Department of Commerce, Bureau of the Census. *See also* United States Census Bureau; U.S. Census Bureau; U.S. Department of Commerce, Bureau of the Census.

United States Department of Justice, Civil Rights Division. *Investigation of the Ferguson Police Department*. U.S. Department of Justice, Mar. 4, 2015. https://www.justice.gov/sites/default/files/opa/press-releases/attachments/2015/03/04/ferguson_police_department_report.pdf.

Unnever, James D., and Shaun L. Gabbidon. *A Theory of African American Offending: Race, Racism and Crime*. Criminology and Justice Studies. New York: Routledge, 2011.

U.S. Bureau of Economic Analysis. "Table 1.4. Chain-Type Quantity Indexes for Depreciation of Fixed Assets and Consumer Durable Goods." BEA, last revised Oct. 2, 2004. https://apps.bea.gov/iTable/?reqid=10&step=2&isuri=1#eyJhcHBpZCI6MTAsInNoZXBz IjpbMSwyLDNdLCJkYXRhIjpbWyJDYXRlZ29yaWVzIiwiUHVibGljRkFCIlosWyJU YWJsZV9MaXNoIiwiODciXV19.

U.S. Census Bureau. *Current Population Survey: 2019 Annual Social and Economic (ASEC) Supplement*. Washington, DC: U.S. Census Bureau, 2019. https://www2.census.gov/programs-surveys/cps/techdocs/cpsmar19.pdf.

U.S. Census Bureau. *See also* United States Census Bureau; United States Department of Commerce, Bureau of the Census; U.S. Department of Commerce, Bureau of the Census.

USDA Food and Nutrition Service. "Program Data Overview." USDA Food and Nutrition Service, last updated July 14, 2025. https://www.fns.usda.gov/pd/overview.

———. "SNAP Data Tables." USDA Food and Nutrition Service, last updated July 14, 2025. https://www.fns.usda.gov/pd/supplemental-nutrition-assistance-program-snap.

———. "WIC Data Tables." USDA Food and Nutrition Service, last updated July 14, 2025. https://www.fns.usda.gov/pd/wic-program.

U.S. Department of Commerce, Bureau of the Census. *1990 Census of Population: General Population Characteristics; United States*. CP-1-1. Washington, DC: U.S. Government, 1992. https://www.census.gov/library/publications/1992/dec/cp-1.html.

———. *1997 Economic Census: Survey of Minority-Owned Business Enterprises.* EC97CS-3. Company Statistics. Washington, DC: U.S. Government, 2001. https://www2.census.gov/library/publications/economic-census/1997/company-statistics/e97cs-3.pdf?#.

———. *Employment and Personal Characteristics.* Edited by Howard G. Brunsman. Vol. 4 of *United States Census of Population: 1950.* Report P-E no. 1A. Washington, DC: U.S. Government, 1953. https://www.census.gov/library/publications/1953/dec/population-vol-04.html.

———. *Historical Statistics of the United States: Colonial Times to 1970; Part 1.* Edited by William Lerner. Bicentennial ed. Washington, DC: U.S. Government, 1975. https://www2.census.gov/library/publications/1975/compendia/hist_stats_colonial-1970/hist_stats_colonial-1970p1-start.pdf.

———. *Historical Statistics of the United States, Colonial Times to 1970; Part 2.* Edited by William Lerner. Bicentennial ed. Washington, DC: U.S. Government, 1975. https://www2.census.gov/library/publications/1975/compendia/hist_stats_colonial-1970/hist_stats_colonial-1970p2-start.pdf.

———. *Money Income of Households, Families, and Persons in the United States: 1987.* Current Population Reports: Consumer Income, series P-60, no. 162. Washington, DC: U.S. Government, 1989. https://www2.census.gov/prod2/popscan/p60-162.pdf.

———. *Occupations, by States: Reports by States, Giving Statistics for Cities of 25,000 or More.* Edited by Alba M. Edwards, with Leon E. Truesdell. Vol. 4 of *Population: Fifteenth Census of the United States: 1930.* Washington, DC: U.S. Government, 1933. https://www.census.gov/library/publications/1933/dec/1930a-vol-04-occupations.html.

———. *Subject Reports: Occupational Characteristics.* Unnumbered vol. of *1970 Census of Population.* PC(2)-7A. Washington, DC: U.S. Government, 1973. https://www.census.gov/library/publications/1973/dec/pc-2-7a.html.

———. *Subject Reports: Occupation by Industry.* Vol. 2 of *1980 Census of Population.* PC80-2-7C. Washington, DC: U.S. Government, 1984. https://www2.census.gov/prod2/decennial/documents/1980/1980censusofpopu8027unse_bw.pdf.

U.S. Department of Commerce, Bureau of the Census. *See also* United States Census Bureau; United States Department of Commerce, Bureau of the Census; U.S. Census Bureau.

U.S. Department of Health and Human Services. *HHS Pandemic Influenza Plan.* CDC, Nov. 2005. https://www.cdc.gov/pandemic-flu/media/hhspandemicinfluenzaplan.pdf.

U.S. Department of Health and Human Services, Office of the Assistant Secretary for Preparedness and Response. *Crimson Contagion 2019 Functional Exercise Draft After-Action Report.* Government Attic, Jan. 2020. https://www.governmentattic.org/38docs/HHSaarCrimsonContAAR_2020.pdf.

U.S. Department of Justice, Immigration and Naturalization Service. *1998 Statistical Yearbook of the Immigration and Naturalization Service.* Office of Homeland Security Statistics, Nov. 2000. M-367. https://ohss.dhs.gov/sites/default/files/2023-12/Yearbook_Immigration_Statistics_1998.pdf.

———. *2001 Statistical Yearbook of the Immigration and Naturalization Service.* Office of Homeland Security Statistics, Feb. 2003. M-367. https://ohss.dhs.gov/sites/default/files/2023-12/Yearbook_Immigration_Statistics_2001.pdf.

BIBLIOGRAPHY

U.S. Equal Employment Opportunity Commission. "2018 Job Patterns for Minorities and Women in Private Industry (EEO-1)." EEOC, 2018. https://www.eeoc.gov/statistics/employment/jobpatterns/eeo1/2018.

———. "EEOC Budget and Staffing History 1980 to Present." EEOC, 2024. https://www.eeoc.gov/eeoc-budget-and-staffing-history-1980-present.

U.S. Small Business Administration, Office of Advocacy. "Private Firms, Establishments, Employment, Annual Payroll and Receipts by Firm Size, 1988–2000." Branding & Marketing, n.d. https://www.brandandmarket.com/advo/research/us88_06.pdf.

Vaca, Nicolás C. *The Presumed Alliance: The Unspoken Conflict Between Latinos and Blacks and What It Means for America*. New York: HarperCollins, 2004.

Van Dyke, Jon M. "Reparations for the Descendants of American Slaves Under International Law." In *Should America Pay? Slavery and the Raging Debate on Reparations*, edited by Raymond A. Winbush, 57–78. New York: HarperCollins, 2003.

Van Kleeck, Mary. "Foreword." In *The Negro in American Civilization: A Study of the Negro Life and Race Relations in the Light of Social Research*, by Charles S. Johnson, v–xi. New York: Holt, 1930.

Vedder, Richard, et al. "Black Exploitation and White Benefits: The Civil War Income Revolution." In *The Wealth of Races: The Present Value of Benefits from Past Injustices*, edited by Richard F. America, 125–37. New York: Greenwood, 1990.

Walker, David. "Our Wretchedness in Consequence of the Preachers of Religion." In *African American Religious History: Documentary Witness*, edited by Milton Sernett, 193–201. 2nd ed. C. Eric Lincoln Series on the Black Experience. Durham: Duke University Press, 1999.

Wallenstein, Peter. *Tell the Court I Love My Wife: Race, Marriage, and Law—an American History*. New York: Palgrave Macmillan, 2002.

Walters, Ronald W. *Black Presidential Politics in America: A Strategic Approach*. Albany: State University of New York Press, 1988.

Washington, James M., ed. *A Testament of Hope: The Essential Writings and Speeches of Martin Luther King, Jr*. New York: HarperCollins, 1986.

Weatherspoon, Floyd. "The Status of African American Males in the Legal Profession: A Pipeline of Institutional Roadblocks and Barriers." *Mississippi Law Journal* 80 (2010) 259–98.

Weiner v. Cuyahoga Community College District, 396 U.S. 1004 (1970).

Weiss, Debra Cassens. "Only 3 Percent of Lawyers in BigLaw Are Black, and Numbers Are Falling." *ABA Journal*, May 30, 2014. https://www.abajournal.com/news/article/only_3_percent_of_lawyers_in_biglaw_are_black_which_firms_were_most_diverse.

Welch, Finis. "Affirmative Action and Discrimination." In *The Question of Discrimination: Racial Inequality in the U.S. Labor Market*, edited by Steven Shulman and William Darity Jr., 153–89. Middletown, CT: Wesleyan University Press, 1989.

Wells, Amy Stuart, and Robert L. Crain. *Stepping Over the Color Line: African-American Students in White Suburban Schools*. New Haven, CT: Yale University Press, 1997.

Weyl, Nathaniel, and William Marina. *American Statesmen on Slavery and the Negro*. New Rochelle, NY: Arlington, 1971.

Wicker, Tom. "Introduction." In *The Kerner Report: The 1968 Report of the National Advisory Commission on Civil Disorders*, xv–xxi. New York: Pantheon, 1988.

———. "Introduction to the 1988 Edition." In *The Kerner Report: The 1968 Report of the National Advisory Commission on Civil Disorders*, xii–xiv. New York: Pantheon, 1988.

Williams, Armstrong. "Presumed Victims." In *Should America Pay? Slavery and the Raging Debate on Reparations*, edited by Raymond A. Winbush, 165–71. New York: HarperCollins, 2003.

Williams, Eric. *Capitalism and Slavery*. Chapel Hill: University of North Carolina, 1994.

Williams, Rhonda M., and Robert E. Kenison. "The Way We Were? Discrimination, Competition, and Inter-Industry Wage Differentials in 1970." *Review of Radical Political Economics* 28 (1996) 1–32.

Wilson, William Julius. *When Work Disappears: The World of the New Urban Poor*. New York: Knopf, 1996.

Winant, Howard. "Dictatorship, Democracy, and Difference: The Historical Construction of Racial Identity." In *The Bubbling Cauldron: Race, Ethnicity, and the Urban Crisis*, edited by Michael Peter Smith and Joe R. Feagin, 31–49. Minneapolis: University of Minnesota, 1995.

Wood, Peter H. *Black Majority: Negroes in Colonial South Carolina from 1670 Through the Stono Rebellion*. New York: Norton, 1974.

World Development Indicators. https://datacatalog.worldbank.org/search/dataset/0037712/World-Development-Indicators.

World Factbook, The. "Field Listing—Infant Mortality Rate." CIA, n.d. https://www.cia.gov/the-world-factbook/field/infant-mortality-rate/.

Wright, Bruce. *Black Robes, White Justice*. Secaucus, NJ: Stuart, 1987.

Wright, Gavin. "Prosperity, Progress, and American Slavery." In *Reckoning with Slavery: A Critical Study in the Quantitative History of American Negro Slavery*, by Paul A. David et al., 302–36. New York: Oxford University Press, 1976.

Yinger, John. *Closed Doors, Opportunities Lost: The Continuing Costs of Housing Discrimination*. New York: Sage, 1995.

Young, J. T. *Democrat Spending Plans Eclipse L. B. J.'s Great Society*. Washington, DC: US Senate Republican Policy Committee, 2000.

Index

Abernathy, David, 44
absolute equality, 20–21
absolute improvements, 74, 76, 328–29
Adarand Constructors, Inc. v. Peña, 88, 147, 176
affirmative action, 146–76
   Black affirmative action, 105, 126, 127–31, 133, 138, 144, 180, 332–33
   California Proposition 16, 236
   Civil Rights Act of 1964, 136–37
   contemporary legal period, 105–7, 110–15
   cost measures merit, 155
   costs over time, 171–74
   cost studies, 156–60
   cultural costs, 19, 104
   discount racial equality programs, 343
   economic costs, 2, 15, 16
   enforcement of Civil Rights laws, 132–35
   GOP party platform, 203
   government contracts/contractors, 164–71
   job performance, 174–76
   knowledge, 146–50
   low-cost equality, 330–34
   medium-cost equality, 334–35, 337
   Philadelphia Plan, 137–43
   political costs, 17
   productivity measures, 161–64
   race neutrality, 117–18
   reparations, 317
   social costs, 18
   wage discrimination costs, 185–86
   white affirmative action, 105, 118–20, 124, 125–27, 133, 144, 192, 331–32
   white cultural beliefs, 86–91
   white opposition, 3–4
   white *versus* Black popular wisdom, 151–54
Affordable Care Act, 85
Agricultural Adjustment Act (AAA), 294
Aid to Dependent Children (ADC), 37, 294, 295–96
Aid to Families with Dependent Children (AFDC), 33, 59–67, 289, 297–98, 307, 328, 347
Alamillo, Rudy, 242–47
Alito, Samuel, 114, 223
Allen, Richard, 128
American Bar Association Journal, 95
American Opportunity Accounts Act, 235
American Society of Newsroom Editors, 95
Amsterdam News (newspaper), 258
Anderson, Carol, 8
antidiscrimination, 2, 4, 13–14, 17, 18, 19, 33, 119, 147, 150, 154, 171, 180, 201, 203–4, 206–9, 225, 247, 287, 324–25, 334, 335, 336–37, 339, 343, 348
antiquity, 43, 284, 316
anti-structuralism, 98–102, 322–23
Arbery, Ahmaud, 10

INDEX

Arizona, 221–25
Armed Forces Qualification Test (AFQT), 182
Armor, David, 272
Arthur Anderson Business Roundtable report, 159–60, 176
Asians, 1, 40, 43, 48, 62, 74, 79, 242, 327, 348
"Assessing Affirmative Action" (Holzer and Neumark), 148
Atlantic Monthly (magazine), 283
Atlantic slave trade, 43–44
atonement, 349–50
audits, 40–41, 45–46, 54, 58, 69, 180, 208–10, 232, 322, 324, 327, 343–44
Avivi, Hadar, 41–42

Banfield, Edward, 34
Barrera, Mario, 19
Barrett, Amy Coney, 105–6, 113, 114, 223
Beard, Charles Austin, 100–101, 119
Beatrice International, 194
Becker, Gary, 152–53
Bell, Sean, 10
Berlin, Ira, 127–28
Bertrand, Marianne, 41
Besco, Randy, 237–38
Bethune, Mary McLeod, 294
bias theories, 34, 36, 44–45, 68–69, 98–99
Biden, Joseph, 2, 3, 12, 13, 100, 106, 113, 116, 204, 230, 247, 261, 345
biological deficiency, 34–36, 68, 98–99, 326–27
Black Americans
   Black children, 2–3, 11, 58, 72, 81, 93–94, 99, 126, 251, 252–53, 255–68, 270–82, 337–39
   Black-on-Black crime, 55–57
   Black optimism, 82
   Black representatives, 233–35, 247
   founding principles of the US, 118–20
   interests/issues, 225–26, 230–35
   lawyers, judges, and prosecutors, 95
   occupational advances, 86–93
   popular wisdom, 151–54, 174–76, 333–34
   strategic improvement, 73–77
   unarmed Black men killed by the police, 8–11
   voting, 2, 17, 128, 132–35, 206–12, 220, 226–35, 235–47, 336–37, 345–46
   white affirmative action, 125–27
   See also reparations; wage discrimination; wealth
Black deficiency, 31–70
   Black to white welfare receipt, 58–64
   causes and solutions to racial inequality, 31–33
   and crime, 55–57
   cultural costs, 33, 68–70
   healthcare, 49–54
   low-cost equality, 326–34
   racial equality studies, 33–49
   railroad-track effect, 68–70
   rising inequality/declining prejudice, 57–58
   welfare reform and the white poor, 64–68
Black Enterprise (magazine), 194
Black Lives Matter movement, 4, 8–9, 180, 205
Black to white family income ratio, 4–5, 37–38, 59–62, 323
Black women, 46–49, 51–53, 57, 58, 87–91, 126, 169, 181, 296, 302–4, 327, 329, 330, 340–41
Blake, Jacob, 10
Booker, Cory, 235, 340
border walls, 57, 322, 323
Boston, Thomas D., 324
Boyle, Ryan, 248–50
Brabri, Mélissa, 276
Brennen, William, 218
Breyer, Stephen, 116, 224
Brinkley, David, 248
Brinsley, Ismaaiyl, 9
Brnovich v. Democratic National Committee, 2, 221–25, 347
Brooks, Roy, 317–18

INDEX

Brown v. Board of Education, 2–3, 81, 91, 93, 115, 117, 119, 253, 267, 271–72, 273, 278, 280–82, 337–38, 344
Buettner, Dan, 52–53
Bunche, Ralph, 294
Bureau of Refugees, Freedmen, and Abandoned Lands. *See* Freedmen's Bureau
Burger, Warren E., 108–9
Burton, Robert, 319
Bush, George H. W., 228
Bush, George W., 219, 228–30, 238, 256, 345
Bushnell, Horace, 44

California, 3–4, 101–2, 176, 236, 254–55, 264
CAMAC (firm), 194
Carson, Ben, 330
Carter, Jimmy, 207, 228, 238, 254
Carter, Samuel Casey, 270
"The Case for Reparations" (Coates), 283
Census Bureau, 77, 85
Centers for Disease Control and Prevention (CDC), 49, 320–21
Charleston, SC, 9
Charlottesville, VA, 9
Chenault, Kenneth, 195
Chicago, IL, 45, 77, 132, 138, 264, 266, 270
Children of the Dream (Johnson and Nazaryan), 279–80
Chubb, John, 269–70, 272
churches, 2, 93–94, 128, 330, 346
Civil Rights Act
  of 1866, 130
  of 1871, 131
  of 1875, 119, 131, 332
  of 1957, 134
  of 1960, 134
  of 1963, 135
  of 1964, 86, 91, 94, 104, 108, 136–37, 137–38, 203, 209, 226, 305, 343
  of 1991, 126
Civil Rights Cases, 119, 131, 332

civil rights legislation, 5, 12, 131–35, 226–30, 234, 300, 337, 346
civil rights movement, 86, 91–93, 130, 142, 202, 220, 281, 330
Civil War amendments to the US Constitution, 118, 331
Clark, Kenneth, 280
Clemmons, Maurice, 10
Clemons, Michael, 242–44
Clinton, Bill, 68, 97, 147, 153, 207–8, 228, 230, 293, 298, 301, 304, 328, 336
Clinton, Hillary, 229, 230, 238
Clyburn, James, 204
CNN, 35, 125
Coalition of Oppressed Peoples of Color (COPOC), 286
Coalition to Defend Affirmative Action, Integration, and Immigration Rights and Fight for Equality by Any Means Necessary (BAMN), 110–11
Coates, Ta-Nehisi, 283
coddling, 329–30
Cohen, Danielle, 281–82
Cole, R. Guy, 111
The Coming Race War (Delgado), 8, 76
The Coming Race War in America (Rowan), 76
commissioned studies. *See* Great Commissions
Commission on Civil Rights, 134
Commission to Study Reparation Proposals for African-Americans Act, 234–35, 236
Committee on Economic Security (CES), 294
Compromise of 1877, 131
Congressional Research Service report, 305
Congress of Racial Equality (CORE), 138, 300
Conyers, John, 234
Coons, John, 127
Coronavirus Aid, Relief, and Economic Security Act (CARES Act), 318

385

INDEX

corporate power, 194–97
Cosby, Bill, 31, 330
cost of racial equality, 1–21
  America's rejection of low-cost solutions, 347–49
  atonement, 349–50
  causes and solutions, 31–33
  cultural costs, 19, 33, 68–70, 72, 77, 81, 86, 103–5, 110, 117, 118, 122, 125, 140, 144, 325–26, 328, 331, 342, 347–48
  destabilization of the state, 5–12
  economic cost, 1–3, 15–17, 57, 104, 150, 209, 317, 323–25, 334, 337, 343–44, 347
  equality and inequality, 20–21
  expertise, cost of, 85–93
  government contracts, 164–71, 333–34
  how cost is measured, 15–21
  incompetence, cost of, 71–73
  no-cost equality, 1–3
  political costs, 2, 4, 15, 17, 103–5, 106, 116, 144, 201, 214–15, 225, 247, 324–25, 336–37, 348
  question of, 4–5
  social costs, 18–19, 103–4, 325
  solution, 12–15
  type and level of, 324–26
  See also affirmative action; high-cost equality; low-cost equality; medium-cost equality
costs of the law, 103–45
  Black affirmative action, 127–31
  claims and counterclaims, 144–45
  contemporary legal period, 105–17
  cotton, 121
  enforcement of Civil Rights laws, 131–35
  founding principles, 118–20
  history of the passage of the 1964 CRA, 136–37
  legal whiteness, 122–24
  Philadelphia Plan, 137–43
  race neutrality, 117–18
  white affirmative action, 125–27
cotton, 121
Council of Economic Advisors, 323

COVID-19 pandemic, 12, 49, 96, 178–80, 204, 220, 293, 318, 320–22, 341
Craemer, Thomas, 313–14
craft occupations, 91, 137–43, 332–33
Crain, Robert, 271–72, 279
criminal justice system, 82–85, 232–33
Crimson Contagion, 322
The Crisis (magazine), 274–77
cultural capital, 62–63, 192
cultural costs, 19, 33, 68–70, 72, 77, 81, 86, 103–5, 110, 117, 118, 122, 125, 140, 144, 325–26, 328, 331, 342, 347–48
cultural deficiencies, 18–19, 32, 34, 55, 68–70, 99, 326, 328
Current Population Survey (CPS), 40–41, 45, 46, 185, 189, 289–92, 327, 336

Dallas, TX, 9
Danko, William, 190–92
Darity, William A., 12, 235, 314–15
Davis, Richard, 125
Dean, Aaron, 10
death penalty, 84, 329
Decennial Census, 45
Defense Education Act (DEA), 250, 322
defense industries, 133
deficiency theories, 34, 37–40, 68–70
Delgado, Richard, 102
Delmont, Matthew F., 2–3, 261
Democratic Party, 2, 202–5, 206–7, 211–14, 223, 226–30, 236, 238–42, 246–47, 336–37, 345–46
Detroit, MI, 278, 300
Diallo, Amadou, 10
Diamond, John, 278–79
Dickey, Jack, 11
"difference principle," Rawls, 20–21
direct testing, 42, 45–46
"Distorted Image of Minorities" (Morin), 32
diversity, equity, and inclusion (DEI), 2, 137, 176, 229, 322, 349
Dole, Robert, 336

Dorner, Christopher, 9–10
Douglass, Frederick, 128
Douglass, William O., 218
Dred Scott v. Sandford, 72, 225, 331
Drug Enforcement Administration (DEA), 57
D'Souza, Dinesh, 330
Du Bois, W. E. B., 7, 274–79
Dunning, David, 71

Eckholm, Erik, 301–2
economic costs, 1–3, 15–17, 57, 104, 150, 209, 317, 323–25, 334, 337, 343–44, 347
economic crisis of 2007–9. *See* Great Recession
Economic Opportunities Act of 1964, 300–301
Education Commission of the States, 269
Education Trust, 265, 267
Eisenhower, Dwight D., 133–34, 248–50, 304
Elementary and Secondary Schools Act of 1965 (ESEA), 250, 256, 257, 263
employment discrimination, 18, 19, 45, 132–35, 174–76, 180, 206–11, 322, 343
Engerman, Stanley, 121
Epstein, Richard, 96
Equal Employment Opportunity Commission (EEOC), 2, 4, 13, 86, 135, 159–60, 171, 206–10, 232, 247, 322, 324, 334, 337, 343–44
Europe, 43–44, 50, 124, 310

Fair Employment Practice Committee (FEPC), 17, 91, 133–35
family incomes, 4–5, 37–39, 59–62, 68, 69, 187–89, 323
Fannie Lou Hamer, Rosa Parks, and Coretta Scott King Voting Rights Act Reauthorization and Amendments Act of 2006, 219
Feagin, Joe, 12, 233

Federal Emergency Relief Administration (FERA), 293–94
Federal Housing Administration (FHA), 126, 192–93, 283, 332
Federal Judicial Center, 95
Federal Reserve, 191, 293–94
female headship for Black women, 46–49, 57, 58, 64–68, 327
Ferguson, Colin, 9
Ferguson, MO, 8–11
Fifteenth Amendment, 118, 130, 215
film industry, 94–95
firm sales, 162–64, 176
Fisher v. University of Texas in 2016 (Fisher I and II), 105–9, 113, 144, 331
Fletcher, Arthur, 139–40, 144
Fletes, Christina, 242–44
Florida, 101, 129, 131, 229, 265
Floyd, George, 10, 286, 348
Fogel, Robert William, 121
Forbes (magazine), 191–92, 195–97, 335
Ford, Gerald, 228, 304
Fortune (magazine), 160, 194–97
Fourteenth Amendment, 110, 118–19, 130–31, 222
Frankenburg, Erica, 205–6
free Blacks, 127–30
Freedmen's Bureau, 129

Gallup poll, 81, 94, 261–62, 284
Garland, Merrick, 105–6, 116
Garner, Eric, 8–9
General Aptitude and Test Battery (GATBY), 126
General Social Survey (GSS), 3, 31–33, 35, 39, 40–41, 45, 80–82, 151–54, 174–75, 190, 244, 262, 326–27
Georgia v. Ashcroft, 218–19, 223
Germany, 284, 315
ghetto enrichment, 252, 254–55, 272, 276, 278–79, 280, 338
GI Bill, 126, 283, 332
Ginsburg, Ruth Bader, 106, 109, 111–12, 144, 220
Goldwater, Barry, 228

INDEX

good theory, 36, 42, 59, 327
GOP, 16, 17, 133, 202–6, 211–12, 213–14, 215, 220, 223, 229–30, 242, 247, 336–37, 345–46
Gordon, David M., 293
Gore, Al, 228, 238
Gorsuch, Neil, 113, 114, 223
government contracts/contractors, 86–90, 138–39, 160, 164–71, 171–73, 176, 332–34
Graves, Joseph, 36
Gray, Freddie, 10, 55
Great Commissions, 44, 98–99, 276–77, 327
Great Depression, 96, 132, 293–94, 340
Great Migration, 132, 258, 286
Great Recession, 96, 177–80, 195, 286, 293, 301–2, 335
Great Society, 8, 13, 37–38, 254, 286, 299–306, 318, 340–42, 347
Greers Ferry Dam, 96
Griffin, Peter, 160, 169–71, 176
Griggs v. Duke Power, 108–9, 117
Grimké, Francis James, 275–76
Gross, Jane, 268
gross domestic product (GDP), 4, 13, 29, 50–51, 209, 306–9, 313, 324, 339–42, 347
Grutter v. Bollinger, 110, 114, 117, 149–50
Guinier, Lani, 125
Gurley, Akai, 10
Guyger, Amber, 10

Hacker, Andrew, 12
Hajnal, Zoltan, 237–38
Hamas, 11
Hamilton, Darrick, 235
Harlan, John Marshall, 115
Harris, Angel, 279
Harris, Cheryl I., 109
Harrison, Jamie, 204
Hart, H. L. A., 20
Harvard University. See *Students for Fair Admissions v. Harvard*
Hayes, Rutherford B., 131
Haynie, Kerry, 238

healthcare, 49–54, 82, 84–85, 189, 208, 232, 286, 307, 322, 329, 348
Heckman, James, 147
Heritage Foundation, 58, 64–65, 269, 272
Herrnstein, Richard, 144, 330
HHS Pandemic Influenza Plan, 321–22
high-cost equality, 15–16, 118, 189, 283–318, 324, 339–42, 347–48
  black welfare versus white welfare, 289–92
  COVID-19 pandemic, 318
  fairness of reparations, 315–18
  Great Society, 299–306
  Jim versus Frank scenario, 284–86
  Malone brothers, 314–15
  Martin Luther King Jr.'s plan, 305–6, 318
  middle-class welfare versus welfare for the poor, 287–89
  political instability, 286–87
  precedents for reparations, 315
  problem with reparations, 283–84
  quality of life, 308–12
  reparations versus welfare, 312–14
  social security, 293–99
  welfare as cheap high-cost equality, 306–8
higher education, 11, 74, 76, 107–10, 117, 129, 149, 154, 250, 343
high-flying schools, 267–68
high-minority school districts, 256, 266, 267–68, 338–39
high-performing-high-poverty schools, 267–69, 338
hiring discrimination, 41–42, 209, 343–44
historical analysis, 42–44
Hitler, Adolf, 72, 103
Hoffer, Peter Charles, 6
Hoffman, David, 248
Holzer, Harry, 147–48
home equity, 126, 191, 193, 258, 336
human capital, 39–40, 46–48, 62, 67, 148, 180–86, 197, 312, 335
Humphrey, Hubert, 228
Hurwitz, Jon, 82–84

INDEX

Ifill, Gwen, 53–54
"I Have a Dream" speech, King, 7, 135, 251–52
immigrants/immigration, 69, 123–24, 181, 202–3, 264, 316–17
income inequality, 37–39, 59, 310–12, 327, 341
incompetence, 71–73, 77, 97–98
independent advantage, 346
infant mortality, 50–51, 310–12
Institute of Medicine (IOM), 44, 53–54, 84, 287
integrated education, 2–3, 80–81, 93–94, 252–53, 255, 261–65, 267, 279–82, 337–39. *See also* segregated schools
Internal Revenue Service (IRS), 190–91
interracial marriage, 57
intrinsic political costs, 2, 4, 15, 17, 104, 201, 202, 209, 211–12, 214–15, 225, 247, 325, 336–37, 342–43
Investigation of the Ferguson Police Department, 8

Jackson, Ketanji Onyika Brown, 114–16
January 6, 2021, 225, 326
Jean, Botham Shem, 10
Jefferson, Atatiana, 10
Jefferson, Thomas, 72, 98, 199, 250–51
Jews, 39, 126, 152, 284, 315, 316, 332
Jim Crow, 5, 7–9, 72, 73, 104, 108, 128, 134, 136, 205, 278, 283, 286, 294, 300, 316, 323–24, 326, 328, 331–32, 340, 348
Jim *versus* Frank scenario, 284–86
job discrimination. *See* hiring discrimination
Jobs Corps, 301
Johns Hopkins Bloomberg School of Public Health, 57, 323
Johns Hopkins Coronavirus Resource Center, 321
Johnson, Andrew, 130
Johnson, Charles, 37, 44, 276–78, 281
Johnson, Lyndon B., 135, 136–37, 138–39, 165, 176, 226, 228, 230, 249–50, 299, 300–305, 332, 346
Johnson, Robert, 196
Johnson, Rucker, 279–80
Johnson Publishing Co., 194
Jones, JoLissa, 106
Jones, Marilee, 125
judges, 95, 103–4, 116

K–12 education, 2–3, 73, 81, 93–94, 97, 100–101, 248–82, 323, 324, 325, 330, 334, 337–39, 344
better, not just equal education, 270
cost of failure, 251–52
declines in white students, 263–65
educational benefits of racial integration, 265–66, 267, 271–72
Elementary and Secondary Schools Act of 1965 (ESEA), 256
equality of education as necessity for freedom and democracy, 252–53
and the founders, 250–51
funding of, 253–54
ghetto enrichment, 254–55
high-performing-high-poverty schools, 267–69
No Child Left Behind (NCLB), 256–61
school bussing, 261–63
school choice, 269–70
segregation is inherently unequal, 273–82
Wyandanch, NY case study, 258–61
Kafer, Krista, 269
Kagan, Elena, 2, 114, 224–25
Kansas City, MO, 262
Karnig, Albert, 237
Katz, Michael, 41–42, 220, 296–97
Katznelson, Ira, 126
Kavanaugh, Brett M., 113, 114, 223
Kennedy, Anthony, 149
Kennedy, John F., 96, 113, 134–35, 228, 249
Kenosha, WI, 10
Kerner Report, 98, 349

INDEX

Kerry, John, 229, 230
Kershnar, Stephen, 284, 285
Kinder, Donald, 12
King, Llewelyn, 248
King, Martin Luther, Jr., 7–9, 20–21, 73, 76, 94, 103–4, 134–35, 145, 200, 225–26, 251–52, 305–6, 318, 327, 341–42, 346, 347–48
King, Martin Luther, Sr., 135
King, Rodney, 55
Kirchhoff, Christopher M., 321–22
Kruger, Justin, 71
Kuklinski, James, 84

labor force participation rates (LFPRs), 188–89
labor markets, 16, 58–62, 97, 148, 154, 174–75, 180–86, 187–89, 312. *See also* employment discrimination
Lakewood, WA, 10
large corporations, 194–95
Latino children, 3, 93, 251, 252, 263–66, 267–68, 272
Latinos, 75, 79, 85, 94–95, 187–89, 235–47, 328–29, 334–39
Launius, Roger, 249
Law Enforcement Assistance Administration (LEAA), 299
law of diminishing returns, 186–87
Lee, Sheila Jackson, 234
Lee-Chin, Michael, 196
Leiter, William and Samuel, 147–48
Leonard, Jonathan, 159–60
Leslie, Charles, 43–44
Lewis, Amanda, 278–79
Lewis, Reginald F., 194
Lieberson, Stanley, 40, 50
life expectancy, 50–53, 69, 327
Lincoln, Abraham, 129, 226
Logan, John, 79–80
Los Angeles, CA, 9–10, 55, 254–55, 264
Los Angeles Times (newspaper), 125
Lott, Trent, 229
low-cost equality, 15–16, 76, 117–18, 324, 326–34, 342, 347–48

low-minority school districts, 256, 266, 268
Lynch, Loretta E., 11

Madison, James, 199–200
magnet schools, 255, 257, 262–63, 269
Mahard, Rita, 279
majority minority, 2, 74, 77, 103–5, 117, 125, 144, 230, 235–36, 239, 252, 323–24, 348
market competition, 96, 261–62, 269, 272, 348
market performance, 161, 172, 175–76
Marketti, James, 306, 312–13
Márquez, Cecilia, 236–37
Marshall, Thurgood, 218, 273
maximum likelihood analysis, 46, 241
McClain, Paula, 237
McConnell, Mitch, 105
McGovern, George, 238
McWhorter, John, 330
Mead, Lawrence, 330
means-tested transfers, 335, 342, 347
means-tested welfare programs, 289–90, 317–18
Medicare and Medicaid, 299, 306–7
medium-cost equality, 15–16, 57, 324, 334–39
Mexicans, 243–47
Michigan, 110–12, 331
middle-class welfare, 287–89, 306–7, 325, 340
Mill, John Stuart, 199–200
Miller, Claire Cain, 41–42
The Millionaire Next Door (Stanley and Danko), 190–91
Minneapolis, MN, 278
minority schools, 254–55, 265–66, 267–69, 337
Missouri v. Jenkins, 273
Mixon, Lovelle, 10
Moe, Terry, 269–70, 272
Mondale, Walter, 238
Morin, Richard, 12, 32, 81, 84–85, 151, 283
Morris, Mary, 339

Mosk, Stanley, 148–49
Moynihan Report, 34
Mullainathan, Sendhil, 41
Mullen, A. Kirsten, 314–15
Multi-City Study of Urban Inequality (MCSUI), 40–41, 45, 62, 154, 181, 327
municipalities, 253–54
Murray, Charles, 144, 151, 330
Myers, Bob, 295
Myers, Samuel, 12

National Academy of Social Insurance, 295
National Advisory Commission on Civil Disorders, 12
National Association for the Advancement of Colored People (NAACP), 132, 276
National Center for Education Statistics (NCES), 265
National Commission on Excellence in Education, 250
National Election Study (NES), 81, 231, 344
National Geographic (magazine), 52–53
National Institutes of Health, 53
National Interracial Conference, 277
National Labor Relations Board (NLRB), 132
National Recovery Administration (NRA), 293–94
National Welfare Rights Organization (NWRO), 296–97
A Nation at Risk report, 250
Native Americans, 190, 221–22, 224–25, 242
natural and physical science experiments, 338–39
naturalization, 123–24
Nazaryan, Alexander, 279–80
Neal, Larry, 312–13
The Negro in American Civilization (Johnson), 276–78
Neiman Marcus, 194
nepotism, 126–27, 332
net financial assets (NFA), 191–94

Neumark, David, 148
New Deal, 37, 226, 230, 294
New Jersey, 265, 277–78
New York City, 258, 264, 266, 268
New York State, 258–61, 265–66, 270
New York Times (newspaper), 36, 41–42, 209, 247, 268, 301–2
New York Times Magazine, 101
The 1968 Report of the National Advisory Commission on Civil Disorder. See Kerner Report
Nixon, Richard, 17, 133–35, 137–39, 202, 228, 238, 332, 345
Nocera, Joe, 209
No Child Left Behind (NCLB), 256–61, 263, 269, 322. *See also* school choice
No Excuses (Carter), 270
non-affirmative action firms, 88, 172, 334
North Charleston, SC, 9
Nozick, Robert, 21

Oakland, CA, 10
Obama, Barack, 3, 96, 97, 105–6, 113, 116, 204, 206–9, 230, 238, 247, 304, 321, 331, 339, 345
O'Connor, Sandra Day, 149, 218, 233
Office for Civil Rights in Action, HHS, 49, 286–87
Office of Economic Opportunity (OEO), 299–301, 305
Office of Federal Contract Compliance (OFCC), 138–40
Office of Federal Contract Compliance Programs (OFCCP), 171
Office of Minority Business Enterprise in the Department of Commerce, 138
Ogletree, Charles, 273
Old-Age and Survivors' Insurance (OASI), 16–17, 292, 293–94, 324
Oliver, Melvin, 126, 192–93, 336
O'Neal, Stanley, 195
one-drop laws, 122
opioid crisis, 55–57, 323, 324, 334, 339

Orfield, Gary, 205–6, 254–55, 261, 264–65, 272, 281, 344
Organisation for Economic Co-Operation and Development (OECD), 308–10

parsimony, 36–38, 42, 69
Parsons, Richard, 195
party platforms, 2, 201–6, 212–13, 336–37
Peffley, Mark, 82–84
perceived political costs, 15, 17, 103–5, 105–6, 116, 201, 202, 209, 211–12, 215, 225, 247, 325, 331, 336–37, 347–48
Perot, Ross, 336
Perry, Tony, 125
personally owned vehicles (POVs), 57, 322
Personal Responsibility and Work Opportunity Reconciliation Act (PRWORA), 298, 301
Philadelphia Plan, 91, 105, 117, 137–43, 144, 286, 332–33
Plessy v. Ferguson, 111, 115, 119, 262, 272, 331–32
points of entry (POEs), 57, 322
Poland, 341
police abuse, 104, 126, 180, 348
political costs, 2, 4, 15, 17, 103–5, 106, 116, 144, 201, 214–15, 225, 247, 324–25, 336–37, 348
politics and voting, 2, 199–247
  Black interests/issues, 225–26, 230–35
  Black representatives, 233–35, 247
  coalitions, 218, 229–30, 235–47
  code words, 202–6
  Equal Employment Opportunity Commission (EEOC), 206–10
  party platforms, 201–6
  perceived political costs, 211–12
  political instability, 286–87
  rainbow coalition, 235–47
  threat of the Black vote, 226–30
  Voting Rights Act of 1965, 214–25
  voting rights and the parties, 212–14

Posner, Richard A., 103
Poussaint, Alvin, 55
poverty, 46, 64–68, 177–98, 259, 263–65, 266, 280–81, 301–3, 327–28, 334–35, 338–39, 341, 344
  corporate power, 194–97
  cost of wage discrimination, 180–86
  education and law of diminishing returns, 186–87
  Great Recession and COVID-19, 177–80
  parents, 189–94
  price of, 187–89
Powell, Colin, 229, 345
Powell, Lewis F. Jr., 148
Power 100, 195–96
PPE procurement and logistics, 321–22
prediction, 36, 40
President's Committee on Equal Employment Opportunity, 135
private schools, 262, 264, 269–70
"A Private School That Thrives on Rules" (Gross), 268
process, 36, 38–39
production function, 155, 160
productivity measures, 161–64, 166–71, 173, 333–34
"Proposed Priorities" (Ryder), 3, 99–102, 347
protests, 8–11, 179–80
public schools, 113, 252, 253–54, 261, 263–64, 268, 269–70, 278, 338

Quadagno, Jill, 296
quality of life, 308–12, 348
quotas, 105, 109, 137–40, 233

race neutrality, 104, 107, 109–10, 117–18, 130, 331
"race norming," 126
racial discrimination, 38–42
"racialized" candidates, Besco, 237
racial mixing, 107–9, 267
racial profiling, 83–84, 202–3, 329
railroad-track effect, 64, 68–70, 172, 178, 327–28, 335, 343

INDEX

rainbow coalition, 235–47
Raines, Franklin, 195
Randolph, A. Phillip, 133
Ransier, Alonzo J., 129
Ransom, Reverdy, 7
Rawls, John, 20–21
reading scores, 265, 272
Reagan, Michele, 221
Reagan, Ronald, 93, 97, 208, 238, 337–39
Reconstruction, 104, 118–19, 128–31
Reed, Katie, 318
Regents diplomas, 259–60, 282
Regents of University of California v. Bakke, 148–49
regression analysis, 46, 89, 161–62, 166, 241, 269
Rehnquist, William, 149
Reich, David, 35–36, 330
relative improvement, 75–76, 328–29
Reno v. Bossier Parish School Board I and II, 217–19
reparations, 234, 283–89, 306, 312–18, 340–42
residential segregation, 77–80, 329
return on assets, capital, or equity, 161, 166–67, 169–70, 172
reverse discrimination, 151, 154, 333, 342
Rice, Condoleezza, 229
Rice, Susan, 321–22
Rittenhouse, Kyle, 10
Roberts, John, 114–15, 219–20, 223
Romney, Mitt, 230
Roof, Dylann, 9, 11
Roosevelt, Franklin D., 37, 133, 293, 298
Roosevelt, Theodore, 294
Rowan, Carl, 76, 102
Rushton, J. Philippe, 34, 42–44, 330

sales per employee, 161–64, 166, 176
Sanders, Lynn, 12
San Francisco, CA, 255
Savoy (magazine), 195
Scalia, Antonin, 105, 149, 331
school bussing, 2–3, 16, 233, 252, 255, 261–63, 272, 338, 344

school choice, 205–6, 261–62, 269–70
schools under registration review (SURR), 265–66
Schuette v. Coalition to Defend Affirmative Action, 111–12
Schulteis, Monica, 318
Scott, Rick, 9
Scott, Walter, 9, 10
SCOTUS Report, 116–17
Screen Actors Guild, 94–95
seasonal restrictions, 296, 340
Second Reconstruction. *See* civil rights movement
"The Secrets of Long Life" (Buettner), 52–53
segregated schools, 104, 255, 263–65, 266, 267, 271–82, 330, 337–39
self-help, 31–32, 326
self-identification, 244, 314–15, 317
Senate, 105–6, 113, 116–17, 131, 305, 318, 331
Seventh-day Adventists (SDAs), 52–53
Shapiro, Thomas, 126, 192–93, 336
Shelby County v. Holder, 2, 213, 214, 219–20
Shultz, George P., 139
Sikes, Melvin, 12
1619 Project, 101
Sixteenth Street Baptist Church, AL, 135
Slager, Michael, 9
slavery, 37, 44, 68–69, 72, 118–20, 121, 128–30, 192, 316. *See also* reparations
Smith, Abraham, 129
Smith, Howard K., 248
Smith, Robert, 196–97
Sniderman, Paul, 84, 152
Snowden, Frank, 43
social costs, 18–19, 103–4, 325
social deficiencies, 18–19, 34, 68
social insurance, 288–90, 307–8, 317
social science, 34, 36–42, 46, 59, 68–69, 71–73, 82, 97, 152, 188, 329, 338
social security, 18, 126, 292, 293–99, 340

393

INDEX

Social Security Act of 1935, 37, 293–96, 299, 332, 340
Social Security Administration, 307
Social Security Disability Insurance (DI), 307
social well-being, 50, 310–11. *See also* infant mortality
socioeconomic status (SES), 44, 125, 191, 216, 269
Sos, Zak, 125
Sotomayor, Sonia, 111, 114–16, 224
Souter, David, 218–19
South Carolina, 9, 129–31, 236
Southern Christian Leadership Conference (SCLC), 286, 300
Soviet Union, 248–52
Sowell, Thomas, 39–40, 86, 91, 93, 330
Spanish flu of 1918, 320–21
Spath, Stefan, 284, 316–18
spatial movement, 252
Spencer, Richard, 9
Sputnik, 248–52
Sputnik Mania (Hoffman), 248
Stakeman, Randy and Jackson, 274
Stanley, Thomas, 190–92
statistical analysis, 42
statistical models, 181–86
Stay-in-School program, 299
Steele, Shelby, 42–43, 330
Steelworkers v. Weber, 117
St. Louis, MO, 255, 257, 263, 271
Stono Rebellion, 6
strategic equality, 76–77, 150, 194, 348
strategic improvement, 73–77, 328–29
Strauder v. West Virginia, 118, 331–32
structural theories, 34, 36, 44–45, 98–101
Student Nonviolent Coordinating Committee (SNCC), 299–300
Students for Fair Admissions (SFFA), 113–16, 148
Students for Fair Admissions v. Harvard, 113–16, 144, 146–48, 194, 331, 347
Stults, Brian, 79–80

Sunday Times of London (newspaper), 35
Survey of Income and Program Participation (SIPP), 190–91
Survey of Minority-Owned Business Enterprises, 194–95
surveys, 42, 44–45
Swain, Carol, 233–34
Swinton, David, 312
Sylvester, Edward C., 138–39
systematic racism, 203

Taylor, Breonna, 10
Temporary Assistance to Needy Families (TANF), 33, 62, 288–89, 297–98, 328, 347
testing tools, 36–42
Thernstrom, Stephan and Abigail, 86, 91–93, 144, 330
Thomas, Clarence, 114, 149, 223, 273–74
Thomas, Melvin, 193
Thomas, Sidney R., 222
Thurgood Marshall Law Review, 106
Thurmond, Strom, 229
Thurow, Lester, 180, 185, 343
Tilden, Samuel J., 131
Tillery, Alvin, 304
timing, 36–37, 59, 69
tip factors, 113–14
Tobin's Q, 161, 165–66
Tocqueville, Alexis de, 128
Troupe, Quincy, 125
Trump, Donald, 13, 57, 113–14, 137, 176, 204, 220, 229, 230, 238, 243, 247, 320, 322, 326, 345–46, 348–49
Turner, Frederick Jackson, 100–101, 119–20
Turner, Henry McNeal, 7, 132
Tyson, Karolyn, 279

unarmed Black men killed by the police, 8–11. *See also* police abuse
unemployment insurance (UI), 293, 306–7
Unequal Treatment (Smedley), 53–54

INDEX

unfair labor practices, 132–33
Unheavenly City (Banfield), 34
universal suffrage, 128
University of Southern California, 94–95
University of Texas at Austin, 106–9
Urban League, 132
US Constitution, 94, 110, 118–20, 130, 331
US Department of Education, 99–102, 255, 256, 272
US Department of Health and Human Services, 286–87, 321–22
US economy, 121, 300
US Historical Statistics, 312

Vaca, Nicolás, 235–36
value of a statistical life (VSL), 56–57
Vanderpool, John, 129
Vanguard, 249
van Kleeck, Mary, 277
Vietnam War, 302–5
voting. *See* politics and voting
Voting Rights Act of 1965, 2, 214–25, 336, 347

wage discrimination, 177–98, 302, 312–13, 322, 334–35, 343–44
  corporate power, 194–97
  education and law of diminishing returns, 186–87
  Great Recession and COVID-19, 177–80
  measuring cost of, 180–86
  parents, 189–94
  price of poverty, 187–89
Wagner, Robert F., 132
Wagner Labor Relations Act of 1935, 18, 132–33
Walker, David, 7, 128
Wallace, George, 228
Walters, Ron, 346
Walton, Hanes, 304
War on Poverty, 301, 303
Warren, Earl, 282
Washington, DC, 264
Washington Post (newspaper), 11, 32, 84–85, 151, 326

Watson, James, 35
wealth, 177–98, 283–84, 334–36
  corporate power, 194–97
  cost of wage discrimination, 180–86
  education and law of diminishing returns, 186–87
  Great Recession and COVID-19, 177–80
  parents, 189–94
  price of poverty, 187–89
Weiss, Debra Cassens, 95
welfare, 16–18, 31–32, 32–33, 36–37, 58–64, 64–70, 126, 287–92, 296–98, 306–14, 317, 324–25, 326–28, 340–41
Wells, Amy Stuart, 271–72
West Babylon, NY, 258–61, 265, 282
West-Faulcon, Kimberly, 109
Wheeler, McArthur, 71
Where Do We Go from Here (King), 20–21
White, Walter Francis, 274–76
white Americans
  cause of racial inequality, 31–33
  cost of expertise, 85–93
  knowledge of affirmative action, 146–50
  school bussing, 261–63
  voting, 202–3, 226–30, 238–41, 336
  white affirmative action, 105, 118–20, 124, 125–27, 133, 144, 192, 331–32
  white opposition, 3–4, 128–29, 151–54, 232–33
  white popular wisdom, 151–54, 174–76, 333–34
  white racial ideas, 80–85
  white rage, 8–11
  white women, 87–93, 303
  See also wage discrimination; wealth
white cultural beliefs, 71–102, 330, 348
  anti-structuralism, 98–102, 322–23
  Black to white male unemployment ratio, 96–97

INDEX

(white cultural beliefs continued)
   departure from social science, 82–85
   dual burden, 97–98
   glass half empty, 93–95
   high cost of expertise, 85–93
   incompetence, cost of, 71–73
   spatial isolation, 77–80, 99, 329
   strategic improvement, 74–77
whiteness, 122–24, 279, 346
white privilege(s), 2, 5, 19, 104, 112, 220, 316–17, 335, 349
white racial identity, 243–44
white students, 252, 256, 261, 263–65, 271–72, 273–82, 337–38
white supremacy, 8–11, 104, 109, 118–19, 205, 225, 349

Wicker, Tom, 98, 349
Wilke, Joy, 231
Williams, Armstrong, 314
Williams, Eric, 316
Wilson, George H., 131
Wilson, William Julius, 192
Winfrey, Oprah, 196–97
Wood, Peter, 6
Wyandanch, NY, 258–61, 265, 269, 282, 299–300

year indicator variables, 242
"A Year of Reckoning" (Kindy), 11
Yinger, Johnny, 41
YouGov survey, 283–84, 315–16

www.ingramcontent.com/pod-product-compliance
Lightning Source LLC
Chambersburg PA
CBHW021929290426
44108CB00012B/773